Kingston
University
London

7-day loan

■INFORMATION SERVICES

www.kingston.ac.uk/library

Law Reform and Financial Markets

ELGAR FINANCIAL LAW

Series editor: Takis Tridimas, *Queen Mary, University of London, UK*

This important new series comprises of high quality monographs on a wide range of topics in the field of financial law, hosting work by established authors of international reputation, alongside younger and more emerging authors. The series is synonymous with original thinking and new, challenging research. The subjects under consideration range from financial services law, through securities regulation, to banking law and from financial fraud, through legal aspects of European Monetary Union and the single currency, to the legal workings of international financial institutions.

Titles in the series include:

Law and Corporate Finance
Frank B. Cross and Robert A. Prentice

Secured Transactions Reform and Access to Credit
Edited by Frederique Dahan and John Simpson

Financial Regulation in Crisis?
The Role of the Law and the Failure of Northern Rock
Edited by Joanna Gray and Orkun Akseli

Law Reform and Financial Markets
Edited by Kern Alexander and Niamh Moloney

Law Reform and Financial Markets

Edited by

Kern Alexander

Professor of Law and Finance, University of Zurich, Switzerland

Niamh Moloney

Professor, London School of Economics and Political Science, UK

ELGAR FINANCIAL LAW

Edward Elgar

Cheltenham, UK • Northampton, MA, USA

Published by
Edward Elgar Publishing Limited
The Lypiatts
15 Lansdown Road
Cheltenham
Glos GL50 2JA
UK

Edward Elgar Publishing, Inc.
William Pratt House
9 Dewey Court
Northampton
Massachusetts 01060
USA

A catalogue record for this book
is available from the British Library

Library of Congress Control Number: 2011926848

MIX
Paper from
responsible sources
FSC® C018575

ISBN 978 0 85793 662 2

Typeset by Servis Filmsetting Ltd, Stockport, Cheshire
Printed and bound by MPG Books Group, UK

Contents

Contributors

Professor Kern Alexander, University of Zurich, Switzerland and Centre for Financial Analysis and Policy, University of Cambridge, UK.

Professor Emilios Avgouleas, University of Manchester, UK.

Professor Julia Black, London School of Economics and Political Science, UK.

Professor Michael A.H. Dempster, Professor Emeritus at the Centre for Financial Research, University of Cambridge.

Professor Nicholas Dorn, Professor of International Safety and Governance, Criminology Department, Erasmus School of Law, Erasmus University Rotterdam, The Netherlands.

Professor Christian A. Johnson, University of Utah, US.

Dr Elena A. Medova, Senior Visiting Fellow at the Centre for Financial Research, Statistical Laboratory, University of Cambridge.

Professor Niamh Moloney, London School of Economics and Political Science, UK.

Philip Morris, Independent Researcher, Jersey.

Professor Iain Ramsay, University of Kent, UK.

Julian Roberts, Barrister and Rechtsanwalte at the Bar in London and in Munich, and Professor of philosophy at the Ludwig–Maximilians–University in Munich.

Agata Waclawik-Wejman, INPRIS Institute, Warsaw and Polish-German Banking Law Center, Jagiellonian University, Cracow, Poland. Member of the Legal Certainty Group of the European Commission.

Professor Toni Williams, University of Kent, UK.

Dr Sanzhu Zhu, School of Oriental and African Studies, University of London, UK.

Introduction

Kern Alexander and Niamh Moloney

The recent history of financial markets suggests that financial crises are recurring more frequently, that traditional regulatory controls have failed to control risk, including systemic risk, and that legal and regulatory reforms are necessary to control the huge social costs that can be imposed on the economy and society by excessive financial risk-taking. Regulation must become more adaptive. One of the important lessons of the global financial crisis is that the effective regulation and supervision of financial markets requires continuous adaptation of rules and supervisory practices as the markets themselves evolve: the nature of the instruments traded, the efficacy of institutional structures and the degree to which national and international markets are integrated, for example, must all be reflected in regulatory and supervisory systems. In the past decade the speed of change has accelerated and has had wide-reaching effects on global markets. This was particularly evident in how the risks that were growing in the US sub-prime mortgage market just prior to the outbreak of the crisis in 2007 were transmitted via the structured finance markets to European banks and to other investors globally.

Law and regulation, both 'on the books', in terms of regulatory design, and 'in action', in terms of supervisory practices and enforcement, were notably deficient in responding to changes to financial markets over the global financial crisis. Private law and public law were both implicated. Weaknesses in private law and contracting frameworks, such as the model contracts governing the vast over-the-counter derivatives market, and in the corporate law doctrine of separate legal personality, which allowed banks to shift massive risks to shell corporations to evade regulatory controls, were exacerbated by prudential regulation frameworks that allowed process-based regulations, such as Basel II, to eviscerate prudential controls and put the global financial system at risk. Legal and regulatory frameworks had an overriding – and disproportionate – focus on reducing transaction costs between market participants, so that they could enter into an increasing array of complex transactions with the expectation of greater returns. But these transactions also carried greater risks, most of which have been externalised, or shifted on to society at large. Regulation and private contracting essentially permitted private parties to reap huge gains from private risk-taking while, at the same time, socializing the losses.

But reform is not easy. An extensive 'law and finance' literature already charts the troublesome and contested relationship between law and financial market development and the uncertainties as to which rules matter and why they do. Massive reform, on an international scale, and with potentially unhelpful influences, including international dynamics in the form of efforts to control the emerging international rule book, institutional competition as domestic institutional structures are reformed, and the risk of group-think, is all the more challenging. As is well known, regulatory reform in the wake of crisis can also suffer from over-reaction as regulators and politicians are gripped by the imperative to 'do something'. The financial crisis has also sharply exposed the difficulties regulation faces in capturing dynamic risks, in crafting appropriate rules and, in particular, in supporting innovative, flexible and imaginative supervisory practices. Even over the relatively short time frame of the current reform movement the nature of systemic risk, for example, has remained contested. Product regulation, to take another example, has come in and out of the regulatory focus as a means for addressing the risks that retail investors face in complex markets; the UK Financial Services Authority's initial reaction post-crisis to difficulties in the retail structured products markets was to focus on distribution; it has since focused more closely on product regulation. Similarly, in the US, initial efforts to require regulatory approval of 'plain vanilla' consumer finance products did not acquire traction.

The theme of this book, accordingly, is law reform in the financial markets. It relies heavily, of course, on the global financial crisis as a rich case study, although not all contributions address the crisis, with some considering the theme of law reform and markets more generally. It seeks to contribute to the global financial crisis literature by ranging across public and private law frameworks, and by using different theoretical, doctrinal and contextual approaches to examine the main weaknesses in the public and private law frameworks for controlling excessive financial risk-taking. Its major theme is law reform, however, and so it adopts a remedial as well as a diagnostic approach and examines the particular areas of financial market law reform that are necessary to build a more efficient financial system with enhanced social welfare.

The volume consists of contributions that were initially presented in 2009 at the W.G. Hart Legal Workshop at the Institute of Advanced Legal Studies, University of London, which addressed the theme of 'Law Reform and the Financial Markets'. The conference's theme was forward-looking in addressing what role law reform can play in building more robust and vibrant financial markets. The workshop was generously supported by the Institute of Advanced Legal Studies, Cambridge Finance, and the ESRC's World Economy & Finance Research Programme. It opened with a plenary lecture by Sean Hagan, General Counsel of the IMF, chaired by London School of Economics and Political Science Director Sir Howard Davies. A series of plenary sessions followed, during which a range of distinguished speakers from the international academic, regulatory (the Bank for International Settlements, BaFin (the German supervisor), CONSOB (the Italian market supervisor), the European Commission, the US Federal Deposit Insurance Corporation, the UK Financial Services Authority, and the Swiss National Bank were all represented) and practitioner communities debated the financial crisis and law reform. The complexities of legal intervention in the financial markets and the related economics and finance issues were discussed in panel sessions over the following two days, with participants including representatives of the Federal Reserve Bank of Chicago and legal practitioners who had brought actions against certain issuers of complex structured finance products. The workshop was characterized by wide-ranging and stimulating debate on a range of issues of central importance to the current international reform movement, including how best to redesign regulation, the international dimension of regulation and the role of private law in financial markets.

This volume reflects the contributions at the conference but it is also designed to reflect the first wave of law reform driven by the global financial crisis, where possible. Most of the chapters reflect developments as at November/December 2010, and so cover, for example, the Dodd-Frank Act 2010, the ongoing UK reforms to the institutional structure of regulation and supervision and the EU sovereign debt crisis. As such, the book aims to consider emerging themes from the 'post-crisis world', as it were. As is traditional with the Hart Workshop, the volume also combines the contributions of established scholars with those from newer, 'early career' scholars.

The book is divided into four parts: I) Redesigning Financial Regulation, II) The Challenges of Capital Market Law Reform, III) Consumer and Depositor Protection, and IV) The Role of the Lender of Last Resort and EU Sovereign Debt Restructuring.

Although much initial attention focused on the broadly-cast reform 'road maps' produced by, inter alia, the G20 and the EU's European Council, the global financial crisis has raised law reform issues of great substantive and technical detail. The EU's efforts to capture the risks of alternative investment funds (particularly hedge funds), and to manage the difficult political and market interests generated by hedge fund regulation, have, for example, led to a harmonizing measure of great technical detail and complexity being adopted by the EU in late 2010. Efforts to capture systemic risk, identify the optimum design for regulatory capital, and recalibrate accounting standards have also preoccupied policymakers nationally, regionally and in the major international fora, including the Financial Stability Board, the Basel Committee and the International Accounting Standards Board. The vast reach of the behemoth Dodd-Frank Act across all sectors of financial market regulation is leading to a new US rule book that has major implications for all market sectors.

But in all this, the very large questions that the crisis has generated with respect to the role of law and supervision must not be overlooked in the 'rush to regulate'. Part I accordingly considers the wider design issues raised by financial regulation. Chapter 1, by Professor Julia Black, who presented one of the workshop's plenary lectures, opens the part by examining one of the core questions that the crisis has prompted: the fate of principles-based regulation (PBR). As Professor Black notes, prior to the financial crisis 'new governance' techniques of financial regulation received close and positive attention from scholars and from exponents of 'smart' regulation, and so their performance over and since the financial crisis merits close review. She focuses in particular on PBR, a prominent member of the family of 'smart' governance techniques that, along with risk-based regulation, reliance on internal management and controls, and market-based regulation, has suffered some reputational damage and has become associated with prejudicial 'light touch' regulation. Professor Black examines the nature of PBR, including how it operates formally and substantively and in different regulatory settings, and charts the recent change in its fortunes. Prior to the financial crisis, not only were the merits of PBR much lauded by regulator and regulatee, but PBR also became an instrument of international regulatory competition. The fall, however, was sharp and steep, particularly in the UK, reflecting a wider shift in the dominant economic and political philosophies away from a reliance on the ability of markets to self-correct and the belief that regulation should be 'light touch'. Professor Black suggests that the future of PBR is mixed; the current emphasis on prescriptive rule-making limits the reach of PBR, for example, but PBR remains important at the international level. She concludes by warning that, while the financial crisis tested the effectiveness of a wide range of regulatory techniques and institutional structures, including traditional rule-based intervention, it is the weaknesses that the crisis exposed in PBR and in other techniques of 'new governance' that should prompt the greatest thought, not least given the support new governance enjoyed prior to the crisis.

Professor Nicholas Dorn argues in Chapter 2 for more democratic accountability in financial regulation and rejects many of the conventional theories (such as convergence theory) that have justified the independence of central banks, financial supervisors and other technical experts who oversee financial market operations. He discusses how convergence in regulatory practices arises from international regulatory networking among national authorities possessed of technical expertise, and suggests that this has undermined effective regulation by insulating regulators and other technical specialists from the moral and social questions prompted by regulation. He applies the work of social theorists such as Pierre Bourdieu, whose theories recognized the tension between cultural capital and economic capital. Most financial regulatory models in market economies lean heavily in favour of the economic capital model, which relies on market models and on forms of technical knowledge developed by private interests. But it often leads to socially undesirable outcomes because it does not reflect the broader values of society, and its governing institutions may not be democratically accountable. He concludes that regulatory reforms have not struck the right balance because they continue to rely on a technical one-dimensional knowledge base for financial market regulation that threatens the broader economic and social values of society. Only by establishing democratically accountable regulatory frameworks can regulators hope to achieve the public good of systemic stability.

The global financial crisis, unlike the earlier Enron-era equity market crisis, originated in the credit rather than the capital markets. But it exposed the risks of silo-based regulation and the extent to which credit and securities markets are interdependent. Capital/securities market regulation has been a subsidiary concern of the reform movement, but it has, nonetheless, been the subject of an important range of reforms, and is the subject of Part II. This part opens with Professor Emilios Avgouleas's discussion of the vexed issue of short sale regulation in Chapter 3. He dismisses the view of many policymakers that short selling leads to increased volatility and financial instability, examining the large number of studies on the market impact of the prohibitions on short sales over the financial crisis. He suggests that the huge falls in the price of financial stocks, which prompted the prohibitions, were more the result of a rational reaction to bad news, funding pressures, and irrational loss aversion, fuelled by herding behaviour, and less the result of short selling itself. The focus of short sales regulation should therefore be to protect against market irrationality and to assist rational traders in moving quickly (through short sales) to protect their positions against the arrival of bad news. But care must be taken to ensure that short sales are not used to perpetrate market abuse. He suggests that these objectives can be achieved by means of enhanced disclosure requirements and a sophisticated circuit breaker system. Professor Avgouleas also calls for better international coordination and criticizes recent reforms and reform proposals from the US SEC, the EU Commission, and EU Member States as obstructing international convergence. The wider lesson is that law reform should be restrained and based on limited controls, such as, in the short-selling context, tailored disclosure requirements. The prohibitions on short selling over the crisis stand as a cautionary lesson for law reform as they seem to have adversely affected liquidity and pricing efficiency in the securities concerned and to have damaged the market's informational efficiency.

The structured product market emerged as one of the most problematic capital market sectors in the wake of the crisis – both for professional and retail investors. The questions for law reform raised by this product sector are reflected in Chapter 4, which examines, from a private law perspective, what causes of action might be possible for investors seeking damages against issuers and third party banks who are involved in the sale of structured finance products. The authors (Professor Michael Dempster, Dr Elena Medova and Julian Roberts) provide an analysis of these issues from a theory of finance perspective. They argue that the *caveat emptor* defence asserted by defendant issuers and banks against claimants who are presumed to be sophisticated (such as institutional investors, pension funds and local city and state governments) may not protect defendants against private law claims. In particular, it may not be sufficient for issuers and banks to have their non-retail clients sign a release against any claims (except those related to fraud) relating to the sale of risky financial products when the products themselves are so risky, from a statistical point of view, that there is very little, if any, chance of recovery. The authors review the recent case law in the US, the UK and Germany and show that the German courts have been more receptive to private law claims in this area, based on the German Civil Code's principles of good faith and negligence. The authors suggest that UK and US courts might depart from a strict application of the *caveat emptor* doctrine in wholesale securities markets to permit more claims to be reviewed based on these principles.

The difficulties generated by private causes of action with respect to claims of mis-selling are also raised in Chapter 5, albeit in the context of the fast-developing regulatory regime that underpins China's capital market. In a wide-ranging examination of the capital market law reform process in China, Dr Sanzhu Zhu argues that one of the most serious problems facing China's capital markets authority, and the Chinese courts, since the emergence of China's capital market, has been how best to tackle various forms of securities fraud in order to protect the interests of investors and to maintain the integrity of China's securities market. This chapter examines in particular the role played by the people's courts in investors' civil compensation claims arising from false statements made on the securities market. Dr Zhu's examination demonstrates the importance of a supportive and accommodating court, with a set of appropriate judicial rules and procedures, to investor protection and the development of securities markets. Dr Zhu argues that the limited role played by the people's courts and the restrictive procedures adopted by the Supreme People's Court suggest that, despite the progress made by the courts in accommodating these types of action, the people's courts are constrained by external as well as internal factors, including resource restrictions and wider concerns about social stability, which may limit further legal reform in this area. The chapter concludes, however, that the legal, regulatory and judicial changes in China over the last few decades have enabled it to achieve sustainable growth levels in its capital markets. The chapter also demonstrates the importance of the embedding of the rule of law in its capital markets to the development of China's markets and to its overall economic development.

Corporate governance-related reforms have emerged as a major theme of the current law reform movement, with corporate governance techniques becoming a key device for supporting better risk management by financial institutions. The EU, for example, has laid down a gauntlet internationally in the form of the high and prescriptive standards that now apply to executive pay in financial institutions under the Capital Requirements Directive III (2010). Efforts are also being made to engage institutional investors more actively as monitors of risk-taking by boards, as reflected in the reforms to shareholder voting on pay that the Dodd-Frank Act 2010 has introduced in the US. The debate concerning shareholder engagement is a long-standing one, however, which pre-dates the crisis. Shareholder voting has, for example, for some time been a concern of the EU, which regards the ease with which cross-border shareholders can vote as a key element of its efforts to construct a deep, liquid and efficient securities market. In Chapter 6, Agata Waclawik-Wejman examines recent developments in the EU legal framework governing cross-border shareholder voting and how voting procedures and safeguards are being strengthened in the intermediated securities environment. The chapter focuses on the technical legal problems that arise where securities are held in cross-border intermediated settlement systems, and the conflicts that can arise between different legal concepts across the EU and that hinder law reform. The chapter also examines the Shareholder Rights Directive, which came into force in 2009, and how it aims to improve communications between issuers and shareholders and strengthen cross-border share-holders' voting rights. The chapter concludes with an overview of the most important initiatives on the removal of the remaining legal barriers to the exercise of voting rights in the EU and considers the reforms that remain necessary if an efficient framework for the cross-border exercise of voting rights in Europe is to be achieved.

The earliest phases of the global financial crisis reform agenda saw the retail investor and the consumer of financial services largely over-looked as policy attention focused on the management of systemic risk and the stabilization of markets. This omission reflects a wider weakness in financial regulation; the consumer financial services markets can be overlooked, including in scholarship and as new tools are developed for examining financial regulation. The insights of the extensive law and finance scholarship in the capital markets field, for example, have not been used to explore weaknesses in consumer market regulation, although the findings of behavioural finance are increasingly shedding a sharp light on design failures in consumer regulation. Governance difficulties also beset the consumer sector; the difficulties the consumer interest faces in accessing policy debates and the law-making process on financial market regulation are well known. More recently, however, law reform has focused more closely on the consumer interest. The passage of the Dodd-Frank Act 2010, for example, saw heated discussion on what would become the new Consumer Financial Protection Bureau and on the scope of its powers, particularly with respect to the authorization of products.

Part III accordingly addresses issues relating to consumer and deposi-tor protection. It opens with Chapter 7, in which Professor Iain Ramsay and Professor Toni Williams explore the implications of the influential neo-liberal approach to consumer credit regulation, based on 'availability and safety', which is promoted by the World Bank, in particular. The chapter examines how this influential model, which assumes that con-sumers can act as agents of market discipline, makes it difficult to design consumer credit regulation that is fair and distributionally progressive. Using this model, the chapter considers the public regulation of consumer credit markets more generally, including recent developments under the Dodd-Frank Act 2010 and the establishment of the Consumer Financial Protection Bureau, with respect to the UK FSA's 'Treating Customers Fairly' supervisory model, and relating to the institutional reorganiza-tion of supervision and regulation in the UK. The authors conclude that there are limits on the ability of consumers to exert discipline on credit markets and, in particular, that financial literacy remains a relatively untested method for 'upskilling' consumers. They suggest that regulation of the supply side remains crucial for achieving fairness, and call for an outcomes-based approach to the regulation of products and product marketing. They point, however, to the limitations of intervention, warning that, while regulation may promise greater safety, and may lead to slightly lower prices and greater choice for lower income consumers, it does not prevent the poor from paying more than middle income consumers for credit, and call for efforts to promote affordable access to credit for low income consumers.

In Chapter 8, Philip Morris explores the particular issues raised by deposit protection in the specific context of the Crown Dependency jurisdictions and with particular reference to international competitiveness. The Isle of Man has operated a deposit protection scheme since 1991 (which has been triggered on two occasions), whilst Guernsey has recently enacted a scheme with distinctive features and Jersey adopted a revised guarantee scheme that became operational in 2009. He examines how these jurisdictions are competing for new financial business in light of the global crisis, and how this dynamic has shaped and influenced the development of their policies and regulatory objectives regarding deposit guarantee schemes.

Part IV addresses the systemic stability risks that have dominated law reform discussions. In Chapter 9, Professor Christian Johnson addresses the legal reforms adopted by the US Congress to enhance the Federal Reserve's ability to provide liquidity to financial institutions during periods of crisis or loss of investor confidence. During the crisis, the Board of Governors of the Federal Reserve System, through the Federal Reserve Bank of New York and other Federal Reserve Banks, embarked upon a series of unparalleled and unprecedented actions, repeatedly injecting massive volumes of liquidity into the US credit markets. Some of the most innovative approaches occurred during the extraordinarily volatile months of September and October 2008. Measured in the tens and hundreds of billions of dollars, all of the actions were bold and innovative, and raised controversial issues regarding the Federal Reserve's authority to act under such circumstances. The chapter provides a thorough review of the Federal Reserve's statutory and regulatory authority as a lender of last resort and discusses how Congress has enhanced its authority under recent legislation, including the Dodd-Frank Act, to allow it to achieve more fully its regulatory and oversight objectives.

The book concludes with Chapter 10, in which Professor Kern Alexander examines the issues raised by law reform in the context of the EU sovereign debt markets. The financial crisis has led to a dramatic reshaping of EU financial market regulation, of the relationship between the Member States and the EU, and of the institutional structures that support EU financial market regulation. Chief among the reforms is the establishment of the new European System of Financial Supervision, which is based on local operational supervision by domestic supervisors and on coordination through four new EU authorities, who are endowed with a range of new supervisory and rule-making powers. In January 2011, three new supervisory authorities, the European Securities and Markets Authority, the European Insurance and Occupational Pensions Authority and the European Banking Authority, were established, together with the new European Systemic Risk Board (ESRB). Although it remains to be seen, the new Authorities and the ESRB should make considerable progress in enhancing prudential supervision and with respect to the surveillance of systemic risk. The European Central Bank, however, has also played a critical role in stabilizing EU markets. Since August 2007, the scale of the ECB's operation to inject liquidity into the EU financial system has been unprecedented in size and scope. It has also been remarkably smooth. The Bank's focus has been on preserving stability in the euro money markets and on supporting the integrity of the EU financial markets. The smooth operation owes much to the competency of the ECB, but also to a more relaxed approach to acceptable collateral than the Bank of England or US Federal Reserve require. But despite the ECB's success in providing exceptional liquidity support to eurozone banks and sovereigns, the eurozone and the EU institutions have not made sufficient progress in redesigning the crisis management procedures of EU Member States and central banks, and in reforming central banks' 'lender of last resort' function, especially in the eurozone.

Professor Alexander addresses some of these issues as they relate to the EU sovereign debt crisis and to how a more harmonized, but decentralized, legal regime governing sovereign bond contracts can achieve more efficiency and stability in EU sovereign debt markets. Over the recent sovereign debt crisis, the EU has not had a legal or formal institutional framework to resolve a sovereign debt default or restructuring. The Greek crisis and the growing sovereign debt problems of other EU states raise important questions about whether EU policymakers should establish a formalized institutional process across the EU to promote more orderly sovereign debt restructurings. Professor Alexander also analyses a number of corollary questions concerning how such a process could work without undermining market discipline; what powers, if any, should be allocated to the EU institutions to oversee sovereign debt restructurings; what set of principles should guide policymakers in devising such an institutional framework; and whether this could help indebted countries avoid a damaging loss of investor confidence and destabilizing market volatility.

Overall, the book seeks to examine the theme of law reform from a range of different theoretical perspectives, with respect to public and private law, and across a variety of jurisdictions and market sectors.

The editors would like to thank the contributors, participants in the 2009 W.G. Hart Legal Workshop and the Workshop's generous sponsors. We would also like to thank Edward Elgar and the Series Editor, Professor Takis Tridimas. Finally, we would like to express our gratitude to Professor Eilis Ferran, who was a member of the Workshop Organizing Committee and provided valuable advice and support.

PART I

Redesigning financial regulation

1.   The rise, fall and fate of principles-based regulation

Julia Black[1]

INTRODUCTION

The financial crisis did not only bring into sharp relief the limitations of the structures of financial markets and the behaviour of their participants; it also called into question some critical aspects of international and national financial regulation. Many of the questions it prompted relate to highly technical matters, for example of prudential regulation and financial stability. Others, however, are more fundamental questions as to the appropriate nature of the relationship between markets and regulators, and the role that each should play in the regulatory regime. In particular, the reputations of four broad categories of regulatory approach and technique have suffered heavy casualties: principles-based regulation, risk-based regulation, reliance on internal management and controls, and market-based regulation. It must be said that detailed, rules-based regulation did not fare particularly well either, but, as such a regulatory approach is largely unfashionable in the regulatory literature, few commentators would have expected it to do so. In contrast, each of the former set is a key example of 'new governance' techniques of regulation,[2] which are far more strongly lauded by academics and 'smart' regulation policymakers alike. Their fate

[1]   Professor of Law, London School of Economics. This chapter was first presented at the Hart Legal Workshop, Institute of Advanced Legal Studies, London in June 2009 and takes into account events up to October 2010. I am grateful to the participants for their comments and reactions, and to David Roach for comments on a previous draft. The usual responsibilities remain my own.
[2]   C. Ford, 'New Governance, Compliance and Principles-Based Securities Regulation', 45 *American Business Law Journal*, 1 (2008); J. Black, 'Decentring Regulation: Understanding the Role of Regulation and Self Regulation in a "Post-Regulatory" World', 54 *Current Legal Problems*, 103 (2002); J. Braithwaite, 'The New Regulatory State and the Transformation of Criminology', 40 *British Journal of Criminology*, 222 (2000); C. Scott, 'Regulation in the Age of Governance: The Rise of the Post Regulatory State', in J. Jordana and D. Levi-Faur (eds),

in the financial crisis should therefore cause us to look long and hard at what has become increasingly accepted wisdom amongst regulatory scholars and 'better regulation' practitioners over the last decade or so.

This chapter focuses on just one of those techniques: principles-based regulation. It asks what lessons can be learned from the crisis as to the effectiveness and appropriate role of principles-based regulation, and what future it may have. Principles-based regulation (PBR) is a moniker that is loosely applied to a number of regulatory regimes, however, and has no clear definition.[3] The chapter therefore first sets out four 'ideal types' of PBR in the Weberian sense: analytical constructs that are rationalized abstractions of particular practices.[4] It then charts the rise and fall of PBR in financial regulation over the last few years and offers some tentative predictions for its future.

WHAT IS PRINCIPLES-BASED REGULATION?

Rules, standards and principles come in different forms and much academic time and debate has been spent delineating the differences among them. Considerable efforts have been made, including by this author, to detail the advantages and disadvantages of each type of norm (detailed, vague, legal, non-legal, specifying processes or outcomes), to analyse when each should be used and how they can be used in combination, and, to a lesser extent, to test their effects empirically.[5] The question of when to use rules, principles or standards has also become a policy issue in its

---

The Politics of Regulation: Institutions and Regulatory Reforms for the Age of Governance (Cheltenham: Edward Elgar, 2004).

[3]   L. Cunningham, *A Prescription to Retire the Rhetoric of 'Principles Based Systems' in Corporate Law, Securities Law and Accounting*, Boston College Law School Research Paper No. 127 (2007), available at http://ssrn.com/abstract=970646.

[4]   M. Weber, *The Methodology of the Social Sciences* (E.A. Shils and H.A. Finch, trans. and eds) (New York: Free Press, 1997) at 88.

[5]   See e.g. C.S. Diver, 'The Optimal Precision of Administrative Rules', 93 *Yale Law Journal*, 65 (1983); C. Sunstein, 'Problems with Rules', 83 *California Law Review*, 953 (1995); F. Schauer, 'The Tyranny of Choice and the Rulification of Standards', 14 *Journal of Contemporary Legal Issues*, 803 (2005); R. Korobkin, 'Behavioral Analysis and Legal Form: Rules vs. Principles Revisited', 79 *Oregon Law Review*, 23 (2000); F. Schauer, 'The Convergence of Rules and Standards', *New Zealand Law Review*, 303 (2003); R. Baldwin, 'Why Rules Don't Work', 53 *Modern Law Review*, 321 (1990); J. Black, *Rules and Regulators* (Oxford: Oxford University Press, 1997); J. Braithwaite, 'A Theory of Legal Certainty', 27 *Australian Journal of Legal Philosophy*, 38 (2002); J. Black, M. Hopper and

own right. In some policy areas, though by no means all, they have been recognised as being particular 'technologies' of regulation and as having particular properties, properties that policymakers in some areas have consciously sought to use and exploit for a variety of ends.[6]

In financial regulation, the UK Financial Services Authority is notable for elevating PBR to a regulatory art form. But it is not alone. As Cunningham documents, in North America regulatory regimes for securities, corporations and accounting have been described as, and have positioned themselves as, being 'principles based'.[7] These monikers are more than just descriptions, however; they also carry significant normative content. Being 'rules-based' is usually denigrated as equating with nitpicking bureaucracy in which compliance with detailed provisions is more important than the attainment of an overall outcome. 'Principles-based', in contrast, evokes images of outcome orientated, flexible regulators fostering ethical standards in largely responsible corporations.

At least, that is the picture that was conjured up pre-crisis. Pre-crisis, PBR was seen as the solution that firms and regulators were looking for to deliver an effective and responsive regulatory regime. Post-crisis, PBR is seen as being the source of the problem: light touch regulation that placed too much reliance on firms themselves to behave responsibly. Having been one of the regulators most committed to PBR, it is no surprise that the FSA responded with such force against the markets' betrayal. It had had so much reputational capital invested in PBR that when the crisis came it had no option but to withdraw it from the market. In its place the FSA launched a new product under a different strapline (to use its own terms): 'outcome based regulation'. Meanwhile, other regulators are climbing on the PBR bandwagon just as it appears to be abandoned by one of its main proponents. In Japan, for example, the head of their Financial Services Authority asserts that it will seek to adopt the right balance between principles and rules in its drive for 'better regulation'.[8] In the US, President Obama's blueprint for regulatory reform was committed to using principles-based regulation in some form.[9] The OECD continues to

---

C. Band, 'Making a Success of Principles Based Regulation', 1 *Law and Financial Markets Review*, 3 (2007) at 191; Ford, above n 2.

   [6] For discussion see Black, above n 5, and J. Black, '"Which Arrow?" Regulatory Policy and Rule Type', *Public Law*, 77 (1998).

   [7] Cunningham, above n 3.

   [8] T. Sato, *Global Reform of Financial Regulation and its Implications*, Speech delivered to the 4th Annual Japan Investment Forum (Tokyo, June 2009).

   [9] Department of the Treasury, *Financial Regulatory Reform: A New Foundation* (2009), proposed that a new Consumer Financial Protection Agency

support the strengths of principles-based regulation although ultimately cautions that the appropriate balance between rules and principles will depend on a number of country-specific factors.[10] The advocation of PBR is not confined to financial regulation. In the UK, the Legal Services Board has stated that it will be a 'principles based regulator', for example.[11] Both the Solicitors Regulation Authority and the Financial Reporting Council (FRC) adopted a similar approach, but called it 'outcomes-focused'.[12] The Walker review of corporate governance enunciated more principles for institutional investors, further developed in the FRC's Stewardship Code, issued in July 2010.[13]

So what is PBR? I suggest that, by adopting a two-dimensional analysis, four 'ideal types' of PBR can be constructed. The first dimension is the approach taken by the regulator: whether principles play a formal role in the rulebooks of regulation or whether the regulators' approach has certain substantive characteristics. The second dimension is the institutional setting and relationship in which principles are mainly being deployed: this could be in the dyadic setting of regulator–regulatee, which is the normal focus of debates on PBR, where principles are used in attempts to change the behaviour of individual regulatees. Principles can also be deployed in a decentred or polycentric regulatory regime as tools of orchestration or network management, amongst other things. For example, they are used in the global financial regulatory regime to set out core normative requirements that other regulators are meant to observe, elaborate and implement.

Together, these form four variations or types of PBR: formal and substantive; and dyadic and polycentric (see Figure 1.1).[14] Although

---

should use a principle-based approach to disclosure to consumers (at 64), and that the SEC and CFTC should seek a harmonized approach to their rules, in which the CFTC's principles should become more detailed (akin to those of IOSCO) and the SEC's rules should become more flexible (at 50).

[10]   OECD, 'Policy Framework for Effective and Efficient Financial Regulation: General Guidance and High-Level Checklist', *OECD Journal, Financial Market Trends*, 2 (2009) at 21–2.

[11]   Legal Services Board, *Business Plan 2009/10* (London: Legal Services Board, 2009) at para 30.

[12]   Solicitors Regulation Authority, *Achieving the Right Outcomes* (London: Solicitors Regulation Authority, 2010).

[13]   Sir David Walker, *A Review of Corporate Governance of UK Banks and Other Financial Industry Entities* (London: HM Treasury, FRC, *Stewardship Code* (London, 16 July 2010)).

[14]   This is an elaboration of the argument made in J. Black, 'Forms and Paradoxes of Principles Based Regulation', 3(4) *Capital Markets Law Journal*, 425 (2008).

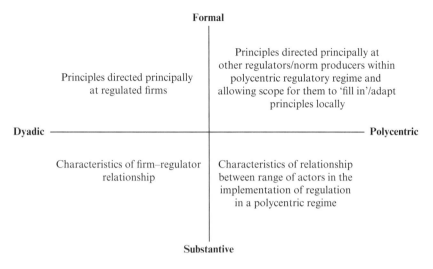

Formal

Principles directed principally
at regulated firms

Principles directed principally at
other regulators/norm producers within
polycentric regulatory regime and
allowing scope for them to 'fill in'/adapt
principles locally

Dyadic ———————————————————————— **Polycentric**

Characteristics of firm–regulator
relationship

Characteristics of relationship
between range of actors in the
implementation of regulation
in a polycentric regime

Substantive

Figure 1.1   Forms of PBR

portrayed diagrammatically as being in separate boxes, in practice the distinctions among the categories are not always clear cut. And, of course, a regulatory regime may have both formal and substantive PBR together, operating in dyadic and polycentric settings.

PBR AND REGULATORY STYLE: FORMAL AND SUBSTANTIVE PBR

Regulatory styles can vary considerably across the various regulatory tasks of standard setting, monitoring and changing behaviour or managing risks. Principles may play only a formal role: existing at the level of the rule books. Alternatively a regulatory style may in practice have some of the characteristics that are often ascribed to PBR regimes, what I term here substantive PBR. The point about separating them is to distinguish what the rule books look like from how regulation actually operates in practice.

Formal PBR is PBR at the level of the rule book. By this I do not mean that a regulator regulates only through using principles. Very few regulatory regimes rely wholly on principles. In practice they are usually accompanied by guidance, written explanations and, often, more detailed rules. These rules may be written by regulators or firms (in dyadic PBR relationships) or by other actors (in polycentric PBR relationships), such as trade associations, other regulators, for example at national

level in multi-level regulatory regimes, or other market actors, such as
credit rating agencies, insurance companies, NGOs (non-governmental
organizations), or standard setters such as the ISO, as discussed further
below. The number of rules written to 'fill out' the principles can be
great: in the FSA's case, these rules ran to several thousand pages. But
the chief characteristics of formal PBR is that principles have a dominant place in the organization and interpretation of regulatory norms
throughout the regulatory regime. Detailed rules or guidance flow from
the principles and the principles are used to interpret and apply those
norms.

In substantive PBR, regulators adopt particular approaches to regulation. These approaches can be adopted irrespective of the form the rules
take. In the debates on rules-based versus principle-based regimes, the
focus is often on these substantive aspects, even if only implicitly, as each
type of rule is asserted to be associated with particular forms of regulatory practice. However, it is important to note that regulatory practices
can be quite divorced from the nature of the rules being implemented.
The substantive character and nature of a regulatory regime cannot be
discerned simply by analysing the types of norms it uses. Substantive
PBR can operate without principles being present in the rule books;
formal PBR need not be accompanied by any of the characteristics of
substantive PBR.

There are a number of reasons why the substantive character of a
regulatory regime may depart from its formal character. A key reason
is that the regulator is not necessarily the author, or at least not the sole
author, of the norms it has to implement. Regulators can be recipients
of a rule-making process or co-authors within it, but they may not have
autonomy to write their own rules. Rather, these rules can be formulated
by legislatures that do not wish to confer on regulators the discretion to
elaborate on principles, but wish to stipulate provisions in considerable
detail,[15] or by other rule-making bodies within the regulatory regime
whose rules the regulator has to abide by or incorporate in its own rules.
Thus, even though it has extensive rule-making powers, the FSA is constrained in the extent to which it can adopt PBR in its rule books by EU
legislation.[16] Nevertheless, substantive PBR can be achieved through the
flexible implementation and enforcement of a highly detailed set of rules

---

[15]   For discussion with respect to the British Columbia Securities Commission,
see Ford, above n. 2.

[16]   A fact emphasized in a paper accompanying the FSA's Turner Review. See
Financial Services Authority (FSA), *Discussion Paper 09/2: A Regulatory Response
to the Global Banking Crisis* (London: FSA, 2009) at para 11.8.

(and conversely, PBR in practice may end up as no better than detailed box ticking if the principles are given particularly 'hard edges' in the way they are interpreted by regulators or courts, or are coupled with a highly deterrence-based and unpredictable enforcement regime that prompts very conservative behaviour by firms).

Given the variety of regimes that are styled, or style themselves, as PBR regimes, the construction of an ideal type necessarily means that some regimes will accord more strongly with certain features than others. However, substantive PBR regimes may be said to have one or more of five key characteristics. These pertain to modes of interpretation, enforcement, compliance focus, distribution of responsibilities within the regulatory regime and conscious reliance on internal management, or meta-regulation. To reiterate, each of these characteristics can be present independently of the presence of principles in the rule books.

First, substantive PBR regimes are characterized by a dense network of 'regulatory conversations': repeated and reasoned interchanges, conversations, between regulator, regulatee and others as to the purpose and application of the principle. Others can play a key role in these conversations in practice, in particular consultants and advisors (but rarely consumers). In these conversations, it is not the case that any interpretation that the parties can agree upon will suffice; the interpretation is always structured by the goal the principle is trying to achieve or the value that it is expressing: to act fairly, or with integrity, or with due care and diligence, for example. Disputes over the application of principles are resolved not through detailed linguistic (legal) interpretive approaches but through purposive interpretations and consequentialist reasoning. The interpretive approach in resolving disputes ultimately depends on the approach adopted by the final arbiter of the rule's interpretation (court, regulator, ombudsman, or all three in different fora); the 'battle for interpretive control' can thus be critical. Further, responsibility for developing interpretations and applications is shared between regulator and regulatee, though each have somewhat different roles. Firms have to take responsibility for thinking through the application of the principle to specific circumstances; regulators have the responsibility to give clear guidance.

Second, substantive PBR regimes adopt particular approaches to enforcement. Under PBR, firms are required to think through the application of the provisions to particular situations to a far greater degree than they are with respect to a detailed rule. There is thus a greater exposure to 'interpretative risk': the risk that they will make the wrong assessment. A 'wrong' assessment is here simply judged in pragmatic terms: it is one with which the ultimate arbiter of interpretation (regulator, tribunal or court) does not agree.[17] Those subject to the principles (or rules) will seek to minimize this risk by calling for greater clarification or even prescription from the regulator. In the absence of that clarification, the enforcement approach is critical. Regulators can manage firms' interpretive risk in two ways: by minimizing its probability through issuing guidance or other aids to interpretation, or by minimizing its impact through the approach to enforcement. Minimizing its impact means minimizing the impact of the firms' interpretation not matching that of the regulator or final arbiter of the rule's/principle's interpretation, for example through due diligence defences. In a regime with a tough, punitive approach in which every minor infraction is met with a sanction, PBR will not survive. It will transform into a system of detailed requirements, as that is what firms will need. They will demand rules to provide them, and the regulator, with clear boundaries. In order to maintain the central role of principles in a PBR regime, enforcement therefore has to be responsive to the firm's own attitude and behaviour.

A 'responsive' enforcement approach is not contingent on any particular rule design, however.[18] It can operate in systems of highly detailed rules, or where the rules are mainly principles, or where there is a combination of the two. That said, different rule types make it easier for regulatory officials to deal with certain types of regulated firm, as Baldwin has pointed out. Those who know what they are meant to be doing and are generally inclined to do it (the well intentioned and well informed) are best dealt with using a negotiating strategy, which is easier to do using principles. In contrast, those who do not know what they are meant to be doing and even if they did would not be inclined to do it (the ill intentioned and ill informed) are best dealt with using a strategy that is more targeted, for which bright line rules are more effective. A supervisor can simply tell those firms: 'just do this because that is what the rule says.'[19]

The point here, however, is not which rule type is most effective for which type of regulated firm, though that is relevant, but which enforcement approach is used. Substantive PBR requires a broadly 'responsive'

---

[17]   Again, this is not to say that the normatively 'right' answer is simply one that the parties agree amongst themselves irrespective of the rule or principle; the point being made is a practical and operational one, not one that expresses a particular interpretive philosophy.

[18]   In Ayres and Braithwaite's original exposition there is no discussion of rule type; the issue is the nature of the dyadic interaction of regulator and regulatee: I. Ayres and J. Braithwaite, *Responsive Regulation* (Oxford: Oxford University Press, 1992).

[19]   R. Baldwin, *Rules and Government* (Oxford: Oxford University Press, 1995).

mode of supervision and enforcement, in which negotiation as to the meaning, application and purpose of the rule plays a central role, and in which the focus is on the outcome that is to be achieved.[20] However, whilst a 'responsive' approach to enforcement may be facilitated by rules of certain types, it is not contingent on them. So in the area of enforcement there can be, at least in this sense, substantive PBR without the form. The British Columbia Securities Commission provides a good example. As Ford explains, even though the BCSC has not been able to introduce principles, it has introduced the substantive aspect of PBR through changes to the manner in which it monitors and enforces its regulatory requirements.[21]

A third characteristic of substantive PBR is a focus on outcomes throughout the whole regulatory process. Again, there is no analytical correlation between using rules of a particular type (principles) and outcome-based supervision, but having formal PBR facilitates outcome-based supervision. It depends how the outcomes are defined (and whether they really are outcomes rather than outputs). Targets, for example, can be extremely precisely defined, and, as such, are as open to gaming and 'creative compliance' as detailed rules. Studies of how hospitals and other public service providers 'game' the performance targets set for them by central government illustrate this very clearly.[22] In the telling phrase, those subject to targets 'can hit the target and miss the point'[23] just as firms can engage in 'creative compliance' or the gaming of detailed rules: complying with the letter but not the spirit of the rule. Outcomes that are defined in qualitative and/or behavioural terms – for example to act 'with integrity', 'fairly', 'in the best interests of the client'[24] – are far harder to game. It is possible to have outcome-based supervision without having formal PBR if the outcomes are identified and adopted as operational supervisory and enforcement norms in the course of regulatory practice. However, the absence of any formal principles articulating those outcomes or the values from which they are derived can hinder formal enforcement processes. For if a firm fails to achieve those outcomes but there is no breach of a detailed rule, that is, gaming strategies are employed, then the regulator is largely impotent as there is nothing on which to base enforcement actions.

---

[20]   What 'responsive' can consist of is elaborated in R. Baldwin and J. Black, 'Really Responsive Regulation', 71 *Modern Law Review*, 59 (2008).

[21]   Ford, above n. 2.

[22]   C. Hood, 'Gaming in Targetworld: The Targets Approach to Managing British Public Services', 66(4) *Public Administration Review*, 515 (2006).

[23]   Ibid.

[24]   Outcomes are usually distinguished from outputs in performance evaluations: outputs are easier to game than outcomes.

The fourth characteristic of substantive PBR is that the responsibility for ensuring that the objectives of the principles are met is shifted, in part, from the regulator to the regulated. More general rules (principles) allow firms greater discretion as to what to do. With that discretion comes the need, and responsibility, for working out what they should do. Where the balance should be struck between firms thinking for themselves and the regulators providing guidance is endlessly contested; each thinks the other should be doing more. Firms want more specific guidance; regulators think firms should work it out for themselves. Firms do not want to do the regulators' job for them; regulators do not want to become unpaid consultants. This tension in their relationship, as to what the regulatory compact entails, is not unique to PBR regimes. Regulators implementing detailed rules face the same tension, as the NAO's review of the five largest regulators in the UK illustrates.[25] But PBR involves a significant shift in responsibility to firms, and requires a substantially different set of skills on the part of inspectors and compliance staff to engage in the negotiations and qualitative judgements that are entailed.

The final characteristic of substantive PBR is a conscious and deliberate focus by the regulator on the firm's internal systems of management and controls – referred to in the regulatory literature as 'meta-regulation' or management-based regulation.[26] As with enforcement, meta-regulation can and does operate in systems where there are detailed rules. Given that any regulatory regime requires firms to internalize the regulatory requirements into their own systems and processes for it to be complied with, meta-regulation could be argued to be not so much a radical new strategy as regulators making a virtue out of a necessity, or at least recognizing that necessity. Regulators always have to rely on firms' internal management regimes even for one-man firms simply because regulators cannot be continually present in all the firms they are responsible for all the time. However, in management-based or meta-regulatory regimes, reliance on internal management is 'designed in' to the regulatory regime and the regulator consciously and deliberately focuses its attention on ensuring that the firms' own internal rules, systems and processes are

---

[25] National Audit Office, *Regulatory Quality: How Regulators are Implementing the Hampton Vision* (London: National Audit Office, 2008) at para 4.5, notes that 'Regulators with direct inspection responsibilities face [the] challenge of determining where to draw the line between their preferred stance of neutral guidance provider and educator of business and the more hands on consultant-cum-management role many businesses seem to want.'

[26] C. Parker, *The Open Corporation* (Cambridge: Cambridge University Press, 2000), ch 9.

such that they will ensure compliance. As Power comments, internal management systems become the critical interface between regulatory and business values, and hence between society's and the organization's goals and operations.[27] Again the emphasis is on substance not form, under the substantive model. Regulators and firms should be focused on the outcomes those systems and processes deliver, not just on the form they take.

PBR AND REGULATORY SETTINGS: DYADIC AND POLYCENTRIC/NETWORKED PBR

Regulators stand in different institutional positions and relationships vis-à-vis other actors in a regulatory regime. Usually when we talk of regulatory regimes we think in terms of a dyadic relationship of regulator–regulatee. The regulator can be state or non-state, as can the regulatee, and they can exist in any combination (state regulating non-state; non-state regulating state; state regulating state; non-state regulating non-state). In dyadic PBR, the focus of analysis (and use of the principles) is to affect the behaviour of the regulatee. This is the normal focus of analysis and debates on PBR, and as explained above, PBR can exist simply at the level of the rule books, and/or can be manifested in particular regulatory approaches.

But regulatory regimes are often composed of dense, polycentric networks of actors. All or some of these actors can be regulators themselves, depending on which aspect of the overall regime we are focusing on. In polycentric PBR, principles are used in the management of networks of regulators. PBR in this context can also be substantive or formal. Principles can be used explicitly or implicitly to manage a network of regulators by distributing formal powers, responsibility and discretion within the regulatory regime. Principles implicitly or explicitly confer discretion on other regulators, as well as firms, to develop more detailed interpretations and applications. The extent to which they do so depends significantly on the space that they allow through their phrasing. One of the critical aspects of rules or principles is that they can both structure and distribute discretion, conferring space not just between rules/principles but within them, in which actors can exercise choice.[28] To give an obvious

---

[27] M. Power, *Organized Uncertainty: Designing a World of Risk Management* (Oxford: Oxford University Press, 2007) at 42.
[28] Black, above n 5, ch 1.

example, a norm that requires me to drive at a maximum of 30 miles per hour gives me less discretion to determine at which speed to go than one that requires me to drive at a reasonable speed. One of the contested issues within EU financial regulation, for example, is whether EU directives leave enough, or too much, room for national regulators to adapt the provisions to local markets or political preferences, and whether its provisions impose minimum or maximum harmonization.

These more detailed interpretations could be developed by other 'interpretive intermediaries', for example non-state regulatory organizations, trade associations and others who produce guidance on the meaning and application of the principles. In the UK, this is a strategy that the FSA had been using to an increasing degree. In the area of money laundering, it reduced its rules to two pages, preferring to rely instead on the provisions of the Joint Money Laundering Steering Group (JMLSG). Reducing the amount of rules in the area of money laundering was worthwhile, but the equivalent of picking low hanging fruit – the rules, as they were, mainly reiterated the provisions of either the statutory instruments or the JMSLG's guidance. There are other examples where the FSA actively facilitated the production of guidance by requiring representatives from different parts of the industry to agree on the contested issue of soft commissions. As part of its PBR initiative, the FSA also introduced a system of 'confirmed' guidance, whereby it would 'confirm' industry guidance on the application of the principles. The status of such guidance, the FSA stated, was that it will act as a 'shield' not a 'sword'. In other words, conduct in accordance with the guidance could be used as a 'shield' against enforcement action (though it did not have the formal status of a safe harbour), but non-conformity with the guidance would not be used as a 'sword' by the FSA with which to impale firms.[29]

Polycentric or network PBR is also manifested at the international level. Transnational financial regulation is characterized by such a dense network of regulatory actors, both state and non-state, operating at the global, regional and national level, and by a network of principles. Formal PBR is manifested in the plethora of principles issued by the various international committees. The transnational network of principles is denser in some areas than others. Some sets of principles interact through their inter-textuality, interconnecting through the incorporation of definitions or provisions from each other, or incorporation of entire codes themselves, or through cross-referencing, producing particularly

[29]   FSA, *Principles Based Regulation: Focusing on the Outcomes that Matter* (London: FSA, 2007).

dense networks of norms. Others do not interact at the formal level (that is, in their texts) but are brought together through mechanisms of implementation and enforcement, including systems of peer review. A notable example is the Financial Sector Assessment Programme, the review (inter alia) of the compliance of financial regulators and their national governments with a compendium of codes and principles issued by the main international standard-setting bodies. Under this programme, regulators and governments are assessed by a peer group of regulators as to the degree to which they have implemented the codes. In the wake of the financial crisis, the newly reformulated Financial Stability Board announced it will enhance and reinforce this process.[30] Other principles or codes are less integrated into the network, and simply exist side by side with other sets of principles with no explicit cross-referencing or common enforcement mechanism, but represent attempts by their authors to establish a place in the international dialogue and to position themselves in the institutional domain.[31]

Although the degree of density and interaction may vary, as do the individual reasons for their production, many uses of principles at the international level share a common aim: it is through the network of principles, and increasingly through their enforcement, that regulators seek to regulate other regulators. In networked or polycentric PBR principles can be used in an attempt both to confer and to structure the discretion of regulators and set the terms of their inter-regulator relationships, as they are in the more familiar regulator–firm relationships. As in that more familiar relationship, networked or polycentric PBR can have formal and substantive elements. Formally, polycentric PBR can exist at the level of rules. Substantively, it can be manifested in the operation of the management of the regulatory network. However, there can be a gap between formal enunciation of principles and their implementation in any regulatory regime. In financial regulation this is particularly manifested at the international level. The international financial regulatory regime exhibits strong formal PBR in so far as there are any number of principles of regulation. As to the substance, of course, one of the criticisms of international financial regulation is that there is surfeit of norms but at least until now no systematic means for ensuring their implementation; there was only weak substantive regulation of any form.

---

[30] Financial Stability Board, *Framework to Strengthen Adherence to International Standards* (Basel: BIS, 2010).

[31] E.g. OECD, *Principles for Efficient and Effective Financial Regulation* (Paris: OECD, 2009).

CHARTING THE RISE (AND FALL?) OF PBR

The Rise

In the period before the financial crisis, the attractiveness of PBR was significantly on the rise both in terms of regulatory practice and in political rhetoric. PBR has some obvious attractions, and, as noted above, resonated well with the new governance strategies being propounded by academics and some policymakers alike. In providing the framework in which firms can organize their own processes to achieve the substantive outcomes the regulator seeks, PBR both relies on and reinforces the image of the self-observing, responsible organization that is a central feature of governance strategies.[32] Regulatory conversations take centre stage as the meaning and application of principles is elaborated in iterated communications between regulator and regulated.[33] Rigid divisions of responsibility for producing rules between public and private actors are eschewed as third parties to the regulator–regulatee relationship such as trade associations are brought in to develop interpretations and guidance on their meaning. The strategy links with another key 'new governance' strategy, that of 'meta-regulation' or management-based regulation, in which regulators focus not on detailed compliance but on whether the firm's internal systems and processes can deliver the outcomes that the regulator seeks.[34] Principles impose outcomes to be achieved, not detailed processes for achieving them, thus allowing room for local or 'bottom up' elaboration and customization. They can thus help to overcome the problems of scale that all regulatory systems face: the move from the aggregate and the general, which is the level at which rules and principles operate,[35] to the local and the particular, which is the site of their application.[36]

The FSA had styled itself as an evidence-based, risk-based and principles-based regulator, but it was the last of these self-descriptions that caught political attention. The FSA itself put forward cogent reasons for adopting PBR, which accord with the advantages of principles often noted in aca-

---

[32] On those strategies, see Parker, above n 26, ch 9; Power, above n 27, at 41–2.

[33] See, further, J. Black, 'Talking about Regulation', *Public Law*, 77 (1998).

[34] Parker, above n 26; C Coglianese and D. Lazer, 'Management Based Regulation: Prescribing Private Management to Achieve Public Goals', 37(4) *Law and Society Review*, 691 (2003).

[35] As do policymakers.

[36] Black, above n. 5.

demic commentaries, and indeed echoed in the OECD's recent Principles.[37] It offered four main reasons for adopting a more principles-based approach. Firstly, effectiveness: detailed rules, it argued, have been incapable of preventing misconduct in a range of areas, such as misselling of retail financial products. Secondly, durability: regulation that focuses on outcomes is more able to adapt to a rapidly changing market environment than one which is based on prescriptive rules. Thirdly, accessibility: principles are far more accessible to senior management and smaller firms, in particular, than a bewildering mass of detailed requirements. Fourthly, fostering substantive compliance: a large volume of detailed provisions can divert attention towards adhering to the letter rather than the spirit of the rules, making it less likely that the FSA will achieve its regulatory objectives.[38]

However, there was more to the PBR debate pre-crisis than regulatory functionality. In the US–UK context, and to an extent in the EU–UK context, PBR became intimately embroiled in a competition among regulators (and their governments) for business. There is no doubt that, at least at the rhetorical level, PBR was a weapon in the fierce battle for business between London and New York.[39] The political attraction of principles-based regulation lay in its rhetorical invocation of a Utopian world. In this regulatory Utopia, regulation is targeted and focused, and preferably harmonized across jurisdictions; regulated firms are given the flexibility they need to get on with running their businesses; and consequently regulatory outcomes are achieved with no undue cost to business. It is a world in which regulators have sufficient perspective on and understanding of the problems and issues that they confront to be selective, and to identify the key issues, principles and purposes on which regulation should focus to agree a common framework. It is also a world in which regulated firms are given the flexibility and responsibility to develop their own systems for ensuring that the regulatory principles are adhered to, but in a way that means their businesses can operate efficiently and innovatively in a stable regulatory environment.

The rhetoric of principles-based regulation thus invoked, not deregulation, but a re-framing of the regulatory relationship from one of directing and controlling to one based on responsibility, mutuality and trust. Regulators and regulatees move from a directing relationship of telling and doing, to a relationship of responsibility, mutuality and trust in which regulators communicate their goals and expectations clearly in principles

---

[37]   OECD Principles, above n. 31.
[38]   FSA, above n. 29, at 6.
[39]   The rhetorical battle has led Cunningham to argue that the debate should be abandoned and refocused on fundamentals. See Cunningham, above n. 3.

and apply those principles predictably, regulatees adopt a self-reflective approach to the development of processes and practices to ensure that these goals are substantively met, and, critically, both trust each other to fulfil their side of this new regulatory bargain.

This is a powerful vision with obvious political appeal for politicians, regulators and firms alike. In less Utopian visions, of course, PBR is either simply a licence for backsliding – for allowing regulatees to do what they want with regulators' pandering not kept in check by detailed rules that they have to enforce – or, conversely, PBR is simply a licence for regulators to put the boot in retrospectively when they decide that a firm's conduct is not up to scratch, with regulators' arbitrariness not kept in check by detailed rules to which they can be held accountable.

The Fall

The higher the climb, the bigger the fall, and the reputation of PBR suffered a significant setback in the wake of the crisis. The FSA was forced into a 'product recall', and re-launched itself under the new strapline of an 'outcomes based regulator'. In the Discussion Paper that accompanied the Turner Report, it described the change thus:

> The FSA has always considered itself to be principles-based in carrying out its supervisory work, preferring, where appropriate, a high-level articulation of what is expected of regulated firms over prescriptive rules. This enables firms to decide how to align their business objectives with the specified regulatory outcomes. The focus is not on the principles themselves but on judging the results of the actions of the firms and the individuals that the FSA supervises. In this way, a better articulation of the FSA's philosophy is that it is an outcomes-focused regulator, firmly committed to a risk-based and proportionate approach.[40]

As Hector Sants, the FSA's chief executive, explained:

> The whole point of outcomes . . . is that we want the supervisors to supervise, ie, to give consideration to whether the actions which companies are taking are leading to consequences which work in the best interests of society, consumer and the markets. We want them to think ahead, anticipate, think what is going to happen next, think whether what is going to happen next is going to work for society. That is what we mean by outcomes-based regulation. It is always difficult to capture that in one word but the point is clear. They need to be forward-thinking, braver, intrusive and get involved.[41]

---

[40]   FSA, above n. 16, at para 1.64.
[41]   Treasury Select Committee, Minutes of Evidence (25 February 2009), Response to Q2235.

So what has changed in the FSA's approach? What has not changed is the rule book, or at least not in ways that change its character. The 11 Principles for Business are still in place. Although its ability to use principles throughout its rule book is heavily circumscribed by the need to implement European legislation, the FSA relies extensively on a variety of other codes and principles embedded within the Handbook wherever it can. Notable amongst these are the Statement of Principles for Approved Persons, which the FSA is proposing to enhance in a number of respects,[42] and its recently introduced Remuneration Code, discussed further below.[43]

PBR has been retained in the sense that the FSA still seeks, where it can, to move away from prescriptive rules to a higher level articulation of what the FSA expects firms to do. As Sants explained again: 'In other words, it [principles-based regulation] helps emphasise that what really matters is not that any particular box has been ticked but rather that when making decisions, executives know they will be judged on the consequences – the results of those actions.'[44]

However, the FSA no longer looked to the Principles to be the means to achieve its outcomes, and withdrew from the strategy of 'light touch' regulation. Post-crisis, there was a fundamental change in the FSA's supervisory approach, at least (and this is an important qualification) with respect to its supervision of high-impact financial institutions, notably the large banks. The change has been both philosophical, at least in a 'lite' sense, and operational.

At the more ideational level, as Lord Turner, incoming chair of the FSA, explained, the previous regulatory philosophy had been forged in the meeting of two distinct philosophies: one economic, the other political. The dominant economic philosophy, held not just by self-interested market participants but also by independent academic economists in the UK and elsewhere, was that markets were self-correcting and that firms were best placed to manage their own risk.

This economic philosophy was coupled, at least in the UK, with a political attitude that deemed regulation should be 'light touch'. This, Lord Turner argued, had a significant role to play in shaping the FSA's approach, notwithstanding its formal independence. In his evidence,

---

[42]   FSA, *Consultation Paper 10/3: Effective Corporate Governance (Significant Influence Controlled Functions and the Walker Review)* (London: FSA, 2010).

[43]   SYSC 19; for discussion see FSA, *Policy Statement 09/15: Reforming Remuneration Practices in Financial Services* (London: FSA, 2009).

[44]   H. Sants, *Delivering Intensive Supervision and Credible Deterrence*, Speech delivered to the Reuters Newsmakers Event (12 March 2009).

Lord Turner explained: 'I think it is also the case that that [economic philosophy] existed within a political philosophy where all the pressure on the FSA was not to say: "Are you looking more closely at these business models?" but to say: "Why are you being so heavy and intrusive? Can you not make your regulation a bit more light touch?"'[45]

The resulting combination produced a regulatory system based on the twin assumptions of self-correcting markets and responsible management cased in a political context in which the worst offence the regulator could commit was to cause London to lose business. The FSA's regulatory philosophy was therefore to focus on organizational structures, processes and systems and whether the reporting lines were correct. Its view was that it was not the function of the regulator to question the overall business strategy of the institution. In his evidence to the Treasury Select Committee, Lord Turner explained:

> I think there was a philosophy of regulation which emerged, not just in this country but in other countries, which was based upon too extreme a form of confidence in markets and confidence in the ideas that markets were self-correcting, which therefore believed that the fundamental role of the supervision of financial institutions, in particular banks, was to make sure that processes and procedures and systems were in place, while leaving it to the judgment of individual management to make fundamentally sensible decisions. As Alan Greenspan said, that is the intellectual framework which has received an extraordinary challenge.[46]

The FSA still focuses on internal management and controls, but in a more substantive and less formalistic way than before. To quote Turner again, its approach shifted from one focusing on structured systems and procedures 'to one which is focused on understanding the fundamental economics of the banks we are dealing with'.[47] The mantra changed to 'intensive supervision', in which the FSA 'make[s] judgements of the judgements of firms' senior management and require action if, in their view, the latter pose risks to the FSA's objectives'.[48]

There are four strands, in effect, to the FSA's model of 'intensive super-

---

[45]   Treasury Select Committee, Minutes of Evidence (25 February 2009), Lord Turner Response to Q2145. See also his response to Q2160: 'it [the political philosophy] was expressed in speeches on both sides of the House but which suggested that the key priority in regulation was to keep it light rather than to ask ever more searching questions'.

[46]   Treasury Select Committee, Minutes of Evidence (25 February 2009), Lord Turner Response to Q2156.

[47]   Response to Q2148.

[48]   FSA, above n. 16, at para. 1.66.

vision'. The first is a much closer attention to the implementation of its risk-based system of supervision and a greater focus on risk identification and the integration of macro-prudential analysis into firm-specific supervision. The lesson of Northern Rock was that the FSA was operating as an organization in which there was considerable bifurcation between the supervision that Northern Rock was meant to receive and that which it received in practice. It was meant to be monitored on a 'close and continuous' basis, though ranked as relatively low impact in the risk-based system in place at the time. The 'close and continuous' monitoring was meant, amongst other things, to provide a window on the bank through which supervisors could see whether there were any risks emerging. In practice, far from being 'close and continuous', the monitoring was remote and ad hoc. As a result, the regulator as a whole had a view of the bank in which it assumed that far more monitoring was occurring than actually was.[49]

Northern Rock was a massive shock to the FSA, and it fundamentally reshaped the implementation of its risk-based approach to high-impact firms as a consequence. The Risk Division was moved from the periphery to the centre of the organization. It has also become the organization's own compliance division. Key internal supervisory meetings are organized by the Risk Division, and are not quorate unless a member of the Risk Division is present. The Risk Division signs off on all supervisory plans, and also assesses the participation of each member present for the purposes of their own internal review and promotion. Supervisory planning meetings for high-impact firms are attended by those from all divisions responsible for monitoring it, as well as by economic specialists. Macro-prudential issues are integrated into each supervisory plan, and into the firms' day-to-day supervision. It has developed a highly complex system of internal governance, involving significant numbers of senior people from across the organization in the supervision of high-impact institutions with a considerable impact on resource allocation within the organization, and supervisory staff have increased by 30 per cent.[50]

The second strand is a shift in the manner in which the FSA relies on senior management. That reliance is now much more sceptical and far less trusting than it was before. In Hector Sants's memorable phrase, 'a

---

[49]   FSA, *Internal Audit Report, The Supervision of Northern Rock: A Lessons Learned Review* (London: FSA, 2008).
[50]   There has also been a shift in resource allocation from a roughly 60:40 split between conduct of business and prudential divisions to a direct reversal of those proportions. Communications between FSA officials and author; notes on file with author.

principles-based approach does not work with individuals who have no principles'.[51] Pre-crisis, there was a far more accepting culture within the FSA that they could trust the picture that the large firms painted of themselves. Now, there is a far more intensive and sceptical supervisory process that looks at how those systems operate in practice, a change that is linked to the increased focus on outcomes, discussed below. Underlying this is a significant reduction in the trust that the FSA is prepared to place in firms' senior management to do the job they are appointed (and extremely well paid) to do, and indeed to appoint people to positions that they are competent to hold.

One example of this shift is its increased role in approving internal appointments to those occupying 'significant influence functions' under the Approved Persons regime, and the extension of the positions to which the code applies.[52] The FSA has always imposed corporate governance provisions on regulated firms that are significantly above those imposed through the UK Corporate Governance Code and company law. Since its inception it has required those occupying certain strategic and operational functions within authorized firms to have separate regulatory approval under a 'fit and proper' test, and has subjected them to individual responsibilities set out in the Approved Persons regime. However, the process of approval had been largely administrative and had focused primarily on the 'properness' of the person, investigating whether they had criminal convictions no matter how minor or irrelevant (for example, driving offences). Indeed, the FSA had within the last couple of years revised the regime to reduce the number of times that approval needed to be sought for more client-facing functions to reduce the administrative burdens on firms. This reduction had been much lauded in its 'better regulation' approach outlined in 2007. Post-crisis, the FSA started taking the approval role far more seriously for those who are applying to occupy 'significant influence functions' within authorized firms, focusing on their 'fitness' and competence, not just on their 'properness'. It has started interviewing those to take significant influence functions (SIFs), and between October 2008 and January 2010 had conducted 332 interviews, rejecting 25 applicants,[53] and, if anecdotal evidence is to be believed, refusing to shortlist even more. This focus on competence in appointment is matched by a policy to take enforcement actions against individuals not just for breach of probity but

---

[51]   Sants, above n. 44.

[52]   FSA, *Dear CEO Letter, Approving and Supervising Significant Influence Functions: Our New Intrusive Approach* (London: FSA, 12 October 2009), FSA, above n. 42.

[53]   FSA, *Press Notice/015/2010* (London: FSA, 28 January 2010).

also of competence.[54] As with other regulators, it also started scrutinizing remuneration structures within financial institutions.[55]

There is also a notable extension here in the focus of who takes the responsibility for managing the firm. Pre-crisis, the focus was on senior management. Post-crisis there is a shift, at least in the UK, to placing greater responsibility on non-executive directors and on shareholders, as evidenced by the FRC's Stewardship Code, noted above.[56] As the FSA is careful to point out, there are limits to what regulation can achieve: 'regulators make no claim to be infallible'. Moreover, regulation should not be about restricting firms' risk-taking per se. However, the emphasis is now not only on firms' senior management, but also on their non-executive directors, shareholders and auditors, who *together* 'carry primary responsibility for their actions and resulting consequences'.[57]

The third dimension to the FSA's changed approach is its focus on outcomes. The FSA states that it is now far more concerned with testing whether firms have delivered the right regulatory outcomes, and, to an extent, with anticipating whether they will deliver those outcomes in the near future. It is a 'move from regulation based on facts to regulation based on judgements about the future'.[58] Here, again, caution is merited. The FSA's 'treating customers fairly' (TCF) initiative was all about focusing on outcomes, which had led to both firms and the FSA having to grapple with what 'fairness' meant in the context of the firm–customer relationship. The difference between the two perspectives was well illustrated in the debate between 'suitability' and 'satisfaction'. Firms argued that they could use customer surveys of 'satisfaction' as evidence that they delivered suitability; the FSA in contrast argued that, as the products are opaque and customers cannot assess suitability for themselves, customers may be satisfied even if sold an unsuitable product.[59]

So the move to 'outcomes' is not without precedence; rather, again, it provides an illustration of the twin-track approach that the FSA adopted

---

[54] See M Cole, *Speech to Enforcement Law Conference* (18 June 2008). It imposed its first fine against a chief executive of a publicly quoted firm in May 2008: a fine of £14,000 imposed on Paul Briant of Land of Leather for allowing untrained sales staff to sell payment protection insurance (PPI). The firm was fined £210 000.

[55] FSA, *Code on Remuneration* (London: FSA, 2009).

[56] See, e.g., P Myners, Financial Services Secretary to the Treasury, *Speech to the NAPF Corporate Governance Seminar*, *HM Treasury PN 14/10 9* (February 2010); Walker, above n 13.

[57] FSA, above n. 16, at para. 11.10.

[58] Ibid.

[59] FSA, *Treating Customers Fairly: Progress Update* (London: FSA, 2008) at 13.

pre-crisis between retail and wholesale regulation. The increased focus on outcomes across the board is linked, as noted above, to the manner in which the FSA assesses firms' ability to manage the risks they are taking. The crisis revealed significant flaws in the risk-management systems of all large financial institutions, not just those in the UK. At fault were not only inadequate risk models or organizational structures and reporting lines, but entire organizational cultures. 'Risk' and 'compliance' were the Cinderella enclaves of large financial institutions, relatively underpaid and significantly overlooked both in the day-to-day operations of the firm and in its strategic management.[60] Just as the FSA found that having pristine processes on paper does not guarantee their implementation within its own organization, so it has recognized that the same is true for those it regulates. So there is reliance on senior management, but now that reliance is more sceptically held and is focused on the delivery of outcomes, not on the presentation of structures and processes.

Finally, it has adopted a policy of what it terms 'credible deterrence'. The FSA has long been criticized for failing to take any successful enforcement actions against insider dealing and market abuse. These are notoriously difficult to prove offences, and so lack of successful actions does not necessarily point to inadequate investigations or lax enforcement processes. However, even with respect to less complex breaches of the regulatory rules, its fines have not always been particularly high, with a few notable exceptions, and have certainly been lower than in the US. Again, internal organizational changes have been focused on producing a more integrated organization in which the enforcement division is beginning to be brought in earlier in the overall monitoring and supervisory processes, and not regarded as an 'end of pipe' division. Fines levels have been increasing, rising 53 per cent in 2009/10. Further, as noted above, a critical policy decision has been taken to take enforcement action against senior individuals, not just the companies they run. In March 2010, the FSA announced that it would adopt a policy of raising fine levels. Under the new framework, fines will be linked more closely to income and be based on up to 20 per cent of a firm's revenue from the product or business area linked to the breach over the relevant period; up to 40 per cent of an individual's salary and benefits (including bonuses) from their job relating to the breach in non-market abuse cases; and a minimum starting point of £100000 for individuals in serious market abuse cases.[61]

---

[60] See, e.g., UBS, *Shareholders Report on UBS's Writedowns* (2008); G Kirkpatrick, 'The Corporate Governance Lessons from the Financial Crisis', *Financial Market Trends*, 2009/1 (Paris: OECD, 2009).

[61] FSA, *Policy Statement 10/4: Enforcement Financial Penalties* (London: FSA, 2009).

A number of things have not changed, but this does not indicate that the FSA is still 'light touch'. Rather, it is that there were pockets of highly intensive supervision going on within the FSA, but that the political context at the time meant that these could not be trumpeted as examples of principles-based regulation as loudly as the 'light touch' message could. A lot of the PBR rhetoric has been just that, rhetoric. In fact, when the FSA decided in 2007 to launch the PBR strapline and construct its identity as a 'principles based regulator', it used as a basis for demonstrating that this was not such a major change in approach an initiative that it had launched in the retail sector the previous year: the Treating Customers Fairly initiative, or TCF. TCF was based on Principle 6 of the Principles for Business, which requires firms to 'treat customers fairly'. Under a deliberate quirk of drafting, 'customers' means only retail customers, and so this was firmly a retail markets conduct of business initiative. As such it was far removed from the wholesale financial institutions, and thus from the battle for that wholesale market business among international financial centres in which the 'light touch' mantra, deployed by politicians, played such a role.

TCF was in practice very far from light touch.[62] It had a set of six outcomes that firms were required to deliver, developed quite separately from the individual rules to which they were also subject (though with some overlap, for example in relation to suitability). Firms were required to produce management information demonstrating that they were meeting these outcomes. They also had to put in place novel ways of collecting that information, in particular through having mandatory 'mystery shopping' checks on their sales teams. Moreover, the FSA required firms to demonstrate that they were treating customers fairly at all points in the product chain, not just in the sales process. Rather, at every stage, from product development, through marketing, through commission and remuneration structures through to the sales and post-sales processes, firms were required to demonstrate that they achieved the TCF outcomes. This has far more in common with the newly heralded 'intensive supervision'. Why could the FSA 'get away' with such an intrusive approach here and not with respect to the wholesale activities of the big banks? A very different political context is one reason: there has been a long history of misselling in the retail markets, and consumers are constituents. Further, the retail and wholesale markets have different geo-economic profiles: there is no

---

62 Contrast the Coalition Government's consultation paper, which criticised the FSA for not focusing sufficiently on retail regulation: HM Treasury, *A New Approach to Financial Regulation: Judgement, Focus and Stability*, Cm 7874 (London: TSO, 2010).

intense international battle for retail business, but there is for the high octane, high numbers wholesale business. Retail markets are also far less integrated than the wholesale markets, even in the EU,[63] and not nearly as peripatetic, and so less able to respond to more intensive supervision by moving jurisdiction.

Prior to the crisis, therefore, the FSA was thus already performing intensive, outcomes-focused supervision based almost entirely on one Principle. Moreover, it had also been changing its enforcement approach to taking enforcement actions based on breach of Principles alone. This was a significant change from when it was first formed, when its initial chair and chief executive reassured firms that the FSA would not take enforcement action on the breach of a principle alone. In fact, the levels of enforcement actions based solely on principles had risen from 30 per cent in 2006/7 to 44 per cent in 2007/8.[64] Fine levels had also been increasing prior to 2009.

Neither of these examples is put forward to deny that the FSA has had a fundamental change of approach. Rather, they are put forward as warnings not to take the rhetoric of regulators, and in particular the rhetoric of politicians about regulators, too seriously. Both of these initiatives were not only taking place whilst the FSA was styling itself as a 'principles based regulator'. They were used by the FSA as examples of what it did as a 'principles based regulator'. What is the case, however, is that neither approach, and particularly not the TCF model of supervision, spilled over into prudential supervision. If TCF and the changing patterns of enforcement were illustrations of what the FSA meant by being 'principles based', one of the problems was arguably not that the FSA was 'too' principles-based, but that it was not principles-based enough.

THE FATE OF PBR

Formal PBR

The fate of formal PBR looks better than the fate of one of its key proponents, the FSA. The fate of the FSA is, at the time of writing, not looking particularly rosy. The Coalition Government is currently consulting on

---

[63] European Commission, Staff Working Document, *European Financial Integration Report 2009*, SEC(2009) 1702 final (Brussels: European Commission, 2009).

[64] Figures taken from FSA Annual Reports 2006/7 and 2007/8.

proposals to move prudential supervision to the Bank of England and create an agency for retail and markets regulation. Whatever emerges, it is by no means clear that the label 'principles-based regulator' will be deployed in the near future, though this may change. The Government's consultation paper is actively seeking ways in which to ensure that the new prudential regulator has a 'new, more judgement-led style' of prudential regulation[65] (newspeak, perhaps, for substantive PBR). Elsewhere, however, national governments and the EU are devising increasingly prescriptive requirements for market participants to adhere to. In the current political climate, the worst thing a regulator can be criticized for is not that it causes its financial centre to lose business, but that its regulatory approach is so favourable that it is openly celebrated as somewhere that financial institutions want to be.

So what is the fate of PBR? Certainly, it has a mixed future, at least in financial regulation. Focusing first on formal PBR, here the fate of PBR depends on where you look. At the UK level, as mentioned above, the Principles for Business still occupy a central role in the FSA Handbook. Moreover, wherever it is not constrained by EU legislation, the FSA has a distinct preference for framing rules in terms of broadly framed requirements supplemented by guidance. The OECD has recently produced its Principles for Efficient and Effective Financial Regulation. In Japan, as noted above, there is clear interest in PBR as an element of a move to 'better regulation'.

In the EU, however, the idea(s) of principles-based regulation has never really taken hold, and, if the debates on the regulation of hedge funds are any indicator, it will be a long time before it does. At the formal level, the rationale of the Lamfalussy reforms was, of course, to have a tiered system of rule design, with the Level 1 directives expressing the main principles, and the details being contained in the Level 2 legislative measures and in guidance issued by the Level 3 committees.[66] Whilst there are examples of individual provisions within Directives that are more 'principles' in character than others, overall the network of legislative provisions that comprises financial regulation within the EU is hard to characterize as 'principles based', at least not without so many qualifications that the label becomes almost meaningless.

At the international level, however, formal PBR is alive and well. What

---

[65]   HM Treasury, above n. 62, at para. 3.3.
[66]   European Commission, *Final Report of the Committee of Wise Men on the Regulation of European Securities Markets* (Brussels: European Commission, 2001); Inter-Institutional Monitoring Group, *Final Report* (Brussels: European Commission, 2007).

slows the production of principles at this level is not a preference for detailed rules but the difficulty of securing international agreement on fundamental and difficult questions. The delicate international consensus that initially developed with respect to the thorny question of whether banks should be limited in size or in their activities, for example, was broken with the unilateral announcement by the Obama administration in January 2010 that it would adopt the 'Volker rule', that no deposit-taking banks should engage in proprietary trading.[67] The issue is currently being reviewed in the UK by the Independent Commission on Banking, due to report in September 2011.

However, as discussed above, principles play a number of roles in regulation, particularly but not uniquely in polycentric settings. They are not simply regulatory instruments used in an attempt to affect behaviour. They can have a broader significance. As the FSAP review process, noted above, illustrates, they are increasingly being used as criteria of accountability, benchmarks of performance against which national regulatory regimes are assessed. Principles are also used to establish their authors' own institutional position within the regulatory regime. It is notable, for example, that the newly reformulated Financial Stability Board, which is being positioned and positioning itself as the lead coordinator of global financial regulation, has issued two sets of Principles within its first 18 months,[68] more than it did in the last 10 years in its old formulation as the Financial Stability Forum, in which it issued recommendations, but otherwise simply compiled a compendium of principles issued by others.

Principles are, of course, also used for a more obvious purpose as part of the drive for harmonization of regulation across jurisdictional boundaries. However, the manner in which they are formed can be disjointed and uncoordinated. A good recent illustration of the dynamics of 'principles production' in the polycentric system of financial regulation is the development of codes on remuneration at the international, EU and national (UK) level. In this case, despite the rhetoric of the need for greater international coordination and harmonization, the FSA was a 'first mover', declaring that it was prepared to act unilaterally. It issued its draft code on remuneration in February 2009. This was followed (at least in time) by the communiqué from the G20 that principles governing remuneration should be developed. As a consequence, the Financial Stability Forum

---

[67] President Barack Obama, *Remarks by the President on Financial Reform*, White House Press Conference, 21 January 2010 (on file with author), now enacted in the Dodd-Frank Wall Street Reform and Consumer Protection Act (2010).

[68] FSB, *Principles for Sound Compensation Practice* (Basel: BIS, 2009); FSB, *Principles for Cross-border Cooperation on Crisis Management* (Basel: BIS, 2009).

(as it still was) issued its Principles on Sound Compensation Practices on 2 April 2009, followed by Implementation Standards for the Principles in September 2009, which charged two of the international committees of regulators, IOSCO (securities) and the BCBS (banking), with the task of developing implementation proposals. Separately, regulators in Australia, Switzerland, France and the Netherlands published principles on remuneration practices, broadly following the FSF's, and the US indicated its intention to do so.

Meanwhile, various initiatives were emanating from the EU. The Committee of European Banking Supervisors (CEBS) issued the final version of its high-level principles on remuneration on 20 April. Supervisors and firms were asked to implement them by the end of the third quarter.[69] A few days later, the EU Commission published two non-binding Recommendations. The first updated its disclosure requirements for the pay of executive directors of all EU listed companies. The other addressed remuneration policies in the financial sector and recommended that Member States should ensure that financial institutions have remuneration policies for risk-taking staff that are consistent with and promote sound and effective risk management.[70] The Commission also published for consultation draft amendments to the Capital Requirements Directive (CRD), which included provisions on remuneration, and which were formalized and sent to the EU Parliament and Council in July 2009.[71] None of these sets of principles is exactly aligned with another. The FSA code, for example, is broadly aligned with the FSB's principles, but is 'super-equivalent' in a number of respects.[72] Further, notwithstanding the fact that the FSA ultimately had to implement the CRD's eventual provisions on remuneration, it initially decided that it should act unilaterally and in advance of any EU provisions that would eventually emerge. The FSA's Code on Remuneration was finalized in October 2009 and came into force in January 2010.

---

[69] Committee of European Banking Supervisors (CEBS), *High-Level Principles for Remuneration Policies* (London: CEBS, 2009).

[70] European Commission, Commission Recommendation on Remuneration Policies in the Financial Services Sector, C(2009) 3159 (Brussels: European Commission, 2009).

[71] Proposal for a Directive of the European Parliament and of the Council amending Directives 2006/48/EC and 2006/49/EC as regards capital requirements for the trading book and for re-securitisations, and the supervisory review of remuneration policies, SEC(2009) 974 final, SEC(2009) 975 final. Now enacted as Directive 2010/76/EU OJ (2010) L329/3.

[72] For discussion, see FSA, *Policy Statement 09/15: Reforming Remuneration Practices in Financial Services* (London: FSA, 2009).

The process demonstrates a number of aspects of the dynamics of norm production in polycentric regimes. First, it illustrates the persistent use of formal PBR as a regulatory tool, both in a dyadic, firm–regulator setting (for example, the FSA's Remuneration Code) and in a polycentric setting (FSB principles are directed at national regulators and at the other international committees of financial regulators, positioning the FSB and distributing discretion and attempting to define 'subordinate' roles for national regulators to implement at the local level). Secondly, it demonstrates the 'multi-authorship' of principles, and the multiple roles that individual regulators play in each of these rule-writing fora: the FSA, for example, is both contributing author of and subject to the principles then emanating from the FSB, IOSCO, the BCBS and CEBS. Thirdly, it provides an example of the problems of system management and the lack of coordination that can characterize norm formation in polycentric systems, as each regulator wants to develop its own norms to suit its own local conditions and priorities. Finally, it shows that there is no hierarchy of norm formation for soft law norms: national principles do not necessarily flow from regional ones, and regional principles do not necessarily flow from the transnational. Rather the development of principles at each level can be contemporaneous; or international can follow national or regional or vice versa, and may be only loosely coordinated among the levels, if at all.

Substantive PBR

What of substantive or operational PBR? Here the verdict is just as mixed. The 'ideal type' constructed above consisted of five elements, not all of which need be present: modes of interpretation, enforcement, compliance focus, distribution of responsibilities within the regulatory regime and conscious reliance on internal management, or meta-regulation. At the international level, the increased emphasis on implementation clearly opens the possibility for substantive PBR to be adopted, but proper evaluation of that system has to be left for another time. Focusing again on the dyadic context of substantive PBR, the regulator–regulatee relationship, and on the UK, then the interpretive approach has not changed: interpretation of both rules and principles within the FSA Handbook is still characterized by purposive interpretation and consequentialist reasoning, in fact perhaps even more than it was pre-crisis. The FSA's enforcement activities have certainly intensified, but the trend for taking actions for breaches of Principles alone continues. The main shift here has been with respect to the target of enforcement actions, with senior individuals of large institutions now being targeted when they were not before, and fine levels being raised.

Central to PBR is a reliance on firms' internal management (or in polycentric PBR, on the governance infrastructure of national states or other actors in the regime). Here the FSA has had an interesting journey, and one which is instructive for proponents of meta-regulation or management-based regulation. One of the statutory principles of 'good regulation' that the FSA is required to observe requires it to have regard to 'the responsibilities of those who manage the affairs of authorised persons'.[73] As the FSA explained early on in its life, '[t]his principle is designed to guard against unnecessary intrusion by the regulator into firms' business and requires us to hold senior management responsible for risk management and controls within firms'.[74] The provision was used increasingly by the FSA to defend the deferential approach that it has taken to senior management, and in particular for not intervening in firms' business decisions.[75] As noted above, focus on monitoring the existence of systems and processes has now been replaced with a far more intensive focus on ensuring that those systems and processes are delivering the right outcomes. Far from trusting senior management, the attitude is now that such an important aspect of PBR is not possible: to reiterate Hector Sants's memorable phrase, principles-based regulation is not possible for people who have no principles. So to the extent that PBR meant a focus on outcomes, then that is retained and indeed enhanced. However, a central element of PBR is trust, and that trust has gone. Its disappearance has cast substantive PBR a potentially fatal blow.

PBR AND RISK-BASED REGULATION

Finally, as an aside, it is worth considering the relationship between PBR and risk-based regulation (RBR), at least within the FSA. The FSA has maintained that it is an evidence-based, risk-based, principles-based and now outcomes-focused regulator, all at the same time. By evidence-based, it means that it will only regulate where there is an identifiable market failure and where the costs of intervention are less than the benefits to be gained from intervening. It does not always have the room to do this given the extent to which policy and legislation emanate from the EU, but it has nonetheless conducted cost–benefit analyses routinely since its inception, as indeed it is required to do under its statutory duties. By risk-based, it

---

73   Financial Services and Markets Act s. 2(3)(b).
74   FSA, *A New Regulator for a New Millennium* (London: FSA, 2000).
75   See e.g. Turner Review, above n. 16.

means that it will focus its supervisory resources on matters that pose the greatest risk to its statutory objectives.[76] It has never been particularly clear how its risk-based models of supervision tie in with principles-based regulation. The risk indicators do not interact with the principles; in fact, they do not particularly interact with the Handbook at all. This can partly be explained by historical development: the FSA's risk-based regime is built around risks to its four statutory objectives. It was being formulated more or less at the same time as the Principles for Business, but in a separate part of the organization and led by individuals who came out of different parts of the pre-FSA institutional structure: one from the old Securities and Investments Board, the other from the Bank of England.[77]

But timing is not the only reason for the dissonance. There is potentially an operational mismatch between PBR and RBR that arises from the logic of RBR itself. One of the key points of risk-based regulation is that regulators often have more rules to ensure compliance with than they have resources available. Consequently, one of the first messages of RBR is that regulators should start with 'risks not rules'. This framing of supervision in terms of 'risks not rules' is to help regulators move away from a 'tick box' attitude to compliance, when it checks compliance with every rule, to a more outcomes-based and risk-based approach to supervision.[78] The rules themselves, including any principles, play a rather ambivalent role in risk-based regulation. Their point of entry into the supervisory process is not in the design of the risk-based system, or even its implementation. Rather, it comes later, when a regulator is considering taking enforcement action against conduct or activities that it considers to be posing too high a risk. The danger, of course, then, is that there will be found to be a mismatch between the rules and the risks: that the rules do not focus on the risks and thus there is a critical lacuna in the regulatory regime.

In principle, PBR should complement RBR, for one of the advantages of principles is that they can usually be called upon to fill the gap between risks and detailed rules. However, in the FSA's case, Principles are not used to frame the 'risk to objectives' that are assessed in the risk-based supervisory framework. Rather, they are brought in at the enforcement stage, once it has been decided that a risk has crystallized. This difference is partly due to the contrasting natures of the regulatory interventions:

---

[76]   Both of these were set out early in its life: about, n. 74.

[77]   J. Black, 'The Emergence of Risk Based Regulation and the New Public Management in the UK', *Public Law*, 512 (2005).

[78]   For discussion, see J. Black, *Risk Based Regulation: Choices, Practices and Lessons Being Learned*, paper prepared for the OECD (December 2008) (on file with author).

enforcement is an *ex post* process that looks backwards; risk-based supervision is *ex ante*, and is meant to look forwards. However, there is no analytical reason why the Principles could not be used more clearly to set the supervisory agenda. That they do not suggests the persistence of the 'twin track' operation of PBR and RBR in the FSA's supervisory process.

CONCLUSIONS

Although this discussion has focused on PBR, in orientating its discussion around the 'ideal types' proposed at the outset it risks taking regulators' rhetoric too seriously. In practice, characterizing a regulatory regime as rules based or principles based does not take us very far, descriptively or normatively. It is hard to classify any one regulatory regime as being either entirely rule based or entirely principles based; the better question is what are, and should be, the relative roles of each. Neither principles nor rules usually function particularly successfully without the other.[79] However, debates on PBR are in fact rarely about the linguistic structure of written norms. They are usually much more about the nature of regulatory practices and of regulatory relationships, and about who should have the final say in interpreting the rule or principle. Moreover, it is the substantive nature of these relationships and practices that is far more relevant for understanding the operation of a regulatory regime than what the rule books look like. Furthermore, the rhetoric needs to be separated from the reality, and not necessarily believed. PBR can be used as a marketing label – used to conjure up a regulatory Utopia – as it was by politicians in the pre-crisis battle for market share. Conversely, it can be a derogatory label used to conjure up regulatory ineffectiveness – as it is post-crisis to explain what went wrong.

However, as a (constructed) set of substantive strategies of regulation, in practice PBR is complex and often paradoxical.[80] As for its future: for the moment, its fate is bound up with the association that PBR is light touch regulation. As has been illustrated above, PBR need not equate to 'light touch' regulation, but that more complex and tempering message is not one that politicians set on increasing their control over banks, and over regulators, currently want to hear. PBR, both formal and substantive, and

---

[79] See, e.g., J. Braithwaite, 'A Theory of Legal Certainty', 27 *Australian Journal of Legal Philosophy*, 47 (2002).

[80] J. Black, 'The Forms and Paradoxes of Principles Based Regulation', *Capital Markets Law Journal*, 425 (2008).

in both dyadic and polycentric relationships, is predicated, however, on extensive trust among the actors in the regulatory regime. Wherever that trust is lacking there is little scope for PBR to operate in any substantive way, and little chance that others will be afforded much discretion through the use of principles in the rule books. As for which strategy or set of regulatory strategies is the more effective: the financial crisis was a global experiment in the effectiveness of a wide range of regulatory techniques and institutional structures of financial regulation. All of them failed at least once. Governance and regulatory scholars and 'better regulation' practitioners rarely hold out much hope for the effectiveness of 'command and control' or detailed rules-based regulation, so failures of those techniques will come as no surprise. In contrast, it is the failure of many of the 'new governance' techniques of regulation that should prompt the greatest thought.

2. Policy stances in financial market regulation: Market rapture, club rules or democracy?[1]

Nicholas Dorn

INTRODUCTION

This chapter argues in favour of democratisation of financial market regulation – a topic resisted by many market participants and by some in regulation, yet one that is being explored by policymakers in the US and the EU, notably the UK.[2] Two reasons are advanced. First, active democratic oversight of financial market regulation is merited on grounds of principle. Second, accountability to national and regional parliaments would result in regulatory diversity, resulting in more robust market systems at global level. The current de facto 'independence' of financial market regulators allows them to network globally yet privately, to negotiate on the basis of market demands (each national regulator championing its home industry) and to converge their rules accordingly – producing common blind spots, systemic vulnerabilities and heightened potential for global crisis.

Clearly this analysis cuts against the grain of much regulatory thinking. Before the systemic crisis manifested itself, regulatory thinking was explicitly favourable to regulatory convergence and it remains so (or perhaps is

[1]   The author thanks interdisciplinary masters students on the 2008/9 course on global governance at Erasmus University Rotterdam and senior colleagues in the law faculty; Michael Levi at Cardiff University and Tom Vander Beken at Gent University, both of whom commentated on an earlier version; participants in at the 23–25 June 2009 W G Hart Legal Workshop on Law Reform and Financial Markets, held at IALS, London; Simone White, IALS Research Fellow, who critiqued successive drafts; and the editors of this volume, particular Kern Alexander. Needless to say the opinions expressed remain the responsibility of the author.

[Editors' note: the analysis in this chapter reflects reform developments prior to autumn 2009.]

[2]   HM Treasury, *Reforming Financial Markets*, Cm 7667 (London: HMSO, 2009) at 176.

even more deeply committed, see below). Convergence thrives on and reinforces regulatory independence from democratic oversight and steering – since such steering, based mainly in national and sometimes to a very limited extent in regional parliaments, hinders convergence. Also, at least prior to the crisis, the technical models deployed by regulators had been imported from the private sector and were legitimised by a particular form of rational choice theory (see below). Clearly, these political objectives, technical models and legitimising theory were, as Fourcade and Healy characterise market theory, 'saturated with normativity'.[3] The questions are, whose norms and with what consequences?

The form of rational choice perspective underpinning regulation prior to the crisis had a mood, identified here as rapture, building on Anderson's ironic reinterpretation and *dépassement* of the well-established but contentious idea of regulatory capture.[4] In rapture, regulatory agencies are seen not simply as having conflicts of interest and as slipping under the influence of particular firms within the sector that they are supposed to regulate (the case in capture), but rather as being politically committed to 'their' industry from the start, so doing whatever may possibly advance short-term opportunities for competitive advantage, profit and market positioning. In regulatory rapture, pre-crisis regulatory agencies were no longer 'conflicted' (in the American parlance), they were cheerleaders; although post-crash the mood has moderated.

The emerging corpus of regulators' reflections on the ways in which they were implicated in the crisis, through their acts and omissions, can be sharpened into a critique through deployment of the notion of rapture, as the following paragraphs will suggest. However, this does not offer us an intellectually compelling alternative to the thinking that has brought us here. To move beyond descriptive, critical and contrarian accounts, and to develop a forward basis for the reform of financial market regulation, one needs to locate events within an analysis of the wider structural and political conditions. In the second half of the chapter, an application of the socio-cultural work of Pierre Bourdieu (considered alongside well-known Anglophone work on the historical demise of 'club' regulation) deepens our understanding of how regulatory thinking became so one-dimensional, so lacking in cultural and intellectual checks and balances. Eschewing nostalgic solutions, the chapter points to re-politicisation of

---

[3] M. Fourcade and K. Healy, 'Moral Views of Market Society', 33 *Annual Review of Sociology*, 285 (2007) at 300.

[4] J. Anderson, 'The Public Utility Commission of Texas: A Case of Capture or Rapture?', 1(3) *Policy Studies Review*, 48 (1982).

financial market regulation, and democratic steering, as means of reintroducing intellectual challenge, regulatory diversity and systemic stability of global markets. First, however, the chapter picks up the understanding of the crisis generated within mainstream regulatory thinking.

THE RATIONALITY POSTULATE

> I do not deny the possible importance of irrationality in economic life. However, it seems that the best research strategy is to push the rationality postulate as far as it will go. (Ben Bernanke, Chairman of the Federal Reserve)[5]

In the event, the postulate was pushed quite far. Rational choice analysis underpinned the thinking of regulators before the crisis and it continues to inform their thinking on the origins of the crisis and on how to respond to it.[6] Therefore it is sensible to start with an appreciation and critique of this perspective.

The problem does not seem to be that market participants and regulators do not act rationally; indeed, they do act rationally, albeit always within certain assumptions. No doubt the President of Citibank was thinking rationally, within certain parameters, when he said as recently as July 2008: 'As long as the music is playing [markets are booming], you've got to get up and dance. We're still dancing.' The bank was rescued by the US Government in November of the same year and, as it turned out, that rescue was only the first of three thought necessary by March 2009. This and other rescues – and the reluctance of government majority shareholders to act as such – may all be perfectly rational, depending on the assumptions entertained and the calculations (cultural as well as economic) made.

---

[5]　B. Bernanke, 'Nonmonetary Effects in the Propagation of the Financial Crisis in the Great Depression', 73(3) *American Economic Review*, 257 (1983) at 258.

[6]　Rational choice has a long heritage in the social and economic sciences, including applications and critiques within criminology at local and international levels (see, for example, L. Holmes, 'Good Guys, Bad Guys: Transnational Corporations, Rational Choice Theory and Power Crime', 51(8) *Crime, Law and Social Change*, 383 (2008). For the behavioural finance critique of rational choice, see, inter alia, E Avgouleas, *Financial Regulation, Behavioural Finance, and the Global Credit Crisis: In Search of a New Regulatory Model* (2008), available at http://ssrn.com/abstract=1132665, at 9–10 (also published as E Avgouleas, 'The Global Financial Crisis, Behavioural Finance and Financial Regulation: In Search of a New Orthodoxy', 9 *Journal of Corporate Law Studies*, 23 (2009)) and M. Statman, 'Behavioral Finance, Past Battles and Future Engagements', *Financial Analysts Journal*, 18 (November/December 1999). These, however, are not the focus for this chapter.

Likewise, the regulators also acted rationally, within the limited span of their concerns at the time. Clearly, all regulatory perspectives invoke, either explicitly or implicitly, a sense of context, culture and sentiment, as these construct and interpret available information. Crucially, and as now widely recognised, the regulators were reliant on financial market models and data drawn from the private sector. These are now widely recognised as being inadequate to the task of systemic regulation. As the Governor of the Bank of France has put it, industry-standard risk models turned out to be 'insufficiently robust, comprehensive and disciplined', since they 'fail to produce estimates commensurate with market reality'.[7] Reliance on such models meant that regulators were surprised when 'market reality' took a sharp downward turn. These problems, previously of interest only to those working in and around financial markets, became front-page news in 2008, following the deepening of the crisis after Lehman Brothers was allowed to fail, causing a drying up of financial liquidity between banks and other financial traders. Central Banks stepped in to prop up remaining major financial firms – at least those whose failure it was considered would have further, highly deleterious, systemic effects.

The Rational Choice Self-Critique

As one consequence of the crisis, the central banks and other regulators have faced the delicate issue of theorising what went wrong under their watch. US Federal Reserve Chairman Ben Bernanke summarised the findings of the 'President's Working Group on Financial Markets', focussing particularly on the so-called 'originate-to-distribute' model of financial trading.[8] This example, focussing upon mortgages, equally applies to the creation of and trading in other types of debt: car purchase plans, credit card debt, company bonds, etc. The three stages are origination, securitisation and distribution.

> In the first stage of the process the originator – a lender or a broker serving as a lender's agent – extends the mortgage loan to a potential homebuyer. The originator is responsible for the underwriting – that is, for ensuring that the borrower is creditworthy and that the terms of the mortgage appropriately reflect the risks of the transaction.[9]

---

[7]   C. Noyer, 'Valuation Challenges in a Changing Financial Stability Review', 12 *Valuation and Financial Stability*, 156 (2008) at ii.

[8]   B. Bernanke, *Addressing Weaknesses in the Global Financial Markets: The Report of the President's Working Group on Financial Markets,* speech delivered at Richmond, Virginia, 10 April 2008, available at http://www.federalreserve.gov/newsevents/speech/bernanke20080410a.htm, at 4.

[9]   Ibid. at 2.

Then follows securitisation, in which:

> the originator sells the mortgage to another financial institution, let's call it the packager, which combines the mortgage with many other loans to create a marketable security . . . However, much more complex securities can also be created, backed for example by a mix of different types of loans or other assets combined with various guarantees or hedges; in recent years the issuance of these so-called structured credit products increased sharply. Importantly, the newly created securities may be broken into pieces, or tranches, of varying seniority and credit quality.[10]

Finally, the products are sold into the market.

> In the third stage of the originate-to-distribute process, these tranches are rated separately by one or more credit rating agencies, then sold to investors with differing preferences for risk or retained by the lender. In principle, the originate-to-distribute model spreads risk . . .[11]

And so it proved, to some extent. Although many of the financial institutions that aimed to pass on their risks found that they still were holding much risk when market conditions sharply deteriorated, large amounts had indeed been passed on to a range of investors throughout the world. The latter – pension funds, local government, private investors, etc – had been attracted by the prospect of reconciling strong income flow and apparent safety offered by these instruments.

Financial markets regulators observed, and allowed, the emergence of new, innovative, markets that, being new, were outside the scope of existing regulation. Not only the (in)famous hedge funds (speculative investment vehicles), but also many elements of the originate-to-distribute securitisation process, and new 'off-balance-sheet' financial vehicles of the banks (outlined below), opened up new and largely unregulated spaces.

Why did the regulators not enlarge the scope of regulation in order to bring these activities within the net? Possibly because they were preoccupied with competition among national financial centres and interests – market participants were said to indulge in 'regulatory arbitrage', meaning they would relocate trading operations to less burdensome regulatory centres.[12] Thus, although regulators were fully aware that much or most

---

[10]   Ibid.

[11]   Ibid.

[12]   For a critical review, see R. Prentice, 'Regulatory Competition in Securities Law: A Dream (That Should Be) Deferred', 66(6) *Ohio State Law Journal*, 1156 (2005).

of the international financial system was escaping regulation, there were pressures upon them, both from the market and from policymakers, not to bring regulation to the new market spaces and products.

Considerable intellectual effort went into debates on these matters. Much of the specialist debate on financial market regulation prior to 2007/8 focussed on the distinctions between 'rule-based' regulation (of which New York was taken as the paradigm) and 'principles-based' regulation (London), and on the question of whether the former is more constraining than the latter. As Coffee and Sale[13] summarise:

> Until the current crisis struck, [some US] critics of regulation had been arguing that the U.S. was losing its capital market competitiveness because it was taking a more aggressive posture towards regulation, and particularly towards enforcement, compared to the other major capital markets. At one pole in this debate, some academics even urged that issuers should be able to choose both the corporate and securities law applicable to them, opting from an inventory that would include at the least the corporate and securities laws of the major markets. Such choice, it was argued, would drive a process of regulatory arbitrage[14] until, in theory, the optimal level of regulation was reached. The current crisis is likely to mute this demand for investor choice, because in a world of collapsing and insolvent financial institutions, few favor giving them the right to choose their level of supervision.[15]

However, that debate primarily concerned the listing of firms on stock exchanges,[16] which is not the arena in which the 'credit crunch' problems emerged. In relation to two structural features of credit markets that are clearly implicated in the crisis – off-balance-sheet vehicles, especially

---

[13]   J. Coffee and H. Sale, 'Redesigning the SEC: Does the Treasury Have a Better Idea?' (2008), available at http://ssrn.com/absrtact=1309776 (also published in 95 *Virginia Law Review,* 707 (2009).

[14]   Regulatory arbitrage in its jurisdictional form is a process in which traders are free to relocate to whichever financial centres provide the most favourable regulatory framework, inducing regulators to compete to provide that ideal framework. Some observers advocate a minimum regulatory framework (see, for example, M. Flamée and P. Windels, 'Restructuring Financial Sector Supervision: Creating a Level Playing Field', 34 *The Geneva Papers,* 9 (2009). Neo-liberals advocate a variety of regulatory frameworks, depending on the needs and preferences of traders (eg, for enforceable contracts, at a minimum). The issue of jurisdictional arbitrage is taken up later in this chapter, being re-positioned within the broader argument for regulatory diversity.

[15]   Coffee and Sale, above n. 13, at 5–6.

[16]   J. Coffee, 'Racing Towards the Top? The Impact of Cross-Listings and Stock Market Competition on International Corporate Governance', *Columbia Law and Economics Working Paper 205* (30 May 2002) available at http://ssrn.com/abstract=315840 (also published in 102 *Columbia Law Review,* 1757 (2002).

of banks, and the formation of rules concerning wholesale financial products including derivatives – there was a *uniformly* 'light touch' regulatory stance, in the US, the UK and elsewhere in the EU (a form of convergence).[17] Off-balance-sheet vehicles had emerged as a known and tolerated way for banks to get round the capital adequacy rules required by the Basle I regime for bank regulation: by transferring debt and risk to a wholly-owned subsidiary, the beneficial owners of banks were able to continue to take on risk.[18] Additionally, even on-balance measures of bank debt shot up in the period to 2008. In the US, regulatory reforms encouraged this for the biggest financial institutions.

[T]he United States, as of the beginning of 2008, had five major investment banks that were not owned by a larger commercial bank: Merrill Lynch, Goldman Sachs, Morgan Stanley, Lehman Brothers and Bear Stearns. By the late Fall of 2008, all of these investment banks had either failed or abandoned their status as independent investment banks . . . each of these five firms voluntarily entered into the SEC's Consolidated Supervised Entity ('CSE') Program, which . . . permitted its members to escape the SEC's traditional net capital rule, which placed a maximum ceiling on their debt to equity ratios, and instead elect into a more relaxed 'alternative net capital rule' that contained no similar limitation. The result was predictable: all five of these major investment banks increased their debt-to-equity leverage ratios significantly . . .[19]

Likewise, European banks took on more risk. For example, as one economist[20] put it:

UK bank assets jumped from a manageable twice gross domestic product in 2001 to almost 4.5 times by 2008. These, then, are [like] undercapitalised hedge funds with liabilities large enough to destroy the solvency of the British state. What on earth were the authorities thinking?

The situations in other European countries varied somewhat; however, the general trend has been the same in all. When one considers the regulators'

---

[17] Coffee and Sale, above n. 13, at 6, stating: 'Why did the crisis begin, and largely devastate the financial landscape, in the United States, which has long had much more aggressive public and private enforcement?' Such 'more aggressive' enforcement does seem not to have been applied in relation to the financial practices and instruments that caused systemic problems.

[18] See P. Mizen, 'The Credit Crunch of 2007–2008: A Discussion of the Background, Market Reactions, and Policy Responses', 90(5) *Federal Reserve Bank of St. Louis Review*, 531 (2008).

[19] Ibid. at 560–561.

[20] M. Wolf, 'What To Do with Britain's Banks?', *Financial Times*, 12 December 2008, 9.

tolerance of banks building up such large debts on their balance sheets, alongside ballooning off-balance-sheet debts, then it is clear that the deregulatory trend in this period was strong.

Meanwhile, the rules (sometimes rather loose and amorphous understandings, as it turned out) for wholesale trading in levered debt instruments were made by private associations, not by regulators. It seems that the view of the regulators was that, where trading occurred between large and sophisticated firms, who should be capable of assessing their own 'risk appetite', they and their private associations could be left to self-regulate in relation to derivatives and other highly levered products such as CDS (credit default swaps, essentially a form of insurance against default on an underlying instrument, such as a bond issued by a company or a country). The one part of the originate-to-distribute system that was nominally within the purview of regulators was the front end, the retail part of mortgage and other loan-giving. However, here standards were increasingly relaxed, resulting inter alia in increasing evidence of mortgage fraud and misrepresentation from 2005 onwards.[21]

In summary, the regulators observed some worrying signs at the retail end, whilst permitting private rule-making in securities and derivative markets, and observing a ballooning of debt by banks and off-balance-sheet entities. It was acknowledged by regulators that some risk might be entailed; however, it was thought that, to the extent to which these had been 'spread' (sold on to other investors, insurers, etc), any problems would be minor – a view first enunciated by Alan Greenspan and reiterated by Timothy Geithner as late as 2007, when president and chief executive officer of the New York Federal Exchange.[22]

Precautionary Principle (Absence of)

In other spheres, such as anti-terrorism and ecological policies, the precautionary principle is widely acknowledged, even though the actions to be taken remain controversial: the principle is at least understood. Not so in relation to the financial markets in the years running up to the recent crisis, even though, as Coffee and Sale observe, 'the unique fact about

---

[21]   See e.g. FinCEN, *Suspected Money Laundering in the Residential Real Estate Industry, An Assessment Based Upon Suspicious Activity: Report Filing Analysis* (Washington: FinCEN, April 2008), at 21.
[22]   T. Geithner, *Credit Markets Innovations and Their Implications*, Remarks made at the 2007 Credit Markets Symposium hosted by the Federal Reserve Bank of Richmond, Charlotte, North Carolina.

financial institutions in general, and investment banks in particular, is their fragility'.[23] This fragility is for the following reason.

> They [financial institutions] finance their business using short-term capital to hold long-term illiquid assets. This mismatch exposes investment banks to liquidity crises, and, as the crisis mounts, their counter-parties back away and refuse to trade with them. This has happened before cyclically, well within the memory of the chief executives running these institutions.[24]

Financial institutions borrow, sometimes on a day-to-day basis, in order to have enough finance to cover the longer-term obligations. Every now and again there is a shortage or withdrawal of that short-term finance and then there is a problem ('crisis'). As Coffee and Sale make clear, this is the way the game has been going on for some time: the crisis-era instability reflects the extent to which this model has been extended from the 1990s onwards. In other words, a precautionary regulatory stance would seem to have been merited but it was not taken.

We are left with the analytical question: *why* was the precautionary perspective so weakly articulated in financial regulation? As we have seen above, rational choice theory gives some clues, in its belated acceptance that perverse incentives were in play across the social spectrum. A quite different type of clue is given by constructivist critiques of rational choice theory, emphasising not technical factors and calculable decisions, but rather the inter-subjective aspect of social interactions.

> Given that the subprime market was worth only $0.7 trillion in mid-2007, out of total capital markets of $175 trillion, the impact of subprime is out of all proportion to its actual weight in the financial system. This strongly implies that an explanation for this systemic crisis cannot be deduced in rationalist terms. [Rather . . .] The paralysis that comes over global finance is a consequence of the social or intersubjective nature of markets, rather than the logical result of relatively minor problems with lending to the working poor. But this analysis of the subprime crisis cannot be assimilated by those socialized into an exclusively rationalist view of markets, in which events have logical causes.[25]

Insofar as this view may have practical value, it suggests that technical attempts to 'fix' economic problems cannot work, once a certain threshold

---

[23] Coffee and Sale, above n. 13, at 29.
[24] Ibid.
[25] T. Sinclair 'Round Up the Usual Suspects: Blame and the Subprime Crisis', 15 *New Political Economy*, 91 (2010). On the quantitative observation made by Sinclair, see also: T. Adrian and H S Shin (2008), 'Liquidity and Financial Contagion', 11 *Financial Stability Review*, 108 (2008) (Special issue on liquidity).

of uncertainty has been passed. Rather, the framework of thinking and interaction, and the flip in mentality – from shared expectations to crisis and uncertainty – would have to be addressed at a social level. From that point of view, purely economic analysis and case-by-case policy responses to manifest problems would be insufficient to turn the situation around.

THE RATINGS, THE RAPTURE

Why were investors so comfortable with innovative financial 'packages', the contents of which few, if any, of them understood? The apparent safety of the securitisation (the very language carries with it some reassurance) was a prime motivation of many investors. Much commentary has been attracted to the ratings agencies, and to their unfortunate joining together of (a) optimistic ratings and (b) misleading symbols (AAA mortgage-backed bonds might be seen by some in the market as meaning something similar to AAA sovereign debt, for example US Treasury bonds).

> Fundamentally, is a rating metric suitable for sovereign bonds, investment, and sub-investment-grade corporate bonds, or project finance also suitable for structured financial products? The International Organization of Securities Commissions (IOSCO) has suggested that agencies should introduce new ratings for mortgage-backed or structured finance products because of the perception that they behave differently than other financial instruments in times of stress.[26]

Nevertheless, some commentators have said that 'the market was not fooled'[27] by this symbolism. Market professionals perfectly understood that an AAA rating on a quite new and highly structured product referred to a comparison within that category of product, rather than being equivalent to dissimilar, longer-established products that promised a lower rate of return.

---

[26] P. Mizen, 'The Credit Crunch of 2007–2008: A Discussion of the Background, Market Reactions, and Policy Responses', 90(5) *Review*, 531 (September/October 2008) at 563.

[27] See J. Danielsson, 'The Emperor Has No Clothes: Limits to Risk Modelling', 26(7) *Journal of Banking & Finance*, 1273 (2002). See also J Danielsson, *Blame the Models* (2008), available at VoxEU.org (policy portal of Centre for Economic Policy Research et al.) at 14.

After all, why would a AAA-rated SIV [structured investment vehicle[28]] earn 200 basis points above a AAA-rated corporate bond? One cannot escape the feeling that many players understood what was going on but happily went along. The pension fund manager buying such SIVs may have been incompetent, but he or she was more likely simply bypassing restrictions on buying high-risk assets.[29]

The implication is that the ratings agencies used the same symbols for esoteric products and more mundane products because this allowed the esoteric products to be sold to a wider base of (risk-averse) investors. Fund managers, who throughout the 1990s were under pressure to improve performance – to attain so-called 'alpha' or out-performance – 'bought the story'. Their high demand in turn stimulated the invention and supply of new securities, etc. As Coffee and Sale put it:

> Correct as the President's Working Group was in noting the connection between the decline of discipline in the mortgage loan origination market and a similar laxity among underwriters in the capital markets, it largely ignored the direction of the causality. In retrospect, irresponsible lending in the mortgage market appears to have been a direct response to the capital markets' increasingly insatiable demand for financial assets to securitize.[30]

Ratings agencies are remunerated only if their rating is accepted by those whose products they rate (more will be said below on this as a conflict of interest). This is widely seen as one cause of 'mispricing' and hence of the crisis. Leaving aside that allegation, a rational choice perspective offers 'technical' reasons why the agencies gave such high ratings to SIVs and similar. Essentially, these reasons revolve around (i) a general assumption of induction – that future events will resemble past events; (ii) an empirical limitation, that data on past events was very short-term in the case of SIVs and many financial products (because they had only recently been invented); and (iii) the comforting assumption that, even if a minority of mortgagees defaulted on their loans, the majority would not (and the SIVs spread that risk widely, so it would be very diluted). In the event:

> The main problem with the ratings of SIVs was the incorrect risk assessment provided by rating agencies, who underestimated the default correlation in mortgages by assuming that mortgage defaults are fairly independent events.

---

[28]   Structured investment vehicles (SIVs) were invented by Citicorp and were widely used until 2008 as a means of profiting from differences in interest rates for short- and long-term debt.

[29]   Danielsson, above n. 27, at 14.

[30]   Coffee and Sale, above n. 13, at 19.

Of course, at the height of the business cycle that may be true, but even a cursory glance at history reveals that mortgage defaults become highly correlated in downturns.[31]

Such explanations – and a broader and (for many) rather contentious critique of statistical modelling, suggesting that 'Black Swan' events expected not to occur or to occur very rarely ('once in a thousand years') are in fact more common – remain within the rational choice framework.[32] These explanations of the crisis assume a rational calculation, but suggest a different technical basis for the decisions made.

Such analyses of the originate-to-distribute model of debt creation form one side of the exploration of the contemporary crisis. The other side of the explanation concerns the regulators. The question arises, where were they? Why did they allow – in some cases encourage – all concerned (originators, retail sellers of mortgages, mortgage-buyers, packagers, sellers-on, re-packagers, raters and so on) to continue to 'dance', given the limited data and optimistic assumptions? It has become apparent that they were thinking that the private sector models gave them the information they needed for public sector policy-making.

Private Risk Models for Public Regulation

> [To] Reduce Reliance on Credit Rating Agencies. PWG [President's Working Group] Review of Regulatory Use of Ratings: Treasury will work with the SEC and the President's Working Group on Financial Markets to determine where references to ratings can be removed from regulations.[33]

This 2009 change of policy signalled a realisation of the danger of basing public rules and regulations on private market negotiations. Not only had the regulators allowed the ratings agencies to develop and maintain client-friendly methods that sent to the market positively-biased signals (the ratings agency got business and got paid only if it could give a rating acceptable to the ratee). More troubling is that the authorities built into regulatory standards a requirement that certain categories of market par-

---

[31] Danielsson, above n. 29.

[32] N. Taleb, *Fooled by Randomness: The Hidden Role of Chance in Life and in the Markets* (New York: Random House, 2004).

[33] US Department of the Treasury, Press Release, 21 July, tg-223, *Fact Sheet: Administration's Regulatory Reform Agenda Moves Forward [–] Credit Rating Agency Reform Legislation Sent to Capitol Hill* (2009), available at http://www.ustreas.gov/press/releases/tg223.htm.

ticipants must take account of ratings from state-licensed agencies – and licensed a very small number of rating agencies.[34] In short:

> Regulatory deference or outsourcing facilitated the manipulation of both the information inputted into models and the selection and design of models to justify predetermined decisions [and so] subverted risk management principles and corrupted risk models.[35]

The result was that many institutional investors, including pension funds and the like, instead of making in-depth enquiries of their own, were obliged all to follow the same advice – thus creating a 'Gadarene swine' effect, deepening collective risk and the depth of the eventual crisis.

> Too much homogeneity among risk management strategies among financial institutions can increase systemic risk. If firms have the same strategies and similar portfolios, market shocks can cause the firms to sell the same types of assets at the same time to cover their positions. A widespread sell-off would cause values of these assets to plummet and trigger a sell-off of yet another class of assets . . . At first blush, it may seem odd that firms can have homogenous risk models and risk management practices. But, widespread reliance on rating agency ratings can create this homogeneity.[36]

Moreover, the regulators in part constructed their own worldview from such data. It must be expected, in any regulatory system, that day-to-day working relations between firms and the regulator, friendships, alliances and criss-crossing career paths produce a net of shared orientations and forms of knowledge.[37] However, the regulators' formal reliance on the same worldview, risk methodologies and market data as those used by market actors must further deepen systemic risk. Even allowing for high levels of professionalism and commitment to independence, still the regulators were compromised and blind-sided by their knowledge base.

Alongside reliance on ratings for purposes of regulation of wise investment choices, and for their own worldview, the regulators came to rely on private sector risk models in relation to banks' needs for capital reserves.

---

[34] For an attack written a decade before the crisis, see F Partnoy, 'The Siskel and Ebert of Financial Markets: Two Thumbs Down for the Credit Rating Agencies,' 77 *Washington University Law Quarterly*, 619 (1999).

[35] Geithner, above n. 22, at 10.

[36] Geithner, above n. 22, at 64–5.

[37] A. Pratt, *The Political Economy of Financial Reform: Effective Regulations Require Effective Regulators,* available at VoxEU.org, tagged under Regulatory Capture (9 March 2009). For a review, see E Bó, 'Regulatory Capture: A Review', 22(2) *Oxford Review of Economic Policy,* 203 (2006).

Martin Hellwig recounts that, when in 1993 the Basel Committee on Banking Supervision consulted on a standard approach to bank capital requirements, 'the banking industry responded with intensive criticism, arguing that such regulation would represent a step back from the very sophisticated risk management procedures that they themselves had started to implement on the basis of quantitative models'.[38] The banks won and their 'model based' approach was codified in 1996. Hellwig suggests that, although the standard approach was 'clumsy' in comparison with the risk management methods that the banks were already using, something was lost at this point.

> [I]n this discussion, the notion that there is a difference between private interests and the public interest in risk management and risk control of a bank seems to have been lost. I think of this process as regulatory capture by sophistication. The question of how to protect the public interest against possible flaws in the quantitative risk modelling does not seem to have been given much attention.[39]

The seriousness of this cannot be overstated. How did the banking industry convince regulators to put individual private interests before collective private and public interests? Hellwig suggests that public policymakers were influenced by consideration of the competitive advantage that might accrue to their countries' banks.

> In particular, for countries with banking institutions at the forefront of change, most prominently the United States, the introduction of the option to rely on a model-based approach seemed like a chance to have 'their' institutions benefit from their advantages in global competition in newly developing markets. Even if the bank regulators involved in the negotiations may have had their doubts about the change, the political environments from which they came provided them with little leeway to express these doubts, let alone have them prevail in the international deliberations.[40]

And in relation to derivatives such as futures:

> A similar logic may have been at work in the late nineties when Federal Reserve Board Chairman Greenspan, Treasury Secretary Rubin, and Securities and Exchange Commission Chairman Levitt, all three of them with strong ties to

---

[38]   M. Hellwig, *Systemic Risk in the Financial Sector: An Analysis of the Subprime-Mortgage Financial Crisis* (2008), Preprint 43, Bonn, Max Planck Institute for Research on Collective Goods, available at http://www.coll.mpg.de/pdf_dat/2008_43online.pdf, at 54.

[39]   Ibid. at 54–5.

[40]   Ibid.

the investment banking community, used their influence to stop attempts to bring derivatives trading into the domain of statutory regulation.[41]

From the point of view of regulators' ability to take an evidence-based view on the level of collective risk in part of the international financial system – and then to build up to an understanding of systemic risk in the system as a whole, through consideration of the interlocking of risks among counterparties – the fundamental issue here is that the regulators should have (and did not have) their own requirement for strategic information. This implies that regulators should define the risk models and methods to be used by the private sector, and the data to be passed to the public sector; yet, as we have seen, the converse was the case. That this very basic requirement of governance was let slip suggests that the regulatory system as a whole was an unwitting (one presumes) captive. If power is knowledge, then the regulators rendered themselves powerless and blind.

Rating Reform Stalls

Following an indication by the Council of the EU that it favoured rating agencies being at least registered ('without prejudice to consideration of its practical application'),[42] an EU regulation was proposed by the European Commission.[43] It was amended by the European Parliament's Committee on Economic and Monetary Affairs,[44] amidst strong lobbying but to the eventual satisfaction of the agencies[45]. The proposed regulation covers inter alia an obligation for agencies whose ratings are used within the EU to register within the appropriate authorities of any Member State; to appoint independent directors whose pay does not depend on the fortunes

---

[41] Ibid.

[42] Council of the European Union, *Press Release [on the] 2882nd Council Meeting, Economic and Financial Affairs*, 8 July 2008 (Brussels: European Council, 2008) at 23.

[43] Commission of the European Communities, *Proposal for a Regulation of the European Parliament and of the Council on Credit Rating Agencies*, COM(2008) 704, at 43. [Editors' Note: The Proposal has been enacted, No. 1060/2009].

[44] Committee on Economic and Monetary Affairs, *Report on the Proposal for a Regulation of the European Parliament and of the Council on Credit Rating Agencies*, COM(2008)0704, C6-0397/2008 & 2008/0217(COD) (Brussels: European Parliament, 2009) at 97.

[45] Editorial, '"Workable" Rules Emerge in Europe', *Financial Times*, 23 July 2009, 27.

of the agency; to be open to questioning by supervisory authorities; and generally 'to prevent conflicts of interest and/or to manage these conflicts adequately where they are unavoidable'.[46] It is this last aspiration – so vaguely expressed – that is key. Unfortunately, European political agreement comes at the cost that it really fails to deal with conflict of interest. The conflict of interest of rating agencies – well known within the European institutions, as shown by the following quotation from the European Economic and Social Committee – has been exacerbated by several factors.

> Moody's went public [listed on the stock exchange] in 2000. After the listing, the change was precipitous. There was a sudden concentration on profit. Management got stock options. The whole centre of gravity shifted. Moody's reported the highest profit margins of any company in the S&P 500 index. . . . In the early days of the millennium it was almost impossible for a CDO to get a triple A rating from Moody's if the collateral was entirely made up of mortgages. The agency had a long-standing 'diversity' score which prevented securities with homogenous collateral from winning the highest rating. As a result Moody's lost market share because the two competitors did not apply such a prudent rule. Moody's withdrew the rule in 2004 after which its market share rocketed.[47]

In other words, the transition from being a private company to being floated on the stock exchange deepened the incentives for ratings inflation. A second and interlocking factor was a side effect of the increase from the 1990s onwards in complexity and non-transparency of the financial instruments being rated. Interesting work by Skreta and Veldkamp[48] suggests that conflict of interest due to payment may not matter all that much when the financial instruments being rated are simple and transparent: in such circumstances all agencies are likely to come to similar conclusions, to do otherwise carrying with it considerable risks of challenge and reputational loss. However, when instruments are complex and opaque, there is genuine uncertainty over how to assess them, so a wider diversity of ratings emerges (assuming non-collusion between the agencies) – of which

---

[46] European Commission, above n. 43, at 6.

[47] EESC, *Opinion of the European Economic and Social Committee on the Credit Rating Agencies*, COM(2008) 704 final & 2008/0217 (COD) (Brussels: European Economic and Social Committee, 2009), paras 1–4.14, cited at paras 2.9 and 2.10.

[48] V. Skreta and L. Veldkamp, *Ratings Shopping and Asset Complexity: A Theory of Ratings Inflation (2009)*, *NBER Working Paper number 14761*, available at http://papers.ssrn.com/sol3/papers.cfm?abstract_id=1295503, at 34.

the issuer takes the most favourable.[49] The other opinions are never made public.

> For simple assets, agencies issue nearly identical forecasts. Asset issuers then disclose all ratings because more information reduces investors' uncertainty and increases the price they are willing to pay for the asset. For complex assets, ratings may differ, creating an incentive to shop for the best rating. There is a threshold level of asset complexity such that once this threshold is crossed, shopping becomes optimal and ratings inflation emerges. [As a result . . .] an issuer who shops for ratings might want to issue an even more complex asset, to get a broader menu of ratings to choose from.[50]

In other words, the increasing complexity and non-transparency of financial products gave the issuers a way to game the ratings system (and also to game the regulators). Up against these incentives, European gestures in the direction of good governance may be expected to do little.

The question of ratings shopping, evaded by the Europeans, seems to be the 'property' of the US, being tentatively picked up in Treasury July 2009 proposals to Congress.

> Require Disclosure Of Preliminary Ratings To Reduce 'Ratings Shopping': Currently, an issuer may attempt to 'shop' among rating agencies by soliciting 'preliminary ratings' from multiple agencies and then only paying for and disclosing the highest rating it received for its product. We would shed light on this practice by requiring an issuer to disclose all of the preliminary ratings it had received from different credit rating agencies so that investors will see how much 'shopping' happened and whether there were discrepancies with the final rating.[51]

A foreseeable problem with that outline proposal would arise from the iterative nature of the ratings process, in which a securities issuer amends the instrument until the desired rating is obtained from one or other of the agencies bidding for the work. It could reasonably be argued that, since the 'preliminary ratings' not accepted/purchased related to an earlier version of the instrument being rated, these less favourable ratings are of limited relevance for the final product. Even so, the proposal to make public 'how much "shopping" happened' and the range of ratings offered does carry some information.

What is striking is that the proposals on both sides of the Atlantic are so minor, with little being done to tackle the inherent conflict of interest

---

[49]　Ibid.
[50]　Ibid. at 2.
[51]　US Department of the Treasury, above n 33.

– leading one financial advisor to 'wonder who the regulators work for'.[52] That comment may be unfair; however, it is striking that the position vis-à-vis the agencies should be so critically debated but with so little effect. The one proposal conspicuous by its absence is prohibiting securities issuers from paying for ratings; instead, ratings could be sought and paid for by potential investors (or associations thereof) and/or by exchanges (in the case of securities traded on exchanges). None of that would prevent securities sellers from offering information on their product; however, it would ensure that any ratings would serve purchasers rather than originators – thus severing the conflict of interest, instead of just moderating and managing it.

Why might it be that authorities on both sides of the Atlantic so readily acknowledge conflict of interest as a worrisome issue – an important locus for and facilitator of the financial crisis – yet do not confront it more directly? This failure may be understood as a consequence of the worldview within which the public good (an assemblage of economic and cultural aspects) is underpinned by private interests (primarily economic). Some of the work of Bourdieu is now used to explore these problems.

THE LOSS OF CULTURAL CAPITAL

> When centrist economists start to blog about Bourdieu, the French structuralist Marxist sociologist, something important is happening.[53]

So claims one commentator, observing the critical turn taken by some economist-journalists, distancing themselves from the hitherto dominant rational choice theory and taking up a variety of ideas on the ways into which cultural phenomena shape, indeed may constitute, financial markets. Bourdieu was a sociologist and more specifically an anthropologist. He himself would have been wary of being called a structuralist (since structuralism implies that things cannot change) or a Marxist (if only because he was too immodest an academic to admit to following anyone, according to a reviewer).[54] For some contemporary commentators, Bourdieu raises more heat than light, being seen first and foremost as a political activist, a critic of neoliberalism as a programme for the

---

[52] A. Cifuentes, 'Time We Rated the Bond Graders', *Financial Times*, 27 July 2009.

[53] T. Price, 'Bourdieu & the Crisis. Leverage Your Social Capital', *OpenDemocracy*, 28 April 2009.

[54] R. Jenkins, *Pierre Bourdieu* (London: Routledge, 1992).

destruction of collective interests. For example, regulator and academic John Braithwaite finds Bourdieu's and others' perceptions of neoliberalism to be just a 'fairy tale', the reality according to Braithwaite being regulatory capitalism.[55] It is certainly the case that in his later life Bourdieu made many public statements hostile to neoliberalism in the sense of deregulation.[56] It is suggested here that there is also a broader sense in which his work can help us to understand regulatory failure.

Here we use Bourdieu's ideas to broaden our perspective on regulatory networking, convergence and 'independence' (from democratic oversight). These developments correspond to a *historical shift*, from regulatory thinking being grounded in a tension and balance between cultural capital (related to ideas about 'club' or gentlemanly regulation) and economic capital (market models and other forms of knowledge developed by private interests), to the unchallenged ascendance of the second. This results in a one-dimensional knowledge base for financial market regulation. It opens the door to regulatory *rapture* – an adoring discourse on the charms of the market (the 'great moderation', the search for risk, etc) and the misapprehension that private sector knowledge and models are suitable for public regulatory use. Regulatory convergence and rapture induced market over-confidence, herding behaviour, shared blind spots and systemic risk. Crucially, not only market participants but also the regulators themselves used the same risk assumptions – derived from private sources.

Bourdieu's theoretical apparatus[57] is at heart very simple,[58] even if his own expositions are at times abstruse.[59] The key concepts are forms of capital (economic property, social networking and cultural resources); habitus (habits derived from background, family and, within and sometimes against these parameters, personal choice); field (the space within which the above are deployed); and reproduction (of all the above).

---

[55] J. Braithwaite, *Regulatory Capitalism: How it Works, Ideas for Making it Work Better* (Cheltenham: Edward Elgar, 2008).

[56] P. Bourdieu, 'The Essence of Neoliberalism', *Le Monde Dipomatique* (1998) (on file with author).

[57] P. Bourdieu, *Distinction: A Social Critique of the Judgment of Taste* (London: Routledge, 1984); P Bourdieu, 'Cultural Reproduction and Social Reproduction', in R. Brown (ed.), *Knowledge, Education and Cultural Change* (London: Tailstock, 1993); and P. Bourdieu, *The State Nobility: Elite Schools in the Field of Power*, trans. by L. Clough (Stanford: Stanford University Press, 1996).

[58] D. Allen, E. McGoun and G. Kester, 'A Sociological Explanation of Financial Market Growth', 9 *International Review of Financial Analysis*, 421 (2002); and A King, 'Structure and Agency', in A Harrington (ed.), *Modern Social Theory: An Introduction* (Oxford: Oxford University Press, 2005) at 215–232.

[59] Jenkins, above n. 54.

Capital is not just static forms of property but rather the potential and power of social strata to reproduce and, to some extent, reinvent themselves. Cultural capital stems from sources including family and schooling (a particular focus in Bourdieu's work) and is acquired as tastes and preferences within the circles within which the individual moves, becoming 'second nature' or habitus.[60]

All strata of society are internally differentiated in terms of having more or less economic capital and cultural capital, those at the top of the tree having more of both than those lower down. Concerning the relationships between economic and cultural capital, the former may be traded for the latter (elite schooling being an important mechanism, especially in Bourdieu's time, see his 'The State Nobility').[61] Once acquired, cultural capital can be deployed to 'open doors': for example, in former times, getting a job in the City was easier for those whose possession of culture meant that they could be expected to 'fit in'. Thus, in certain circumstances, there can be a circular relationship between cultural capital (being 'cultured', highbrow, respectable) and economic capital (a seat on the board).

On the other hand, historically Bourdieu observed something of a struggle between, on the one hand, traders possessing economic capital (for example, the nouveau riche) and, on the other hand, certain historically constructed notions of good taste, breeding and cultural capital. Cultural and economic capital kept each other in check, even as they intermingled. Thus, financial market regulation might be based in part on cultural considerations of 'the done thing', as well as on 'vulgar' market calculation – as illustrated for the UK by the tale about the Governor of the Bank of England ruling out certain behaviour by the merest twitching of his eyebrows. A silly story, perhaps; however, it nicely epitomises what a number of eminent scholars of government and regulation have called 'club' regulation.[62] Prior to the 1970s in the UK, checks and balances were provided (to some extent) by the availability of cultural reservoirs of tastes, knowl-

---

[60] Ibid.

[61] Bourdieu, above n 57.

[62] D. Marquand, *The Unprincipled Society: New Demands and Old Politics* (London: Jonathan Cape, 1988); M. Moran, *The British Regulatory State: High Modernism and Hyper-Innovation* (Oxford and New York: Oxford University Press, 2003); M. Moran, 'The Transformation of the British State: From Club Government to State-Administered High Modernism', in J. Levy, *The State After Statism: New State Activities in the Age of Liberalization* (Harvard: Harvard University Press, 2006); and D. Vogel, 'Private Global Business Regulation', 11 *Annual Review of Political Science*, 261 (2008).

edge and power underpinning rather localist, sectorally specific and indeed idiosyncratic forms of club regulation.

However, that precarious balance between economic and cultural capital was destroyed in the UK in the 1970s, as financial elites turned outwards and began to network globally for their cultural and economic reference points. At that point, economic capital as a way of thinking and social reproduction got the upper hand over cultural capital, leaping across social classes – finance capital, packagers, intermediary strata (retailers) and purchasers – there being inadequate checks and balances at any social level, or between levels. As club regulation, with its particular-istic and nationally-based preferences, was historically undermined, so a double victory was achieved by economic capital: ascendancy both within national boundaries and across them. In the UK and subsequently many other countries with the notable exception of the US, this homogenisa-tion was taken further through the creation of a single regulator.[63] As economic capital as a corpus of knowledge and 'common sense' displaced cultural capital and club regulation, so the state *nominally* took charge, whilst in practice ceding the lead to private sector influences.[64] Regulatory independence, in this context, changed meaning – from sectoral, club, self-regulation (although that is really much too individualist a term) to greater attentiveness to the wishes of international firms[65] and consequently to convergence across market sectors and internationally.

These developments impacted the intellectual resources available to people in the private sector as well as in government and the regulatory agencies. Recent work by Sarah Hall suggests that, when the crisis of 2007 onwards struck, senior persons in the industry had well-developed, highly levered but intellectually narrow resources to fall back upon.

> [I]n contrast to earlier generations of financiers, the power of contemporary investment bankers emerges through their role choreographing transnational networks of financial actors associated with securitised and structured prod-ucts rather than being purely read off their social or education background. I suggest that these networked forms of power relation are significant because, on the one hand, they have prevented investment bankers distancing themselves

---

[63]   As of 2009, considerable energy was being expended on the prospects for fine-tuning these structural arrangements; see inter alia S Pellerin, J Walter and P Wescott, 'The Consolidation of Financial Regulation: Pros, Cons, and Implications for the United States', 95(2) *Economic Quarterly*, 121 (2009).

[64]   Braithwaite, above n. 55.

[65]   C. Briault, A. Haldane and M. King, 'Independence and Accountability', in I. Kuroda (ed.), *Towards More Effective Monetary Policy* (London: Macmillan, 1997).

from the ongoing turbulence and uncertainty within the international financial system. Meanwhile, on the other hand, the ability of investment bankers to (re) produce such networks indicates that suggestions of the demise of 'financialised elites' in the wake of the global credit crunch may be too hasty.[66]

With 'good taste' and 'the done thing' having been relegated to cultural history a quarter of a century earlier, neither private sector managers nor regulators have a distinct cultural (and hence intellectual) position to stand upon, other than the market (common) sense that they share.

> Just like an education in art history is a marker of class distinction that is used to perpetuate class distinction, an education in modern finance is a marker of distinction that sets off those who understand the true importance of Wall Street for the American economy. As long [as] the powerful people in Washington, including the regulators who oversee the financial industry, share that worldview, Wall Street's power and ability to make money will be secure.[67]

The framework for regulatory thinking takes it as 'obvious' that, lacking the conditions thought to be necessary for internationalised finance, there would be no funding for art, art museums or other cultural goods. If maintaining those conditions involves conflicts of interest, they will be tolerated. That this analysis might be flawed (for example, removal of conflict of interest might be a necessary condition for financial stability) might enter the heads of policymakers and regulators, yet fail to progress to being a policy option – because it does not 'make sense' for those whose thinking is structured by the ascendancy of economic capital over cultural capital.

As the above analysis demonstrates, this situation seems not to be changing. On these grounds, the prospects for the reform of regulation therefore look somewhat glum. A restoration of nineteenth-century and early twentieth-century class and cultural contours is hardly feasible, even were it to be desirable. Another stumbling block is that, Bourdieu's analysis of cultural capital being quintessentially European, the implications for *international* financial regulation do not flow smoothly. What needs to be found is some other mooring that might step in and replace historically defunct cultural resources for systemic stability.

---

[66] S. Hall, 'Financialised Elites and the Changing Nature of Finance Capitalism: Investment Bankers in London's Financial District', 13(2) *Competition and Change,* 173 (2009) at 173.

[67] J. Kwak, 'Pierre Bourdieu, Tim Geithner, and Cultural Capital', *The Baseline Scenario* (2009) (blog on file with author).

OUR COMMON FUTURE

The rational choice paradigm was fatally compromised by what Alan Greenspan termed irrational exuberance[68] and what this discussion, drawing on Anderson,[69] terms market rapture. The resulting *rapturous choice* perspective – 'private–public' governance, rather than public–private[70] – became the intellectual repertoire for regulatory thinking, consultations, rule-making, networking and pursuit of international (read 'private–public') standards.

In practical terms, this implied employing regulatory staff of a suitable background and calibre (broadly, economists and other quant-savvy persons) who were able to understand private models and were sufficiently comfortable with them to use them in interacting with their private sector originators (indeed, sometimes they might be the same persons). Rapture meant fine-tuning these private models, by inserting into them greater volumes of data, whilst not challenging assumptions of the models.[71] And it implied networking these human and technical resources internationally in pursuit of increasing regulatory convergence so as to minimise inconveniences to 'too big to fail' financial entities. The public would not, of course, be part of the debate, except sometimes to jeer when something goes manifestly wrong.

However, the rapturous formulation of rational choice theory as a *peon* to large international firms is not its only possible formulation – as critiques available in the literature both before and during the financial market crisis have shown (see above text and of course the behavioural finance movement). Rational choice perspectives (plural), when applied in an open and transparent manner, can yield insights into some of the perverse incentives and unwitting pacts with the devil that characterised the run-up to the crisis, as has been shown. For example, the US citizens who were invited by the finance industry to trade in residential property behaved quite rationally in taking up the offer since, if the market should move against them, they could simply return the keys and thus be free of any further obligation. Likewise, finance industry traders and managers had compensation packages that allowed them to gain on any market rises and yet not to

---

[68] R. Shiller, *Irrational Exuberance* (Princeton: Princeton University Press, 2005).

[69] Ibid.

[70] N. Dorn and M. Levi, 'Private–Public or Public–Private? Strategic Dialogue on Serious Crime and Terrorism in the EU', *Security Journal*, online publication (August 2008) (on file with author).

[71] For critique, see Taleb, above n. 32.

suffer correspondingly on any market falls: they too behaved rationally in pushing things to the limit. Such incentives, spanning what otherwise would have been social chasms, aligned short-term interests so effectively that a cultural symbiosis took place, in this case a dangerous one, all accelerator and no brake. The problem is, what alternatives might we have?

Accountability and Oversight

Increasingly, given the reputation damage suffered by 'independent' (that is, market rapture) regulation – and given that a return to club regulation is not available (nor desirable) – the question of a wider social basis for financial market regulators is raised. In the remainder of the chapter, the position is advanced that democratisation is required, re-politicising regulatory issues. This is for two reasons. First, for reasons of principle, posed in terms of a public good argument; second, for reasons of effectiveness in regulation, posed in terms of an argument about robustness of diversified systems.

The question of democratic accountability is by no means an abstract issue. As a result of the soul-searching provoked by the financial crisis, governments are questioning to what extent regulation can be left solely in specialist hands, lacking grounding in democratic structures. A UK White Paper published in July 2009 refers to setting up a Council for Financial Stability and asks what forms of accountability would be appropriate.

> The Council [for Financial Stability] will consist of the Treasury, the Bank of England and the FSA and will be chaired by the Chancellor of the Exchequer. . . . The Government will consult on options for broadening and strengthening channels of democratic accountability and will work with the Treasury Select Committee to consider whether and how emerging options should be implemented.[72]

The White Paper put up for consultation the following questions:

> What are the benefits in creating a more formal and transparent body to coordinate the authorities' more systemic approach to financial regulation? . . . In addition to the input of non-executives from the governing bodies of the FSA and the Bank, what other ways could external advice and commentary be incorporated in this process? What mechanisms might be used for enhancing democratic accountability? Is this important?[73]

---

[72]   HM Treasury, above n. 2, at 138–9. [Editors' Note: UK institutional reform is proceeding: HM Treasury, *A New Approach to Financial Regulation: The Blueprint for reform* (London: HM Treasury, 2011).]

[73]   Ibid. at 139.

These are analytically interesting and practically relevant questions. As Picciotto has observed of general trends in regulation nationally and internationally, 'networked governance disrupts the channels of democratic accountability, which in the classical liberal system are through national constitutional structures, ideally parliamentary representative democracy'.[74] Others have made a similar point: regulatory networking might be good for regulatory networking but at what political cost?

> Braithwaite and Drahos contend [that] webs of dialogue are relatively good (compared to more coercive mechanisms) at delivering effective forms of global regulation because the dialogue: (1) defines issues; (2) enhances the contracting environment so that complex interdependency and issue linkage can motivate agreement and compliance; (3) constitutes normative commitments; (4) institutionalises habits of compliance; and (5) institutionalises informal praise and shame for defection from the regime. [However . . .] resulting decisions may lack democratic legitimacy because the process is too opaque.[75]

It is encouraging to see signs of some awareness of this problem emerging at official level and the prospect of some (albeit possibly minor) compensation for it. What is needed is some way of connecting up the quite general question put up for consultation by government – 'What mechanisms might be used for enhancing democratic accountability?'[76] – with some plausible criteria for answering this question. Two criteria may be advanced: public goods and policy effectiveness.

Public Goods Argument

A public goods perspective forefronts aspects of life that all actors rely upon, even if few have an incentive in the short term to ensure they are in place.[77] This perspective is similar to the idea, commonplace in

---

[74] S. Picciotto, *Regulatory Networks and Global Governance*, Paper presented at conference on The Retreat of the State: Challenges to Law and Lawyers (27–29 June 2006), at 11 (London: Institute of Advanced Legal Studies, 2006) (on file with author).

[75] K. Alexander, E. Ferran, H. Jackson and N. Moloney, *A Report on the Transatlantic Financial Services Regulatory Dialogue* (2007), at 7 and 8, available at http://?.ssrn.com/abstract=961269, at 7 and 8 (also published in 7 *European Business Organization Law Review*, 647 (2006).

[76] HM Treasury, above n. 2.

[77] I. Loader and N. Walker, 'Necessary Virtues: The Legitimate Place of the State in the Production of Security', in W. Wood and B. Dupont (eds), *Democracy, Society and the Governance of Security* (Cambridge: Cambridge University Press, 2006) at 165–95. Loader and Walker draw upon I. Kaul, P. Conceicao, K. Le

the international comparative literature on law and markets,[78] that a
robust legal framework is needed to underpin market development.
From political economy comes an equivalent sentiment, that 'The time
is over-due for a strong reassertion of the crucial importance of a positive public role in regulating financial markets, not simply to prevent
economic collapse, but to ensure that they operate in the broader public
interest.'[79] In short, the public goods perspective identifies the broad
contours of market regulation as being matters for public debate. Of
course, detailed service planning and implementation would remain a
matter for those with the stomach for it, as in lawyering, doctoring and
other specialised work.

This leads to the question of what form accountability should take. To
whom is accountability owed – who bears the public interest? From the
literature, three possibilities may be discerned:

- a minimalist approach, in which regulators would network
  and bargain in closed settings – in other words, the present situation;
- a middling approach, associated with John Braithwaite and others,
  admitting NGOs as bearers of the public interest whilst not envisag-
  ing direct democratic oversight; and
- a maximalist approach – democratic steering – which we will
  advance on grounds of principle and consequences.

The middling approach to regulatory accountability is set out in oft-cited
work by Ian Ayres and John Braithwaite on 'tripartism'.[80] This develops
the proposition that, in order to ensure that regulators do their job properly (and are not captured by their industry), NGOs could be introduced
into the relationship between an industry and its regulators, as watchdogs.
At an initial glance, such tripartism might have some attractions; however,
in the context of financial service regulators it seems not very robust. Up
to now, in the UK at least, tripartism seems to have been operationalised

---

Goulven and R. Mendoza, *Providing Global Public Goods: Managing Globalisation*
(Oxford: Oxford University Press, 2003) ch. 1.

[78] R. La Porta, F. Lopez-de-Silanes and A. Shleifer, 'The Economic
Consequences of Legal Origins', 46 *Journal of Economic Literature,* 285 (2008).

[79] S. Picciotto and J. Haines, 'Regulating Global Financial Markets', 26(3)
Journal of Law & Society, 351 (1999) at 368.

[80] I. Ayres and J. Braithwaite, 'Tripartism: Regulatory Capture and
Empowerment', 16(3) *Law and Social Enquiry,* 435 (1991). See also I. Ayres and
J. Braithwaite, *Responsive Regulation: Transcending the Deregulation Debate*
(Oxford and New York: Oxford University Press, 1992).

more in terms of consultations with consumers, and education of them, than in terms of powerful public interest groups holding the regulator to account. Indeed, the prospects for tripartism seem modest in relation to financial market regulation, where such powerful forces are ranged on the side of private interests.

More fundamentally, tripartite propositions beg the question of why the public interest should not be represented more directly in financial regulation.[81] Surely the starting point should be that there are *prima facie* grounds for democratic oversight of all forms of regulation – that is to say, oversight by elected representatives, with accompanying public debate on broad principles – unless perhaps there can be shown strong grounds for an exception. Exception claims have been advanced from time to time, for example recent years have seen claims that aspects of 'national security' merit exception from democratic oversight; however, such claims are now widely regarded as having been discredited.[82] Exception claims are generally advanced on the basis that there is a 'trade-off' between security and democracy, legitimising curtailment of the latter; however, it must fall to the proponents of such curtailment to make the case for it. Such claims may be difficult to make in the context of the continuing fallout from the financial market crisis.[83]

As a matter of principle, therefore, many will wish a fair wind to proposals to introduce an element of democratic accountability into financial market regulation. Some commentators extend the analysis of democracy from legislative committees to the broader political climate.

> [T]he Scandinavian countries place substantial emphasis on the transparency of decision-making as the primary mechanism to ensure both the independence and accountability of their regulatory agencies. But this approach is premised on the existence of a political culture that prizes openness and transparency.[84]

---

[81]   F. Snyder, 'Economic Globalisation and the Law in the 21st Century', in A. Sarat (ed.), *The Blackwell Companion to Law and Society* (New York and Oxford: Blackwell, 2008) at 624–40.

[82]   See C. Aradau and R. van Munster, 'Exceptionalism and the "War On Terror": Criminology Meets International Relations', 49 *British Journal of Criminology*, 686 (2009). See also A. Cumming, *Sensitive Covert Action Notifications: Oversight Options For Congress* (Washington DC: Congressional Research Service, 7 July 2009) at 15.

[83]   D. Pesendorfer, 'Good-Bye Neoliberalism? Contested Policy Responses to Uncertain Consequences of the 2007–2009 Financial crisis', Paper presented at the W G Hart Legal Workshop on Law Reform and Financial Markets (London: IALS, 23–25 June 2009).

[84]   M. Taylor and A. Fleming, *World Bank Policy Research Working Paper No. 2223, Integrated Financial Supervision: Lessons of Northern European Experience* (1999), available at http://ssrn.com/abstract=623981, at 29.

In other words, democratic oversight is not only a structural arrangement; it lives and breathes through the broader civic culture. We turn now to the question of its possible consequences.

Systemic Protection Argument

Here we pass from a broad in-principle argument about the merits of democratic oversight to discussion of its consequences. In a highly accessible paper on potential agendas for regulatory renewal, Eric Helleiner helpfully distinguishes five broad strategies:[85]

- regulatory *catch-up*, meaning that regulation should be extended to cover financial activities and instruments that at present escape regulation;
- *reform*, meaning that certain aspects of regulation have been positively implicated in the production of the crisis and that changes should be made accordingly;
- *de-regulation*, on the grounds that the market would do better if not interfered with;
- *down-sizing* of the international financial sector, by international imposition of controls on cross-border movements of capital; and
- regulatory *decentralisation*.

A case is now made in favour of the last of these agendas: regulatory decentralisation, anchored in democratic steering of regulatory policy, and leaving open the possibility of regulatory diversity (since political constituencies may differ in their understanding of the issues and in their policy preferences). In short, regulatory decentralisation offers something implied by none of the other regulatory strategies summarised by Helleiner: it offers the prospect of diversity in regional and national regulatory regimes.

Why should this be preferable from the point of view of systemic stability? Clearly, the regulatory condition for the systemic crisis of 2007 onwards – the global sharing of assumptions and models, the reliance on a few ratings agencies, other shared vulnerabilities – was regulatory convergence. Such convergence was possible because financial regulation 'floated off' from its potential moorings in democratic politics. Had

---

[85]   E. Helleiner, *Crisis and Response, the Story So Far: Five Regulatory Agendas in Search of an Outcome,* Paper presented at CIGI workshop (26–27 September 2008) (Waterloo, Canada: Centre for International Governance Innovation).

financial regulators at national and/or regional (eg, EU) levels been held democratically accountable (through elected representatives, even by referenda on controversial issues), then inevitably regulators would have been somewhat constrained from convergence with their professional constituencies at international level. Ergo, there would have been greater diversity in national regulatory systems, weakening the conditions for the particular type of crisis that erupted from 2007 onwards. For the sake of stability as a public good, political diversity can and must intervene against the convergence of markets.

As for how democratic oversight would be exercised, parliamentary or Congressional committees are the conventional route.[86] It has to be admitted, however, that oversight by committees – whose members self-select according to their interests – is by itself no guarantee of good regulation. It rather depends on one's concept of good regulation, on how committee oversight functions in practice, and whether the broader political climate in the country encourages transparency and public involvement. In this chapter, concerned with systemic stability of global financial markets, regulation has been analysed in terms of tendencies to convergence (private good) and divergence (public good), the former being criticised as the condition for regulatory and hence market herding and systemic instability. From this precautionary, diversity-favouring perspective, one could look for differences in the political requirements for regulation among different national (and possibly regional) legislatures. Also, one could look for and seek to enhance mechanisms that create changes within legislatures – such as those occurring when parliamentary committee membership changes, owing to retirement of sitting committee members and/or political shifts following elections. Active national legislative oversight of financial regulation could counteract undue international regulatory convergence.

Towards a Re-evaluation of Regulatory Arbitrage

Several possible objections have already been anticipated in the text; however, there is one other that is especially interesting to discuss: jurisdictional arbitrage.[87]

---

[86] HM Treasury, above n. 2.

[87] We are referring here to arbitrage across regulatory jurisdictions – not across types of regulatory category, which is implicated in current market difficulties: see preceding pages and C Calomiris and J Mason, 'Credit Card Securitization and Regulatory Arbitrage', 26(1) *Journal of Financial Services Research*, 5 (2004).

Jurisdictional arbitrage is commonly regarded as being problematic for investors and customers, since some jurisdictions will provide less protection than others. Some firms will indulge in forum stopping (mentioned above) and will seek to position their operations in jurisdictions where regulation is less onerous to them (not always the case, for reputational and other reasons; however, let us take the proposition at face value). In the light of the events reviewed in this book, any such problems are dwarfed by recent failures in the convergence models of regulation, which impacted adversely on all. Moreover, a strategy of democratic accountability for financial market regulation allows citizens (everyday customers of banks, etc, as well as sophisticated investors) to take part in setting the standards they prefer. This 'responsibilisation' of citizens seems as defensible in this sphere as it would be in, say, health protection. Electorates may choose the forms and level of protection that they prefer, balancing this against other factors. The resulting regulatory patchwork would be more robust than increasing convergence.

An 'uneven playing field' is an issue for the largest global players, who seek a homogeneous working environment in which they may leverage their advantages of scale. Yet, those firms and their competitive advantage are not the primary concern for a global regulatory policy that seeks stability as its primary objective. If there were to be losers from regulatory diversity, then there would also be winners – regulatory diversity could alter the balance of advantage between large, 'too big to fail' firms, medium size firms, 'niche' players, some hedge funds, mutually owned firms, etc. Although it is not the objective of this chapter, some commentators at least would regard discouragement of 'too big to fail' firms as an acceptable side effect of regulatory policy (whilst, of course, others would not[88]).

Jurisdictional arbitrage may pose workload challenges to regulators – since they have to understand dissimilar rules, questions of equivalence and non-equivalence, and regulatory issues involving trading across geographical and regulatory boundaries: a complex working environment for sure. Perhaps, however, the first concern should be the outcomes of the policy, even if that requires intellectual effort from regulators.

For all these reasons, jurisdictional arbitrage, which has hitherto been put forward as a public bad, could be rehabilitated as a servant of the

---

[88]   J. Ackermann, 'Smaller Banks Will Not Make Us Safer', *Financial Times*, 30 July 2009, at 9.

public good. Such arbitrage is a sign of diversity, which is the precondition of systemic robustness.

To sum up, the prospect of serious parliamentary oversight of financial market regulators, with the prospect of national (and, where appropriate, regional) policy reversals, adding to the diversification of the regulatory patchwork, would not be welcomed by some private interests that have a stake in convergence and in managing its path. Nevertheless, there is a broader public interest, within which nestles the common interest of all firms, avoiding systemic collapse.

A Coda on the EU

Too easily the agenda for regulatory reform reduces to proposals for institutional re-shuffling and intensification of networking, as seen in the US and the EU in 2009. One might hope that the EU would dig a little deeper; however, that seems not so far to have been the case, witness the report of the High-Level Group on Financial Supervision, headed by banker Jacques de Larosière.[89] The group repeats the now-standard understanding of the causes of the crisis in terms of the rational choice model, as earlier assembled by the US President's group (see above), drawing the implication that 'profound review of regulatory policy is therefore needed'.[90] The Group's report discusses cooperation, convergence and subsidiarity issues concerning national and EU level regulation, and makes a number of comitology recommendations, reflecting political as well as practical considerations.[91] On prevention of financial market instability, the Group says that greater efforts should be put into surveillance, early warning and risk mapping,[92] in order to reduce systemic risk. This should be done (i) at the international level though the International Monetary Fund and (ii) at a European level through creation of a European Systemic Risk Council. This Council would be chaired by the president of the European Central Bank and composed of the members of the General Council of the Bank and heads of the various EU market supervision committees (and possibly national supervisory authorities).[93] The report presents a diagram

---

[89]   High-Level Group on Financial Supervision in the EU, *Report* (chaired by Jacques de Larosière) (2009), available at http://ec.europa.eu/internal_market/finances/docs/de_larosiere_report_en.pdf, at 86.

[90]   Ibid. at 15.

[91]   Ibid. at 62.

[92]   Ibid. at 64.

[93]   Ibid. at 45. Editors' Note: the European Systemic Risk Board was established in January 2011.

showing how levels and types of supervisors would interrelate:[94] in other words, the same stakeholders and forms of expertise, just institutionally re-configured.

There would be no overt political element; indeed, 'independence' of the regulators is stressed. Whilst there would be 'transmission mechanisms' and 'channels' between regulators and policymakers, these would be one-way, from the regulators to the politicians. No doubt the public could participate by reading press releases.

Subsequent announcements by the European Commission do nothing to give hope for greater transparency, accountability and oversight. For example, concerning stress-testing of banks, the Director-General for Competition, Philip Lowe, referred to the Commission as being 'wary of a public debate'.[95] Whether the European Parliament might be less wary, and how national parliaments will take up their responsibilities in financial market regulation, are issues to be tracked in coming years.

CONCLUSION

This chapter calls for democratic accountability and steering of financial market regulation, supporting national/regional diversity in regulatory institutions, frameworks and rules. It argues that the form taken by the systemic market crisis of 2007 onwards – contagion between market sectors and financial centres – has been in part a result of the process of regulatory convergence and independence.[96]

Convergence arises from international regulatory networking between those possessing technical expertise, separated off from moral questions, public politics and democratic accountability. At a deeper, societal level, Pierre Bourdieu's ideas illuminate a historical shift, from a tension

---

[94]   Ibid. at 57.
[95]   'EU to Require Stress-Testing of Banks', *Financial Times*, 24 July 2009, at 4.
[96]   The concern here is regulation, its cultural basis and political options. The forward-pointing claim is that democratically-fuelled regulatory diversity can and should act as a safeguard against the recently experienced 'Gadarene swine' tendencies in global financial regulation and markets. This chapter does not put forward a macro theory of capitalist crises in general, nor any micro theory about particular financial brands or products. Such macro and micro theories can be found in several timely books on the financial market crisis, each of which constructs its own history of the crisis. All, some or none of the above analyses may be valid, none of which would adversely affect the argument being put forward here: that regulatory convergence heightened systemic risk, by putting everyone in the same rowing boat, and that a diversity of boats and captains would be safer.

between cultural capital (related to 'club' or gentlemanly regulation) and economic capital (market models and other forms of knowledge developed by private interests), to the unchallenged ascendance of the second. This resulted in a one-dimensional knowledge base for financial market regulation, regulatory convergence and rapture, market over-confidence, herding behaviour, shared blind spots and vulnerability to systemic risk.

That discourse has now been punctured, yet we lack a new paradigm. As the economic crisis reconstructs political difference (and hence reintroduces possibilities for real policy choice), there is a tussle among three forces: (a) the damaged but still very strong rapture crowd, favouring a continuation and indeed deepening of international, technocratic networking and private–public governance; (b) nostalgic voices calling for a return to 'club' regulation through institutions independent of both the market and democracy (proposals for central banks or other new 'independent' institutions to become systemic risk regulators fall into this category); and (c) those seeking the broader public good of systemic stability through democratic accountability of financial market regulators. The extent to which these forces will shape the new regulatory environment will have important ramifications in the future.

PART II

The challenges of capital market law reform

3. The vexed issue of short sales regulation when prohibition is inefficient and disclosure insufficient

Emilios Avgouleas[1]

INTRODUCTION

Overview

Short selling normally describes the sale of securities that the seller does not own.[2] In the most common scenario, the seller borrows the securities concerned and engages in relevant transactions against a commitment to buy the securities back later at a lower price, returning also any borrowed shares to the lender. Apart from moral concerns, the main economic issues arising from trading securities that an investor does not own[3] relate to short

---

[1]   Professor of Financial Law and International Financial Markets, School of Law, University of Manchester. Although some sections of this chapter draw on an earlier article, published in the *Stanford Journal of Law, Business and Finance*, this is a totally revised and updated work. The revision of this chapter was completed in May 2011. The chapter does not discuss critical market and regulatory developments beyond this point.
[2]   IOSCO's Consultation Paper on the regulation of short selling suggests that short sales should generally be understood as transactions characterized by the presence of two factors: '(i) a sale of stock that (ii) the seller does not own at the point of sale'. IOSCO, Technical Committee, *Regulation of Short Selling – Consultation Report* (IOSCO, 2009) (IOSCO Report), Appendix III, at 24.
[3]   IOSCO's Report suggests that a trader should be regarded as owning the securities in which she trades when: '(i) the seller has purchased or entered into an unconditional contract to purchase the stock but has not yet received delivery; (ii) the seller has a title to other securities which are convertible into or exchangeable for the stock to which the order relates (and has tendered the application to convert or exchange); (iii) the seller has an option (and has exercised such an option) to acquire the stock to which the order relates; (iv) the seller has rights or warrants (and has exercised such rights or warrants) to subscribe to and to receive the stock to which the order relates; (v) the seller is making a sale of a stock that trades on a "when issued"° basis and has entered into a binding contract to purchase such

sales' ability to destabilize orderly markets and increase market volatility. This becomes a very serious problem when short selling pushes prices further downwards in a falling market, a so-called 'bear raid'. Another very important concern is the possibility of using short sales in order to manipulate the market in a stock or act profitably on inside information.

Short selling is often castigated by the press and politicians (as well as by the directors of affected companies) as the ugly face of 'casino' capitalism. Yet a large number of empirical studies indicate that short selling is an important driver of market efficiency, because it allows all buying and selling interest in the market, including trading interest based on inside information, to be revealed and so to be better reflected into security prices.

Traditionally, the regulatory treatment of short sales has been either hesitantly heavy-handed, such as the US uptick rule under Rule 10a-1,[4] which, in a modified form, was in force from 1938 to July 2007[5] (reinstated in another form in April 2010), or quite relaxed, relying on convoluted disclosure arrangements of stock-lending data, as was the case in the pre-crisis UK regime.[6] The watershed moment in the regulation of short selling was the market price crash of listed financial sector stocks, following the bankruptcy of Lehman Brothers and the revaluation of the losses of American International Group (AIG), the world's biggest insurer,[7] in the first two weeks of September 2008. During that period, stock markets witnessed a massive increase of short selling orders in financial sector stocks; this increase was widely identified as the main reason for the amplification of downward price pressures in what was already a falling market.

Following a serious public backlash against short selling, stoked by the press, and under strong pressure from governments and finan-

---

security, subject only to the condition of issuance of the security; and (vi) the seller has bought the stock in one market and then sells the same stock in another market (regardless of whether it is an overseas market)': ibid.

[4]   Rule 10a-1(a)(1) provided that, subject to exceptions, a listed security could be sold short (A) at a price above the price at which the immediately preceding sale was effected (plus tick), or (B) at the last sale price if it was higher than the last different price (zero-plus tick). Short sales were not permitted on minus ticks or zero-minus ticks, subject to narrow exceptions. This was the 'tick test'. In the case of NASDAQ, instead of the last reported sale price, the 'tick test' was based on the last bid: NASD Rule 5100.

[5]   SEC, 17 CFR PARTS 240 and 242 [Release No. 34-55970; File No. S7-21-06] (Regulation SHO and Rule 10a-1) (effective 3 July 2007).

[6]   See FSA, *Discussion Paper 17, Short Selling* (London: FSA, 2002).

[7]   S. Foley, 'US Fed Rides to the Rescue of AIG with $85bn Bail-out', *The Independent*, 18 September 2008.

cial sector firms and shareholders, the US Securities and Exchange Commission (SEC), the UK Financial Services Authority (FSA), and most European and other developed market regulators issued orders banning short selling in financial sector firms,[8] which came into effect on 21 September 2009. However, the global ban was more of a 'knee-jerk' reaction to the precipitous price falls and less a comprehensive regulatory response to the challenges posed by short selling. Predictably, the various regulatory orders contained several loopholes and were rather asymmetric, both in their reach and with respect to their various exemptions, causing accordingly distortions to cross-border securities trading. For instance, the FSA's ban extended to short-selling positions accumulated through the use of derivatives,[9] but the SEC's did not. The ban expired in most affected markets in January 2009. However, the advent of the sovereign debt crisis in the eurozone in April and May 2010 opened a new cycle of debate and prohibitions, which focused on naked short sales on both sovereign bonds and financial sector stocks. This resulted in a permanent prohibition of 'naked' short sales in Germany.[10]

---

[8] Securities Exchange Act Release No. 34-58592 (18 September 2008) (Emergency Order Pursuant to Section 12(k)(2) of the Securities Exchange Act of 1934 Taking Temporary Action to Respond to Market Developments); FSA, *Short Selling (No. 2) Instrument 2008* (relating to UK Financial Sector companies), FSA 2008/50, 18 September 2008 (London: FSA, 2008). For a description of short sales restrictions in all EU jurisdictions see CESR, *CESR/08-742, Measures recently adopted by CESR Members on short-selling,* 22 (Paris: CESR, September 2008; Updated: 9 January 2009; 31 March 2009; 1 February 2010).

[9] There are various derivative instruments that allow investors to take a short position in a particular security in order to hedge or speculate. Use of these derivatives generally results in a short sale of the related securities further down the chain of transactions in order to hedge the position.

[10] On 18 May 2010, BaFin, Germany's financial services regulator, introduced a temporary ban on 'naked' short selling and 'naked' credit-default swaps of euro-area government bonds. The ban also extended to the naked short selling of the shares of ten of the leading German banks and insurers until 31 March 2011. On 2 June 2010 the cabinet passed a draft bill to ban indefinitely 'naked' short selling of eurozone government bonds and German shares that was endorsed by the German Lower House of Parliament on 2 July and entered the statutory book on 27 July 2010, which meant the repealing of BaFin's General Decree of 18 May 2010. This ban is much wider than the BaFin order of May 2010. See BaFin, *General Decree of 26 July 2010 by the Federal Financial Supervisory Authority (BaFin) to revoke the General Decrees banning naked short-selling transactions in shares and debt securities as well as naked credit default swaps,* 26 July 2010, available at http://www.bafin.de/cln_161/nn_720788/SharedDocs/Aufsichtsrecht/EN/Verfuegungen/vf__100726__leerverkauf__widerruf__en.html.

The Vexed Issue of Short Sales Regulation

While the September 2008 ban clearly intended to provide a temporary relief to the much maligned financial sector, recent studies of the ban's impact on US and UK markets show that short selling was not the main driver of the precipitous price falls in financial sector stocks.[11] Arguably, other factors, such as news about a very serious deterioration of the quality of bank assets, due to the credit crisis and the ensuing economic crisis, de-leveraging by hedge funds, and genuine market panic, amplified by strategic trade behaviour (so-called herding),[12] had a much bigger impact on falling market prices than increased volumes of short selling.

Furthermore, while short sales may be implicated in market abuse, this is usually where short selling represents an implementing strategy in the context of wider schemes to manipulate the market through the use of false rumours. Regulatory efforts should therefore concentrate on the latter context. Only 'naked' short sales[13] and short sales before seasoned offerings have the potential to manipulate market prices without the aid of false rumours. However, regulators have at their disposal a multitude of other means to battle market manipulation without eliminating the liquidity and information and pricing efficiency benefits that short selling seems to bring on many occasions. In particular, extensive disclosure, short trading halts, in the case of highly precipitous market price falls, and strict penalties for non-settlement, may be sufficient to contain the adverse impact of these practices; prohibitions on short sales may not therefore be required.[14]

---

[11] E.g., a study on the impact of the short sales ban in the US conducted by the Office of Economic Analysis found that long sellers, that is traders and investors who sell a stock they actually own, were primarily responsible for price declines during the high volatility period. Office of Economic Analysis, *Analysis of a short sale price test using intraday quote and trade data*, 17 December 2008. The FSA's study on the impact of its own ban also shows that this brought very little benefit and had an adverse impact on liquidity. See FSA, *Discussion paper 09/1, Short selling* (London: FSA, 2009), Annex 2.

[12] On the causes and mechanics of herding see DS Scharfstein and J Stein, 'Herd Behavior and Investment', 80 *American Economic Review,* 465 (1990).

[13] 'Naked' short sales is a term used to describe transactions in securities the seller does not hold at all. The most complete definition of 'naked short sales' is offered by Lecce et al. who describe them as a market practice where: 'the participant, either proprietary or on behalf of a client, enters an order in the market and do not have in place arrangements for delivery of the securities': below n. 79, 2, n. 2.

[14] See also London Stock Exchange Group, *Letter: Response to CESR Call for Evidence on the Regulation of Short Selling*, 20 January 2009, available at http://www.londonstockexchange.com/

The market abuse prevention rationale for banning short sales is therefore unconvincing.

Given the failure of the September 2008 short sales ban to curb market volatility, the vexed issue of short selling regulation still calls for a well designed and far reaching solution, which would also lead to symmetric/compatible national short selling regimes. Most developed market regulators[15] have consulted on the best way to regulate short selling. Moreover, the Commission of European Securities Regulators (CESR)[16] (since January 2011 CESR's work has been taken over by the European Securities and Markets Authority) and the International Organization of Securities Commissions (IOSCO) have, following such consultation, released high level principles for the regulation of short sales,[17] and the SEC has reinstated the uptick rule.[18] The latest round of consultations has been conducted by the EU Commission, which in September 2010 produced a Commission proposal for a Regulation for the harmonization of member states' short selling regimes in the EU.[19]

A New Global Framework for Short Sales Regulation

Following a discussion of the IOSCO Principles and the CESR (ESMA) and EU Commission proposals for the regulation of short sales, this chapter argues that a combination of properly calibrated disclosure requirements and of sophisticated circuit breaker trading halts, instead of a ban or an uptick rule, is sufficient to control the undesirable effects of short selling. When this two-pronged strategy is complemented by a strict settlement regime, such as that proposed by the IOSCO Principles, it may protect issuers of securities, rational investors, semi-rational investors and the market from the undesirable consequences of heavy short selling, which may trigger herding behaviour leading to severe downward

---

[15] SEC 17 CFR PART 242 [Release No. 34-59748; File No. S7-08-09] (Amendments to Regulation SHO); FSA, Discussion Paper, above n. 11.

[16] CESR, CESR/10-088, *Model for a Pan-European Short Selling Disclosure Regime* (Paris: CESR, 2010).

[17] IOSCO, *Final Report on Regulation of Short Selling* (IOSCO, 2009) (the IOSCO Principles).

[18] SEC Press Release, *2010-26, SEC Approves Short Selling Restrictions*, 24 February 2010; SEC 17 CFR PART 242 [Release No. 34-61595; File No. S7-08-09] Amendments to Regulation SHO.

[19] See European Commission, *COM(2010) 482 Proposal for a Regulation on Short Selling and Certain Aspects of Credit Default Swaps* (Brussels: European Commission, 2010) (Short Selling Proposal) and *MEMO/10/255, Public Consultation on Short Selling* (Brussels: European Commission, 2010).

price spirals that destabilize the market, without eliminating the efficiency benefits of short sales.

In particular, the circuit breaker[20] halt rule that stops short trading on the stock concerned for the rest of the trading day, if the market price falls below a certain threshold, must be a much more sophisticated mechanism than the mechanism adopted by the SEC[21] and should not be confused with the general circuit breaker mechanisms securities exchanges normally operate. Therefore, it is suggested in this chapter that a special short sales trading halts system should be designed which incorporates the features proposed below.

First, a relevant system must ascertain whether there is an absolute increase in the volume and value of short sales. Once this test is met, a second test, examining the level of falls in market prices, should be triggered. The price test should refer to a percentage fall in the market price as compared to a weighted average price comprising the previous day's closing price, which should be assigned the biggest weight, the average closing price of the preceding week, assigned the middle weight, and the average closing price of the preceding month, assigned the lowest weight. Setting the price threshold as a percentage fall over a weighted average would allow the circuit breaker to capture market trends that extend beyond a day's trading and thus be more restrictive of sudden price falls, possibly caused by a 'wild' swing in investor sentiment, the so-called 'animal spirits' of the market.[22] It would also allow the circuit breaker system to be less restrictive in the case of market price falls that are closer to market expectations over a short- and medium-term period.

It follows that, in order to take into account actual differences in price fluctuations of very liquid, less liquid, and relatively illiquid stocks, and facilitate the implementation, through symmetric national regulations, of an effective global regime governing short sales, the price threshold should be set at the same level (for example, 10 per cent fall from the weighted average price) for all stocks belonging to the main indices of developed markets, for example, the FTSE 350, S&P 500, Nikkei 500. A similar uniform threshold should apply to lower cap stocks that are not part of

---

[20] The FSA offers the following general definition of circuit breakers: 'A circuit-breaker involves a suspension of trading in a share whenever there is an abnormal rise or fall in its price. For example, if a share price fell by more than 10% in a single day, the exchanges could be required to discontinue trading in the stock for the rest of the day': FSA, Discussion Paper, above n. 11, at 21, para. 4.28.

[21] See SEC Release No. 34-61595, above n. 18.

[22] J.M. Keynes, *General Theory of Employment, Interest and Money* (1936) (republished, Basingstoke: Palgrave Macmillan, 2007).

the main index of a developed market and to stocks traded in developing markets. Admittedly, stocks participating in one of the major market indices are much more liquid and less prone to wild price swings than stocks included on the small cap market indices or stocks listed on developing markets. Moreover, the same uniform principles may be applied to thresholds triggering the disclosure of short positions as part of local regulations.

The proposed strategy is easily transferable from jurisdiction to jurisdiction, allowing IOSCO and ESMA to build standards and rules that may lead, through national implementation, to symmetric national regimes governing short sales. Therefore, it may be used as the foundation of a new global framework for the regulation of short sales that would eliminate the obstacles to cross-border trading created by the current regulatory asymmetry in this area. As a result, costs of compliance and other costs of cross-border equity trading would be lowered.

The introduction of symmetric or harmonized national short selling regimes in order to lower the costs of cross-border equity trading is demanded by all major institutional investors. In addition, a combination of lower costs of equity trading and a reduced possibility of overpricing, which is related to the legalization of short selling activity, essentially means a lower cost of capital. The cost of capital is, of course, a very important determinant of capital investment.[23] This means that the cost of capital is also a crucial factor in attracting higher volumes of Foreign Direct Investment,[24] fostering growth in developing countries.

This chapter is divided into six sections beginning with this introduction. The next section describes the ambit of the SEC and FSA September 2008 bans on short sales and the implications these created for cross-border trading. The third section analyses the moral concerns raised by short selling and explains the mechanics of short selling in contemporary securities markets, which are viewed as 'adaptive' markets that incorporate elements of both modern finance theory and behavioural finance. Furthermore, it examines the efficiency gains that short selling brings and reviews relevant empirical studies. It also considers the potential of short sales to destabilize orderly markets and discusses the risk that short sales present to issuers in the context of seasoned equity offerings, including rights issues. The fourth section provides an outline of the current proposals for the regulation of short sales set out by IOSCO, the SEC and the EU. The fifth section analyses the mechanisms proposed in

---

[23]   For a recent study see S. Gilchrist and E. Zakrajsek, *NBER Working Paper No. 13174, Investment and the Cost of Capital: New Evidence from the Corporate Bond Market* (2007).
[24]   I.A. Moosa, *Foreign Direct Investment: Theory, Evidence and Practice* (Basingstoke: Palgrave Macmillan, 2002), at 189–93.

this chapter for the regulation of short selling. It explains why a dual strategy of disclosure and short trading halts is superior to prohibition or the imposition of uptick rules. It also sets out the parameters of the proposed disclosure regime and circuit breaker system. The last section concludes.

THE SEPTEMBER 2008 BANS AND DISCLOSURE OF SHORT SALES ORDERS

The Short Sales Ban in the US

On 18 September 2008, the SEC issued an Order ('Financial Firms Order'),[25] which temporarily prohibited all short sales of publicly traded common equity securities of 799 financial services firms. The SEC's order extended only to positions in equity securities and did not cover convertible bonds and short positions created through the use of derivatives, although the ban did affect the ability of traders to physically settle such positions. The ban expired on 17 October 2008, following the adoption of the so-called Troubled Assets Relief Program (TARP),[26] a bank rescue package that essentially vindicated the fears of, and defensive positions taken by short sellers in September 2008. According to the SEC, the emergency action was intended to, first, prevent short selling from being used to drive down the share prices of issuers even where there was no fundamental basis for a price decline other than general market conditions and, second, prevent market abuse.

The second action adopted by the SEC was to significantly tighten disclosure requirements for trading in shares.[27] The SEC 'Reporting Order' obliged every institutional investment manager that: (a) exercised investment discretion with respect to accounts holding section 13(f) securities and (b) had filed or was required to file a Form 13F for the calendar quarter ended 30 June 2008, to file the new Form SH with the Commission.[28]

---

[25]   See Securities Exchange Act Release No. 34-58611 (21 September 2008) (Amendment to Emergency Order Pursuant to Section 12(k)(2) of the Securities Exchange Act of 1934 Taking Temporary Action to Respond to Market Developments).

[26]   Emergency Economic Stabilization Act of 2008 (US) (PL 110-343).

[27]   Securities Exchange Act Release No. 34-58591 (18 September 2008) (Emergency Order Pursuant to Section 12(k)(2) of the Securities Exchange Act of 1934 Taking Temporary Action to Respond to Market Developments) (SEC Reporting Order).

[28]   Form SH requires investment managers to disclose the number and value of securities sold short for each section 13(f) security, except for short sales in options,

The third SEC action in this context was, in an attempt to boost liquidity on the demand side, to issue an Order easing restrictions on the ability of securities issuers to repurchase their securities,[29] in accordance with Exchange Act Rule 10b-18. This provision granted issuers a safe harbour to effect repurchases subject to certain restrictions.

The UK Short Sales Ban

The UK's ban of short selling in financial sector stocks was based on the market abuse and investor confidence rationales; the FSA's reasoning for the ban[30] was accordingly broadly the same as the SEC's. Thus, on 18 September 2008 the FSA issued *Short Selling (No. 2) Instrument 2008*,[31] which amended its Code of Market Conduct (the FSA's principal rule book for dealing with behaviour that amounts to market abuse). The FSA's Instrument proscribed as market abuse (attracting a penalty) any transaction (whether alone or in conjunction with other transactions) that had the effect of creating or increasing a 'net short position' in the issued share capital of any 'UK financial sector company', defined widely to include designated publicly quoted UK incorporated banks and insurers (in total 32 stocks). The FSA defined as 'net short position' any 'net short position' that gave rise 'to an economic exposure to the issued share capital of a listed company'. Thus, every economic interest or exposure to the shares of a company, including derivatives positions, was taken into account in calculating a 'net short position'.[32] The FSA Instrument covered the creation or increase of economic net short positions through any mechanism whatever, including any kind of derivatives contract (such

---

as well as the opening short position, closing short position, largest intraday short position, and the time of the largest intraday short position, for that security during each calendar day of the prior week. Ibid.

[29] Securities Exchange Act Release No. 34-58588 (18 September 2008) (Emergency Order Pursuant to Section 12(k)(2) of the Securities Exchange Act of 1934 Taking Temporary Action to Respond to Market Developments – Easing Restrictions on the Ability of Issuers to Repurchase Securities) (Issuer Order).

[30] FSA, *Consultation Paper 09/1, Temporary Short Selling Measures* (London: FSA, 2009), at 4. The FSA also cited as a reason for its prohibition that the crisis of confidence brought about by heavy short selling in financial sector stocks could impair the liquidity and ultimate viability of an issuer.

[31] FSA, *Short Selling (No. 3) Instrument 2008*, FSA 2008/51, 23 September 2008 (London: FSA, 2008).

[32] FSA 2008/50, 18 September 2008. For guidance on the application of FSA's decision see FSA, *Short Selling (No. 2) Instrument 2008 – FAQs Version 5* (London: FSA, 2008).

contracts were not included in the SEC Order). Like the SEC Order the FSA Instrument exempted market makers that provided bid and offer prices to brokers for shares so that they could meet client demand.

The FSA ban had a global reach, covering shorting of shares in the list anywhere, for example, on the Deutsche Börse or the New York Stock Exchange. Accordingly, while the criterion for the SEC's ban was that the stocks be traded on a US securities exchange, the FSA's criterion was the place of incorporation, regardless of the location of the market where the securities of the firms in the list were traded. The ban included intraday trading, when a short position was generated and then closed in the same day. The prohibition covered new short positions, however created, while existing short positions did not have to be closed; they just could not be increased. The ban expired on 17 January 2009.

The FSA also required (daily) disclosure of pre-existing short positions (including convertible bonds) in financial sector companies of more than 0.25 per cent. The FSA had already issued its first emergency rules in July 2008, which required disclosure of short positions over 0.25 per cent in (all) companies undergoing rights offers,[33] which, however, did not extend to convertible bonds.

The Cost of Asymmetric National Short Selling Restrictions

Most EU Member States adopted regulations dealing with short sales at around the same time as the SEC and the FSA. Yet, both the scope of such regulations and the exemptions differed widely. As a result of the disparity of regulatory responses to short sales throughout the EU, CESR issued a paper providing a summary to market participants to facilitate compliance.[34] The market maker exemption, in particular, was a source of serious difficulty. Most Member States either did not have a market maker exemption or relied on a uniform definition of the kind of market actors which qualified as market makers. The asymmetric restrictions meant a serious increase in the costs of compliance for institutional investors. This comment by the Association of British Insurers in the context of CESR's consultation on short sales is typical:[35]

---

[33] FSA, *Short Selling (No. 1) Instrument 2008* (relating to companies in rights issue periods), FSA 2008/27, 13 July 2008 (London: FSA, 2008).

[34] CESR, Measures recently adopted, above n. 8.

[35] Association of British Insurers (ABI), *Regulation of Short Selling by CESR Members – The ABI's Response to CESR 08/1010*. See also European Forum of Securities Associations (EFSA), *CESR's Call for Evidence (CESR 08-1010) concerning the Regulation of Short Selling by CESR Members – Response by the*

[T]he disparity of approaches taken not just in the EU but globally has represented a significant cost. For example, one large firm, which operates in several jurisdictions, reports that the annual legal and consultancy fees paid merely for identifying and tracking changes run to tens of thousands of pounds.

The European Fund and Asset Management Association (EFAMA) also noted in its response to CESR's consultation with respect to the short sales ban that: 'EFAMA regrets the lack of coordination among regulators and the lack of harmonization of these measures'. According to EFAMA, these failings had three main effects for its members:[36] (a) increased costs for investment managers to track and comply with the many different rules in all jurisdictions; (b) a significant increase in *legal uncertainty*, due to the lack of harmonization and to the lack of guidance on implementation; and (c) the above loopholes created regulatory arbitrage possibilities, 'due to the many differences in the short selling regimes and the cross-border nature of equity markets . . . [which sometimes caused] . . . *distortions that negatively impacted the trading in specific shares or markets*'.[37]

Accordingly, there is a pressing need for new international standards that will lead to coordinated implementation of compatible national regimes in order to reduce the costs of cross-border equity trading. This objective has not been achieved so far for three reasons. First, because the IOSCO Principles are very high level, they struggle to support the meaningful harmonization of national regimes; second, the regulatory model proposed by the EU contains a blanket prohibition of 'naked' short sales,[38] which may not be acceptable to non-EU markets; and third, the SEC has reintroduced a form of the uptick rule, ignoring both the defects of this measure and the potential for international coordination, which the uptick rule precludes.[39] To answer the pressing need for international coordination, this chapter provides in Section 5 a comprehensive model of short selling regulation that may lead to the adoption of symmetrical short selling regimes by IOSCO members with respect to stock markets. The same may be said about bonds markets and especially the global sovereign

---

European Forum of Securities Associations (2009), available at http://www.liba.org.uk/issues/2009/Feb/EFSA%20letter%20to%20CESR%20SS%20finaldoc.pdf.

[36] EFAMA, *Reply to CESR's Call for Evidence on Regulation of Short Selling by CESR Members* (2009) .

[37] Ibid. (emphasis added).

[38] Short Selling Proposal, above n. 19.

[39] This is due to the fact that it is very hard to modify trading systems outside the US in a way that would make the introduction of the uptick rule cost effective.

debt markets, but a close examination of those markets is outside of the ambit of this chapter.

SHOULD SHORT SALES BE BANNED? A COST–BENEFIT ANALYSIS

Short Sales in Contemporary Financial Markets

In order to ascertain whether short selling should be banned, we should first consider whether this practice is strongly objectionable on moral grounds. The efficiency benefits of short selling and the results of the prohibitions of short sales in various jurisdictions must then be evaluated. In this context, consideration must also be given to the ability of short sales to destabilize the market in a specific stock, particularly in the context of seasoned equity offerings, including rights issues, and its link to market abuse.

Moral considerations
As mentioned in the introduction to this chapter, one of the reasons that short selling is often regarded as an extreme form of speculation, associated with the dark side of financial capitalism, is that politicians, a large part of society, and the media regard it as a risk-free, one-way bet that destabilizes markets and brings large profit to 'unscrupulous' traders. The fact that hedge funds are often among the most aggressive short sellers only helps to reinforce this view, which at the height of the crisis was shared by regulators, policymakers and senior bankers whose share prices suffered from heavy short selling.[40]

Furthermore, selling something that the trader does not own on the spot market runs counter to one of the deepest rooted traditions of Western (free market) economies, namely that parties in spot asset markets entering, for profit, into any kind of economic exchange must have property rights, probably title, of some form over the traded asset. This is normally not the case with short sales, at least with 'naked' short sales.

Difficulties also arise from the passive approach of big institutional investors like insurance companies and pension funds to short selling. Institutional stock holdings – kept for safe keeping, or for settling transactions, or as collateral – are lent by custodians (or even prime brokers)

---

[40]   D. Wighton, 'Bankers Take a Billhook to the Hedge Funds', *The Times*, 11 October 2008.

to short sellers. Therefore, for a stock-lending fee institutions facilitate a practice that can have a negative impact (falling prices) on the value of their holdings.

Accordingly, it might be argued that it is only where there is evidence of serious welfare gains that a regime in which short sales are permitted can be justified. In addition, any relevant regulations must be sufficiently calibrated so as to make sure that the financial markets are not turned into 'casinos', with certain investors taking risk-free bets. The first criterion may be met if it can be shown that the efficiency gains from free short sales are sufficiently important to market welfare to override the aforementioned moral concerns. The second criterion calls for a regulatory design that allows the efficiency gains of short selling to accrue while, at the same time, controlling its undesirable consequences, especially in terms of market stability. A consideration is first required, however, of how short selling interacts with other market mechanisms and, second, of the socio-psychological factors in contemporary financial markets.

Herding and short sales in 'efficient' and 'adaptive' securities markets

Modern finance theory, and its offspring the Efficient Markets Hypothesis (EMH), has been the predominant method for interpreting market behaviour for the past four decades. The EMH, as the brainchild of rational choice theory,[41] assumes that asset prices are set by rational investors.[42] Thus, market prices reflect/equal fundamental value and react to new information.[43] Most of the assumptions relating to the EMH have been challenged by behavioural finance theory that incorporates insights from so-called psychology of choice and judgement[44] into analysis of

---

[41] For the theoretical foundations of the EMH see P.A. Samuelson, 'Proof that Properly Anticipated Prices Fluctuate Randomly', 6 *Industrial Management Review*, 41 (1965) and B. Mandelbrot, 'Forecasts of Future Prices, Unbiased Markets, and Martingale Models', 39 *Journal of Business*, 242 (1966).

[42] M. Friedman, *The Methodology of Positive Economics*, Essays in Positive Economics, 3–43 (Chicago: University of Chicago Press, 1953).

[43] University of Chicago Professor Eugene Fama has been a major contributor to the empirical foundations of the EMH. See E.F. Fama, 'Efficient Capital Markets: A Review of Theory and Empirical Work', 25 *Journal of Finance*, 383 (1970) and id., 'Efficient Capital Markets II', 46 *Journal of Finance*, 1575 (1991).

[44] The founders of psychology of choice and judgement were Daniel Kahneman and Amos Tversky. Representative publications include: D Kahneman and A Tversky, 'Judgment under Uncertainty: Heuristics and Biases', 185 *Science*, 1124 (1974); id., 'Prospect Theory: An Analysis of Decision under Risk', 47 *Econometrica*, 263 (1979); id., 'Rational Choice and the Framing

market behaviour.[45] According to behavioural finance, many of the market 'anomalies' that cannot be explained by the EMH can be explained by reference to individuals' use of their cognitive attributes such as heuristics[46] and their likely results, so-called cognitive biases.[47]

One of the core assumptions of the EMH is that, in an efficient market, no investment strategy can yield average returns that are higher than the risk assumed and no trader can consistently outperform the market or accurately predict future price levels, as new information is instantly absorbed by market prices. Therefore, since in efficient markets transaction costs are relatively low, 'professionally-informed traders' have the opportunity to quickly observe and exploit through arbitrage trading any price deviations from fundamental value, since such discrepancy creates a profit opportunity. The result of arbitrage activity is that prices reach a new equilibrium, which reflects more accurately the traded asset's value, and corrects any mis-pricings.[48] Short selling is a highly efficient mechanism for arbitrage trading. However, when what calls for correction is not a price spike but a precipitous price fall, arbitrageurs must engage in much more expensive (as compared to unrestricted short sales) share purchases. Thus, in this case, the corrective power of arbitrage trading is limited owing to higher transaction costs. It follows that, if arbitrage activity fails to 'correct' a precipitous price fall caused by short selling, the majority of

---

of Decisions', 59 *Journal of Business*, S251 (1986); and id., 'Loss Aversion in Riskless Choice: A Reference-Dependent Model', 106 *Quarterly Journal of Economics*, 1039 (1991).

[45]   See, in general, N.C. Barberis and R. Thaler, *A Survey of Behavioral Finance, National Bureau of Economic Research, Working Paper No. 9222* (2002), 4, 13; W F M DeBondt and R H Thaler, 'Does the Stock Market Overreact?', 40 *Journal of Finance*, 557 (1985); D Hirschliefer, 'Investor Psychology and Asset Pricing', 56 *Journal of Finance*, 1533 (2001); cf. E.F. Fama, 'Market Efficiency, Long-Term Returns, and Behavioral Finance', 49 *Journal Financial Economics*, 283 (1998).

[46]   'Heuristics' are cognitive processes that allow individuals to reduce the complex tasks of assessing probabilities and predicting values to simpler judgemental operations. For this reason, they are also called 'mental shortcuts'. In general, these heuristics are quite useful, but sometimes they lead to severe and systematic errors. See Kahneman and Tversky, 'Judgment under Uncertainty', above n. 44.

[47]   Cognitive biases are the results of the use of heuristics, when they lead to: (a) systematic errors in estimations of known quantities and statistical facts and (b) systematic departures of intuitive judgements from the principles of probability theory. Ibid.

[48]   B.G. Malkiel, 'The Efficient Market Hypothesis and Its Critics', 17 *Journal of Economic Perspectives*, 59 (2003).

market actors may feel compelled to imitate short sellers' trades, adding further downward pressure on prices.

Furthermore, the corrective influence that the EMH attributes to arbitrage is strongly disputed by behavioural finance, because, apart from transaction cost restrictions,[49] the EMH assumes that all market players are rational. Behavioural finance assumes two kinds of investors in the market: (a) rational speculators or arbitrageurs who trade on the basis of information and (b) quasi-rational investors, called 'noise' traders. As a result, a number of investors ('noise' traders) act on imperfect information[50] and may cause prices to deviate from their equilibrium values. This framework, combined with the fact that upwards arbitrage trading may have limited corrective power, can explain why short sales can sometimes trigger investor herding and cause widespread market price falls. However, a more convincing explanation of why short sales may trigger strategic trading behaviour, justifying the introduction of circuit breaker trading halts, is offered by theories that claim to replace the EMH and behavioural finance.

Despite the powerful and ultimately successful challenge that behavioural finance has mounted on the EMH, it may not serve as the successor to the EMH, since sometimes investors do behave rationally and prices take a 'random walk'. Behavioural finance also lacks predictive value. Thus, it seems that other more sophisticated theories, which view markets as evolutionary and adaptive systems that are also susceptible to irrational behaviour, owing to investors' cognitive limitations and limited self-control, and to strategic trade behaviour (herding), caused by socio-psychological or narrow self-interest factors, provide a better understanding of actual market conditions and investor behaviour.

Andrew Lo of MIT has offered the best alternative so far to the battling rivals of modern finance theory and behavioural finance. Lo's theory, the Adaptive Markets Hypothesis (AMH),[51] incorporates several of the assumptions of both theories in an evolutionary framework. Lo submits that markets can often be efficient, but can also display strong deviations caused by behavioural factors. These are caused by the fact that market actors' computational ability is limited and cognitive biases do play a role in their investment decisions. The predominant theme of the AMH

---

[49] See A. Shleifer and R.W. Vishny, 'Limits of Arbitrage', 52 *Journal of Finance*, 35 (1997).

[50] A. Shleifer and L.H. Summers, 'The Noise Trader Approach to Finance', 4 *Journal of Economic Perspectives*, 19 (1990).

[51] A. Lo, 'Reconciling Efficient Markets with Behavioral Finance: The Adaptive Markets Hypothesis', 7 *Journal of Investment Consulting*, 21 (2005).

is that market actors ultimately struggle not for optimal returns (as the EMH holds) – optimization is costly – but for survival, like all living species in an evolutionary framework. Namely, the AMH holds that market actors behave rationally at times, and irrationally at other times, depending on which strategy best suits their struggle for survival. For the reasons explained in the next few paragraphs, herding may become the only survival strategy in a falling market, even for professional (rational) investors.

If the more accurate assumption is that markets are complex adaptive systems that encompass both rational and quasi-rational investors,[52] and the latter cause prices to deviate from their equilibrium values, and for the aforementioned reasons upward pressure through arbitrage trading is either not strong or fast enough, then the majority of investors may just follow the herd, joining the 'momentum' game. Namely, they may resort to the safest short-term survival strategy.

The assumption that herding may merely constitute a survival strategy sits well with recent research that herding does not have to be the result of irrational panic. Peer pressure, or attachment to short-term gains for career, and other reasons relating to the reputation and compensation of traders or fund managers, are also sufficient and likely factors,[53] because of the agency relationship, the so-called 'separation of brains from capital'. The agency relationship means that fund managers' and fund investors' interests may be misaligned. Reputations, salaries and career progress are often determined on the basis of short-term profit and comparability with competitors' returns.[54] As a result, fund managers, in fear of the irrational behaviour of 'noise traders' that may force further market falls, and require them to post losses, are likely to decide that foregoing arbitrage opportunities and following the herd is a safer option for themselves.[55] This possibility fully justifies the use of the circuit breaker system as a supplement to disclosure and settlement rules.

---

[52]   See also R.H. Thaler, 'The End of Behavioral Finance', *Financial Analysts Journal*, 12 (November/December 1999), 12–13.

[53]   P.M. Healy and K.G. Palepu, 'Governance and Intermediation Problems in Capital Markets: Evidence from the Fall of Enron', 17 *Journal of Economic Perspectives*, 3 (2003).

[54]   J. Chevalier and G. Ellison, 'Career Concerns of Mutual Fund Managers', 114 *Quarterly Journal of Economics*, 389 (1999).

[55]   J.R. Nofsinger and R.W. Sias, 'Herding and Feedback Trading by Institutional and Individual Investors', 54 *Journal of Finance*, 2263 (1999). This short termism has been widely castigated as one of the fundamental causes of the global financial crisis. See E. Avgouleas, 'The Global Financial Crisis, Behavioural

The Efficiency Benefits of Short Selling

IOSCO has recognized that short selling may bring significant efficiency gains particularly with respect to: (a) efficient price discovery, because short selling facilitates 'a more rapid re-pricing of over-valued securities than would otherwise be the case'; (b) mitigation of price bubbles, because it helps 'contrarian investors' to mitigate, through rapid sales, steep, temporary price spikes (mini 'bubbles'); (c) increasing market liquidity; and (d) facilitating hedging and other risk management activities.[56]

IOSCO's view reflects economic theory-based perceptions of short selling,[57] endorsed subsequently by a significant number of empirical studies. These studies show that short selling can facilitate better valuation of securities by controlling overpricing,[58] enable the market to adjust faster to bad news,[59] and enhance pricing efficiency.[60] In addition, there is some evidence that an absence of short selling restrictions may boost liquidity, because short traders and their counterparties find it easier to trade, and may also facilitate hedging strategies based on short selling. This translates into a bigger number of trading parties for a specific stock, higher trading volume, and lower bid ask spreads.

A number of empirical studies indicate that an increase in short positions also signals genuine bad news relating to the stock[61] and heavily shorted

---

Finance and Financial Market Regulation: In Search of a New Orthodoxy', 9 *Journal of Corporate Law Studies*, 23 (2009), at 39–44.

[56]   IOSCO Report, above n. 2, at 5, 22.

[57]   E.M. Miller, 'Risk, Uncertainty, and Divergence of Opinion', 32 *Journal of Finance*, 1151 (1977); D.W. Diamond and R.E. Verrecchia, 'Constraints on Short-selling and Asset Price Adjustment to Private Information', 18 *Journal of Financial Economics*, 277 (1987).

[58]   In fact, there is evidence that stocks can be overpriced when securities are subject to short sale constraints. See C.M. Jones and O.A. Lamont, 'Short Sale Constraints and Stock Returns', 66 *Journal of Financial Economics*, 207 (2002); and A. Charoenrook and H. Daouk, *A study of market-wide short-selling restrictions*, Unpublished working paper, Vanderbilt University, Tennessee (2005), available at http://ssrn,com/abstract=687562.

[59]   Y. Bai, E. Chang and J. Wang, 'Asset Prices under Short-Sale Constraints', University of Hong Kong and MIT Working Paper (2006), available at http://web.mit.edu/wangj/www/pap/BCW_061112.pdf.

[60]   A. Bris, W.N. Goetzmann and N. Zhu, 'Efficiency and the Bear: Short Sales and Markets Around the World', 62 *Journal of Finance*, 1029 (2007).

[61]   A.J. Senchack and L.T. Starks, 'Short-sale Restrictions and Market Reaction to Short-Interest Announcement', 28 *Journal of Financial and Quantitative Analysis*, 177 (1993).

stocks tend to exhibit, following the trades, negative returns.[62] The latter finding suggests that short sales probably convey negative information about a stock, which feeds into its valuation for a considerable period.[63]

Boehmer, Jones and Zhang examined NYSE short sale order flow data in the period from January 2000 to April 2004. They showed that short sellers as a group tend to be well informed and to trade on fundamentals. Furthermore, they found that those engaging in a higher volume of short sales (5000 shares or more) were very well informed, unlike those entering a lower volume of short sales (500 shares or less), who tended to be less well informed.[64]

Arguably, the most convincing evidence of the beneficial impact of short sales on market efficiency arises from the studies that examined the impact of the SEC and FSA bans on price volatility and trading liquidity, both among the most important indicators of market efficiency. From the studies conducted by the US Office of Economic Analysis (OEA), it is evident that the price impact of the short selling ban was minimal[65] and that long sellers were more responsible for price declines during the period under consideration.[66] Another study on the impact of the SEC's ban by Boehmer, Jones and Zhang compared a selection of NYSE-listed stocks on the restricted list with comparable NYSE-listed stocks not subject to the ban. The study showed that stocks on the restricted list experienced a share price increase at the start of the ban and a temporary share price decline when shorting resumed after the end of the ban. However, market quality for these stocks, as measured by spreads, the five-minute price impact of trades, and intraday volatility, decreased. Namely, the ban gave a temporary boost to the share prices of financial companies in the restricted list, which proved to be short-lived.[67]

---

[62]   H. Desai, K. Ramesh, S. Ramu Thiagarajan and B.V. Balachandran, 'An Investigation of the Informational Role of Short Interest in the Nasdaq Market', 57 *Journal of Finance*, 2263 (2002).

[63]   P. Asquith and L. Meulbroek, *An Empirical Investigation of Short Interest*, Harvard Business School Working Paper (1995), available at www.hbs.edu/research/facpubs/workingpapers/abstracts/9596/96-012.html.

[64]   E. Boehmer, C.M. Jones and X. Zhang, 'Which Shorts Are Informed?' 63 *Journal of Finance*, 491 (2008).

[65]   Office of Economic Analysis, *Analysis of Short Selling Activity during the First Weeks of September 2008*, 16 December 2008.

[66]   Office of Economic Analysis, *Analysis of a short sale price test using intraday quote and trade data*, 17 December 2008.

[67]   E. Boehmer, C.M. Jones and X. Zhang, *Shackling Short Sellers: The 2008 Shorting Ban*, Working Paper, Columbia University (2008), available at http://www2.gsb.columbia.edu/faculty/cjones/ShortingBan.pdf.

An independent study, commissioned by the London Stock Exchange to evaluate the impact of the ban on market quality (defined as market volatility and liquidity) for the stocks affected by the ban, also produced very interesting findings that strongly argue against a prohibition on short selling.[68] In particular, Clifton and Snape (the authors of the study) compared quality of trading in 15 FTSE 100 stocks from the restricted list (affected stocks) and in 78 stocks outside the restricted list (control stocks) during 3 separate 30-day trading periods: 2 prior to the FSA ban and 1 after the ban. They found that liquidity in affected stocks, measured by reference to the size of bid ask spreads, order depth, number of trades and trading volume, deteriorated. According to the authors of this study, the two separate regression analyses that they conducted showed that the marked decline in liquidity occurred 'independently of market-wide changes and increased volatility'.[69] Thus, the reduction of liquidity levels may be attributed to the ban. These findings are also in accordance with the conclusions of a study conducted by the FSA regarding the impact of its own ban on short sales.[70]

The results of the above studies are further corroborated by independent research conducted by Marsh and Niemer, who examined the impact of the September 2008 short selling restrictions in a number of countries, including the UK, the US, France and Germany.[71] Using stock return data over the period 1 January 2008 to 31 October 2008, they compared, inter alia, mean and median daily returns,[72] for companies subject to the restrictions and companies not subject to the restrictions in each of the surveyed countries, for companies subject to the restrictions before and after the restrictions were imposed in a surveyed country, and for similar companies subject to different short selling restrictions in different countries, where restrictions were less binding. The three separate studies were necessary as the report has, essentially, tried to identify the counterfactual: to produce evidence of what the behaviour of 'the returns on stocks

---

[68]   M. Clifton and M. Snape, *The Effect of Short-selling Restrictions on Liquidity: Evidence from the London Stock Exchange* (2008), available at http://www.londonstockexchange.com/

[69]   Ibid.

[70]   FSA, Discussion Paper, above n 11, at Annex 2, 1.

[71]   I.W. Marsh and N. Niemer, *The Impact of Short Sales Restrictions* (2008), available at http://www.cass.city.ac.uk/media/stories/resources/the-impact-of-short-sales-restrictions.pdf.

[72]   In total, Marsh and Niemer examine: (a) mean daily return, (b) median daily returns, (c) standard deviation of daily returns, (d) skewness of daily returns, (e) kurtosis of daily returns, (f) first order autocorrelation of daily returns, (g) goodness of fit for the market model of daily returns. Ibid., at 4.

subject to the short sales restrictions would have been in the absence of those restrictions'.[73] Marsh and Niemeyer found no strong evidence that restrictions on short selling in the UK or elsewhere changed the behaviour of stock returns.

In summary, the overwhelming majority of relevant empirical studies show that short selling brings considerable efficiency gains to the market. On the other hand, short selling prohibitions failed to stabilize securities markets and bring about reductions in price volatility. At the same time, they seem to have adversely affected liquidity and thus pricing efficiency in the securities concerned and the market's information efficiency.

Destabilization of Orderly Markets

The most potent of the perceived threats that short selling presents is its ability to destabilize orderly securities markets. Owing to their large volume and speed of implementation, short sales may create downward price spirals.[74] These may be the result of other traders' inability to insert buying orders in a rapidly falling market or their unwillingness to take a long position, since the market's continuous decline may generate large losses on such long positions. Furthermore, short selling that causes a significant price fall may also force long traders to liquidate their positions because of funding pressures, for example margin calls, feeding further downward price spirals, or in order to avoid losses due to strategic trade behaviour, namely, herding.

A free falling share price affects issuers' standing among investors and impairs issuers' ability to raise fresh capital or obtain credit. Also, the precipitous collapse in the market price of a security may have implications for the wider market in terms of investor confidence. A precipitous collapse in the market price of a stock, due to short selling, may have a contagious effect, spreading downward price pressures to the rest of the market and destabilizing market prices in all stocks of the same sector or the market as a whole,[75] a danger that has intensified with the advent of rapid computer-driven programme trading.

The aforementioned study by Bris, Goetzmann and Zhu tried to ascertain whether short sales have a destabilizing impact on securities markets. The study analysed cross-sectional and time-series information from 46 equity

---

[73] Ibid.
[74] IOSCO Report, above n. 2, at 22.
[75] FSA, Discussion Paper, above n. 11, at 12.

markets around the world for the period 1990–2001.[76] Its results suggest that short sales do not affect the frequency of extreme negative returns. However, without short selling restrictions, extreme returns become even more negative. The Bris, Goetzmann and Zhu study also found evidence that short selling amplifies price swings, which means that downward price pressures are fed faster to the market and may be stronger.[77] Furthermore, despite BaFin's ban on 'naked' short sales for financial sector stocks, there was scant evidence that the volatility experienced by the stocks of those institutions was based on heavy short selling rather than on investor sales driven by a generalized concern about the health of Eurozone financial institutions.[78]

On the other hand, there is strong evidence that 'naked' short sales do not lead to more efficient prices, but instead increase the volatility of stock returns and create a serious settlement risk. They may also lead to a deterioration of liquidity, through wider bid ask spreads, decreased order depth and reduced trading volumes, and to an increase in the volatility of stock returns.[79] Nonetheless, a combination of a sophisticated circuit breaker system and a tight disclosure regime, such as the one proposed in this chapter, with the addition of a strict timeline for the settlement of transactions with steep penalties for non-settlement, is, arguably, sufficient to contain both the risk of 'contagion' to other stocks, feared by the FSA, and the risk posed by 'naked' short sales.

Settlement Risk

Short selling may also raise concerns in the context of the settlement of relevant transactions. 'Naked' short sales, where the short seller has not

---

[76]   Bris et al., above n. 60. To assess better the impact of short selling on volatility, the study looked at both the frequency of extreme negative market returns and the skewness of market returns.

[77]   Ibid.

[78]   E.g., from the ten protected institutions there was a sizable short position in the stock of only one institution. Perhaps not surprisingly, that institution was Commerzbank, which was one of the German institutions that suffered the heaviest losses during the global financial crisis: 'Data shows as of Monday's close 5.1 per cent of stock was on loan.' In the case of all other institutions short positions were negligible: 'Next is Deutsche Bank with only 1 per cent of stock on loan. Combined all the other eight stocks have less than 2 per cent on loan.' See blog entry:'Germany Short Selling Ban and Short Sale Definition – EURUSD Trading and Swaps Trading Communication', available at http://hubpages.com/hub/Short-Selling-Ban.

[79]   S. Lecce, A. Lepone and R. Segara, *The Impact of Naked Short-Sales on Returns, Volatility and Liquidity: Evidence from the Australian Securities Exchange* (2008), available at http://ssrn.com/abstract=1253176.

arranged borrowing ahead of the sale, in particular, may lead to settlement default, if either the short seller does not have strong incentive to settle or the stock lending market has become illiquid and does not allow the seller to borrow the shares sold short to fulfil the settlement obligations. Also, it is possible that short sellers may have overextended their positions and become vulnerable to a price upsurge or a squeeze[80] by the long traders, as was the case with the Volkswagen shares.[81]

A settlement failure is a serious matter, because it may cause serious disruption to the orderly operation of the market in the securities concerned. In addition, it might trigger a chain of defaults among highly leveraged market participants, threatening the stability of the system.[82] Even more serious is the risk to the buyer, who may wish to exercise voting rights over the securities concerned, or to meet obligations in respect of an onward chain of transactions, and is prevented from doing so because the shares sold short were not registered in a timely manner.

However, even settlement risk, arising from 'naked' short sales, does not warrant an outright ban. A combined strategy of tight settlement periods, for example maximum three days after trading day (T+3), and heavy penalties for failure to settle can eliminate trader incentives not to settle. Furthermore, full disclosure of the aggregate volume of short sales

---

[80]   The FSA describes this risk to short sellers as follows: 'Short sellers must, at some point in the future, buy back an equivalent number of shares to those that were sold short. This would be true whether they were to replace the number of borrowed shares in the case of covered short selling or simply close out the short position in the case of naked short selling. In either scenario, the short seller is exposed to the risk that the shorted shares will go up in price. If the price rises while the short position is open, then the short seller will be required to either close out the position at a loss or to pledge more cash to keep the position open. Stock prices may rise for any number of reasons and if this occurs quickly and is sustained for a period of time then short sellers are caught in what is called a "short squeeze", with the covering of short positions driving up prices further.' FSA, Discussion Paper, above n 11, at 7, para. 2.5.

[81]   See A.J. Kammel, 'The Dilemma of Blind Spots in Capital Markets – How to Make Efficient Use of Regulatory Loopholes?', 10 *German Law Journal*, 605 (2009). This article describes the VW 'squeeze' as follows: 'On a Sunday late in October 2008, on the 26th to be precise, Porsche published a statement in which it informed the public that it had raised its stake in VW to 42.6 per cent from before 35 per cent, and that it held options for another 31.5 per cent. In case of exercising those options Porsche would be put within spitting distance of the 75 per cent threshold, which [meant] it could control every major decision at its much larger rival, Volkswagen . . . This statement had tremendous effects: VW shares shot up to a momentary high of \$ 1,276, making it for once moment the most expensive share worldwide on Tuesday, 28 October 2008' (notes omitted), at 605-606.

[82]   IOSCO Report, above n. 2.

in regular intervals should be sufficient to prevent any serious market disruption. The combination of the above measures, as well as the possibility of a squeeze of the shorts, would mean that 'naked' short sales would take place only when there are serious information grounds that warrant resorting to this technique. Therefore, the possibility for extreme speculation to destabilize the market is drastically reduced without losing the information benefits that short sales may bring.

Rights Issues

Rights issues and other seasoned offerings are particularly vulnerable to short selling, as short sellers, who attempt to drive down the share price below the offer or the rights issue price, can later cover their positions at profit.[83] The perception of short selling as a destabilizing factor in the context of seasoned equity offerings, including rights issues, is very well entrenched. It is also believed that large volumes of short sales in the same context may lead to the perpetration of a successful market manipulation. Yet relevant empirical studies provide a more mixed view.

A study by Christophe et al.,[84] which examined short sales transactions in the five days prior to earnings announcements of 913 Nasdaq-listed firms, provided 'evidence of informed trading in pre-announcement short-selling', which would justify wide price movements before the announcement of seasoned equity offerings. In another study Safieddine and Wilhelm[85] examined whether short selling around seasoned equity offerings for NYSE and Amex-listed firms during the period 1980–1991 led to issue discounts. They also examined the effects of the SEC's adoption of (former) Rule 10b-21 in 1988.[86] The study found that seasoned equity offers were, indeed, preceded by abnormally high levels of short selling. It also showed that higher levels of short selling were associated with lower offer prices and thus reduced proceeds from the equity issue. Saffiedine and Wilhelm concluded that (former) Rule 10b-21 constrained short

---

[83]   FSA, Discussion Paper, above n. 11, at 11–12.

[84]   S.E. Christophe, M.G. Ferri and J.J. Angel, 'Short-Selling Prior to Earnings Announcements', 59 *Journal of Finance*, 1845 (2004).

[85]   A. Safieddine and W. Wilhelm, 'An Empirical Investigation of Short-selling Activity prior to Seasoned Equity Offerings', 51 *Journal of Finance*, 729 (1996).

[86]   This Rule prohibited short sales where the short position was covered by purchasing shares from the new offering, if the short position was established between the filing of the registration statement and the beginning of the distribution of the offering.

selling activity prior to seasoned equity offerings and therefore reduced the cost of seasoned offerings.

A more recent study undertaken by Kim and Shin also examined the effects of the introduction of (former) Rule 10b-21, using a larger sample of US equity offerings, covering the period 1983 to 1998,[87] and reached an opposite conclusion. The Kim and Shin study postulated that the observed significant seasoned equity offer discounts that became distinguishable after 1988, the year (former) Rule 10b-21 went into effect, were the result of *ex ante* uncertainty about the offer price. Since (former) Rule 10b-21 restricted short sales, it reduced the informativeness of seasoned equity offer prices, raising levels of uncertainty and thus causing greater discounts.

Another major study on the impact of short sales on seasoned offers' discounts was conducted by Autore in 2006.[88] Autore compared price discounting in US traditional and shelf-registered seasoned equity offerings during the period 1982–2004. This comparison could provide useful conclusions, because shelf-registered seasoned equity offerings were exempt from (former) Rule 10b-21, unlike traditional seasoned equity offerings, enabling Autore to use shelf-registered offers as a control group. His study showed that (former) Rule 10b-21 did not lead to an increase in seasoned offer discounts, contradicting the conclusions of Kim and Shin's study.

The most recent study is by Henry and Koski,[89] who examined whether short sales around seasoned equity offerings were the result of informed or manipulative trading. Henry and Koski examined a sample of US seasoned equity offers in the period 2005–2006. However, unlike other studies, they used daily short selling data. Their study found evidence of manipulative short selling in traditional seasoned offers, which could not be fully contained by SEC Rule 105,[90] which replaced Rule 10b-21. Henry and Koski argue that the wide discrepancy between the findings of their study and those of other studies is explained by the fact that they used daily rather than monthly short selling data.

---

[87]　A.K. Kim and H.-H. Shin, 'The Puzzling Increase in the Underpricing of Seasoned Equity Offerings', 39 *The Financial Review*, 343 (2004).

[88]　D. Autore, *Seasoned Offer Discounting and Rule 10b-21: What Can We Learn from the Shelf Exception?* (2006) available at http://www.fma.org/SLC/Papers/seasoned_offer_discounting_fma_paper.pdf.

[89]　T.R. Henry and J.L. Koski, *Short-selling Around Seasoned Equity Offerings* (2008), available at http://ssrn.com/abstract=972076.

[90]　SEC Rule 105 prohibited traders from covering short sales made within five days of the seasoned offer with shares purchased through a subscription to the offer.

Although empirical studies provide a mixed view, the special circumstances surrounding seasoned equity offerings, including rights issues, would seem to justify a ban on 'naked' short sales rather than a restriction on the ability of short sellers to cover their positions in the newly issued shares.[91] Mere use of increased disclosure, in line with the FSA's rule in July 2008,[92] would not seem to bring any relief in this case since the incentives for determined speculators to carry out their scheme and manipulate the price of newly issued shares are very high

Does Short Selling Amount to Market Abuse?

The second of the main rationales offered by the FSA and the SEC for the short selling ban of September 2008 was short selling's role in the perpetration of market abuse. First, short selling may help insiders to profit from information they possess, which if made public would have an adverse impact on the price of the issuer's securities. Second, it may be used as an implementing tool in the context of a wider scheme to manipulate the market through spreading of false rumours. Finally, 'naked' short sales may in some cases become an effective way to manipulate downwards market prices,[93] a possibility that seems quite serious in the case of seasoned securities offerings.

As regards the relationship of short sales to insider dealing, Christophe, Ferri and Angel conducted a study of short selling in a period (five trading days) leading to earnings announcements in the autumn of 2000 for 913 firms listed on NASDAQ. The hypothesis they tested was that, if short sellers possess inside information, short selling activity should increase prior to negative earnings announcements and decrease before positive earnings announcements. Their tests found that there is a negative relationship between short selling prior to an announcement and the post-announcement change in share prices and that abnormally large changes in short selling volume are often followed by substantial post-announcement share price movements. This shows that short sellers are overall better informed, evidencing the existence of insider dealing in short selling before earnings announcements.[94]

However, none of these concerns justifies a ban on short sales. First,

---

[91] See E. Avgouleas, 'Short-Sales Regulation in Seasoned Equity Offerings: What Are the Issues?' in D. Prentice and A. Reisberg (eds), *EU Corporate Law and Finance* (Oxford: OUP, 2010), ch. 5, at 117–139.

[92] FSA, *Short Selling (No. 1) Instrument 2008,* above n. 31.

[93] Lecce et al., above n. 79.

[94] See Christophe et al., above n. 84.

regulatory authorities in the US, the EU and the UK have many other weapons to deal with insider dealing and market manipulation through the spreading of false rumours; banning short sales on grounds of market abuse would seem unjustified. For instance, as regards the possibility of insider dealing through short sales prior to earnings announcements, a more extensive and timely disclosure of short selling activity would decrease the insider's scope to make profit, as other market participants would also start selling and so increase the market's information efficiency. Second, the fact that short selling may be used by traders to profit from the circulation of false rumours does not make it an abusive practice per se.[95] On the contrary, short sales serve as an effective market tool in battling market manipulations that push the price upwards. Of course, regulators should be extra vigilant in periods of increased market turbulence, which provide a fertile ground for the dissemination of false rumours and perpetration of market manipulation.

If 'naked' short sales are used as an independent means to depress the market,[96] it is doubtful whether such trade-based manipulation[97] should be deterred by means of an *ex ante* prohibition. Trade-based manipulations are difficult to achieve for a variety of reasons,[98] and are also very risky for the short seller who is vulnerable to a swing in market sentiment that pushes prices upwards or leads to a squeeze of the shorts. Porsche's building of a significant stake in fellow German car-maker Volkswagen (VW) in October 2008 through share options, for example, pushed VW's valuation as high as $370 billion and resulted in a very big squeeze of the holders of short positions, which, on this occasion, were mostly aggressively trading hedge funds.[99] Arguably, a close to real time regime for the

---

[95]   IOSCO's paper, in general, concurs with this point: '. . . short selling [is not] abusive in itself. But its ability to add incremental weight to a downtrend, or to be used in conjunction with insider dealing by those with adverse information about an issuer, could make it a potentially useful tool for those who are intent on abusing a market.' IOSCO Report, above n 2, at 23.

[96]   Lecce et al., above n. 79.

[97]   See E. Avgouleas, *The Mechanics and Regulation of Market Abuse, A Legal and Economic Analysis* (Oxford: OUP, 2005), ch. 4.

[98]   See D.R. Fischell and D.J. Ross, 'Should the Law Prohibit Manipulation in Financial Markets?' 105 *Harvard Law Review*, 503 (1991).

[99]   'BaFin, Germany's financial-markets regulator, is monitoring trading after Volkswagen rose more than fourfold in two days . . . [a]t its high today, Wolfsburg, Germany-based Volkswagen's common shares were valued at 296 billion euros ($370 billion), more than Exxon Mobil Corp.'s $343 billion at yesterday's closing price . . . The gains follow Porsche's Oct. 26 announcement that the maker plans to increase its Volkswagen holding from 42.6 per cent, spurring short-sellers to buy from a shrinking pool of stock to close their positions in a so-called squeeze.' A.

disclosure of short sales to the regulator and a strict settlement framework with severe penalties for failure to settle, such as that suggested by IOSCO, would suffice, making an outright prohibition of 'naked' short sales, as suggested by the EU Commission, rather unnecessary.

Similarly, while the possibility of manipulating the premium of CDS over sovereign bonds through 'naked' short selling on sovereign bonds must be recognized, it is doubtful that this risk cannot be contained by a short settlement cycle. As a result, the link between naked short selling and manipulation of spreads of sovereign bonds and attendant CDS premia may be broken by means of harmonization and strengthening of the settlement cycle applicable to all major on exchange and OTC markets for those bonds, rather than by means of an outright prohibition. Therefore, the approach adopted by German government legislation and the EU Commission proposals (discussed in the next section) with respect to 'naked' short sales could be considered very restrictive and an impediment to international efforts to integrate short selling regimes beyond the boundaries of the EU.

IOSCO PRINCIPLES, EU COMMISSION PROPOSALS AND SEC RULES

IOSCO Principles

In June 2009, IOSCO's Technical Committee issued the final set of Principles for the regulation of short sales.[100] This was preceded by the publication of a Consultation Paper on the appropriate regulation of short selling.[101] According to the Committee the main objectives of the regulation of short selling should be to protect the beneficial role short selling plays in capital markets especially with respect to (a) efficient price discovery, (b) mitigating price bubbles, (c) increasing market liquidity, and (d) facilitating hedging and other risk management activities.[102]

At the same time, regulation must ensure that, especially in extreme market conditions, certain types of short selling, or the use of short selling in combination with certain abusive strategies, do not destabilize orderly

---

Xydias, 'Volkswagen Overtakes Exxon as Most Valuable Company', *Bloomberg*, 28 October 2008, available at http://www.bloomberg.com/apps/news?pid=newsar chiveandsid=aWeWGIPhKfnk. See also Kammel, above n. 81.

[100] IOSCO Principles, above n. 17.
[101] IOSCO Report, above n. 2.
[102] Ibid., at 5.

markets. Thus, the 'principles have been developed with a view to striking a balance between realising the potential benefits of short selling and reducing the adverse impact on financial markets that may arise from abusive short selling'.[103] Following consultation, IOSCO published its four high level general principles on the regulation of short selling in June 2009.[104] These provide that short sales must be regulated by means of:

a. appropriate controls to reduce or minimize the potential risks that could affect the orderly and efficient functioning and stability of financial markets;
b. a reporting regime that provides timely information to the market or to market authorities;
c. an effective compliance and enforcement system; and
d. appropriate exceptions for certain types of transactions for efficient market functioning and development.

According to IOSCO, the first principle mostly refers to appropriate arrangements for the settlement of short selling transactions, including strict settlement requirements (such as compulsory buy-in) for failed trades.[105] Yet much more is required to ensure that short selling does not disrupt the 'orderly and efficient functioning and stability of financial markets' and IOSCO's interpretation here is markedly light touch, possibly in order to secure international consensus. IOSCO has clarified that the objectives of the second principle, provision of ready access to information on short selling, are to: (a) deter market abuse; (b) contain the potential of aggressive short selling to disrupt the orderly function of the market; (c) provide regulators and the market with early warning signs of the building up of large short positions and alert regulators to promptly investigate suspicious activities that may be potentially abusive or disruptive to the orderly functioning or stability of the markets; and (d) provide evidence to assist post-event investigations and disciplinary actions.[106]

Evidently the conflicting attitudes towards short selling of IOSCO members have prevented it from producing a more concrete and detailed set of principles. However, it is doubtful whether the objective of international harmonization may be achieved by means of very high level

---

[103] Ibid., at 6. It should be noted here that IOSCO does not take a position for or against short selling; the high level principles are addressed to jurisdictions where a decision has been made to allow short selling. Id.

[104] IOSCO Principles, above n. 17, at 4, 6.

[105] Ibid. at 8–10.

[106] Ibid. 9–12.

principles. Furthermore, although a short settlement cycle combined with severe monetary penalties for failure to settle may successfully contain the settlement risk posed by 'naked' short sales, it may not prove sufficient, on a self-standing basis, to prevent market instability in the event of a 'bear raid'. Thus, a strict settlement framework should be supplemented by the two-pronged regime of enhanced disclosure and trading halts.

CESR Recommendations and the EU Commission Proposal for an EU Regulation

Following extensive consultation, CESR published its report in March 2010 recommending to the EU institutions a pan-European short selling regime 'based on a two-tier model for disclosure of significant individual net short positions' in all shares that are admitted to trading on an EEA regulated market and/or an EEA alternative trading system, Multilateral Trading Facility.[107] First, at the lower threshold, positions would be disclosed to the relevant regulator once they reached the 0.2 per cent threshold. Second, at the higher threshold, positions would be disclosed both to the regulator and to the market as a whole once they reached the 0.5 per cent threshold. All changes of position would be reported at increments of 0.1 per cent, first to the regulator (from 0.3 per cent to 0.4 per cent) and then to the regulator and the market. In calculating whether a disclosure was required, market participants would have to take account of any transaction that provided an economic exposure to a particular share. Hence transactions in exchange-traded and OTC derivatives would need to be covered alongside short positions in the cash markets. All disclosure reports of short positions – whether to the regulator or to the market – would be made on the trading day following that on which the relevant trigger threshold had been crossed, a requirement that could greatly reduce the value of relevant information.

CESR's Recommendations (now within ESMA's sphere of action) are a major step towards the establishment of a consistent pan-EU disclosure regime governing short selling and have been endorsed by the EU Commission Proposal for an EU Regulation on Short Sales and CDS matters.[108] Yet its disclosure standards may not be sufficient to counter the destabilization effect of aggressive speculation by means of 'naked' short sales.

Recognizing this reality, the EU Commission Proposal swings to the

---

[107] CESR Report, above n. 16.
[108] Short Selling Proposal, above n. 19.

other end of the regulatory rigidity and, reflecting recent German legislation (discussed in the introduction), calls for the total ban of 'uncovered' ('naked') short sales.[109] This prohibition is, as explained in the previous section, both inefficient and unnecessary to the extent that it covers 'naked' short selling beyond the context of seasoned equity offerings. The second requirement included in the Commission Proposal, the requirement that trading venues have in place 'buy-in' procedures to contain settlement risk,[110] while possibly impractical, is certainly a useful if drastic measure to eliminate risks associated with settlement failure.

The SEC Rule

The SEC issued a Consultation Paper in April 2009 that set out two approaches to short sales regulation. The SEC Paper proposed two alternatives measures: permanent *market-wide (price) tests* triggering an uptick rule and temporary *security-specific price tests* that would trigger either a short trading halt (circuit breaker) or an uptick regime.[111] In particular, the SEC's Permanent Market-Wide Approach provided for two options:[112] (a) *a Proposed Modified Uptick Rule* under which a market-wide price test based on the national best bid would allow short sales only at par or equal to the current bid, when this was higher than the immediately preceding bid and (b) a *Proposed Uptick Rule*, which meant a market-wide price test based on the last sale price, which would allow short sales only at par or higher than the immediately preceding sale price.

The Temporary Security-Specific Approach referred to a circuit breaker mechanism that would halt short selling in a particular security for the remainder of the trading day, if there was a significant decline in the price of that security (*proposed circuit breaker halt rule*).[113] The SEC suggested that the *proposed circuit breaker halt rule* should be based either on: (a) a short sale price test based on the *national best bid* in a particular security

---

[109] '[N]natural or legal persons entering into short sales of such instruments must at the time of the sale have borrowed the instruments, entered into an agreement to borrow the shares or made other arrangements which ensure that the security can be borrowed so that settlement can be effected when it is due': ibid., at 8.

[110] '[T]rading venues must ensure that there are adequate arrangements in place for buy-in of shares or sovereign debt where there is a failure to settle a transaction. In case of non-settlement, daily fines must be imposed. In addition, trading venues will have the power to prohibit a natural or legal person who failed to settle to enter into further short sales': ibid., at 8.

[111] SEC Release No. 34-59748.

[112] Ibid. at 5.

[113] Ibid. at 5–6.

(*proposed circuit breaker modified uptick rule*), or (b) a short sale price test based on the *last sale price* in a particular security (*proposed circuit breaker uptick rule*).

Following the receipt of comments on the above SEC proposals highlighting the many problems associated with them, the SEC reopened consultation with regard to the so-called *alternative uptick rule*.[114] Consistent with the SEC's original Proposal, the *alternative uptick rule* is structured as either a market-wide and permanent price restriction or as a price test imposed once a circuit breaker threshold is triggered. A circuit breaker that would impose the alternative uptick rule would be triggered by an intraday decline in the price of an individual equity security by a set percentage (for example 10, 15 or 20 per cent) from the previous day's closing price.[115]

Finally, the SEC (in a 3–2 vote) adopted the so-called *alternative uptick rule* on 24 February 2010, which is 'designed to restrict short selling from further driving down the price of a stock that has dropped more than 10 per cent in one day'. The rule 'will enable long sellers to stand in the front of the line and sell their shares before any short sellers once the circuit breaker is triggered'.[116] Essentially, a 'circuit-breaker' will be triggered any day in which a stock's price falls by 10 per cent or more from the previous day's closing price. Once the circuit breaker is triggered, the 'alternative uptick rule' will apply to short sale orders in the affected security for the remainder of that day as well as the following day, only allowing short sales where the price is above the current national best bid. However, the adoption of the *alternative uptick* rule constitutes a serious interference with the markets' price formation mechanism, as it would essentially 'dictate' the price of short sales in rising markets and not only halt downward price spirals.[117]

---

[114] SEC 17 CFR PART 242 [Release No. 34-60509; File No. S7-08-09] RIN 3235-AK35 (Amendments to Regulation SHO – Proposed rule; notice of reopening of comment period and supplemental request for comment).

[115] Ibid.

[116] '[T]he Rule requires that a trading center establish, maintain, and enforce written policies and procedures reasonably designed to prevent the execution or display of a short sale order of a covered security at a price that is less than or equal to the current national best bid if the price of that covered security decreases by 10% or more from the covered security's closing price as determined by the listing market for the covered security as of the end of regular trading hours on the prior day.' SEC 17 CFR PART 242 [Release No. 34-61595; File No. S7-08-09], above n. 18, at 2.

[117] N. Mehta, 'SEC Short-Sale Rule May Cut Confidence, White Cap's Selway Says', *Business Week*, 25 February 2010, available at http://www.businessweek.

RECONFIGURING THE REGULATION OF SHORT SELLING

Disclosure and Trading Halts or Uptick Rules?

As explained above, short selling brings valuable information to the market and increases liquidity. Thus, it enhances, in some measure, market efficiency. The possibility of short sales leading to a massive downward price spiral, in contexts other than new rights issues, is, arguably, the combination of two factors: rational investor response to bad news and socio-psychological reactions to falling prices, especially if the volume of short sales is significant, triggering herding behaviour by non-information-seeking 'noise' traders. Therefore, the true challenge financial regulators face is not how to ban short selling, if it is agreed, in principle, that the ethical concerns short selling creates are outweighed by its beneficial impact on market efficiency. Rather, policymakers and regulators have a dual duty. First, they must create a transparent market that allows traders to have information on the volume of short sales with respect to a tradable stock and its potential price impact. Second, they must check the socio-psychological factors that would potentially cause a market overreaction, which would destabilize the price formation mechanism.

The first objective can be achieved through increased disclosure, which would also create an information barrier to the successful implementation of designs to manipulate the market. The second objective could be achieved through the introduction of a circuit breaker system that would halt short trading for the day once the price of the stock on which there is a heavy volume of short selling falls below a certain threshold.

To put it simply, a regulatory strategy that merely focuses on disclosure, such as that endorsed by CESR, will lead to unsatisfactory results. As explained above, the presence in the market of 'noise' traders and of high transaction costs for actual stock purchases means that arbitrage trading on the demand side, triggered by increased availability of information about the volume and price limits of short sales, may not materialize in such a quantity as to provide a counterbalance to the downward price trends initiated by sizeable short sales and in particular 'naked' short sales. The inability of the market to provide stabilizers to unnecessary downward price movements, in spite of increased availability of information, will trigger further sales owing to herding with professionals joining

---

com/news/2010-02-25/sec-short-sale-rule-may-cut-confidence-white-cap-s-selway-says.html.

the herd to strengthen downward pressures. Yet a blanket prohibition of 'naked' short sales in accordance with the EU proposals, while curbing speculation, might, at the same time, harm market information efficiency and levels of liquidity. Therefore, a circuit breaker halt rule that operates on the basis of a sophisticated price threshold is a necessary supplement to disclosure and possibly the only way to keep in 'check' the destructive 'animal spirits', preventing price falls from destabilizing the market.[118]

The price limits incorporated in a circuit breaker halt rule should not exclusively calculate the fall in the market price of a specific stock just by reference to the previous day's closing price or on the basis of intraday price fluctuations. It is fairer to all market participants if the threshold also incorporates relatively longer-term price trends. Moreover, if the circuit breaker rule is to act as a proper market stabilizer, the price threshold must be set in such a way as to take into account levels of liquidity. These levels are different for stocks composing a developed market's main index and for those in the periphery, as well as for stocks traded OTC.

This two-pronged strategy excludes the use of uptick rules, which the SEC has just reintroduced. The US has long had in place an uptick rule, which it repealed in July 2007 with all other restrictions on short sales[119] and reinstated (in a modified form) in April 2010 (as discussed above). The uptick rule had come under sustained attack as being unable to fulfil its stated objectives well before its repeal.[120] Also, empirical studies that subsequently examined the impact of the repeal of the uptick rule found that, while the repeal led to a significant increase in the volume of short sales, nevertheless, it had no impact on the increased volatility experienced by the US markets in July and August 2007.[121] In general, most empirical studies on the impact of the uptick rule were critical of its effect. One study found that the rule had an (adverse) influence on the quality of execution

---

[118] FSA, Temporary Short Selling Measures, above n. 30, at 4.

[119] This repeal was preceded by extensive SEC consultation. SEC17 CFR PART 240 Release No. 34-42037, File No. S7-24-99 (Short Sales).

[120] E.g., J.R. Macey, M. Mitchell and J. Netter, 'Restrictions on Short Sales: an Analysis of the Uptick Rule and its Role in View of the October 1987 Stock Market Crash', 74 *Cornell Law Review*, 799 (1989).

[121] E. Boehmer, C.M. Jones and X. Zhang, 'Unshackling Short Sellers: The Repeal of the Uptick Rule' (11 December 2008) (investigating whether the repeal of the uptick rule and of other short sale price tests by the SEC in July 2007 contributed to the subsequent bout of volatility in US stocks in late July and early August 2007, when the effects of the credit crunch became evident), available at http://mysite.verizon.net/ekki9999/UptickRepealDec11.pdf.

of short sales,[122] which the original uptick rule did not intend to restrict. Other studies found that the uptick rule played no serious role in preventing price declines,[123] and, in fact, that the price behaviour of stocks subject to the uptick rule was not substantially different to that of stocks not subject to such restriction.[124]

Another problem that the application of the uptick rule poses is that it is not clear what is the most suitable criterion for an uptick rule: the last sale price or the last bid? In the context of shares traded on a multitude of markets it is difficult to identify the best bid outside the US National Markets System. On the other hand, for any important stock traded on a cross-border basis, it is not difficult to identify price falls larger than 10 per cent over a (uniform) price threshold, due to heavy short selling in any of the markets concerned.

Moreover, a sophisticated circuit breaker system that temporarily halts short trading, unlike an uptick rule, generates only minimal interference with the market's price formation mechanism, one of the most important welfare functions of securities markets. It also provides short selling arbitrageurs with ample room to minimize a price bubble, without allowing them to destabilize the market; the uptick rule, however, does not give any room to short sellers to counter a price spike, unless it is suspended. However, any such suspension has to be implemented on a case by case basis, creating serious challenges in terms of regulatory coordination for cross-listed stocks. This is yet another reason why the uptick rule is patently unsuitable as the foundation of national short sales regimes that lead to a de facto implementation of a symmetrical global framework.

Finally, given existing strong disagreement as to the benefits of the uptick rule,[125] it is unlikely that such an approach to short selling regulation would be widely endorsed by national regulators; it would, rather, perpetuate the regulatory gaps and attendant obstacles to cross-border securities trading, discussed in the second section. Therefore, the uptick rule cannot be the foundation of a global short sales regime that is based

---

[122] G.J. Alexander and M.A. Peterson, 'Short Selling on the New York Stock Exchange and the Effects of the Uptick Rule', 8 *Journal of Financial Intermediation*, 90 (1999).

[123] L. Bai, *The Uptick Rule of Short Sale Regulation – Can it Alleviate Downward Price Pressure from Negative Earnings Shocks?*, University of Cincinnati Public Law Research Paper No. 07-20 (2007), available at http://ssrn.com/abstract=956106.

[124] G.J. Alexander and M.A. Peterson, *Does the Uptick Rule Constrain Short Selling?* (2006), available at http://ssrn.com/abstract=891478.

[125] See LSEG, above n. 14.

on symmetric national regulations. Yet symmetric/harmonized national short sales regimes are the only way to lower the costs of cross-border equity trading, which, as mentioned above, is called for by significant institutional investors with global equity portfolios.

Disclosure of Short Sales

This chapter suggests that short selling should be subject to a two-pronged regulatory regime based on strict disclosure requirements and a sophisticated circuit breaker system that would halt short trading for the day in the stock concerned. The first prong is based on an obligation imposed on short sellers to disclose to their brokers, who in turn would notify the regulator and the market, net short sales that exceed a certain threshold of an issuer's outstanding share capital. The disclosure thresholds would inevitably be set at an arbitrary level. Of course, an enhanced disclosure regime for short sales entails substantial compliance costs, for example, direct costs to firms that conduct short selling to implement and operate relevant systems (staff hours, funds needed to set up and maintain disclosure systems, and so on).[126] As a result, the only effective way to implement a disclosure regime without hindering cross-border trade is if relevant thresholds are uniform for stocks of comparable liquidity.

Accordingly, unlike the uniformity adopted by CESR's proposals on disclosure of short selling positions,[127] the threshold for listed securities in a market's main index should be lower (for example, 0.3 per cent) than that for less liquid stocks outside the main market index (for example, 0.6 per cent), and for stocks exclusively traded OTC (for example, 1 per cent). The different thresholds reflect the differences in the liquidity of the stocks and protect short sellers' trades against competitors taking opposite positions, in order to frustrate their trading strategy. Short sellers should also be required to provide a new notification every time that they exceed the set thresholds or reduce their holdings by, for example, 0.25 per cent for all listed shares and 0.5 per cent for off exchange traded shares.

Another thorny issue in the context of disclosure of short sales data is whether individual short selling positions should be disclosed to the market. The FSA's Discussion Paper accurately notes that 'disclosure of individual significant short positions and of the identity of significant short sellers to the regulator or to the market can facilitate detection of

126 FSA, Discussion Paper, above n. 11, at 23–5.
127 See CESR Report, above n. 16.

short selling that is connected to market abuse'.[128] This is because such
disclosure allows the regulator to identify in a timely manner the holder
of significant positions and 'as necessary follow up any enquiries with that
market participant',[129] preventing attempts to manipulate the market or
to profit from inside information. It also allows the market to reflect on
the meaning of such trades and to expose manipulators by taking opposite
positions. Therefore, disclosure of individual short positions above a set
threshold is an effective way to address the risk of market abuse through
short sales.

On the other hand, the disclosure of individual significant short positions on a real time or nearly real time basis 'may dissipate the liquidity
benefits of short-sales'.[130] As the market may take opposite positions
frustrating the short seller's investment strategy, it is possible that short
traders may switch to other strategies in order to minimize this risk. Short
traders will be particularly careful not to reveal their strategies. As a result,
they might be hiding short sale orders in order not to reach the disclosure
threshold. Thus, the volume of short sale orders entered into the market
may be lower, leading to substantial liquidity losses and a potentially
adverse impact on the price formation mechanism and the information
efficiency of the market.

The FSA notes that on balance: '[t]he benefits of reducing disorderly
markets and abusive short selling can outweigh the costs associated with
impaired market efficiency which may occur through any reduction of
liquidity'.[131] However, this need not be the case. Although it is not a
low cost exercise, disclosure of aggregate short positions several times
throughout the day, instead of publication of this data just once at the
beginning of the trading day, would be sufficient to serve the public interest objectives of disclosure-based regulation of short sales without having
to disclose on a real time, or nearly real time basis, individual significant
short positions. On the other hand, real time or nearly real time disclosure
of individual short positions to the regulator is not affected by any concerns of the short sellers being squeezed, and gives the regulator the ability
to monitor real time market activity and intervene in a timely manner, if
suspicious activity is taking place. Subsequently, data about individual
short positions may be released to the market by the regulator or the securities exchanges (on an anonymous basis) with a two hours' or more lag.

---

128   Ibid. at 29, para 5.28.
129   Ibid.
130   For a good exposition of this risk see IOSCO, *Report on Transparency of
Short Selling, Report of the Technical Committee of IOSCO* (IOSCO, 2003).
131   FSA, Discussion Paper, above n. 11, at 27, para. 5.10.

This time lag would be large enough to allow short traders to unwind their trades without any fear of the market taking an opposite position. Also, the disclosure rules may grant to short sellers the right to request from the regulator or the exchange that data about their individual short sale positions is withheld for another two hours because of exceptional market conditions.

The Proposed Circuit Breaker Mechanism

The second prong of the proposed regulatory strategy is a circuit breaker system that would halt short trading on the stock concerned for the remainder of the trading day.[132] The purpose of the circuit breaker halt is to control extreme speculation, when, for the reasons discussed above, the market's reaction to price falls is not rational. The design of the circuit breaker rule is an issue of cardinal importance. Thus, an effective circuit breaker rule should lead to a trading halt when two tests are met. First, it should be asked whether there is an increase in the aggregate volume and value of short sale orders as compared to the previous day's aggregate size. If the answer to this test is positive, then the regulator/market operator must apply a price test.

Of course, setting the circuit breaker price test would inevitably be a somewhat arbitrary exercise. Yet the test should clearly measure the movement in the market price of any security in a way that takes account of short- to medium-term price trends and not only the previous day's closing price. The price limit should therefore be based on a percentage fall against a weighted price average. The latter must take into account the price behaviour of the stock over longer periods of time and not only in the course of a single day's trading. The price limit should also take into account the fact that shares in the main market indices of developed markets, such as the FTSE 350, S&P 500, Nikkei 500, Hang Seng, etc.,[133] are more liquid and more resilient to downward price pressures than listed

---

[132] For a more extensive description of the circuit breaker mechanism see E Avgouleas, 'A New Framework for the Global Regulation of Short Sales: Why Prohibition is Inefficient and Disclosure Insufficient' (2010) *Stanford Journal of Law, Business and Finance*.

[133] Respectively the main indices for stocks traded on the London Stock Exchange, US Exchanges and NASDAQ, Tokyo Stock Exchange, and the Hong Kong Stock Exchange. The main indices of other major stock exchanges such as the DAX (Deutsche Börse), CAC 40 (Paris, part of Euronext), and S and P/ TSX (Toronto Stock Exchange) are the other obvious candidates for inclusion in this list.

stocks that are outside the main indices of developed markets. The latter stocks, whether they are stocks traded in developing markets or in small cap markets, are more susceptible to downward price pressures and thus the price threshold for them must be set at a higher level.

Accordingly, the suggested price threshold for stocks in the main indices of developed markets could be set at a 10 per cent fall of current market price over a weighted price average comprising the previous day's closing price (attracting a weight of 50 per cent), the average closing price of the preceding week (attracting a weight of 35 per cent), and the average closing price of the preceding month (attracting a weight of 15 per cent). The price threshold could be set at 15 per cent for all other listed stocks, or stocks listed on developing markets, which are more volatile than developed markets,[134] and 20 per cent for unlisted stocks, which are, normally, less liquid.

To provide an example of how the above model would work, assume that for listed stock X, which is a component of the S&P 500, the previous day's closing price was $13, the week's average closing price was $15, and the preceding month's average closing price was $17: then the weighted average price for this stock is $14.3 and the price fall threshold $1.43. Therefore, the lowest price threshold for the day's trading before the circuit breaker is triggered is $11.57.[135] As a result, if the current market price is $11.55, short trading in this stock should be halted, provided that the short sales volume tests have already been met.

Having such a sophisticated price threshold may also be an effective means to counter the so-called 'magnet effect', namely a rushing through of short sales before the circuit breaker is triggered.[136] If the price test calculated only a fall over the previous day's trading price, short trading would have to be halted at $11.7: $13 - (13 \times 10\%)$. In the above example, the suggested system allows the market to fall further, but not uncontrollably, accounting for the fact that overall there is a falling price trend for the stock concerned. However, the actual force of the 'magnet effect' itself

---

[134] See G. Bekaert, C.R. Harvey and C. Lundblad, *Liquidity and Expected Returns: Lessons from Emerging Markets, NBER Working Paper No. 11413* (2005); and I. Domowitz, J. Glen and A. Madhavan, *Liquidity, Volatility, and Equity Trading Costs Across Countries and Over Time,* William Davidson Institute, University of Michigan, Working Paper No. 322 (2000), available at http://www.wdi.umich.edu/files/Publications/WorkingPapers/wp322.pdf.

[135] $(17 \times 15\%) + (15 \times 35\%) + (13 \times 50\%) \times 10\% = 1.43$.

[136] For a comprehensive discussion of the 'magnet' effect see SEC Consultation, above n. 18, at 93–4.

is not uncontroversial and serious doubts have been expressed concerning its existence.

The use of a circuit breaker mechanism to regulate short sales presents two further advantages. First, it minimizes intervention in the market, since it is triggered only in the event of serious downward pressure ('a bear raid'). Second, as it would only trigger a halt in short selling for the remainder of the trading day, it would not lead to the build-up of significant positions in futures markets. This is normally the consequence of a ban on short sales, which both makes it difficult in some cases to unwind/settle future positions afterwards and leads to serious discrepancies between the spot price for the stock and the price at which futures contracts are concluded for the same asset. In contrast, a circuit breaker mechanism would allow short trading to resume the next day. So if there is a genuine downward trend in the stock, based on undisclosed information or other factors, the price may keep falling either until the market stabilizes or until the circuit breaker price threshold is triggered again. Given that the suggested thresholds will have also taken into account the fall in market price observed in the preceding trading day, before the halt in short trading, the next day's trading would allow the market price to fall significantly further, but not uncontrollably. So there is no serious incentive to build significant positions in the futures markets and no serious difficulty is posed in unwinding/settling those positions, even by means of physical settlement. It may just take a few hours longer. This is a trade-off that rational traders would probably find acceptable, in exchange for some protection against the 'animal spirits' of the market.[137]

CONCLUSION

Short selling is often associated with some of the most objectionable aspects of financial capitalism. Yet it may also be a significant source of market efficiency. The results of a large number of studies considering the market impact of the September 2008 bans have shown that the huge falls in the price of financial stocks were more due to a rational reaction to bad news, funding pressures, and irrational loss aversion, fuelled by herding

---

[137] A famous and seasoned futures trader has recently remarked: '[T]he crucial problem bedevilling all markets these days was a lack of price limits . . . [which] would force "all participants to take a more deliberate approach to external shocks that can only be accurately assessed with more time to gather information"': G. Tett, 'Why Regulators Should Heed Hedge Fund Call for Price Limits', *Financial Times*, 22 October 2010, 32.

behaviour, and less the result of short selling per se. Therefore, what is required to resolve the vexed issue of short sales regulation is a strategy that protects against market irrationality and assists rational traders to move quickly (through short sales) to protect their positions against the arrival of bad news. The same strategy must ensure that short sales are unlikely to be used to perpetrate market abuse.

It has been argued here that these objectives may be achieved through a mix of enhanced disclosure requirements and a sophisticated circuit breaker system that, once a three-pronged test is satisfied, leads to daily short trading halts. In addition, if international consensus is built on this dual track strategy, then it should not prove difficult to devise rules that may have a global reach. However, the IOSCO Principles are overly high level to provide the certainty required in the coordination of national regulatory efforts in this area, and the EU proposals are poised to be unappealing to non-EU jurisdictions that would not adopt a generalized prohibition of 'naked' short sales. Finally, the reinstatement of the controversial uptick rule (in a modified form) by the SEC will further impede regulatory coordination efforts.

Sophisticated price limits operating through circuit breakers are a very powerful mechanism for containing destabilizing speculation and preventing the implementation of abusive strategies. They also restrain market actors, who may feel compelled to herd, increasing the volume of short sale orders and driving market prices lower. Arguably, this mixed approach to short sales regulation is a much less paternalistic intervention in securities markets than an outright ban or an uptick rule regime, which tinkers with the market's price formation mechanism to a greater extent than a temporary halt. Finally, if the disclosure and circuit breaker regime is complemented by a tight time frame for settlement of trades and strict penalties for non-settlement, as suggested by the IOSCO Principles, then the threat of 'naked' short sales is fully contained, protecting the market from the harmful effects of this practice.

Resolving one of the main legal uncertainties investors encounter in the context of cross-border securities trading would decrease the cost of cross-border equity trading, improving liquidity. A combination of lower costs of equity trading and reduced possibilities for overpricing essentially translates into lower cost of capital, fostering economic growth.

4. Regulating complex derivatives: Can the opaque be made transparent?

Michael A.H. Dempster, Elena A. Medova and Julian Roberts[1]

INTRODUCTION

The response to the financial crisis of 2007–2009 has so far been largely concerned with proposals for sharpening the national and international regulatory framework, for example, by restricting institutions like hedge funds and private equity firms and practices like short selling and credit default swap (CDS) trading, requiring exchange trading of complex derivatives like CDSs, or increasing the regulatory capital requirements on financial institutions. But it may well be that the deregulation of Thatcher and Reagan and their successors throughout the Greenspan years led to a situation that had less to do with Schumpeterian 'creative destruction' than with the abuse of market power. In the words of Robert Khuzami, SEC Enforcement Director, regarding the recent civil fraud suit involving a subprime mortgage bond or collateralised debt obligation (CDO) brought against Goldman Sachs, 'the product was new and complex but the deception and conflicts (of interest) are old and simple'.

The exact role played by derivatives in the financial crisis is of course controversial.[2] However, derivative deals of many kinds have been

---

[1] This chapter was presented at the Law Reform and Financial Markets W.G. Hart Legal Workshop at the Institute for Advanced Legal Studies of the University of London on 24 June 2009 and at the Münchner Kompetenz Zentrum Ethik Seminar of the Ludwig Maximilians Universität, Munich on 9 July 2009. We are grateful to the participants and the associate editor for helpful comments and criticism.

[2] See, e.g., S.K. Henderson, 'Regulation of Credit Derivatives: To What Effect and For Whose Benefit?', 11 *Journal of International Banking and Financial Law*, 679 (2009).

associated with abuses that raise important regulatory issues. In a highly sophisticated industry such as modern investment banking, specific rules are of only limited use. Markets depend for their efficiency on flexibility. This suggests that future regulation must first get the underlying market and institutional structures right and then efficiency is best guaranteed not by regulatory interference in the detail of negotiations, but by applying the founding principles of commercial life. They are *caveat emptor*, the principle that it is always the buyer who is responsible for evaluating the terms of a deal offered to him,[3] and good faith, the principle that contracts do not permit deliberate harm of one party by the other. Markets depend on these two principles being held in the right balance to one another and seen to be so held, which is probably impossible without supporting legislation.[4] Ultimately, however, they are judicial principles. They are applied not by regulators, but by courts.

Be that as it may, many of the biggest market disturbances were obviously unleashed by mispriced credit derivatives (notably in the cases of Citigroup, Lehmans, Merrill Lynch, AIG and AMBAC). Credit default swaps (CDSs) – in any event in their commercially bona fide form – are a form of insurance. The constraints normally applicable to insurance (in particular, that indemnification is restricted to 'insurable interest', i.e. real loss) significantly limit the risks of the insurer. However, contracts for credit derivatives invariably specify that they are not insurance (and are therefore outside the rules for that industry). This inevitably increases the risk of the party writing the CDS – to a massive degree, as is now

---

[3] 'Contracts between banks for the sale and purchase of complicated structured products work perfectly well on the basis of the principle of the caveat emptor'. Hamblen J. in *Cassa Rispanmio di San Marino v. Barclays* [2011] EWHC 484 (Comm), at para. 544.

[4] The US Dodd-Frank Act defines an OTC 'swap' as virtually any derivative product written on other broadly defined securities, commodities, funds, indices, financial events, and so on and a 'security-based swap' as one written on a single security, loan, narrowly based index or event. It specifically sets high business conduct standards on issues of these product regarding the client disclosure of their material risks, incentives (for example, 'teaser' features), conflicts of interest and mark–to–market information. The Act further explicitly sets higher standards regarding advisors and counterparties of governments at all levels, pension plans and foundations by requiring actions in the 'best interests' of the client, thus putting US law in line with similar legislation in some other jurisdictions (for example, Italy). However, the details of the nature of required client disclosure are still open at the time of writing, and unfortunately the subject of fierce lobbying and political activity. It is not clear at this juncture that the US SEC and CFTC will succeed in removing the natural information asymmetry between issues and non-bank client by the methods proposed in this article, or otherwise.

evident. AIG, itself traditionally an insurer, appears not to have taken this into account in accumulating its own huge exposure to CDSs. At the very least, the speculative element of what is after all 'fake' insurance needs to be adequately reflected in the price of the deal. Beyond that, perhaps disclaiming the 'insurance' element in CDSs should be banned altogether. That would be an example of an abuse that may be amenable to regulatory reforms.

In this chapter we examine the case for applying general principles to such instrument-specific regulation. In the next section, we shall discuss the specific consequences for derivatives litigation of informational asymmetry arising from the market power of global investment banks. These insights are based on a large number of cases currently in progress involving major European and US financial institutions in the fields of fixed income, asset management and foreign exchange hedging as well as credit derivatives. To set the stage for the subsequent discussion, the representative instruments involved are described from the plaintiff's viewpoint in a general way in the section entitled, 'Some representative structured derivative deals'. In the section entitled, 'Legal aspects of failed derivative deals' we attempt to draw appropriate legal principles from these failed derivative deals and their regulatory implications and likely consequences. There is, then, a conclusion at the end of the chapter.

INFORMATIONAL ASYMMETRY

In a significant number of derivatives cases it is clear that the initiators of the over-the-counter (OTC), i.e. bespoke, deals have been able to take advantage of their contract partner's ignorance or inexperience. Indeed, it has been said in the City of London that '30 per cent of OTC derivatives are bought and 70 per cent are sold', meaning that 30 per cent of the deals are between counterparties who are professionally able to assess the risks involved while 70 per cent are sold by the issuer to a counterparty who has no idea in detail of what they are buying. Does the latter, in any particular case, exceed those limits set on *caveat emptor* by good faith? Under what circumstances is a participant in a sophisticated market entitled to assume that everyone understands what is going on?

Three kinds of ignorance or 'informational failure' have played a role in dysfunctional derivative contracts in recent years, namely:

- commercial innocence
- documentary misunderstanding
- technical ignorance.

To some extent, each is involved in all the various disasters that have recently befallen incautious investors. However, each element raises slightly different legal issues and we shall consider them separately.

Commercial Innocence

Commercial innocence sounds like the kind of element that a mature market should not have to accommodate. Nonetheless, it has clearly played a major role in the context of the rapid development of the financial markets over the last half century. The most important change has been to remove, as far as possible, questions of capacity to contract from the functioning of the markets.

All markets are dangerous places for the uninitiated, and this is particularly true of the financial markets. Under German law, for example, access to derivatives trading was long restricted to persons qualified, for example by virtue of their status as 'Kaufmann' (i.e. commercial trader, see § 53 of the Stock Exchange Act of 1908).[5]

However, restricting entry is alien to modern conceptions of market freedom. MiFID (the Markets in Financial Instruments Directive), which sets the terms of participation in EU financial markets, represents the current high point in opening them up. Participants are still categorised in terms of capacity to contract – retail, professional, eligible counterparty – but these categories are negotiable in any particular case, and even at the most protected level (retail customers) the duties of care are now relatively abstract.[6]

Whatever the merits or demerits of this development – and in most Member States of the EU the regulatory bodies still closely supervise at least the retail markets – there has been a marked change in the attitude of banks to their customers. Whereas in the past bank managers fell into the same category as solicitors or doctors – they were professionals charged with duties of loyalty and personal responsibility[7] – this has now given way to a relationship in which bank staff are under the same pressures as any other salesman. It has taken a little time for popular perceptions to catch up with this, and only now, after the mayhem wrought by the financial crisis, has it become widely apparent that banks should be entered with the same degree of caution as used car showrooms.

---

[5] H.-D. Assmann and R. Schütze, *Handbuch des Kapitalanlagerechts* (3rd Ed., München: Beck, 2007), 6.

[6] H.-D. Assmann and U. Schneider, *WpHG – Wertpapierhandelsgesetz* (5th Ed., Cologne: O. Schmidt, 2009), § 31a.

[7] In Germany bank employees were called 'Bankbeamte', which put them on a level with civil servants.

The change of the banking business model has posed problems for customers who were previously not accustomed to scrutinising offers from their bank in much detail. This is particularly true of municipalities, who throughout the world suffer from not having the resources for expert staff in their treasurers' departments. The fact that they are also solid credit risks makes them especially attractive to predators from new-style banks. The consequences of this combination of characteristics have been visible in a series of cases, ranging from classics like the *Hammersmith*[8] case and *Orange County* to more recent contretemps such as *Kenosha USD v Royal Bank of Canada*,[9] and *Stadt Hagen v Deutsche Bank*.[10] The latter is only one of a series of disputes between municipalities and banks that have been exercising the German courts. Similar disagreements about structured derivatives have recently surfaced in relation to municipalities or public bodies in Greece and Italy, including the current pressing of criminal fraud charges against several global banks on behalf of the City of Milan involving swaps of the type discussed in the next section.[11] Such controversies have also arisen in America, where the sums involved are even higher and threaten to bankrupt municipalities such as Detroit.[12]

Legal Misunderstanding

The second category of problems is that of *legal misunderstanding*. By this we mean a failure to understand the legal import of an agreement.

It is a feature of some modern derivatives that the documentation is extremely voluminous. Early, and now notorious, examples of this were the so-called 'cross-border-leasing' deals struck by numerous municipalities and utilities in the late 1990s. Despite their name, many of these were in reality a combination of tax shelter and credit default swap. In exchange for a payment of several millions, municipalities would agree to 'sell' capital items to US investors and then to lease them back for a certain period. The deals were structured so that only a relatively small amount of money genuinely changed hands, and all the incidents of ownership remained where they were, that is, with the municipalities.

---

[8] [1991] 1 All ER 545.
[9] [2009] EWHC 2227 (Comm).
[10] L.G. Wuppertal 16 July 2008.
[11] E. Martinelli, 'Milan Swaps Banks Failed to Shop Around, Witness Says', *Bloomberg News*, 11 November 2010, available at: www.bloomberg.com/news.
[12] T. Francis, B. Levisohn, C. Palmieri and J. Silver-Greenberg, 'Wall Street vs. America', *Business Week*, 20 November 2009, 34–9.

The arrangement was allegedly intended to provide US investors with a tax shelter, although this is doubtful, since the IRS had already declined the model well before many of the deals were concluded. In fact, hidden among dozens of interlinked agreements and sub-agreements covering well in excess of 1000 pages was a credit default swap written on either AIG, AMBAC or another US insurer. Many of these deals duly blew up in 2008, to the dismay of the municipalities who had bought the 'leasing' agreements. So far, at least, this aspect has been only substantively litigated in the US,[13] but the issue has involved numerous European municipalities.[14]

Technical Misunderstanding

The third category is technical misunderstanding. The principal example of this lies in the valuation of the performance to which each party commits itself. Banks do not gamble, or at least they should not. Not only that: they are obliged by law to keep a close watch on the value of the assets and obligations they hold on their books.

Techniques for valuing structured products have developed in the last 30 years or so, and it is only to that degree that banks have been able to start trading them. This applies especially to exotic products – that is, structured instruments that can only be valued in terms of the parameters of a statistical distribution. Creating a model to value such an instrument is generally outside the competence of anyone who is not a financial mathematician (or 'quant'). Even though it is possible nowadays to obtain values for exotic products from specialist suppliers, and this method is frequently used by traders, such information is too expensive to be used by client counterparties to a bank's offered product.

More to the point – quite apart from the problem of knowing where to go for information, or having the money to pay for it – most people who are not themselves regularly trading in the markets do not even know what it means to value something in terms of statistical parameters like 'mean' or 'standard deviation'. 'Price' in traditional parlance derives from the record of a concrete agreement reached in a liquid market between a willing buyer and a willing seller. By contrast, a statistical distribution generated from a computer simulation *seems* to bear more relation to a forecast than to

---

[13]   *Hoosier Energy v John Hancock,* Southern District of Indiana, 25 November 2008 – 1:08-cv-1560-DFH-DML.

[14]   See, e.g., *AWG Leasing Trust v United States of America,* Northern District of Ohio, 28 May 2008 – 1:07-CV-857.

an empirical fact. A statistical distribution, however, is typically required to specify the value/price of an instrument in relation to its opposing forward income streams. A 'fair market value' will be the mean of such a distribution after adjustment for risk. With or without this adjustment the distribution's variance will give a measure of how risky it would be to rely on one outcome as opposed to another and, as we shall see in the next section, other simple measures may be more appropriate. All such ideas are extremely useful, and can no more be dismissed as mere 'forecasting' than the statement that the chance of throwing a four on a single throw of a die is one in six. Establishing regularity in terms of probability has nothing unfamiliar about it to particle physicists (a typical source of 'quants'[15]). These techniques do not, however, record 'a price', and to anyone operating within a deterministic world view their entire conceptual basis remains essentially foreign.

Ignorance of statistical pricing methods and of how they underlie derivative trading values has exposed numerous town hall treasurers to some highly unfavourable deals. Instruments that were variously presented as 'techniques for optimising interest rate payments' and 'modern debt management' were, in fact, no more than badly priced wagers on the yield curve. Losses were considerable (the German city of Hagen, for example, ended up €47m under water on its rates deal with Deutsche Bank, LG Wuppertal and the current Milan case involves alleged total losses of €101m).

A worrying aspect of these cases, of which there were many, was the evasive representation of valuation and risk. In the out-turn – for example, when calling the instrument – the banks made it clear that they were using statistical techniques to set prices. Giving evidence in court, they explained that they bargained for the deal by first obtaining a fair market value from statistical models and then moving the strike (i.e. essentially the line dividing the two parties' expected returns) as far in their favour as the customer would tolerate.[16] It was accepted by defendant banks that the 'profit margin' envisaged by this technique was in the region of 5 per cent of nominal (though 'nominal' is an abstract magnitude given the

---

[15]   R.R. Lindsey and B. Schachter (2007), *How I Became a Quant: Insights from 25 of Wall Street's Elite* (Hoboken, NJ: John Wiley & Sons, 2007), 58.

[16]   OLG Stuttgart 9 U 111/08 (settlement protocol). See also OLG Stuttgart, 9 U 164/08 and OLG Stuttgart 9 U 148/08. A similar procedure in the context of CDO structuring was described in a recent English case as positioning a portfolio in the 'arbitrage spectrum' – see *Casadi Risparmio di San Marino v. Barclays* [2011] EWHC 484 (Comm.), para. 322 (5).

considerable leverage structured into the products).[17] When asked how the customer was supposed to bargain without knowing the fair market price, or even that such a thing existed, the witness in the Stuttgart case indicated that customers could always ask for terms from other banks. This was obviously a rather theoretical possibility, however, not least in view of the fact that the products were individually customised (OTC).

In relation to risk, obscuring the basis for valuation was almost a systematic part of the sales information. In their term sheets, banks emphasised that risk and return were not amenable to certain forms of valuation. They said, for example, that writers of options (most of the disputed rate swaps involved the customer writing an option) were exposed to 'theoretically infinite' risk. They also claimed that a 'worst case' could not be quantified.

Whether or not these comments constitute fair warning, they certainly obscure the reality of the instruments from the professional traders' point of view. The suggestion – frequently made by the banks' representatives in court – was that rate swaps were entirely unpredictable and the bank had nothing more reliable to go on than the customer. This is, of course, wrong. Nobody has a deterministic forecast for future interest rate developments. It is quite true that anything might happen. But it is not true that all outcomes are equally probable. And the financial markets price probabilistically, not deterministically (more on this in the next section).

So, statistically speaking, deterministic concepts like 'theoretical' risk and maximal 'worst case' are not relevant. Statistical pricing quantifies the relative probability of various outcomes so that, given a distribution, an investor can decide, for example, whether the possible return is worth the risk, whether a hedge is required, and so on. The banks had access to computer-generated statistical distributions because without them they would not have been able to establish the products' fair market values. And they needed to quantify the risk in order to manage the client credit risk as well as their own market risk. In view of this knowledge, which would have been available to the bank in (for example) quantified value at risk (VaR) figures, telling the client that her risk was 'theoretically infinite' sounds like deliberately pointing someone in the wrong direction.

Cumulative Misunderstanding

The most striking calamities have, as widely reported in the press, taken place in the area of collateralised debt obligations (CDOs). Here, too,

---

[17]　LG Frankfurt/M 10 March 2008 – 2-4 O 388/06.

there have been celebrated victims among public bodies, for example the Austrian state railways and the local transport system in Berlin, who together seem to have accumulated losses approaching €1b. Disasters of this kind are probably only explicable in terms of all three forms of informational imbalance coming together.

As is now generally known, CDOs serve to set exposure (risk and return) in line with the preferences of investors. They do this by channelling the risks arising from a portfolio of securities. Instead of sharing risk out evenly among a portfolio's investors (everyone takes a pro rata share of losses), losses flow sequentially to a hierarchy of 'tranches'. The lowest tranche takes losses first. If losses are so great that this one gets knocked out, the next tranche up gets attacked. In compensation for this, investors in the lower tranches reap a correspondingly higher rate of return, at least for as long as each tranche still exists – and so on up the hierarchy.

The CDOs that caused so much damage to European institutional investors were synthetic and structured around credit default swaps (CDSs). This means that the portfolio did not consist of actually owned obligations, but is better compared to a group of racehorses on which the investors bet. Misfortunes befalling the obligations, such as default, restructuring and the like (these are called 'credit events') trigger certain previously agreed consequences for the CDS counterparty, and these losses then flow into the CDO itself. A portfolio that escapes 'credit events' during the lifetime of the note may be compared to having all one's horses complete the season unscathed. Obviously such a result would be highly desirable for those holding the 'lower' tranches.

As with interest rate swaps, modern financial mathematics makes it possible to calculate the risk adjusted net present value and the risk profile of each tranche.[18] For the prudent investor, doing this should really precede engagement at any particular level. Such a procedure is, as with interest rate swaps, not easy for anyone outside the markets, because it requires access to credit risk data for all obligations in the portfolio. Such data is expensive and in any event the mathematical challenge remains.

One example of a CDO that was bought by German public bodies in the early summer of 2007, and that subsequently nosedived, is the Volante CDO Class A2E credit linked notes issued by Barclays Capital with a total volume of €100m for listing on the Dublin Stock Exchange. The

---

[18]   See, e.g., M.A.H. Dempster, E.A. Medova and M. Villaverde (2010), 'Long-Term Interest Rates and Consol Bond Valuation', 11(2–3) *Journal of Asset Management*, 113 (2010), 113–135.

instrument was sold with an 'expected' S&P rating of AA and paid out 0.78 per cent over Euribor. By September 2009 it was rated at CCC−.

From the start, it had three features that perhaps give pause for thought. First, the tranche was only 1 per cent thick. The problem with such a thin tranche is that it can be wiped out by a correspondingly small incidence of losses in the portfolio.

Second, at 5.44 per cent to 6.44 per cent it was deeply subordinated. That is to say, it was low down in the hierarchy – not quite first loss, but not far away from first loss, and thus exposed to attack after even a relatively small number of defaults in the reference portfolio. The reference portfolio consisted of 100 obligations, all roughly equal in weighting. This meant that the Volante notes could be under water even if only 7 of the 100 reference obligations generated 'credit events'.

The third feature was less visible from the prospectus, but lay concealed in the indicative portfolio. The portfolio consisted, at first glance, of securities from worthy issuers including Allianz, AT&T, Berkshire Hathaway, Deutsche Telekom and others. Also present, however, were the names Countrywide, Fannie May, GMAC LLC, Lehman Brothers, HSBC Finance, Merrill Lynch, Residential Capital, and Bear Stearns. By 8 June 2007, when the product was offered to investors, the subprime crisis had already been gathering momentum for four months, and the press had reported negatively about all eight of these names. A further ten names in the portfolio were in subprime trouble by the end of the year: AMBAC, Capital One, Centex, CIT, Freddie Mac, Financial Security Assurance, MBIA, MGIC, PMI, and XL Capital.

In view of this, it is hardly surprising that the Volante A2E notes are now largely worthless. Eight of the 100 portfolio names were known to be risky even when the product was sold; but by 6 months later, 18 fell into this category. A slender tranche at 5.44 per cent to 6.44 per cent was clearly in considerable danger from the start.

It is not unknown for CDO investors to criticise the composition of portfolios that have led to losses. This generally relates to substitutions made during the term of the note by the portfolio manager.[19] The Volante A2E portfolio was managed, but that does not seem to be the problem: the constituents of the portfolio were 'toxic' from the start. Why this should have been so may have something to do with Barclays' alleged $9b exposure in the

---

[19]   See *HSH Nordbank v UBS* ([2008] EWHC 1529 (Comm)) and HSH's earlier dispute with Barclays (J. Treanor, 'Barclays "Toxic Waste" Row with German Bank Settled', *The Guardian*, 15 February 2005, and more recently, P. Aldrick, 'Suspicions Grow over Barclays Toxic Debt Move', *The Telegraph*, 12 January 2011.

subprime market.[20] The question for us in the fourth section, 'Legal Aspects of Failed Derivative Deals', however, is what legal consequences, if any, such a miscalculation should have for the parties – that is, for the German institutions that bought Volante on the one hand, and for Volante's seller on the other. But first we will discuss losing structured derivative deals for banks' clients in fixed income, portfolio management and FX.

SOME REPRESENTATIVE STRUCTURED DERIVATIVE DEALS

This section attempts to illustrate the issues raised in the previous section in terms of various representative OTC structured derivatives sold to clients by banks in the 2004–2006 boom period with maturities ranging from three years to indefinite-lived consol bonds. The clients investing in these products were wealthy individuals, SMEs and local authorities in Continental Europe. The contracts between counterparties involved structured versions of swaps, bonds raising Tier 1 capital for financial institutions under Basel II and foreign exchange (FX) hedging programmes. Representation to clients of the risks involved in these investments was typically termed 'unlimited', as noted above, and/or ignored egregious features of the contracts such as embedded one-sided cancellation options without compensation.

Structured Swaps

A par interest rate swap is a standard contract between two counterparties to exchange cash flows. At set time intervals, termed reset dates, one party pays a predetermined fixed rate of interest on the nominal value, the other a floating rate, until the maturity date of the contract. The floating leg of swap fixes the interest rates for each payment at the rate of a published interest rate. The fixed rate, known as the swap rate, is that interest rate which makes the fair value of the par swap 0 at inception. Thus the cash flows of the two legs of a par swap are those of a pair of bonds with face value of the swap nominal, one fixed rate, and the other floating rate.

Since the swap market is highly liquid with many par swaps traded every day, it is possible to obtain rates for swaps of a set of constant maturities

---

[20] A. Gangahar, 'Fortress Unit Moves to Cut Subprime Links', *Financial Times*, 25 September 2007.

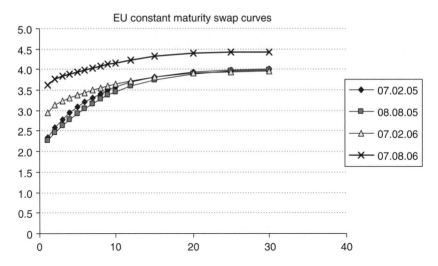

Figure 4.1   Illustrative swap curve movements

from 1 to 30 years from the market each day.[21] From the market swap rates a swap curve that gives the rates for constant maturity swaps (CMS) of all durations may be constructed each day. This market determined curve may be used to price OTC swaps between a dealer and specific client counterparty. Illustrative swap curve movements over time are depicted in Figure 4.1.

A standard corporate treasury hedging situation for such an OTC swap is that the client, rather than the bank, pays fixed and receives floating to cover floating rate loan payments on a principal amount, matched by the swap nominal, in order to hedge floating interest rate risk. However, in most of the CMS-spread ladder swaps issued to clients the bank pays fixed and receives floating.[22] These payments are illustrated for a representative CMS swap payment illustration in the conventional way in Figure 4.2, which shows the typical few (here two) initial fixed payment exchanges in the client's favour. These are typically followed by structured floating payments whose precise details need not concern us here except to note that at each payment date the spread shown in Figure 4.2 depends on the swap rates at different maturities and the strike and the gearing (here 3) are chosen by the bank to structure

---

[21]   This is by contrast with the market yields for Treasury bonds whose actual maturities each day depend on a discrete number of previous auction dates and must be adjusted to approximate constant maturity.

[22]   Usually a swap rate from Reuters with resets at three- or six-month intervals.

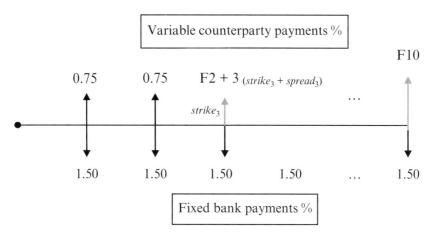

Figure 4.2   CMS swap payment illustration

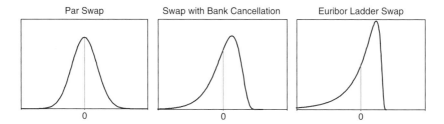

Figure 4.3   NPV distributions of three types of swaps

the product. The term ladder refers to the fact that at each payment period a term depending on these parameters and the current market spread is added to or subtracted from the interest payment of the previous period. We shall see that this can lead to an alarming rate of increase in the client's payments to the bank that is paying fixed payments to the client.

Suffice it to say here for our purposes that it is possible with a suitable mathematical model to conduct a Monte Carlo simulation for possible swap forward cash flows to maturity which upon time (and possibly risk) discounting yields a net present value (NPV) distribution for the security as illustrated in Figure 4.3.[23] The expected value of this distribution with risk discounting is the so-called fair market *price* of the security; without risk discounting the distribution corresponds to the ordinary NPV values

---

[23]   For more details and further references see Dempster et al., above n. 16.

used by corporate treasurers and illustrates the relative likelihoods (probabilities) of the NPVs of possible future cash flows.

The NPV distribution on the left is that of an exchange traded par swap that has a symmetric NPV distribution about zero after transaction costs. That in the middle shows the effect of the OTC swap client granting the bank an option to cancel without compensation in the contract, which skews the losses in favour of the bank. The rightmost diagram gives an indication of how much this skew is further moved against the client and in favour of the bank by adding the structured CMS-spread ladder feature to the client's floating payment.[24]

In essence, owing to the structuring of the swaps in the 2005–2006 issuing period, the counterparty gave the dealer a call option on the flattening of the swap curve shown in Figure 4.2, which normally follows sharp rises in short-term rates. Global macroeconomic conditions in the period in which these contracts were issued clearly indicated sharply increasing short rates, a process that had already begun in the US at the time and followed in the EU only shortly thereafter. Figure 4.4 shows the declining CMS 2–10 year spread from the inception of the euro to the end of 2006. The levered laddered payment formulae used to calculate a client's interest payment in CMS-spread ladder swaps issued in this period had the same intent as the infamous 'inverse floating' floating notes issued by Orange County, California, to Merrill Lynch in 1994 and which led to its bankruptcy. The 'laddered' dependence of the current client payment on the previous for the more recent CMS-spread ladder swaps have, however, an additional acceleration effect not present in inverse floaters.

The typical effects of this structuring in steadily increasing net client payments forecast for valuation purposes (as described above) at inception can be seen in Figure 4.5, which shows the expected payments and those at plus or minus one standard deviation from the mean of their forecast distribution in per cent of nominal for a specific swap. Even though a positive net payment stream in favour of the client is possible, it is capped at a relative low value by a floor in favour of the issuer. In the vast majority of cases, when such valuation forecasts were conducted after several floating payments by the client had actually been made to the bank, their realised values fell close to the negative red line. In short, the declining spread increased client payments substantially.

The potential results of this at inception in terms of the NPV of simu-

---

[24]   We shall see a number of these Monte Carlo NPV distributions for actual instruments in the sequel.

CMS 2, CMS 10 and spread

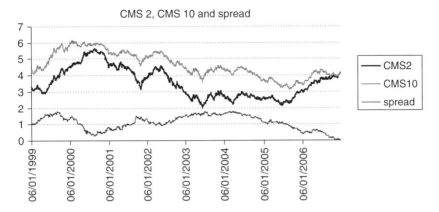

Figure 4.4   Base CMS rates and spread evolution 1999–2006

Net payments to client over swap maturity at inception (30.8.2005)

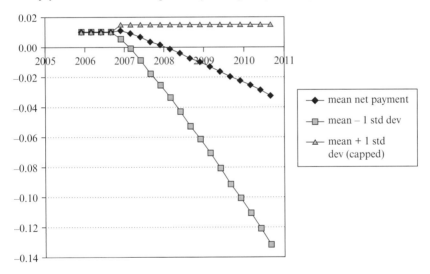

Figure 4.5   View of client net payments distribution at inception

lated future cash flows distribution are shown in Figure 4.6 where both the distribution with and without the bank's cancellation without compensation option are shown. Note that the bank's cancellation option cuts off most of the client's upside (above 0) and skews the client's potential loss tail at the 99 per cent level far to the left while making the bank's corresponding loss level asymmetrically much smaller.

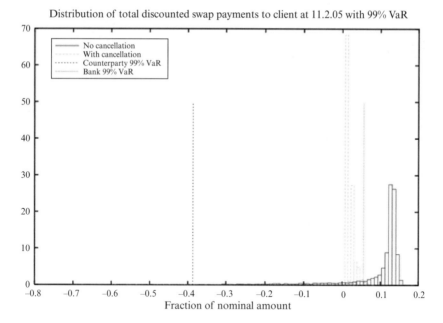

*Figure 4.6   Distribution at inception of total net time discounted swap
            payments to client in per cent of nominal with 99% loss level
            (value at risk) from 0 to client and bank*

Figure 4.7 shows that over time (here one year) this net NPV distribution typically just gets worse (even though here the 99 per cent loss level
remains approximately the same).

Capital Raising Hybrid Bonds

Under the Basel II recommendations it became possible for banks to
raise Tier 1 regulatory capital in the form of so-called hybrid instruments
issued as bonds or notes but ranking in default seniority at the level of
preferred shares. Most European banks, including the European Bank
for Reconstruction and Development (EBRD), used the structuring techniques we have seen above applied to OTC swaps to issue callable bonds
of finite or infinite maturities. As before, these typically had the sweeten-
ing feature of a few fixed payments at higher than current market rate
followed by floating payments by the bank that sank well below expected
market rates represented by the current forward interest rate curve.

Figure 4.8 shows this feature of annual coupon payments for a 30-year

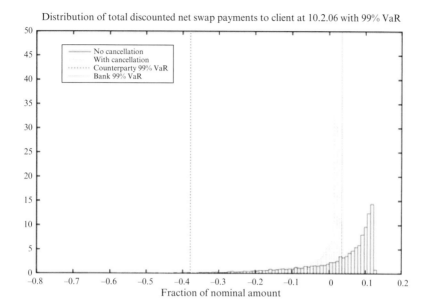

Figure 4.7   Distribution at first anniversary of total net time discounted swap payments to client in per cent of nominal with 99% loss level (value at risk) from 0 to client and bank

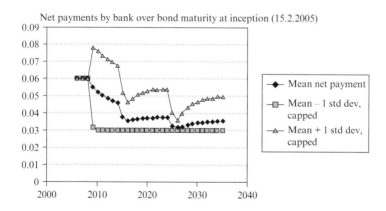

Figure 4.8   Prospective annual coupon payments at inception for a 30-year structured bond with coupon floor at 3%

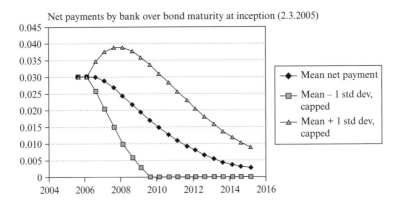

*Figure 4.9   Prospective semi-annual coupon payments at inception for a
20-year structured bond with no coupon floor*

bond only callable at two specific dates in the future. For this bond three
annual coupon payments were at 6 per cent, triple the prevailing market
rate (see Figure 4.14), followed prospectively at inception by a rapid
coupon rate distribution, which was however floored at 3 per cent per
annum. Many such instruments, including those issued by the EBRD,
were, however, not floored. Figure 4.9 shows the features of the prospective semi-annual coupon payment distributions for a 20-year maturity
bond (callable at floating rate payment dates), which at inception has
a significant probability of paying the holder no interest at all after 10
years.

Figure 4.10 shows for a hybrid instrument issued by another bank early
in 2005 the prospective distribution at inception of the NPV of future
coupon payments plus the final repayment of the invested capital as a
fraction of this investment. Thus the value 1 represents the repayment by
the bank to the bond holder of exactly the intitial investment effectively
with *no* any interest but only the capital appreciation that would accrue
to the holder of a zero coupon bond owing to the time value of money.[25]
Outcomes below one represent loss of capital invested and outcomes

---

[25]   An alternative representation would be to show the present value of the
net gain over the initial investment of the bond holder as a percentage of nominal
by subtracting it from the PV of the subsequent cash flows. This would produce
NPV distribution diagrams comparable to those for swaps in which 0 rather than
1 becomes the pivotal value between client gains and losses. We are indebted to
Professor Robert R Bliss for this observation.

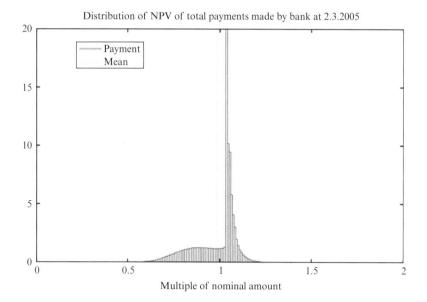

*Figure 4.10   Prospective distribution at inception of the present value
               of future payments of the bank to the hybrid bond holder
               showing possible return on investment*

above one represent the collection of some interest by the investor, taking
account of the bank exercising its call option when market conditions led
to coupon payments becoming too high.

Figure 4.10 shows that, owing to the structured coupon payments, the
prospective situation nearly four years later in late 2008 has become much
worse for the holder of this bond – the investment will almost certainly be
loss making.

As a demonstration of the conflicts of interest inherent in modern
banking institutions, their asset management divisions recommended to
private pension funds and other risk averse investors portfolios of these
loss-making hybrid capital raising 'bond' instruments issued by other
banks, sometimes even including those issued by the investment banking
arm of the portfolio manager's bank.

Subsequently, in 2007, banks extended the maturity of callable hybrid
capital raising instruments to indefinite, thereby reviving a structured
floating rate version of the *consol* fixed rate bonds issued by the British
government in the eighteenth century and still alive today (with reduced
rates). Such floating rate consols raise the issue of the not inconsiderable

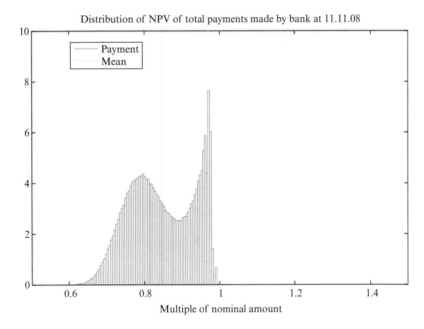

Figure 4.11 *Losing prospective distribution of the present value of future payments of the bank to the bond holder nearly four years from inception*

credit risk of the issuing bank defaulting on the interest payments over the potentially infinite maturity, however structured, and are very difficult to price.[26] Put simply, the issuing bank collects the invested capital up front for these bonds in return for a stream of interest payments terminated only by the bank calling the instrument and repaying its face value in extremely adverse market conditions or defaulting – think of the holders of the Russian Tsar's consols in 1917.[27] Interestingly, at inception, just prior to the credit crisis, these instruments were traded in the secondary market near par, as holders appeared to take the view that the bank would likely call these potentially infinite-lived bonds soon after

[26] See for details Dempster et al., above n. 16. We were unable to find any literature whatsoever on pricing floating rate consol bonds and had to devise appropriate techniques to approximately price these instruments, taking into account all risk factors including default risk.

[27] Some of whose descendants are still trying to make the current Russian Government honour the debt.

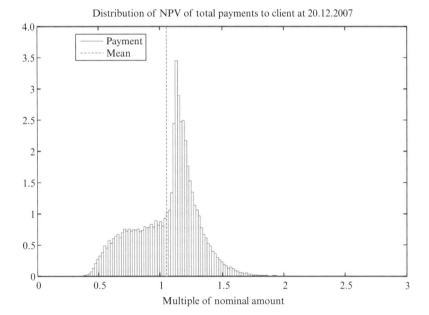

*Figure 4.12   Prospective distribution at inception of the present value
of future payments of the bank to the callable consol bond
holder showing possible return on investment*

the initial favourable fixed payments. With the manifold problems of
the credit crisis, not least the insolvency and government rescue of many
of the issuers, some of whom have suspended interest payments, these
losing hybrid investments are currently trading at discounts ranging from
20 to 80 per cent of face value. Figure 4.12 shows the present value distribution at inception of future payments to the bond holder of such an
investment, which has a high return tail in the relatively unlikely event of
coupon payments continuing over a very long period. To evaluate such
an investment in the absence of credit risk this PV payment distribution
must be compared to that for a fixed rate long maturity sovereign or
consol with the same face value, usually unfavourably.

Foreign Exchange Hedging

One of the most egregious failed derivatives deals we have seen to date
involved a bank's European corporate client with needs to continually purchase US dollars for euros and led eventually to over a 30m euro loss. The
firm had previously been using forward contracts to do this in line with its

Figure 4.13   Evolution of the EUR–USD currency exchange rate from 1999 to 2008

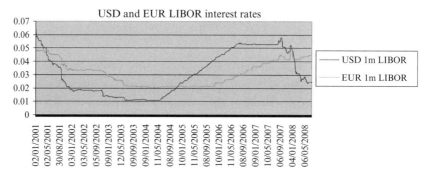

Figure 4.14   Evolution of USD and EUR LIBOR 1 one-month interest rates from 2001 to 2008

anticipated needs, but the bank suggested that this could be more cheaply done using foreign exchange (FX) options to hedge its exchange rate risk.

Figure 4.13 charts the evolution since the introduction of the euro of the EUR–USD exchange rate, giving the value in dollars of one euro. After a short initial weakening period the euro's value enjoyed a steady rise in value from 2001 through the third quarter of 2008.

According to the theory of uncovered interest rate parity the FX rates between two specific currencies responds to short-term interest rates in the two currency areas. However Figure 4.14, which plots the US and EU London interbank offer (LIBOR) one-month rates, suggests that the relationship for EUR–USD is at best complicated and at worst entirely unpredictable.

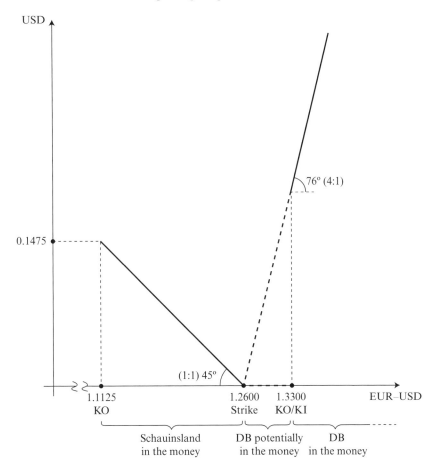

Figure 4.15   Counterparty option pair pay-off diagram in USD on the EUR–USD exchange rate

When the corporate client was initially presented by the bank with a standard FX hedging programme it likely considered the costs too high relative to forward dollar purchase at no up-front cost. The bank therefore came up with a deal to exchange at no up-front cost European (i.e. exercisable only at maturity) FX barrier options whose pay-off diagram in US dollars is shown in Figure 4.15.[28] It is immediately noticeable that

---

[28]   Payments were actually in euros, which results in a non-linear version of this diagram, but the dollar linear version shows the payout structure more clearly.

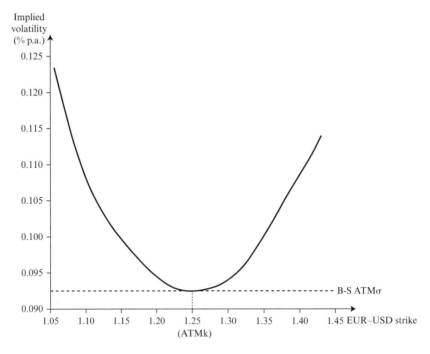

Figure 4.16   A representative EUR–USD implied volatility smile when the current rate is 1.25 USD per EUR

the pay-off structure is asymmetric with a favourable penny change in the dollar value of the euro worth initially four and later six times more to the bank than the client. The structuring of both exchanged options involves a choice of knock-out points for the client's option and knock-in points for the bank's.

Again, pricing of such options is a complex matter that involves adjusting prices to incorporate higher prices for option values away from the rate at inception in terms of the so-called volatility smile depicted in Figure 4.16. Many different methods are available and in use by different traders and banks including the Monte Carlo method.[29]

Over 33 months 70 option pairs were exchanged between the bank and the client, many apparently mispriced in favour of the bank in that the client's options were underpriced, corresponding to negative smile

---

[29] See A. Castanga and F. Mercurio, 'The Vanna-Volga Method for Implied Volatilities', *Risk* (January 2007), 106–111, for a more advanced method often used.

corrections, and the bank's overpriced. Whatever method(s) the bank used, this is entirely inappropriate and leaves the impression of arbitrary pricing. Moreover a large proportion of these deals were restructured by the bank to incorporate the client's mark-to-market losses on the existing deal and postpone any cash changing hands between the counterparties. At such restructurings the bank always took the opportunity to improve the knock-in points for their option (the client's having been knocked out, i.e. dead) in their favour. Nevertheless, no significant cash changed hands for 27 months in these contract exchanges until the deals struck in the last 6 months of the programme when in early 2008 the client was billed over five days for €30.5m even though some of the European options involved, a few struck in the previous weeks, had not yet expired.

OTC Structured Deals Summary

In this section we have described a number of representative failed OTC deals involving structured derivative and bond products. They have in common the features that they all possess an enticement to early client return but their final outcomes are highly skewed in favour of the issuing banks. Moreover the swap and FX deals usually involve (often multiple) restructurings by the issuing bank to incorporate (often mispriced) client mark-to-market losses on the existing deal and postpone the eventual client losses, which always grow substantially. It is clear that a bank's counterparty in this position, like a good trader, should always cut their losses at the first opportunity, but unfortunately they seldom do.

LEGAL ASPECTS OF FAILED DERIVATIVE DEALS

Caveat Emptor and Market Transparency

Obviously the fact that an investor suffers losses from an investment does not of itself ground any claims for compensation. On the face of it, this is a typical case for *caveat emptor.* Markets are highly efficient at the allocation of resources. One of the mechanisms behind that efficiency is the principle that prices are set by the competitive interaction of buyers, not sellers (as is typified by auctions). Sellers are, to a degree, responsible for what they say about their product. If, however, they make no representations about it, then it is up to the buyer to ensure that the purchase makes sense for him. Allowing, or requiring, sellers to set prices counteracts market efficiency. And the criteria for price, fitness for purpose, and the like apply strictly *ex ante* – being wise after the event is irrelevant for the validity of the contract.

Nonetheless, although *caveat emptor* is an effective device for ensuring market efficiency, it is only a device, not the basis of the market itself. Ultimately, the market is a system for generating information about the goods and services society needs at any given moment. Benefits of this sort flow directly from the market's openness and transparency. In contrast, situations where information is being suppressed or perverted contravene market principles at a more fundamental level than any individual departure from *caveat emptor*.

The law promotes transparency and openness in the market with the aid of various principles. First, it can exclude persons who do not have the capacity to deal in the market: the ignorant or those not competent to take risks with the property entrusted to them. Second, it can strike down bargains reached on the basis of false representations or fraud. These restrictions on pure *caveat emptor* are relevant in the cases we have mentioned, and we shall now look at them in more detail.

Capacity to Contract

Capacity is the classic topic of derivatives litigation, having been the central theme of the *Hammersmith* case,[30] and, more recently, of *Haugesund v Depfa*.[31] As a matter of principle, speculation as such is probably never within the 'capacity' of municipalities, which means the contracts are void and that third parties purporting to enter such agreements with municipalities are likely to emerge empty-handed, whether they 'won' or not.

Capacity to contract – or its absence – is a significant part of the law of obligations, though less so than in the past. Today, for example, wives can generally speaking make valid contracts without the consent of their spouses, and it is no longer possible for commercial corporations to avoid obligations to third parties by reference to their terms of incorporation.[32] Municipalities are different, however. The doctrine that they cannot validly perform acts that lie outside the powers granted to them by legislators (ultra vires) is definitely still part of English law and probably also part

---

[30]   *Hazell v Hammersmith and Fulham LBC [1990] 3* All ER 33 (QBD and CA) [1991] 1 All ER 545 (HL).
[31]   4 September 2009 – [2009] EWHC 2227 (Comm).
[32]   First Company Law Directive, 68/151/EEC, Art. 9.

of German law. The 'Fischereiwirtschaft case'[33] explicitly recognised ultra vires as part of German law, though German courts have subsequently been reticent about using the term. Possibly a notion like 'exceeding one's radius of action',[34] which does play a part in German administrative law, identifies an equivalent position.[35]

Whether or not ultra vires as such is valid, the issues in any particular case will have more to do with two further elements.

First, are financial instruments like swaps 'speculation', or are they not simply modern instruments of what is known as 'debt management'? If the latter, surely they can be legitimately deployed as incidental to most municipalities' powers to organise their debts in the best possible way, at least if they are used only to modify the conditions of particular existing debts? Contrary to the tenor of the English decisions,[36] administrative practice in Germany seems willing to countenance the use of swaps subject only to the criterion of 'connexity' – i.e., that swaps must be referable to existing debts (though the precise functioning of this criterion is a matter of some obscurity). No German court has taken the view that swaps were outside the powers of local authorities, though the matter has not so far been fully argued.

Second, what of municipalities or municipal offshoots that are not mere creatures of public law? In *Hammersmith*, for example, there was considerable debate about whether a London borough, which is a corporation set up by royal charter and can thus in principle do anything that an 'ordinary individual' (i.e. a natural person) can do, is subject to the same limits on its power as a local council. In relation to the borough corporation, the English courts rejected the argument that it could speculate even if a council could not, *inter alia* on the grounds that its income was subject to statutory constraints and could only be used subject to those constraints, however 'free' the corporation as such might otherwise be ('the permitted use of council funds [is] not affected by the extent of the theoretical, legal capacity of the corporation').[37]

There are analogous distinctions in German administrative law between municipalities, which are always creatures of some higher legislature, and

---

[33] BGH 28.02.1956, BGHZ 20, 119.

[34] *Überschreitung des Wirkungskreises, Überschreitung des Wirkungsbereichs.*

[35] W. Kewenig and H. Schneider, 'Swap-Geschäfte der öffentlichen Hand in Deutschland', *Wertpapiermitteilungen*, Sonderbeilage 2/1992.

[36] See the House of Lords in *Hazell v Hammersmith & Fulham LBC* [1991] 1 All ER 545.

[37] CA per Sir Stephen Browne, *Hazell v Hammersmith & Fulham LBC* [1991] 1 All ER 545, at 77 f.

sovereign bodies such as the state and federal governments. This has not so far been an issue in swap disputes, though it might conceivably be relevant to situations where state banks (*Landesbanken*) have been involved in swap deals.

Questions of capacity are also relevant to cases in which the swap investor is not the municipality itself, but a private law entity set up by the municipality to perform certain of its functions. Certainly it might be argued that a private company wholly owned by a municipality, set up under powers conferred by statute and performing statutory functions, should in principle be subject to the same constraints on its use of public money as is a purely statutory body (by analogy with *Hammersmith* in the English courts). Hitherto, however, German courts have resisted any attempt to subject a municipality's private law activities to public law rules. This obviously makes a degree of sense in formal terms. Beyond that, it also reflects the fact that German administrative law provides in detail for supervisory bodies to restrain acts in excess of jurisdiction, but with methods that can be invoked only in the context of the administrative structure itself.[38]

The Landesbanken have not, historically, been corporations within Article 9 of Directive 68/151/EEC. The extent to which this would allow them to rely on their statutes as against third parties is unclear, but it seems doubtful whether such statutes would exclude the purchase of any financial instruments, however speculative (see Law establishing the Bavarian State Bank, Art. 2 (3)).[39]

Implied Terms

Financial deals are subject to a number of terms implied by law or statute.

Good faith

A 'fallback' term that is everywhere implied is good faith. This is in some respects more familiar to Continental legal systems[40] but uncontroversially

---

[38] *Genehmigungsbedürftigkeit, schwebende Unwirksamkeit* etc., see § 58 (2) of the Administrative Procedure Act.

[39] It is probably the case, however, that ultra vires applied to Landesbanken in their earlier incarnation, when they more closely resembled public bodies – see Christian Koenig in WM 49 (1995), 317-325.

[40] See the German concept of 'Treu und Glauben', MüKomm BGB, §§ 242 Rn 10; §§ 242 Rn. 1.

also plays a role in the common law treatment of financial relationships.[41] What it means in the present context is probably the same in either system: good faith means honesty and the absence of deception or fraud. It is not acceptable to deceive the counterparty for one's own gain.

How far this gets a claimant in a swap case is doubtful. 'Deception' generally has to be active; failing to clear up the counterparty's misconceptions is not generally dishonest unless there is a duty to do so. A duty arises when good faith requires it, for example because the counterparty is obviously and justifiably depending on information from the defendant.[42] This argument is somewhat circular, however, and leaves open the question of what good faith specifically requires. In the case of professional investors, it might readily be said that it is *not* justifiable, in the absence of explicit provision, for a buyer to rely on the seller to clear up any misconceptions.

Under the MiFID regime,[43] sellers are in any event entitled to assume that 'professional' buyers know what they are doing,[44] though this does not necessarily cover the case when a seller has actual knowledge that a buyer doesn't know what he is doing.

Advice

There is so far no case law on MiFID and it is unclear how much difference it will make to securities sellers' duties, in as far as investors have hitherto been able to invoke them in the individual Member States.[45]

In Germany, this may mean that the courts will continue to imply terms establishing a contract of advice.[46] Under *Bond*, this arises in any case in which a securities dealer engages in any discussion ('Gespräch') with an investor with a view to the purchase of a security. This obviously engages a wide spectrum of cases, though it excludes an 'execution only' scenario.

It is particularly important that, in *Bond* terms, the relationship of advice arises without regard to the status of the customer. If it turns out in the course of the relationship that the customer is experienced (or even professional), then the dealer's advice may be abbreviated accordingly. But

---

[41] *IFE Fund SA v Goldman Sachs* – [2007] EWCA Civ 811 (65 ff); *Socimer International Bank Ltd (in liq) v Standard Bank London Ltd* – [2008] EWCA Civ 116 (106).

[42] *Wendtland*, in: *BeckOK BGB*, §§ 123 Rn 11-12.

[43] Which has only applied since 2007 and is thus not relevant for most of the examples mentioned here.

[44] Directive 2006/73/EC, Art. 36.

[45] See, for Germany, § 31 WpHG.

[46] The so-called *Bond* caselaw – BGH 6 July 1993 – XI ZR 12/93; see Podewils/ Reisich (2009), at 121.

the relationship remains one of advice rather than one of mere 'information'. Thus, if he is aware of it, an adviser may not disregard the fact that his customer is labouring under material misconceptions. The difference between a duty of information and a duty to give advice is that the latter requires active engagement in the customer's individual state of mind and knowledge. In principle, then, that applies just as much when the bank is selling to another bank as it does when the customers are widows and orphans.[47]

Representations

There is clearly a good deal of scope for misrepresentation in deals that come with generous documentation, often amounting to hundreds of pages, and intensive sales presentations.

Causation

Not surprisingly, however, sellers of derivatives usually garnish their documentation with a multitude of disclaimers. Indeed, it is at this point that claims from investors typically fail. However much sellers may misbehave, for example by extolling their products for virtues they do not have, this will not be regarded as causative if the customer was an experienced investor, and if the literature contained clear disclaimers and warnings that were seen and acknowledged by the investor.[48]

German courts have in a number of recent derivatives cases followed a similar line of argument: as long as it is made clear that the product involves a substantial amount of risk, experienced investors cannot claim that their decision was materially influenced by the sales team's representations, whatever these may have contained. The warnings mentioned above ('theoretically infinite risk' and so on) have been held to be more than sufficient by a number of appeal courts.[49]

Representations as to randomness

Warnings as to risk may not be sufficient on their own, however – in particular they may be insufficient if such warnings are not quantified in terms

---

[47]   However, as pointed out in n.3, the US Dodd-Frank Act explicitly addresses the requirement for advice in the best interests of the client only with regard to governmental entities, pension funds and foundations.

[48]   *Bankers Trust v PT Dharmala* [1996] CLC 518; *Morgan Chase v Springwell* [2008] EWHC 1186 (Comm).

[49]   OLG Bamberg, 11 May 2009; OLG Celle, 30 September 2009; OLG Düsseldorf, 29 June 2009, OLG Frankfurt, above n. 15.

of fair value as well as risk and return. At least one German court has now accepted that this may be the case.[50] The argument goes as follows.

As several German courts have accepted, instruments like the swaps described above are, functionally, wagers.[51] Gambling debts are in most European countries irrecoverable.[52] Swap debts are not in general caught by this, because in most countries financial instruments – or, more specifically, contracts for difference, which used to be regarded as bets – have been taken out of the restrictions on betting provided at least one of the parties is a regulated financial institution.[53]

So far, however, German courts have been slow to see the implications of their own viewpoint. They have tended to assume that if the swaps are wagers, and that if this was apparent to both parties, then the customer cannot legitimately complain about the outcome: he knew (or should have known) it was a wager, therefore he obviously wanted a wager, and everyone knows that wagers can be lost. Moreover, because the counter-party was a regulated bank, the debts incurred in the wager were recoverable.

This argument obscures the fact that categorising something as a wager raises a new set of legal consequences that go beyond the question of debt enforceability. Wagering contracts have their own rules or implied terms.

Under German law, for example, a person who proposes a wager represents by his conduct (i.e. even without doing so explicitly) that he has not influenced the random character of the event.[54] Under English law, presumably any undisclosed interference with the randomness of the object of the wager constitutes 'cheating'.[55] In both cases, it is an implied term that the object of the wager has not been interfered with. Generally, in both Germany and England, for gaming or wagering that departs from the principle of 'equal chance' not to be fraudulent, this fact must be disclosed. (Moreover, outside 'equal chance', all gaming and betting is subject to licensing requirements and other restrictions.)

Modern derivatives, as we have seen, are traded on the basis of fair market values. This is the starting point for price negotiations (at least from the bank's point of view, whether or not the customers realise this

---

50 OLG Stuttgart, above n. 14. Some of these issues are expected to be decided by the Federal Supreme Court (BGH) during 2011.

51 OLG Bamberg, above note 46.

52 M Henssler, *Risiko als Vertragsgegenstand* (Tübingen: Mohr Siebeck, 1994).

53 See, e.g., § 37e WpHG; Gambling Act 2005, s 10.

54 Schönke/Schröder, *Strafgesetzbuch*, Kommentar (26th ed, München, 2001), §§ 263 Rn. 16e.

55 Gambling Act 2005, s 42.

is happening). Moreover, the ascertainment of a fair value by statistical means necessarily generates information about risk – which the banks also use for their own trading purposes. Modern derivatives sellers know about the random distribution of their products, and they use this knowledge for pricing and for risk management.

Clearly, diverging from fair value to the benefit of the seller is not just a matter of putting in a profit margin, for it alters the balance of risk and return as between the parties. Setting the strike price at a figure that makes the swap diverge from its fair value is analogous to adding green (zero) pockets to a roulette wheel. Pockets change the odds for the benefit of the casino (and, in the long run, provide its profits). Such an intervention is fair, however, because it is disclosed. The pockets on the casino's wheels are clearly marked by their distinctive colour, and the manipulation of the odds can readily be calculated by anyone anxious to do so. This transparency is not available, however, to derivatives buyers unless they (a) already understand the concept of fair value and how the seller is using it as a basis for his price negotiation, and (b) have a quant department to calculate the odds. Requirement (a) could in principle be met, but in the past clearly has not been for the vast majority of investors, however 'experienced'. As for requirement (b), we assume that it is currently not met even by major institutional investors.

In principle, then, non-disclosure of an intervention materially affecting the chances of a wager must be fraudulent. If, as has happened in all the cases mentioned above, the seller has structured the instrument so as to affect the balance of risk and return to his benefit, then he must say so, and he must put a number on it. Generalised declarations as to 'infinite risk' or 'no worst case can be specified' are certainly not enough, for they not only fail to identify the real question, they actively divert attention from it.

Representation summary
There appear to be two grounds on which investors of any category – i.e. not only 'consumers', but 'professionals' as well – can in principle impugn complex structured finance deals.

Breach of good faith   If investors can establish that the dealer was under a duty to give advice, then any failure by him to clear up material misconceptions that were or should have been evident is dishonest. Such a duty may arise, for example, under an implied term (as in Germany's *Bond* case law). Misunderstanding the nature of price and risk in a complex derivative is a material misconception.

Misrepresentation In the absence of statements to the contrary, the offeror of a wagering contract implicitly represents that the balance of risk has not been manipulated. Even if it is clear to the buyer that the instrument is, functionally, a wager, this does not absolve the seller of a duty to disclose any interference.

Inadequate or false representations as to something that is basically a wagering contract can ground claims in ways that bypass questions of capacity or of causation. In principle, any investor, even including a sophisticated institution, is entitled to be told what risks his counterparty is preparing for him. It is not enough to warn the investor of 'infinite risks', because that, whether true or not, is merely incidental to what the counterparty's interventions have actually achieved for himself.[56] This applies however sophisticated the investor is: if he clearly doesn't know what game he has joined, then the counterparty must tell him. It is difficult to see how that information can avoid including the basic element of the counterparty's pricing – namely, the divergence from fair value.

CONCLUSION

Courts have been relatively slow to move from *caveat emptor* to the considerations above more appropriate to OTC derivatives. It seems, however, that they are nevertheless finally moving towards an understanding of the problems posed by modern derivative instruments, although they are undoubtedly faced with a steep learning curve. Of course, this might become unnecessary if the types of OTC deals we have discussed in this chapter are forced by legislation on to cleared exchanges. However, many tailored OTC products will likely remain in any case.

A cost-effective, relatively simple, risk disclosure legislation in all jurisdictions could in any event alleviate the disclosure problems encountered by OTC banking clients. This would require institutions by law to display the asymmetric risks involved in their structured products along the lines

---

[56] See the recent appeal ruling on this specific point by the German Federal Court of Justice in Karlsruhe in Ille Papier v. Deutsche Bank (International Herald Tribune, 23 March 2011, p. 18). Here, a sales pitch was found to invite reliance by the client on its commercial bank and then any such reliance was disclaimed in the written contract, providing evidence of lack of good faith by the defendant. The similarity with the foreign exchange case treated in this article, with much more at stake, is striking.

of the NPV or PV distribution diagrams we have shown here for OTC swaps, bonds and FX contracts. We maintain that any potential client seeing the figures of this chapter in an OTC term sheet would think twice about signing the contract.[57] The result would be fairer OTC products and encouragement of the proper use of tailored derivatives by clients for hedging various risks. The concomitant would of course be smaller margins for banks, perhaps not a bad thing.

---

[57] Unfortunately, the implementation of the US Dodd-Frank Act by the SES and CFTC, due by the end of 2011 is unlikely to incorporate this simple requirement.

5. The role of law and governance in financial markets: The case of the emerging Chinese securities market

Sanzhu Zhu

INTRODUCTION

In March 2009, the Chinese government endorsed a plan to establish Shanghai as an international financial centre and shipping hub by 2020, ten years earlier than was previously planned.[1] This was good news for Shanghai where, together with numerous banks, insurance and securities establishments, China's three major securities and futures exchanges are located: the Shanghai Stock Exchange,[2] the Shanghai Futures Exchange[3] and the China Financial Futures Exchange.[4] Anticipating a

---

[1]   See The Opinion of the State Council on Promoting Shanghai to Speed up the Development of Modern Services Industry and Advanced Manufacture Industry and Construction of an International Financial Centre and an International Shipping Centre (Guowuyuan Guanyu Tuijin Shanghai Jiakuai Fazhan Xiandai Fuwuye and Xianjin Zhizhaoye Jianshe Guoji Jinrong Zhongxin he Guoji Hangyun Zhongxin de Yijian) (Guofa [2009] No. 19), issued by the State Council on 14 April 2009.

[2]   The Shanghai Stock Exchange was established on 26 November, 1990 and the trading started on 19 December 1990. By the end of 2007, there were 860 listed companies.

[3]   The Shanghai Futures Exchange was established in 1998 by merging the Shanghai Commodity Exchange, the Shanghai Metal Exchange, and the Shanghai Grain & Oil Exchange and business started in December 1999. Futures products currently include copper, aluminium, natural rubber, fuel oil, zinc and gold futures contracts. See Shanghai Futures Exchange Home Page (follow 'About the Futures Exchange' ('Guan Yu Qi Jiao Suo') hyperlink).

[4]   The China Financial Futures Exchange (CFFEX) was established jointly by the five current securities and futures exchanges, namely, the Shanghai Futures Exchange, the Zhengzhou Commodity Exchange, the Dalian Commodity Exchange, the Shanghai Stock Exchange and the Shenzhen Stock Exchange. The CSI 300 index futures contract is a product that CFFEX prepared to launch. The basis of the CSI 300 index futures contract is the CSI 300 index (*hushen 300*

threat to Hong Kong's position as an international financial centre and shipping hub, Hong Kong commentators argued, however, that Hong Kong had little to fear, pointing out, as one of the reasons, Shanghai's 'woefully inadequate regulatory system'.[5] Shortly afterwards at the annual Lujiazui Forum in May 2009, which drew more than 700 top Chinese policymakers and financial industry experts, one of the issues explored by the participants was the regulatory changes needed to transform Shanghai into a peer of Hong Kong, New York and London.[6]

The story of China's emerging securities market tells that the establishment of a healthy and sustainable securities and futures market in China could not go far without a well-established regulatory system, supported by a culture of the rule of law and by good governance. The success of Shanghai as a prominent international financial centre will depend upon, among other factors, a well-established regulatory system and respect for the rule of law and governance. The arguments presented in this chapter reinforce this proposition.

China's securities market is a new and transitional market and emerged in the process of China's transformation from a previous socialist and planned economy to a market economy.[7] In the 1980s, soon after China started economic reform in late 1978, the government and enterprises began to issue government and enterprise bonds.[8] Starting from 1984, joint stock companies were established and shares were issued to the public.[9] In 1990 and 1991, the Shanghai and Shenzhen stock exchanges were, respectively, established, marking an important stage of the establishment

---

zhishu) which comprises 300 A-shares listed on the Shanghai Stock Exchange and the Shenzhen Stock Exchange and represents 60% market capitalization of the Shanghai and Shenzhen markets as a whole. Apart from the CSI 300 index futures contract, CFFEX plans to introduce other index futures, index options, government bonds futures and currency futures, see China Financial Futures Exchange Home Page ('Guan yu Jiao Yi Suo').

[5]   See T. Holland, 'Shaky Shanghai Poses No Threat to Hong Kong', *The Monitor Column, South China Morning Post* (2009), B10.

[6]   See J.T. Areddy, 'China Wrestles With Shaping the Future of Shanghai', *Wall Street Journal*, 6 (2009). (Reporting the event with comments.)

[7]   See generally X. Mei, et al., *The Re-emerging Securities Market in China* (Westport: Quorum Books, 1992); S Zhu, *Securities Regulation in China* (London: Transnational Publishers, Simmonds & Hill Publishing Ltd, 2000); S Green, *The Development of China's Stockmarket, 1984–2002: Equity Politics and Market Institutions* (London, New York: Routledge, 2004).

[8]   Zhu, *Securities Regulation in China*, n. 7 above, at 1–22.

[9]   Ibid.

of China's emerging securities market.[10] In 1998, China's first securities law was enacted.[11] Since the late 1990s, the securities investment fund market has enjoyed sustainable growth,[12] which was further promoted by the promulgation of the Securities Investment Fund Law of the People's Republic of China (PRC) in 2003.[13] This chapter further examines the role played by law, regulation and judicial rules in the regulation of securities markets in China.

China's commodity and financial futures markets, the development of which has undergone a tortuous passage, are a prime example of how important it is that an appropriate and balanced legal, regulatory and judicial framework should be put in place to ensure the healthy and sustainable development of a commodity and financial futures market. China's first commodity futures exchange, the Zhengzhou Commodity Exchange, was created in October 1990, and provided a platform, and facilitated the need, for commodity futures trading arising from China's economic reform, as China moved towards a market economy during the early 1990s.[14] In the futures market's formative years, the number of futures trading disputes increased sharply and flooded the people's courts. In the words of the then deputy president of the Supreme People's Court,

---

[10]   The Shenzhen Stock Exchange was established on 1 December 1990 and the trading started on 3 July 1991.

[11]   The Securities Law of the People's Republic of China was adopted by the Standing Committee of the National People's Congress on 29 December 1998, effective as of 1 July 1999. The drafting of the 1998 Securities Law went through a longer period of time than its sister legislation, the 1993 Company Law. For the drafting process of the 1998 Securities Law, see Zhu, n 7 above, in particular section B of Chapter I, 8–14 (2000).

[12]   In March 1998, the first two investment funds were created after the promulgation of the Provisional Measures on the Administration of Securities Investment Fund in November 1997. By the end of 1998, there were only 5 investment funds, with a total net value 10.74 billion yuan; by the end of 2006, in contrast, there were 307 investment funds, with a net value 856.5 billion yuan. See 'An Outline of the Development of Securities Investment Fund Sector in Our Country' (Woguo Zhengquan Touzi Jijinye Fazhan Gaikuang), *China Securities Daily* (29 July 2008).

[13]   The Securities Investment Fund Law of the People's Republic of China, adopted by the Standing Committee of the National People's Congress on 28 October 2003 and effective as of 1 June 2004.

[14]   Prior to the introduction of futures trading on 28 May 1993, the Zhengzhou Commodity Exchange operated for two years trading cash forward contracts. Currently the futures products traded on the Zhengzhou Commodity Exchange include wheat, cotton, white sugar, pure terephthalic acid (PTA), rapeseed oil and green bean futures contracts. See Zhengzhou Commodity Exchange Homepage (follow 'About the Exchange' ('Guan yu Jiao Yi Suo') (on file with author).

the futures market had become a 'big litigation family' (*susong dahu*), generating a high rate of disputes and litigation.[15] Sixteen years later, the China Financial Futures Exchange was established in Shanghai.[16] This was followed by the opening of gold futures trading on the Shanghai Futures Exchange on 9 January, 2008.[17] This chapter further examines the role played by law, regulation and judicial rules in shaping China's commodity and financial futures market.

One of the serious problems facing China's securities regulatory authority and Chinese courts since the emergence of China's securities market has been how best to tackle various forms of securities fraud in order to protect the interests of investors and to maintain the integrity of China's securities market. This chapter also therefore examines the role played by the people's court in dealing with investors' civil compensation claims resulting from false statements made on the securities market. This is an area which demonstrates the importance of a supportive and accommodating court with a set of appropriate judicial rules and procedures. The limited role played by the people's court and the restrictive procedural rules set out by the Supreme People's Court in this area, as discussed further below, indicate that despite the progress that the people's court made by opening up its doors to accommodate this type of case, the people's courts are constrained by external as well as internal factors, such as resources and concern about social stability.

China's emerging securities market has developed and is regulated within the context of China's overall administrative, economic, legal, social and political systems. The government's clearing-up campaigns in the commodity and financial market in the 1990s, the intervention of administrative authorities and securities regulators in resolving civil securities disputes, an overly-weighted emphasis placed on social stability and financial stability, and the questionable role played by the judicial committee of the people's court in the adjudication of major and complicated securities dispute cases, all show that the regulation

---

[15]   B. Jiang (ed.), *Understanding and Application of 'the 2003 Provisions of the Supreme People's Court on Several Issues Concerning Adjudication of Cases of Futures Disputes'* ('Zuigao Renmin Fayuan Guanyu Shenli Qihuo Jiufen Anjian Ruogan Wenti de Guiding' de Lijie Yu Shiyong), compiled by the Second Division Court of the Supreme People's Court, Preface (Beijing: The People's Court Publishing House, 2003) at 1.

[16]   See above n. 4.

[17]   The launch of gold futures trading was met by enthusiastic investors. See J. Blas and C. Flood, 'Gold Futures Fly High in Shanghai Market', *Financial Times* (9 January 2008).

of China's securities market and the resolution of securities disputes is part and parcel of a legal and regulatory system based on China's current administrative, economic, legal, social and political systems. This chapter also therefore examines the way in which the role of law, the role of courts, and the role of the administrative authorities and their actions are entwined in the regulation of China's securities market, in the context of China's overall administrative, economic, legal, social and political system.

This chapter concludes that the legal, regulatory and judicial steps China has taken in the past decades in building China's emerging securities market have proved to be a fundamentally important part of the policies and actions taken to promote the healthy and sustainable growth of China's emerging securities market. Future development of China's securities market calls for further legal, regulatory and judicial reform in order to support China's securities market in moving to a new level of scale and standards, compatible with China's overall economic development and China's gradual establishment of the rule of law in the twenty-first century.

DEVELOPMENT OF THE LAW, REGULATION AND JUDICIAL RULES OF CHINA'S EMERGING SECURITIES MARKET

The main source of securities law in China is the 1998 Securities Law of the PRC.[18] Before 1998, the 1993 Provisional Regulations on the Administration of Issuing and Trading of Shares played a major role in regulating share issuance and trading.[19] During the 1980s and early 1990s, a range of specific regulations and normative documents were issued on the regulation of various aspects of China's emerging securities and futures market, covering, for example, securities fraud,[20]

---

[18] The Securities Law of the People's Republic of China, adopted by the Standing Committee of the National People's Congress on 29 December 1998 and effective as of 1 July 1999; amended on 27 October 2005 and effective as of 1 January 2006. See Zhu, above n 7, 207–224, together with a translation of full text of the Law. See also above n. 11.

[19] The 1993 Provisional Regulations on the Administration of Issuing and Trading of Shares was promulgated by the State Council on 22 April 1993.

[20] For example, the 1993 Provisional Measures on the Prohibition of Securities Frauds, approved by the State Council on 15 August 1993, promulgated by the State Council Securities Committee on, and effective from 2 September 1993.

government and enterprise bonds,[21] securities repurchases,[22] commodity and financial futures,[23] foreign participation in China's securities market and the overseas listing of Chinese companies.[24] After the establishment of the Shanghai and Shenzhen stock exchanges in 1990 and 1991, the Securities Committee of the State Council (SCSC) and the China Securities Regulatory Commission (CSRC), the principal regulator for the securities and futures market in China, were established in October 1992, moving the institutional development of China's securities regulatory system into a new stage.[25] In 1993, the Company Law of the PRC, the first company law since the founding of the PRC in 1949, was enacted.[26]

The 1998 Securities Law and the 1993 Company Law were both amended substantially in 2005, which was described as a 'legal construction year for China's securities market'.[27] From the judges' point of view, the amendments, which covered 40 per cent of the provisions of the 1998 Securities Law,[28] had a positive impact on securities-related crimi-

---

[21] The 1986 Government Bond Regulations and the 1993 Regulations on the Administration of Enterprise Bonds.

[22] The 1994 Provisional Measures for the Administration of Credit Funds and the 1995 Circular on Reiteration of Relevant Issues Concerning Further Standardization of Securities Repurchase Business.

[23] The 1993 Provisional Measures on the Administration of Registration of Futures Broker Firms and the 1993 Circular of the State Council on Firmly Stopping Blind Development of Futures Market. See further below.

[24] The 1991 Measures on the Administration of Shanghai Special Renminbi Shares, promulgated by the People's Bank of China and the Shanghai Municipal People's Government on, and effective as of 22 November 1991; the 1994 Mandatory Provisions for the Articles of Association of Companies to be Listed Outside China, issued by the State Council Securities Commission and the State Commission for Restructuring the Economic System on 19 September 1994.

[25] For a discussion of the role played by the SCSC and CSRC in the early 1990s, see Zhu, above n 7, at 8–14. Apart from the SCSC and the CSRC, the People's Bank of China, China's central bank, was designated as a watchdog to oversee the securities market in conjunction with various bodies of the central and local government. The SCSC was later dissolved, leaving the CSRC and its local offices as a single national securities regulator.

[26] The 1993 Company Law was adopted by the Standing Committee of the National People's Congress on 29 December 1993, and effective as of 1 July 1994, amended in 1999, 2004 and 2005.

[27] See J. Liu, 'Innovation of Securities Legal System' (Zhengquan Falü de Zhidu Chuangxin), 22 *China Finance (Zhongguo Jinrong)*, 48 (2005) at 50.

[28] See Legal Department of CSRC, 'Landmark of the Development of Chinese Securities Legal System – Background, Process and Significance of Securities Law Amendments'.

nal, administrative and civil litigation procedures.[29] While the previous amendments made to the 1993 Company Law in 1999 and 2004 affected only three articles of the 1993 Company Law, the 2005 amendments effectuated a wide range of important changes.[30]

The legal frameworks established under the 2005 Securities Law and the 2005 Company Law complemented each other. The provisions concerning the issue of new shares, issue of corporate bonds and listing requirements and procedures for joint stock companies, all of which were previously covered by the 1993 Company Law, have now been moved to the 2005 Securities Law. This change, as argued by some scholars, has made China's company law and securities law better-matched with each other.[31] These and other amendments included in the 2005 Securities Law and the 2005 Company Law form a consolidated and improved regulatory framework for listed companies in China's stock market.

Tackling the misuse of clients' money by securities companies, which was a widespread problem, especially in the early formative years of China's securities market, has been one of the continuing regulatory focuses of the securities regulator, the courts and the legislature. Between 1998 and 2005, the CSRC issued a series of regulatory documents setting out regulatory requirements for the management of transaction clearing funds of clients of a securities company.[32] In November 2004, the Supreme People's Court, in consultation with the CSRC, issued a set of judicial

---

[29] See S. Cao, 'Major Contents of Revision of Securities Law and Impact on Litigation' (Zhengquan Fa Xiuding de Zhuyao Neirong Yiji Dui Susong de Yingxiang), 22 *China Law (Zhongguo Falü)*, 23–25 (2006) at 24. (English translation of the article at 81–84.) S. Cao is a senior judge of the Supreme People's Court.

[30] Two articles (Art. 67 and Art. 229) were amended in 1999 and 1 article (Art. 131) in 2004. By contrast, under the 2005 amendments, 46 articles or paragraphs were deleted, 41 articles or paragraphs were added and 137 articles or paragraphs were amended. See an interview with Professor Z. Zhao (2005), (who was a member of the company law revision team), 'Talk by Company Law Revision Expert' (Gongsi Fa Xiugai Zhuanjia Tan), *Legal Daily (Fazhi Ribao)* (30 October).

[31] See J. Liu, 'Innovation of New Company Law System' (Xin Gongsi Fa de Zhidu Chuangxin), *Legal Daily (Fazhi Ribao)* (1 November 2005).

[32] The Measures on the Administration of Client Transaction Clearing Funds (*Kehu Jiaoyi Jiesuan Zijin Guanli Banfa*), issued by the CSRC on 16 May 2001, effective as of 1 January 2002; the Circular of Several Opinions of the CSRC on Implementation of 'The Measures on the Administration of Client Transaction Clearing Funds' (*Guanyu Zhixing 'Kehu Jiaoyi Jiesuan Zijin Guanli Banfa' Ruogan Yijian de Tongzhi*), issued on 8 October 2001; the Circular of the CSRC on Further Strengthening Supervision and Regulation of Client Transaction of Securities Company (*Guanyu Jinyibu Jiaqiang Zhengquan Gongsi Kehu Jiaoyi Jiesuan Zijin Jianguan de Tongzhi*), issued on 12 October 2004.

rules in the Circular on Relevant Issues Concerning Freeze and Transfer of Securities Transaction Clearing Funds, which updated its previous judicial rules in this area and clarified certain issues concerning the freeze and transfer of securities transaction clearing funds by the people's court in enforcement proceedings.[33]

The amended 2005 Securities Law further enhanced the protection of clients' money of securities companies. The 2005 Securities Law requires that the transaction clearing funds of clients of a securities company be deposited with a commercial bank under separate accounts in the names of each client;[34] no securities company may take the clients' transaction clearing funds and securities as their own property;[35] where a securities company is bankrupt or liquidated, the transaction clearing funds and securities of its clients will not belong to its bankrupt property or liquidated property;[36] and no transaction clearing funds and securities of clients may be sealed up, frozen up, transferred or enforced, except in relation to the debts of the clients themselves or other circumstances as stipulated by the law.[37] Further protections are provided for securities and funds in the clearing process.[38] Compared with the 1998 Securities

---

[33] The Circular on Relevant Issues Concerning Freeze and Transfer of Securities Transaction Clearing Funds (*Guanyu Dongjie, Kouhua Zhengquan Jiaoyi Jiesuan Zijin Youguan Wenti de Tongzhi*), issued on 9 November 2004. It superseded a similar circular of the Supreme People's Court issued on 2 December 1997: Circular of the Supreme People's Court on the Issues Concerning Freeze and Transfer Clearing Account Funds of Securities or Futures Exchanges, Securities Registration and Settlement Organization, Securities Companies or Futures Firms (*Zuigao Renmin Fayuan Guanyu Dongjie, Huabo Zhengquan Huo Qihuo Jiaoyisuo, Zhengquan Dengji Jiesuan Jigou, Zhengquan Jingying Huo Qihuo Jingji Jigou Qingsuan Zhanghu Zijin Deng Wenti de Tongzhi*). The new Circular made clear that the people's court may not freeze and transfer the securities or funds that have entered into clearing and delivery procedures following completion of a securities transaction. Point Four of the 2004 Circular on Relevant Issues Concerning Freeze and Transfer of Securities Transaction Clearing Funds.

[34] Art. 139, the 2005 Securities Law.

[35] Ibid.

[36] Ibid.

[37] Ibid.

[38] Art. 167 of the 2005 Securities Law stipulates that no one may, before delivery is completed, use the securities, funds or security pledged for delivery. Article 168 of the 2005 Securities Law stipulates that the clearing funds and securities of various kinds collected by securities registration and settlement organizations according to their business rules must be deposited in designated clearing and delivery accounts, and may only be used for the clearing and delivery following completion of a securities transaction according to the business rules, and shall not be subject to any enforcement.

Law,[39] the 2005 Securities Law moved a step forward by providing more specific, definite and comprehensive provisions in this area.

Corporate governance, which was a problem historically in China's emerging securities market, has been improved in recent years, assisted by the Code of Corporate Governance for Listed Companies in China issued in 2002 (the 2002 Code).[40] The 2002 Code provides, among other standards, that where the resolutions of shareholders' meetings or the resolutions of the board of directors are in breach of laws and administrative regulations, or infringe on shareholders' legal rights and interests, the shareholders have the right to initiate litigation to stop such breach or infringement.[41] The directors, supervisors and managers of the company carry liability to pay compensation where they violate laws, administrative regulations or articles of association and cause damages to the company in the course of the performance of their duties; shareholders have the right to request the company to sue for compensation in accordance with law.[42]

These standards of corporate governance have now been codified in the 2005 Securities Law and the 2005 Company Law. Shareholders have the right to bring an action in the people's court to request the court to cancel a resolution;[43] to request the court to order the company to allow inspection of the accounts of the company;[44] to request the court to dissolve the company;[45] to initiate litigation where the shareholder and the company cannot reach an agreement upon purchase of shareholding of

---

[39]   Art. 132 of the 1998 Securities Law requires that transaction clearing funds of clients are deposited in separate accounts of designated commercial banks.

[40]   The Code of Corporate Governance for Listed Companies in China (*Shangshi Gongsi Zhili Zhunze*), issued jointly by the CSRC and the State Economic and Trade Commission on, and effective as of 7 January 2002.

[41]   The Code of Corporate Governance for Listed Companies in China (*Shangshi Gongsi Zhili Zhunze*), issued jointly by the CSRC and the State Economic and Trade Commission on, and effective as of 7 January 2002, Art. 4.

[42]   Ibid.

[43]   Art. 22 of the 2005 Company Law provides that shareholders have the right to bring an action in the people's court to request the court to cancel a resolution if the resolution is reached in violation of law, administrative regulations or articles of association.

[44]   Art. 34 of the 2005 Company Law provides that shareholders have the right to request the court to order inspection of the accounts of the company if the company refuses the inspection request of the shareholders without reason.

[45]   Art. 183 of the 2005 Company Law provides that shareholders have the right to request the court to dissolve a company where the company is in serious difficulties and the continuous existence of the company will cause major loss to the shareholders.

the shareholder;[46] to request the company to sue for compensation where the directors, supervisors and managers of the company violate laws, administrative regulations or articles of association and cause damage to the company in the course of performance of their duties, or to sue directly in their own name, in the interests of the company, if the board of directors or the supervisory board refuse or fail to start a lawsuit as requested by the shareholders;[47] to sue for compensation where the directors and managers of the company violate laws, administrative regulations or articles of association and the interests of the shareholders are harmed;[48] and to sue in their own name in the interests of the company where the board of directors of a listed company fails to reclaim the profits gained through trading in the company's shares, in violation of the six-month trading restriction imposed on the directors, supervisors, managers and shareholders who hold over 5 per cent of shareholding.[49]

The combined effect of the 2005 Securities Law and the 2005 Company Law means that shareholders of listed, as well as non-listed, companies are provided with improved protection in terms of their rights to take a legal action in the people's court.[50] This in turn calls for a more accommodating people's court to implement and enforce these rights of shareholders, as provided for in the 2005 Securities Law and the 2005 Company Law. In 2006 and 2008, respectively, the Supreme People's Court issued two judicial interpretations concerning the application of the 2005 Company Law by the people's courts in their dealing with cases involving company

---

[46] Art. 75 of the 2005 Company Law provides that shareholders have the right to initiate litigation if a shareholder and the company cannot reach an agreement on purchase of the shareholding of the shareholder who votes against the resolution of the company to, for example, merge, divide or transfer its substantial assets.

[47] Art. 152 of the 2005 Company Law. Further, Article 150 states that 'If the directors, supervisors and senior executive of a company violate the laws, administrative regulations or the articles of association of the company in performance of their functions and thus cause loss to the company, they shall be liable for compensation'.

[48] Art. 153 of the 2005 Company Law.

[49] Art. 47 of the 2005 Securities Law.

[50] For an assessment of the corporate governance provisions under the 2005 Securities Law and the 2005 Company Law, see T. Yang et al., 'Steady as She Goes (2005/2006) – China's New Securities Law', *China Law & Practice* (December 05/ January 06) at 16–17; C Anderson and B Guo, 'Corporate Governance under the New Company Law (Part 1): Fiduciary Duties and Minority Shareholder Protection', *China Law & Practice* (April 2006) at 17–24, and (Part 2): 'Shareholder Lawsuits and Enforcement', *China Law & Practice* (May 2006) at 15–22.

matters.[51] This was a welcome step which provided necessary guidance to local people's courts.

One of the weaknesses of the 1998 Securities Law was that emphasis had been placed on administrative and criminal penalties, while not much attention had been given to civil liability and civil compensation. Compared with the numerous provisions on criminal and administrative penalties, provisions on civil liability and civil compensation were not closely addressed by the 1998 Securities Law.[52] Companies or individuals who committed insider trading or market manipulation were subject only to administrative and criminal penalties.[53] Provisions were absent in the 1998 Securities Law in other areas concerning civil liability and civil compensation, for example, in respect of the activities of securities investment consultant organizations.[54]

The 2005 Securities Law has now enlarged the scope of application of civil liability and civil compensation. Companies or individuals who commit insider trading or market manipulation are now subject not only to administrative and criminal penalties, but also to civil liability and civil compensation where losses are caused to investors.[55] Securities companies and their staff are liable for compensation if they commit fraud on their clients and losses are caused to them.[56] Where a securities company buys or sells securities or handles other transaction matters in violation

---

[51]   The Provisions of the Supreme People's Court on Several Issues in Application of 'the Company Law of the People's Republic of China' (*Zuigao Renmin Fayuan Guanyu Shiyong 'Zhonghua Renmin Gongheguo Gongsifa' Ruogan Wenti de Guiding*), issued by the Supreme People's Court on 28 April 2006, effective as of 9 May 2006; The Provisions of the Supreme People's Court on Several Issues in Application of 'the Company Law of the People's Republic of China' (*Zuigao Renmin Fayuan Guanyu Shiyong 'Zhonghua Renmin Gongheguo Gongsifa' Ruogan Wenti de Guiding*), issued by the Supreme People's Court on 12 May 2008, effective as of 19 May 2008.

[52]   Chapter 11 'Legal Responsibilities' consist of 36 articles, most of which were concerned with administrative and criminal penalties and only 3 articles (Arts 192, 202 and 207) were concerned with civil liability and civil compensation; in the 1998 Securities Law there were no more than 6 articles concerned with civil liability and civil compensation.

[53]   There were no provisions in the 1998 Securities Law that gave rise to civil compensatory consequences for insider trading and market manipulation.

[54]   There was no provision in the 1998 Securities Law concerning civil liability and civil compensation with respect to the activities of securities investment consultant organizations.

[55]   Arts 76 and 77 of the 2005 Securities Law.

[56]   Ibid., Art. 79, which prescribes a list of fraudulent activities of securities companies, such as purchasing or selling securities for a client without authorization from the clients, or purchasing or selling securities under the name of a client.

of instructions of a client, or handles matters other than transactions in violation of the true expression of intent of a client, which causes losses to the client, the securities company is liable for compensation.[57] Securities investment consultant organizations and their staff are held liable for compensation if they engage in an activity which they should not engage in and cause losses to investors.[58] Apart from these amendments, there are some other amendments that have enlarged the scope of the application of civil liability and civil compensation.[59] These amendments are regarded by leading scholars of Chinese securities and company law as significant changes for the protection of investors in China's securities market.[60]

For the first time, the 2005 Securities Law also provides for the establishment of a statutory securities investor protection fund, which is composed of the funds paid in by securities companies and other funds raised according to law.[61] In June 2005, before the promulgation of the 2005 Securities Law, the CSRC issued the Administrative Measures on the Securities Investor Protection Fund, which set out specific measures for raising, managing and using the securities investor protection fund.[62] On 29 September 2005, the China Securities Investor Protection Fund Co. Ltd was launched, which marked another positive step in the improvement of investor protection in China's securities market.[63]

The development of the law, regulations and judicial rules of China's

---

[57]   Ibid., Art. 210.

[58]   Ibid., Art. 171, which prescribes a range of activities that securities investment consultant organizations may not engage in, for example, to trade shares of a listed company that a securities investment consultant organization provides services.

[59]   Arts 190, 191 and 214 of the 2005 Securities Law, which give rise to civil liability and civil compensation in the context of underwriting or takeover activities. In accordance with Art. 190, for example, where a securities company underwrites or acts as an agent in the trading of securities offered publicly without being examined and approved, and has caused losses to the investors, the securities company shall be liable jointly and severally with the issuers.

[60]   See Liu, above n 27, at 48–49.

[61]   Art. 134, the 2005 Securities Law.

[62]   The Administrative Measures on the Securities Investor Protection Fund (*Zhengquan Touzizhe Baohu Jijin Guanli Banfa*), issued by the CSRC on 30 June 2005, effective as of 1 July 2005.

[63]   See a newspaper interview: 'An Important Component Part of Securities Investor Protection System – Answers to the Questions of Correspondence by Senior Member of the China Securities Investor Protection Fund Co. Ltd' (Touzizhe Baohu Tixi de Zhongyao Zucheng Bufen – Zhongguo Zhengquan Touzizhe Baohu Jijin Youxian Zeren Gongsi Fuzeren Da Jizhe Wen), *China Securities Journal (Zhongguo Zhengquan Bao)* (29 September 2005).

emerging securities market cannot be separated from the development of China's legal system and judicial reform since 1978 in response to China's economic and legal transformation.[64] The development of China's legal system and judiciary supports the regulation of China's securities market, while the development of securities law, regulations and judicial rules in turn promotes further reform of China's legal system. Among the primary legislation that is closely relevant to the development of the regulation of China's securities and futures market, the 1986 General Principles of Civil Law (1986 GPCL) lays down the general principles of civil and commercial law[65] and the 1999 Contract Law has transformed the previous separate system of contract laws into a unified system of contract law.[66] Procedurally speaking, the 1982 Civil Procedure Law was replaced by the 1991 Civil Procedure Law, which was further amended in 2007.[67]

All these developments have contributed directly and indirectly to the development of the legal, regulatory and judicial framework for the regulation of China's emerging securities market. The general principles of civil law, agency law, tort law, contract law, security law and civil procedure law form a basic and important part of the legal and procedural rules, in accordance with which the people's courts deal with disputes involving shares, bonds, futures contracts, and other types of securities. The 1995 SPC Futures Judicial Guidelines[68] set forth, for example, specific

---

[64]   For China's legal reform generally, see S. Lubman (ed.), *China's Legal Reform* (Oxford: Oxford University Press, 1996); A Hung-yee Chen, *An Introduction to the Legal System of the People's Republic of China* (3rd edn) (Singapore, Malaysia, Hong Kong: Butterworths Asia, 2004); S Lubman, *Bird in a Cage: Legal Reform in China after Mao* (Stanford: Stanford University Press, 1999).

[65]   The General Principles of Civil Law of the People's Republic of China, adopted by the National People's Congress on 12 April 1986, effective as of 1 January 1987. For the background of the enactment of the 1986 General Principles of Civil Law, see J.E. Epstein, 'The Evolution of China's General Principles of Civil Law', 34 *American Journal of Comparative Law*, 705 (1986) at 705–713.

[66]   The 1999 Contract Law of the People's Republic of China was enacted by the National People's Congress on 15 March 1999, and effective as of 1 October 1999. The contract laws promulgated during the 1980s and repealed by the 1999 Contract Law were the 1981 Economic Contract Law, as amended in 1993, the 1985 Economic Contract Law Involving Foreign Parties, and the 1987 Technology Contract Law. For the process of drafting the 1999 Contract Law, see P. Jiang, 'Drafting the Uniform Contract Law in China', 10 *Columbia Journal of Asian Law*, 245 (1996) at 245–258.

[67]   The Civil Procedure Law of the People's Republic of China, adopted by the National People's Congress and enacted on, and effective as of, 9 April 1991; the amendments were adopted by the Standing Committee of the National People's Congress on 28 October 2007, effective as of 1 April 2008.

[68]   See below n. 106.

principles by which the people's courts are to handle disputes in China's commodity and financial futures market,[69]including with respect to the correct application of law,[70] balancing between risks and interests,[71] balancing between fault and responsibilities,[72] and respecting the agreement of parties.[73] These principles were reiterated in the 2003 SPC Futures Judicial Provisions[74] and continue to guide the people's courts handling futures dispute cases.[75]

In essence, these principles are an extension and application of the legal principles stated in the 1986 GPCL,[76] the 1999 Contract Law,[77] and other

---

[69]   Section 1 the 1995 SPC Futures Judicial Guidelines.

[70]   Section 1(1) states that the people's courts should apply the 1986 General Principles of Civil Law as a primary source of law and also act in light of central and local administrative regulations and normative documents; where the disputes involve foreign, Hong Kong and Macao elements, the people's courts should also refer to international practice. Section One, the 1995 SPC Futures Judicial Guidelines.

[71]   Section 1(2) states that, given the fact that futures trading involves speculation and high risks, the people's courts should protect the lawful interests of trading parties on the one hand, and determine correctly the risks the parties should undertake. Section 1, the 1995 SPC Futures Judicial Guidelines.

[72]   Section 1(3) states that the people's court should analyse carefully whether parties in a dispute are at fault, the nature of the fault, how serious the fault is, and whether there is a causal link between the fault and losses, and on the basis of these findings determine the corresponding responsibilities. Section One, the 1995 SPC Futures Judicial Guidelines.

[73]   Section 1(4) states that the agreement of the parties should be treated as the basis for dealing with disputes between the parties as long as the agreement does not violate laws, regulations and customs of futures trading. Section One, the 1995 SPC Futures Judicial Guidelines.

[74]   Arts 1, 2, 3, the 2003 SPC Futures Judicial Provisions, see below n. 126, 127, 128, 129 and accompanying texts.

[75]   Ibid. Art. 1 of the 2003 SPC Futures Judicial Provisions: When adjudicating futures disputes, the people's courts are to act in accordance with the law to protect the legal rights and interests of the parties, determine correctly the risk and responsibilities each party bears, and uphold the order of futures markets. Art. 2 of the 2003 SPC Futures Judicial Provisions: When adjudicating futures contract disputes, the people's courts shall determine the liability of the party who breaches the contract in strict accordance with the parties' contract and agreements therein, so long as the agreements do not violate statutory law, mandatory administrative and regulatory provisions. Art. 3 of the 2003 SPC Futures Judicial Provisions: When adjudicating disputes, the people's courts shall determine the civil liabilities of the party at fault after an evaluation of the relative faults of the parties, the characteristics of the faults, the magnitude of the faults, and the causal relationship between the faults and loss suffered.

[76]   See above n. 65.

[77]   See above n. 66.

relevant primary laws.[78] The general legal principles of the 1986 GPCL and the 1999 Contract Law apply to all types of civil and commercial activities in China, while other relevant primary laws apply to the activities in their respective areas. Together, they have been and currently are a source of legal principles that the people's courts use to formulate specific principles applicable to certain types of dispute.

To a large extent, the patterns of, and relationships between, the development of the legal, regulatory and judicial framework and procedures in China's securities and futures market are no different from the patterns and relationships found in some other areas of China's commercial law and regulations. That is, legislation begins as tentative, ad hoc or local regulations, which pave the way to formal national regulation,[79] which is then further supplemented by detailed implementing rules from central government regulators.[80] Ultimately, national law is enacted by the National People's Congress or its Standing Committee, China's law-making body.[81] On the judicial side, the Supreme People's Court

---

[78]   Eg, The Securities Law of the PRC (1998 and 2005).

[79]   E.g., in the area of company law, before the enactment of the Company Law of the People's Republic of China by the Standing Committee of the National People's Congress in December 1993 (as amended in 1999, 2004 and 2005), there were a range of regulations, regulatory documents and implementing rules at both local and national level, including, among others, 1980 Measures of Fujian Province for Issuance of Bonds by Fujian Investment Enterprise Company (*Fujian Sheng Fujian Touzi Qiye Gongsi Zhaiquan Faxing Banfa*), adopted by the Standing Committee of Fujian Provincial People's Congress on December 24, 1979 and announced by the Fujian Government on 17 January 1980; 1985 Circular of the State Council on Further Clear-up and Consolidation of Companies (*Guowuyuan Guanyu Jinyibu Qingli he Zhengdun Gongsi de Tongzhi*), issued by the State Council on August 20, 1985; 1986 Regulations of Guangdong Province on Foreign Related Companies in Special Economic Zones (*Guangdong Sheng Jingji Tequ Shewai Gongsi Tiaoli*), adopted by the Standing Committee of Guangdong Provincial Sixth People's Congress on 28 September 1986 and promulgated on 20 October 1986; 1991 Trial Measures of Xiamen City for Establishment of Company Limited by Shares (*Xiamen Shi Zujian Gufen Youxian Gongsi Shidian Banfa*), issued by the Xiamen Government on 24 July 1991; 1992 Tentative Regulations of Shanghai City on Company Limited by Shares (*Shanghai Shi Gufen Youxian Gongsi Zanxing Guiding*), issued by the Shanghai City Government on 18 May 1992; 1992 Opinions on Standardization of Limited Liability Company (*Youxian Zeren Gongsi Guifan Yijian*), issued by the State Commission for Economic System Reform on 15 May 1992; and 1992 Opinions on Standardization of Company Limited by Shares (*Gufen Youxian Gongsi Guifan Yijian*), issued by the State Commission for Economic System Reform on 15 May 1992.

[80]   Ibid.

[81]   Ibid.

formulates jurisdiction-specific procedural principles and guidelines for dispute resolution in accordance with the legal and procedural principles stated in the 1991 Civil Procedure Law, as amended in 2007, the 1986 GPCL, other primary legislation such as the 1999 Contract Law, and special laws and regulations of that area.[82]

Despite these developments and achievements, the securities law, regulations and judicial rules of China's emerging securities market are still at an early stage of development, compared with those markets where the rule of law and governance are well established. Problems, such as those discussed in the following parts of this chapter, give rise to concerns about the future development of the legal, regulatory and judicial framework of China's emerging securities market. On the general level of China's legal system, further legal and judicial reforms are necessary for building the rule of law, good governance, and for improving the operation of the legal system, such as improving the problematic gap between the law on the books and the law in practice with respect to implementation and enforcement of the law.

REGULATION OF THE COMMODITY AND FINANCIAL FUTURES MARKET: TOWARDS A BALANCED LEGAL, REGULATORY AND JUDICIAL FRAMEWORK

The early 1990s witnessed the rapid establishment of futures exchanges in China. At the height of the expansion, 50 futures exchanges were established in major cities throughout the country.[83] In 1993, this blind

---

[82]   E.g., the Supreme People's Court formulated in 2000 Several Provisions of the Supreme People's Court on Hearing Disputes Involving Negotiable Instruments (*Zuigao Renmin Fayuan Guanyu Shenli Piaoju Jiufen Anjian Ruogan Wenti de Guiding*), in 2003 Several Provisions of the Supreme People's Court on Hearing Civil Compensation Cases Arising From False Statement on the Securities Market (*Zuigao Remin Fayuan Guanyu Shenli Zhengquan Shichang Yin Xujiachengshu Yinfa de Minshi Peichang Anjian de Ruogan Guiding*), and in 2005 Interpretations of the Supreme People's Court on Application of Law in Hearing Disputes on Contracts Involving State Owned Land Use Rights (*Zuigao Remin Fayuan Guanyu Shenli Sheji Guoyou Tudi Shiyongquan Hetong Jiufen Anjian Shiyong Falü Wenti de Jieshi*), in accordance with the 1991 Civil Procedural Law, 1986 General Principles of Civil Law, 1999 Contract Law, 1995 Negotiable Law (as amended in 2004), 1998 Securities Law (as amended in 2005), 1993 Company Law (as amended in 1999, 2004 and 2005), 1998 Land Administration Law (as amended in 2004), and 1994 Urban Real Estate Administration Law (as amended in 2007).
[83]   Q. Wu and X. Jiang (eds), *Civil Liabilities of Futures Trading (Qihuo Jiaoyi Minshi Zeren)* (China Legal System Publishing House, 2003), at 1 (looking briefly

expansion led to problems with excessive speculative trading and various illegal activities, which prompted the government to impose tight control over the rapid growth and ensuing activities of the futures market.[84] A consolidation process substantially reduced the number of futures exchanges to 14 by the middle of the 1990s.[85] This consolidation process continued into the late 1990s, whereby the remaining 14 futures exchanges were further consolidated to the 3 current exchanges:[86] the Zhengzhou Commodity Exchange,[87] the Shanghai Futures Exchange,[88] and the Dalian Commodity Exchange.[89] Alongside the expansion of the futures market, over 1000 futures trading firms were founded, although this number has reduced subsequently to fewer than 200.[90]

Between 1993 and 1998, various regulations were issued by the central and local governments, including the 1993 Provisional Measures on the

---

at the history of China's futures market, the author noted that the futures market 'experienced a period of blind expansion during the early stage of trial . . .').

[84] On 14 November 1993, the State Council issued the Notice of the State Council on Firmly Stopping Blind Development of the Futures Market (*Guowuyuan Guanyu Jianjue Zhizhi Qihuo Shichang Mangmu Fazhan de Tongzhi*), which stated, among other things, that 'Futures markets . . . high risk and speculation, . . . according to the actual circumstances of our country at the current stage, except for selecting a few commodities and locations for trial experimentation, must be strictly controlled and may not develop blindly.' See *Guowuyuan guan yu jian jue zhi zhi qi huo shi chang mang mu fa zhan de tong zhi* (Notice of the State Council on Firmly Stopping Blind Development of the Futures Market) (promulgated by the State Council on, and effective as of, 14 November 1993).

[85] See Q. Wu and X. Jiang, above n. 83, at 1.

[86] The Notice of the State Council on Further Consolidation and Standardization of the Futures Market issued on 1 August 1998 set out, among other things, a plan for the consolidation of the existing 14 futures exchanges into 3 by merging or restructuring them. For example, the Notice required that Shanghai Commodity Exchange, Shanghai Metal Exchange and Shanghai Grain & Oil Exchange be merged into one as Shanghai Futures Exchange. See *Guowuyuan guan yu jin yi bu zheng dun he guifan qi huo shi chang de tong zhi* (The Notice of the State Council on Further Consolidation and Standardization of the Futures Market) (promulgated by the State Council on, and effective as of, 1 August 1998).

[87] Above n. 14.

[88] Above n. 3.

[89] Dalian Commodity Exchange, located in Dalian, Liaoning, was established on 28 February 1993. Futures products currently include corn, soybeans No.1 and No.2, soybean meal, soybean oil, linear low density polyethylene (LLDPE) and RBD palm oil futures contracts. Dalian Commodity Exchange Home Page (follow 'About the Exchange' ('Guan Yu Jiao Yi Suo').

[90] See Q. Wu and X. Jiang, above n. 83, at 1.

Administration of Registration of Futures Broker Firms,[91] the 1993 Circular of the State Council on Firmly Stopping Blind Development of the Futures Market,[92] the 1994 Opinion of the State Council Securities Committee on Firmly Stopping Blind Development of the Futures Market,[93] the 1994 Provisional Measures on the Administration of Personnel Working in Futures Business Organizations,[94] the 1994 Regulations on the Administration of Shanghai Futures Market,[95] and the 1998 Circular of the State Council on Further Consolidation and Standardization of the Futures Market.[96] The central purpose of these measures was to develop a futures market in China, but with great caution: on one hand, the futures market was allowed to continue to exist and develop, but, on the other hand, its continued existence and development was tightly controlled and regulated.[97] For instance, some commod-

---

[91] The Provisional Measures on the Administration of Registration of Futures Broker Firms (*Qi huo jing ji gong si deng ji guan li zhan xing ban fa*), promulgated by the State Administration for Industry and Commerce on, and effective as of, 28 April 1993.

[92] See Notice of the State Council on Firmly Stopping Blind Development of the Futures Market (*Guowuyuan guan yu jian jue zhi zhi qi huo shi chang mang mu fa zhan de tong zhi*), promulgated by the State Council on, and effective as of, 14 November 1993.

[93] Notice of the General Office of the State Council Reissuing the Request of the State Council Securities Commission Seeking Instructions on Several Opinions on Firmly Stopping Blind Development of the Futures Market (*Guowuyuan ban gong ting zhuan fa Guowuyuan zheng quan wei yuan hui guan yu jian jue zhi zhi qi huo shi chang mang mu fa zhan ruo gan yi jian qing shi de tong zhi*), promulgated by the General Office of the State Council on, and effective as of, 16 May 1994.

[94] The Provisional Measures on the Administration of Personnel Working in Futures Business Organizations (*Qi huo jing ying ji gou gong ye ren yuan guan li zhan xing ban fa*), promulgated by the State Council Securities Commission on, and effective as of, 7 November 1994.

[95] The Regulations on the Administration of Shanghai Futures Market (*Shanghai shi qi huo shi chang guan li gui ding*), promulgated by the Shanghai Municipal Government on 5 December 1994, effective 1 January 1995 (Notice No. 87).

[96] See The Notice of the State Council on Further Consolidation and Standardization of the Futures Market (*Guowuyuan guan yu jin yi bu zheng dun he guifan qi huo shi chang de tong zhi*), promulgated by the State Council on, and effective as of, 1 August 1998.

[97] One of the principles stated in the 1993 Notice of the State Council on Firmly Stopping Blind Development of Futures Market was 'To start in a standardized manner; to strengthen legislation; to experiment all things . . . ' (*guifan qibu, jiaqiang lifa, yiqie jingguo shiyan he yange kongzhi*). See Notice of the State Council on Firmly Stopping Blind Development of the Futures Market (*Guowuyuan guan yu jian jue zhi zhi qi huo shi chang mang mu fa zhan de tong*

ity futures contracts were removed from the product list of commodity exchanges,[98] trading was suspended with foreign exchange futures[99] and government bond futures,[100] and offshore trading of commodity futures products was cancelled.[101]

A highly visible rise in litigation prompted the Supreme People's Court to develop guidelines to direct the local courts in dealing with futures dispute cases. In April 1995, the Supreme People's Court held a symposium to discuss the issues arising in the adjudication of futures disputes in the people's courts.[102] Judges from 14 high people's courts and 6 intermediate people's courts attended the symposium.[103] Prominent issues of concern included the principles for handling futures cases, the jurisdiction of the people's courts over futures cases, the qualifications necessary to engage in futures trading, the legal status and civil liability of brokers,

---

zhi), promulgated by the State Council on, and effective as of 14 November 1993.

[98]   See The Circular of the State Council Securities Committee Asking for Instructions on Stopping Trading Futures of Steel, Sugar and Coal (*Guowuyuan zheng quan wei yuan hui guan yu ging zhi gang cai, shi tang, mei tan qi huo jiao yi qing shi de tong zhi*), issued by the General Office of the State Council on 6 April 1994 (suspending further trading and listing of standard futures contracts of steel, sugar and coal).

[99]   See The Circular on the Summary of the Meeting Implementing the Circular on Sternly Investigating and Dealing with Illegal Trading Activities in Foreign Exchange Futures and Foreign Exchange Deposit Trading (*Guan yu guan che 'Guan yu yan li cha chu fei fa wai hui qi huo he wai hui an jin jiao yi huo dong de tong zhi' de hui yi ji yao de tong zhi*), issued jointly by the CSRC, the State Administration of Foreign Exchange, the State Administration for Industry and Commerce and the Ministry of Public Security on 14 December 1994. The Circular stated that '. . . in a long period of time in the future, our country will not engage in trials in these areas . . .', at 1.

[100]   See The Urgent Circular on Suspension of Trials of Government Bond Futures Trading (*Guan yu zhan ting guo zhai qi huo jiao yi shi dian de jin ji tong zhi*), issued by the CSRC on 17 May 1995. According to the Circular, the trial of trading government bond futures was suspended with effect as of 18 May 1995, and 31 May 1995 was set as the deadline for clearing out existing positions by exchanges. Ibid.

[101]   See the Circular on Relevant Issues about Cancellation by Futures Broker Firms of Offshore Futures Business (*Guanyu Qihuo Jingji Gongsi Zhuxiao Jingwai Qihuo Yewu Youguan Wenti de Tongzhi*), issued by the CSRC on 12 September 1994. This required futures broker firms to stop their offshore futures business with immediate effect, not to accept new customers, and not to take on new orders.

[102]   The Symposium of the Supreme People's Court on Adjudication of Cases of Futures Disputes (*Zuigao Renmin Fayuan Guanyu Shenli Qihuo Jiufen Anjian Zoutanhui*), held at Chengdu city, Sichuan province, on 18–21 April 1995.

[103]   Ibid.

the nature of contract and tort liability, the invalidity of civil acts relating to futures transactions and the determination of civil liability relating to such acts,[104] the trading of foreign exchange deposits, and the applicable burden of proof in futures cases.[105]

In October 1995, the Supreme People's Court issued futures judicial guidelines (1995 SPC Futures Judicial Guidelines),[106] which enumerated the symposium's positions and represented the Court's comprehensive response to the problematic increase of futures disputes in the people's courts. It emphasized that the people's courts' main tasks were to deal with futures disputes fairly and expediently, to protect the lawful rights and interests of the parties, to punish illegal trading activities, and to maintain order in the futures market.[107] The 1995 SPC Futures Judicial Guidelines were embraced by the people's courts and became the first comprehensive set of provisional guidelines addressing substantial and procedural issues in the adjudication of futures disputes.

In addition to the Supreme People's Court's April symposium, local regulatory bodies held similar seminars and discussions. In Shanghai, the location of several futures exchanges and the site of active and substantial futures trading, the Shanghai Securities Regulatory Office, in conjunction with the Shanghai Commodity Exchange, the Metal Exchange and the Grain & Oil Exchange, organized a seminar in June 1998 to discuss how to deal with futures disputes arising particularly in the futures market of Shanghai.[108] Participants included judges from the Shanghai High

---

[104]   For example, where futures broker firms engage in futures brokerage business without approval and licence, they shall not be held responsible for civil compensation if there is evidence to prove that the broker firm carries out futures trading in accordance with the clients' instruction and the loss suffered by the client was caused by normal market risk. Section Seven, the Notice of the Supreme People's Court on Circulating 'Minutes of the Symposium of the Supreme People's Court on Adjudication of Cases of Futures Disputes' (*Zuigao Renmin Fayuan Yinfa Guanyu Shenli Qihuo Jiufen Anjian Zuotanhui Jiyao de Tongzhi*).

[105]   The Symposium of the Supreme People's Court on Adjudication of Cases of Futures Disputes (*Zuigao Renmin Fayuan Guanyu Shenli Qihuo Jiufen Anjian Zoutanhui*), above n. 102.

[106]   The Notice of the Supreme People's Court on Circulating 'Minutes of the Symposium of the Supreme People's Court on Adjudication of Cases of Futures Disputes' (*Zuigao Renmin Fayuan Yinfa Guanyu Shenli Qihuo Jiufen Anjian Zuotanhui Jiyao de Tongzhi*), issued by the Supreme People's Court on 27 October 1995.

[107]   Section 1, the 1995 SPC Futures Judicial Guidelines.

[108]   The Summary of Shanghai Seminar on Handling Futures Trading Disputes (*Shanghai Qihuo Jiaoyi Jiufen Chuli Yantaohui Jiyao*), 20 July 1998 in Z. Futang et al., *Commentary and Analysis on Futures Trading Dispute Cases* (*Qihuo Jiaoyi Jiufen Anli Pingxi*) (Shanghai: Xuelin Publishing House, 1998) at 226–33.

People's Court and several intermediate and district courts in Shanghai.[109] The seminar was a response to an increasing number of futures disputes in Shanghai and created a forum to address new issues and problems, including those that were not fully addressed by the 1995 SPC Futures Judicial Guidelines.

The Asian financial crisis erupted in 1997–1998, pushing many countries into recession and threatening China's financial system.[110] Two years later, in late 1999, only a limited number of state-owned enterprises were allowed to engage in offshore trading of commodities futures products for hedging purposes, and even those transactions were subject to approval by government regulators.[111] A number of regulatory protocols were issued to regulate and facilitate this activity, including the Circular on Relevant Issues about Application for Offshore Futures Business[112] and the Administrative Measures on Offshore Futures Hedging Business by State-owned Enterprises.[113] Under these protocols, central government approval was required for any engagement in offshore trading of commodities futures products by state-owned enterprises.[114] Such engagements also needed to meet conditions set out in Articles 6,[115] 7 and 8 of

---

[109] Z. Futang et al., *Commentary and Analysis on Futures Trading Dispute Cases* (*Qihuo Jiaoyi Jiufen Anli Pingxi*) (Shanghai: Xuelin Publishing House, 1998) at 226–27.

[110] For a general discussion about the 1997–1998 Asian financial crisis, see G.W. Noble and J. Ravenhill, *The Asian Financial Crisis and the Architecture of Global Finance* (Cambridge: Cambridge University Press, 2000).

[111] See above nn. 114, 115 and 116.

[112] See CSRC, 'The Circular on Relevant Issues about Application for Offshore Futures Business' (*Guanyu Shenqing Jingwai Qihuo Yewu Youguan Wenti de Tongzhi*) (15 October 1999).

[113] CSRC, 'The Administrative Measures on Offshore Futures Hedging Business by State-owned Enterprises' (*Guoyou Qiye Jingwai Qihuo Taoqi Baozhi Yewu Guanli Banfa*), issued jointly with the State Bureau of Foreign Exchange and four other government departments on 24 May 2001.

[114] Art. 5 (1) of the 2001 Administrative Measures on Offshore Futures Hedging Business by State-owned Enterprises states that enterprises engaging in offshore futures business must be approved by the State Council.

[115] Art. 6 sets out a list of conditions for engagement in offshore futures business by state-owned enterprises including, among others, that the enterprise has import and export rights (Art. 6 (2)); there is definitely a hedging need in the offshore futures market for import and export commodities or other commodities purchased or sold on the offshore spot market (Art. 6 (3)); there is a sound and comprehensive management system for offshore futures business (Art. 6 (4)); and there are at least three persons who have offshore futures business experience over one year and who have obtained qualifications certified by the CSRC or offshore futures regulators, including a special futures risk management person, and there

the Administrative Measures on Offshore Futures Hedging Business by State-owned Enterprises:[116] these regulatory requirements and procedures reflected the government's cautious position that offshore trading was necessary only insofar as to hedge against risks arising from fluctuation of exchange rates or other international market risks; otherwise speculative offshore trading was not permissible.[117]

In June 1999, the State Council made an important step in the regulation of the futures market by promulgating the 1999 Provisional Regulations on the Administration of Futures Market (1999 Provisional Regulations),[118] the first formal regulations on futures trading. In August 1999, the CSRC, one of whose functions as the country's securities regulator is to implement the State Council's policy and formulate detailed securities regulatory rules, set forth four provisions in accordance with the 1999 Provisional Regulations. The four provisions addressed the regulation of the futures exchange,[119] the regulation of futures broker firms,[120] enacted qualification requirements for senior managers in futures broker firms,[121] and enacted qualification requirements for entering into the

---

is at least one senior management person who knows offshore futures trading and who has satisfied other requirements of the CSRC (Art. 6 (6)) The Administrative Measures on Offshore Futures Hedging Business by State-owned Enterprises (*Guoyou Qiye Jingwai Qihuo Taoqi Baozhi Yewu Guanli Banfa*).

[116] Art. 7 requires an applicant enterprise to submit a list of application documents including, among others, the business licence and qualification as an import and export enterprise; Article 8 requires the applicant enterprise, once approved, to obtain the relevant licence to register with the relevant authorities before engaging in offshore futures trading. The Administrative Measures on Offshore Futures Hedging Business by State-owned Enterprises (*Guoyou Qiye Jingwai Qihuo Taoqi Baozhi Yewu Guanli Banfa*).

[117] The 2001 Administrative Measures on Offshore Futures Hedging Business by State-owned Enterprises grant the CSRC a power to conduct routine inspections of the state-owned enterprises who have a licence to engage in offshore trading of commodities futures products; one of the matters within such inspection is whether the enterprise concerned carries out speculative trading. Art. 37 (4), the Administrative Measures on Offshore Futures Hedging Business by State-owned Enterprises (*Guoyou Qiye Jingwai Qihuo Taoqi Baozhi Yewu Guanli Banfa*).

[118] The 1999 Provisional Regulations on the Administration of Futures Trading (*Qihuo Jiaoyi Guanli Zanxing Tiaoli*) was promulgated by the State Council on 2 June 1999 and effective from 1 September, 1999.

[119] The Measures on the Administration of Futures Exchanges (*Qihuo Jiaoyisuo Guanli Banfa*), issued by the CSRC on 31 August 1999.

[120] The Measures on the Administration of Futures Broker Firms (*Qihuo Jingji Gongsi Guanli Banfa*), issued by the CSRC on 31 August 1999.

[121] The Measures on the Administration of Qualifications for Appointment of Senior Management Personnel of Futures Broker Firms (*Qihuo Jingji Gongsi*

futures business.[122] In January and May 2002, those four provisions were amended by the CSRC, which changed some regulated areas, such as that of futures broker firms,[123] and added more detailed provisions in others.[124] Altogether, the 1999 Provisional Regulations and the four CSRC provisions served as an impetus to the standardization of China's new futures market and also provided guidance to the people's courts, which were handling the influx of futures disputes.

On the judicial side, the Supreme People's Court constructed a new guideline in July 1999, based on the 1995 SPC Futures Judicial Guidelines and the people's courts' experiences with futures cases. After 4 drafting stages and 28 drafts,[125] the new guideline was finalized in May 2003.[126] The 2003 Provisions of the Supreme People's Court on Several Issues Concerning Adjudication of Cases of Futures Disputes (2003 SPC Futures Judicial Provisions)[127] was the product of careful work based on

---

Gaoji Guanli Renyuan Renzhi Zige Guanli Banfa), issued by the CSRC on 31 August 1999.

[122] The Measures on the Administration of Qualifications for Personnel Engaging in Futures Business (*Qihuoye Congye Renyuan Zige Guanli Banfa*), issued by the CSRC on 31 August 1999.

[123] E.g., futures broker firms were allowed to engage in futures consultancy and training business under Art. 6 (2) of the 2002 Measures on the Administration of Futures Broker Firms while this provision was not spelled out in the 1999 Measures on the Administration of Futures Broker Firms.

[124] E.g., the 2002 Measures on the Administration of Futures Exchanges has more detailed provisions concerning deposits made by members of a futures exchange than in the 1999 Measures on the Administration of Futures Exchanges.

[125] The drafting started on 21 July 1999. The first stage was to work on the new issues and questions that had emerged since 1995 and to incorporate them into the drafts; starting from May 2001, the second stage was to focus on the structure; starting from early 2002, the third stage was to consult with the CSRC, futures exchanges and the Association of Futures Business; during February and May 2003, the fourth stage was to go through several rounds of discussions by the Adjudication Committee of the Supreme People's Court. See B. Jiang (ed.), *Understanding and Application of 'the 2003 Provisions of the Supreme People's Court on Several Issues Concerning Adjudication of Cases of Futures Disputes' ('Zuigao Renmin Fayuan Guanyu Shenli Qihuo Jiufen Anjian Ruogan Wenti de Guiding' de Lijie Yu Shiyong)*, compiled by the Second Division Court of the Supreme People's Court (Beijing: the People's Court Publishing House, 2003) at 18–19.

[126] The 2003 Provisions of the Supreme People's Court on Several Issues Concerning Adjudication of Cases of Futures Disputes (*Zuigao Renmin Fayuan Guanyu Shenli Qihuo Jiufen Anjian Ruogan Wenti de Guiding*), adopted by the Adjudication Committee of the Supreme People's Court on 16 May 2003, effective as of 1 July 2003.

[127] Ibid.

consultation with the futures business sector and market regulators.[128] It represented a unified understanding of major civil law issues concerning the futures market as they were recognized by the people's courts, the regulators and the futures business.[129]

Compared with the 1995 SPC Futures Judicial Guidelines, the 2003 SPC Futures Judicial Provisions provided the people's courts with more mature and settled guidelines for handling futures disputes. For example, the 2003 SPC Futures Judicial Provisions refined the 1995 SPC Futures Judicial Guidelines' position regarding the burden of proof in cases where a futures broker firm may not have carried out a client's trading instruction in the market.[130] Also, the 2003 SPC Futures Judicial Provisions made clear that the amount of positions that a futures exchange or a futures broker firm closes out must equal the margin of that futures broker firm or that of its client; the loss caused by an excessive liquidation would be borne by those forcing liquidation.[131] Such an equity-based principle was absent from the 1995 SPC Futures Judicial Guidelines and the 1999 Provisional Regulations.[132]

In 2007, the 1999 Provisional Regulations were amended comprehensively, including by means of 20 new articles in the 2007 Regulations on the Administration of Futures Trading (2007 Regulations).[133] Important

---

[128] It took nearly four years for the Supreme People's Court to complete the draft, during which period the Supreme People's Court consulted with the CSRC, futures exchanges and the Association of Futures Business.

[129] See an interview by news reporter with Jiang Bixin, deputy president of the Supreme People's Court, on the application of the 2003 Provisions of the Supreme People's Court on Several Issues Concerning Adjudication of Cases of Futures Disputes, J. Bixin (ed.), *Understanding and Application of 'the 2003 Provisions of the Supreme People's Court on Several Issues Concerning Adjudication of Cases of Futures Disputes' ('Zuigao Renmin Fayuan Guanyu Shenli Qihuo Jiufen Anjian Ruogan Wenti de Guiding' de Lijie Yu Shiyong)*, compiled by the Second Division Court of the Supreme People's Court (Beijing: the People's Court Publishing House, 2003) at 19.

[130] See Arts 56 and 57 of the 2003 SPC Futures Judicial Provisions and Section Nine of the 1995 SPC Futures Judicial Guidelines.

[131] Art. 39 of the 2003 SPC Futures Judicial Provisions states that 'the amount of positions that a futures exchange or a futures broker firm close out should be basically equal to the amount of margin that a futures broker firm or a client has to add up. The loss caused by an excessive liquidation shall be borne by those who take the forced liquidation measure.'

[132] Section Five (Point 6) of the 1995 SPC Futures Judicial Guidelines and Article 41 of the 1999 Provisional Regulations addressed the issue of forced liquidation but neither of them addressed the issue of excessive forced liquidation and consequent liabilities.

[133] The 2007 Regulations on the Administration of Futures Trading has 91 articles, an increase from 71 articles in the 1999 Provisional Regulations on the

changes included the relaxation of a previous ban on financial institutions to engage in futures trading,[134] the creation of a futures investor protection fund,[135] and the introduction of a division system[136] between settlement members (*jiesuan huiyuan*) and non-settlement members (*fei jiesuan huiyuan*). On the whole, the 2007 Regulations produced a balanced regulatory framework for China's commodity and financial futures market by lifting some unnecessary restrictions on normal futures trading activities and participants; the 2007 Regulations also cautiously implemented strong government supervision of the market.

Out of the 91 articles in the 2007 Regulations, about 25 articles leave a provision open[137] or refer certain matters to regulations yet to be issued.[138] Apart from the uncertainty and confusion the open provisions create, full operation of the regulatory system under the 2007 Regulations remains dependent on those regulations and provisions not yet issued; this leaves the regulatory system vulnerable to inconsistency amidst the competing interests of government authorities. To mitigate this, the four

---

Administration of Futures Trading. The 2007 Regulations on the Administration of Futures Trading (*Qihuo Jiaoyi Guanli Tiaoli*), promulgated by the State Council on 6 March 2007, effective as of 15 April 2007.

[134]   Art. 30 of the 1999 Provisional Regulations on the Administration of Futures Trading listed a number of institutions and individuals, including financial institutions, who may not engage in futures trading and for whom futures broker firms may not accept entrustments to trade futures. See ibid., Art. 26 of the 2007 Regulations on the Administration of Futures Trading has now removed financial institutions from this list.

[135]   Art. 54 of the 2007 Regulations on the Administration of Futures Trading. See also Provisional Measures on the Administration of Futures Investors Protection Fund (*Qihuo Touzizhe Baozhang Jijin Guanli Zhanxing Banfa*), issued in accordance with Art. 54 the 2007 Regulations on the Administration of Futures Trading by the CSRC and the Ministry of Finance on 19 April 2007, effective as of 1 August 2007.

[136]   In accordance with Art. 8 of the 2007 Regulations on the Administration of Futures Trading, futures exchanges may adopt a system of membership consisting of settlement members and non-settlement members. Articles 61–68 of the 2007 Measures on the Administration of Futures Exchanges provide for further provisions regarding approval and operation of this division system.

[137]   Eg, Art. 16 stipulates a list of conditions for establishment of a futures company, the last one of which is 'other conditions stipulated by the futures regulator of the State Council'.

[138]   Eg, in accordance with Art. 46, measures concerning offshore futures trading by institutions or individuals shall be formulated by the futures regulator of the State Council in consultation with a number of other government departments and regulators, such as a foreign exchange authority, and be approved by the State Council.

implementing provisions of the 1999 Provisional Regulations, as amended in 2002, were again amended to accommodate the 2007 Regulations.[139]

In contrast to the tentative and ad hoc regulations and regulatory measures in the early 1990s, China has since gradually established a legal and regulatory framework for the commodity and financial futures market, with the 2007 Regulations at the centre. However, one remaining issue is whether a special futures law will ultimately be enacted to regulate the market. In the early 1990s, the drafting process for a law governing futures trading started, but was suspended during the government's campaign to stop a blind expansion of China's futures market.[140] In March 2006, a drafting team was set up with the task of drafting the Futures Trading Law.[141] When the Futures Trading Law is passed in the future, China's securities and futures law will be a tripartite body consisting of a Securities Law, Securities Investment Fund Law and Futures Trading Law.

The form of a futures law in China is contested: should a separate futures law operate alongside the 2005 Securities Law and the 2003 Securities Investment Fund Law, or, alternatively, should the regulation of the futures market fall within the purview of the 2005 Securities Law, with supplemental support from further administrative regulations covering specific issues of the futures market and futures trading? Some judges, regulators and scholars advocate a comprehensive futures law so that China may develop a market of the financial futures products, such as foreign exchange futures and share index futures.[142] Given that the

---

[139] The 2002 Measures on the Administration of Qualifications for Appointment of Senior Management Personnel of Futures Broker Firms, amended on and effective as of 4 July 2007, renamed as Measures on the Administration of Qualifications for Appointment of Directors, Supervisors and Senior Management Personnel of Futures Company (*Qihuo Gongsi Dongshi, Jianshi he Gaoji Guanli Renyuan Renzhi Zige Guanli Banfa*). The 2002 Measures on the Administration of Qualifications for Personnel Engaging in Futures Business, amended on and effective as of 4 July 2007, renamed as Measures on the Administration of Personnel Engaging in Futures Business (*Qihuo Congye Renyuan Guanli Banfa*). The 2002 Measures on the Administration of Futures Exchanges, amended on 28 March 2007 and effective as of 15 April 2007. The 2002 Measures on the Administration of Futures Broker Firms, amended on 28 March 2007 and effective as of 15 April, 2007, renamed as Measures on the Administration of Futures Company (*Qihuo Gongsi Guanli Banfa*).

[140] See Wu and Jiang, above n. 83, at 1.

[141] Since then the drafting team has been working on the draft and made substantial progress. See news report: 'Significant Progress has been Made with Legislation of Futures Trading of Our Country' (*Woguo Qihuo Jiaoyi Lifa Qude Zhongda Jinzhan*) (4 December 2007).

[142] Wu and Jiang, above n. 83, at 2–3.

financial futures and commodity futures markets in China are expected to develop substantially in the future in line with China's economic growth and further reform towards a market economy,[143] the promulgation of a futures law represents a sensible step towards promoting a set of uniform principles and rules for the regulation and development of China's futures market, and also for the resolution of disputes arising in the futures market.

The emergence and expansion of a commodity and financial futures market in China went through a rather problematic period in the 1990s. The market was dominated by market manipulation, unauthorized trading by numerous futures firms, irregularities of various kinds and excessive speculation. The government's campaign from 1993 to 1999 to stop such a situation and halt the blind development of China's futures market led to a substantial reduction of futures exchanges, the cancellation of certain futures products, the suspension of offshore futures trading and the closure of the government bond futures market. Arguably, this campaign and the resulting regulations were serious and caused excessive interventions and interruptions in the market. From the government's point of view, such conditions were not conducive to China's growth, beyond a few experimental futures products in a limited number of futures exchanges. Given the seriousness of the problem, its impact on the financial market, on public confidence, and on the economy as a whole, the government's actions proved to be necessary to maintain social stability and public confidence in the fragile financial market.

China's lack of coherent and comprehensive regulation of the commodity and financial futures market in its early years contributed to the frequency of problems. The 1999 Provisional Regulations and the four implementing rules provided an impetus to the standardization of China's new futures market. The revised 2007 Regulations further implemented rules extending the securities and futures regulatory framework established by the 1999 Provisional Regulations and the 2005 Securities Law. The 2007 Regulations represent a step toward building a balanced regulatory framework for

---

[143] Eg, trading of steel futures contracts, which was suspended in 1994, was launched on the Shanghai Futures Exchange on 27 March, 2009. The launch of futures contracts for two construction steel products – reinforcing steel bar and wire rod – is seen as a major event in China, the world's largest producer and consumer of the metal. It is hailed as a sign that China's steel industry has taken an important step forward in the process of marketization. See S. James, 'Chinese Steel Futures Market Scheduled for Launch Today', 27 March 2009 (New York: Reuters); and id., 'Analysis: China's Launch of Steel Futures May Change Global Pricing System', 30 March 2009.

China's commodity and financial futures market. However, full operation of the regulatory system under the 2007 Regulations depends upon further development of regulation and clarification of open provisions. As a result, the framework remains subject to uncertain and confused application.

China's emerging commodity and financial futures market has changed significantly since the establishment of the first commodity futures exchange in Zhengzhou in October 1990. These changes reflect a transition in China's commodity and financial futures market and a regulatory framework that has aligned the market with China's overall economic, legal and judicial reform, and in particular, the development of China's capital market. China's commodity and, financial futures market in the early 1990s demonstrated how crucial an appropriate and balanced legal, regulatory and judicial framework is to ensuring a healthy and sustainable development of commodity and financial futures markets. Despite past government policy and the tight control over securities and futures markets, China's regulatory experiences will be instrumental to accomplishing this goal. The recent regulatory developments in the revised 2007 Regulations, such as the relaxation of a previous ban on financial institutions engaging in futures trading,[144] suggest that China is moving closer to building a well-suited and well-balanced legal, regulatory and judicial framework for its commodity and financial futures exchange markets.[145]

SECURITIES CIVIL LITIGATION ARISING FROM FALSE STATEMENTS: LIMITATION OF THE ROLE OF THE PEOPLE'S COURT

China's securities regulatory authority has been active in the past decades in tackling various forms of securities fraud on the market by means of administrative penalties and criminal charges, in order to protect the interests of investors and to maintain the integrity of China's securities

---

[144]   Above n. 134. As opposed to Art. 30 of the 1999 Provisional Regulations, financial institutions are not included under Art. 26 of the 2007 Regulations on the Administration of Futures Trading. See the 1999 Provisional Regulations on the Admininistration of Futures Trading, above n. 118; see also the 2007 Regulations on the Admininistration of Futures Trading, above n 133.

[145]   For discussion on China's securities regulation and the stages of development since 1980s, see Zhu, above n. 7. See also S. Zhu, *Securities Dispute Resolution in China* (Aldershot, England; Burlington, VT, USA: Ashgate, 2007) in particular ch. 1, 'The Legal, Regulatory and Judicial Framework', at 7–41 and ch. 7, 'The Development of Securities Dispute Resolution in China', at 197–231.

market.[146] The 1993 Provisional Measures on Prohibition of Securities Fraud was promulgated to deal specifically with insider trading, market manipulation, false disclosure of information and other forms of securities fraud.[147] Similar provisions were promulgated in the 1993 Provisional Regulations on Share Issuing and Trading,[148] the 1993 Company Law,[149] and the 1998 Securities Law.[150] The revised 1997 Criminal Law, for the first time, created securities-related criminal offences, targeting various forms of securities fraud.[151] Many firms and individuals who committed securities fraud have been investigated and punished by the CSRC.[152] Where criminal offences were committed, detected and tried, the offenders who were found guilty were subject to punishments by criminal courts.[153]

On the other hand, these laws and regulations failed to provide adequate protection for the civil rights and interests of investors who

---

[146]   See Zhu, above n. 7, at 117–125, 187–206.

[147]   See above n. 20.

[148]   See above n. 19. According to Art. 72, e.g., those who commit insider trading are subject to a fine between 50 000 and 500 000 yuan in addition to confiscation of illegal gain.

[149]   See above n. 26. Art. 212, e.g., states that where companies provide shareholders and the public with false financial reports or conceal material facts the person in charge or other directly responsible person shall be fined between 10 000 and 100 000 yuan and charged where crimes are committed.

[150]   See above n. 11, 18. Art. 5, e.g., states generally that securities fraud, insider trading and market manipulation is prohibited.

[151]   The 1979 Criminal Law was revised by the 8th National People's Congress on 14 March 1997, and effective from 1 October 1997 (as amended in December 1999, August 2001, December 2001 and December 2002 respectively). Arts. 160, 161, 180, 181 and 182 are concerned with offences of false disclosure, insider trading and market manipulation.

[152]   See *Zhengjianhui Gonggao* (CSRC announcement) and *Chufa Jueding* (penalty decisions) where over 300 administrative penalty decisions and related administrative review decisions were made by the CSRC between January 1994 and November 2003, many of which were concerned with securities frauds committed by listed companies, securities companies, accounting firms, law firms, individual directors, managers and other senior persons of these companies.

[153]   According to G. Li, deputy president of the Supreme People's Court, 46 securities fraud cases, including cases involving false statement, insider trading and market manipulation, were charged and tried by the people's courts between 1997 and the end of 2001 in accordance with revised 1997 Criminal Law. See an interview with G. Li by correspondence of *Xinwen Zhoukan* (News Weekly) on 23 July 2002, '*Gaofa Fuyuanzhang Li Guoguang Xishuo Guojia Jinrong Anquan de Sifa Baozhang*' (*Deputy President of the Supreme People's Court Li Guoguang Talks in Detail about Judicial Protection for the State Financial Safety*). The interview report is in Chinese (zhongguo shewai shangshi haishi shenpan wang) (China Foreign-Related Commercial and Maritime Trial Website).

suffered losses as a result of securities fraud, which remained a fundamental weakness of the system. Compared with comprehensive provisions dealing with administrative sanction of securities fraud, there were
very limited provisions in the 1993 Provisional Regulations on Share
Issuing and Trading that dealt with civil liability and civil compensation
related to securities fraud.[154] Although the 1998 Securities Law strengthened the regulation of the securities market and, as the first securities law
in China, brought China's securities market and the regulation into a
new stage, it failed to improve the protection of investors from securities
fraud by strengthening provisions concerning civil liability and related
civil compensation.[155]

In the meantime, the number of listed companies on the Shanghai
and Shenzhen stock exchanges increased from fewer than 20 in the early
1990s to 851 in 1998,[156] and numbers of investors expanded from about
2 million in 1992 to about 40 million in 1998.[157] This rapid development
was accompanied by an increasing number of securities fraud cases and
consequent losses to investors, but the people's courts closed their doors
to the investors who suffered losses as a result of securities fraud and who
brought civil actions to the court.[158] Lawyers, academics and investors
lobbied the Supreme People's Court, calling for the people's court to
accept and hear these cases.[159]

---

[154]   Art. 77 is a brief article in the 1993 Provisional Regulations on Share
Issuing and Trading that relates to the issue of civil liability and compensation,
which states: 'where the provision of this regulation is violated and losses are
caused to others, it shall bear liabilities for civil compensation according to law'.

[155]   Arts 67 to 71, and 183 and 184, deal with market manipulation and insider
trading, which have no stipulations on related civil liabilities. Only Art. 63 men-
tions expressly about civil liability and compensation of losses caused by the false
recording, misleading statement and material omission made by issuers and securities companies.

[156]   The figure comes from an introduction by the CSRC: '*Introduction to
China's Securities Market*'.

[157]   Ibid.

[158]   According to G. Li, deputy president of the Supreme People's Court, none
of the civil claims brought and filed to the people's courts between 1991 and 2002
as a result of insider trading, market manipulation and false statement was continued to the stage of substantial hearing.

[159]   F. Guo, a Beijing-based lawyer and academic who participated in drafting the Securities Law in the early 1990s, actively took part in the campaign
together with others on behalf of grieved investors calling for the people's court
to accept and hear civil compensation claims arising from securities frauds. See
S.V. Lawrence, 'Shareholder Lawsuits: Ally of the People', *Far Eastern Economic
Review* (9 May 2002) at 27.

Under these circumstances, between September 2001 and January 2003, the Supreme People's Court issued three circulars giving instructions to local people's courts on how to deal with civil compensation claims arising from securities fraud on China's securities market.[160] The first circular, issued on 21 September 2001,[161] instructed local people's courts not to accept civil compensation claims arising from insider trading, market manipulation and other securities frauds. The reason given by the Supreme People's Court for not accepting such cases was because 'the people's courts do not have necessary conditions to accept and hear such cases due to current legislative and judicial limitations'.[162]

The second circular, issued just four months later,[163] took a U-turn and partially reversed the position of the first circular of the Supreme People's Court, which instructed local intermediate people's courts to accept and hear cases arising from false statement, but not from insider trading or market manipulation.[164] From 15 January 2002, intermediate people's courts designated by the Supreme People's Court began to accept and hear civil compensation cases arising from false statements, which marked a formal beginning of civil litigation in the people's court in relation to false statement on China's securities market.

The third circular, the Notice of the Supreme People's Court on Relevant Issues of Filing of Civil Tort Dispute Cases Arising from False Statement on the Securities Market (2003 Rules of the SPC), issued on 9 January 2003,[165] followed the basic line of the second circular of the

---

[160] See below nn. 161, 163 and 165.
[161] The Notice of the Supreme People's Court on Temporarily Refusal of Filing of Securities Related Civil Compensation Cases (*Zuigao Remin Fayuan Guanyu She Zhengquan Mishi Peichang Anjian Zan Buyu Shouli de Tongzhi*) (21 September, 2001).
[162] Ibid. The Circular provided no further elaboration on '. . . necessary conditions to accept and hear such cases due to current legislative and judicial limitations'. At that time the 1998 Securities Law had no provisions regarding civil liabilities for insider trading and market manipulation.
[163] The Notice of the Supreme People's Court on Relevant Issues of Filing of Civil Tort Dispute Cases Arising from False Statement on the Securities Market (*Zuigao Renmin Fayuan Guanyu Shouli Zhengquan Shichang Yin Xujiachenshu Yinfa de Minshi Qinquan Jiufen Anjian Youguan Wenti de Tongzhi*), 15 January 2002.
[164] Ibid.
[165] Several Provisions of the Supreme People's Court on Hearing Civil Compensation Cases Arising from False Statement on the Securities Market (*Zuigao Renmin Fayuan Guanyu Shenli Zhengquan Shichang Yin Xujiachenshu Yinfa de Minshi Peichang Anjian de Ruogan Guiding*) (adopted by the Judicial Committee of the Supreme People's Court on 26 December 2002, and promulgated

Supreme People's Court and set out more detailed procedural rules for dealing with cases arising from false statements on China's securities market. These procedural rules, in conjunction with the relevant provisions in the 1991 Civil Procedure Law, the 1998 Securities Law and other relevant laws and regulations, provided local intermediate people's courts with the necessary guidelines for them to deal with compensation claims arising from securities-related false statements.

The 2003 Rules of the SPC was a first and important step towards the establishment of a civil litigation and compensation system for the people's court to deal with securities fraud cases on China's securities market. But it failed to go beyond its predecessors and to transcend their limitations. The restrictive features of the previous circulars were still retained in the 2003 Rules of the SPC concerning prerequisite rules, procedures for joint actions and other aspects of the procedures.

The prerequisite rules introduced in both the second circular and the 2003 Rules of the SPC were one of the problematic aspects of the procedure. In accordance with the second circular and the 2003 Rules of the SPC, the people's court could not accept a civil compensation lawsuit from investors arising from a securities-related false statement unless the alleged false statement had already been investigated by the CSRC or its regional offices and an administrative penalty had consequently been imposed, upon which investors could rely as the factual basis of their actions.[166] In other words, a pre-condition was effectively created to bar plaintiff investors from initiating an action to claim compensations unless this pre-condition was met. The difference between the second circular and the current 2003 Rules of the SPC regarding this prerequisite rule is that the 2003 Rules of the SPC recognized, in addition to the penalty decision made by the CSRC and its regional offices, which was recognized by the second circular, that the criminal judgments made by the people's courts and the administrative penalty decisions made by other competent authorities could also be relied upon as the bases for plaintiff investors to start a civil compensation action.

This prerequisite rule has both procedural and evidential effects. It has a procedural effect in that investors may start litigation if there is an administrative or criminal sanction, regardless of the content of sanction documents; it has an evidential effect in that the facts concluded in

---

on 9 January 2003, effective from 1 February 2003) (Chinalawinfo Co., Ltd. and the Legal Information Centre of Peking University, 2004).

[166] Art. 2, the second circular of the Supreme People's Court; Art. 6, the 2003 Rules of the SPC.

the sanction documents may be treated as evidence in civil litigation.[167] From the critics' point of view, this restrictive prerequisite rule reduces the civil litigation process to the availability of administrative decisions or criminal court judgments and effectively limits and thereby deprives investors of their civil litigation rights.[168] Furthermore, the 2003 Rules of the SPC were criticized on the ground that the Supreme People's Court exceeded its judicial interpretation power beyond the provisions of the 1991 Civil Procedure Law, which require that four conditions need to be met for initiating a civil action.[169] The prerequisite rule creates an additional pre-condition for initiating a civil compensation action and such a pre-condition has no statutory basis in the 1991 Civil Procedure Law.

On the other hand, arguments were put forward to support this prerequisite procedure, particularly by those who were judges from both the Supreme People's Court and local courts.[170] They argued that it was necessary to have this procedure for the time being for two main reasons. First, it was in line with the current limited judicial sources of the people's court; it is otherwise difficult for the people's court to cope with a situation of a 'securities litigation time bomb'.[171] Second, it could help plaintiffs in

---

[167] For more on the procedural and evidential effects of the rule, see S.Yixing, 'Xujia Chenshu Minshi Peichang Susong Zhidu Ruogan Wenti de Sikao' (Thoughts on Several Issues of the Litigation System for Civil Compensation Arising from False Statements), *Falü Shiyong* (*Application of Law*) No.4 (2003) at 9.

[168] See G. Lu, 'Private Enforcement of Securities Fraud Law in China: A Critique of Supreme People's Court 2003 Provisions Concerning Private Securities Litigation', *Pacific Rim Law and Policy Journal* (2003) at 795–8; J. Yin, 'Zhengquan Xujia Chenshu Minshi Zheren Zhidu Lun' (On the System of Civil Liability of Securities-related False Statements), 6 *Faxue* (*Legal Science*) (2003) at 110–111.

[169] Art. 108 of the 1991 Civil Procedure Law states: 'The following conditions must be met when a lawsuit is brought: (1) the plaintiff must be a citizen, legal person or any other organization that has a direct interest in the case; (2) there must be a definite defendant; (3) there must be specific claim or claims, facts, and cause or causes for the suit; and (4) the suit must be within the scope of acceptance for civil actions by the people's court and under the jurisdiction of the people's court where the suit is entertained.'

[170] See L. Kong and J. Ye, 'Zhengquan Shichang Yin Xujia Chenshu Yinfa de Minshi Peichang Anjian de Shouli Tiaojian' (Conditions for Acceptance of Civil Compensation Cases Arising from False Statements on the Securities Market), 4 *Falü Shiyong* (*Application of Law*) (2003) at 21, 22. One of the authors is from the Supreme People's Court. H Sheng and C Zhu, 'Zhengquan Xujia Chenshu Minshi Peichang Yinguo Guanxi Lun' (On Causal Link of Civil Compensation Cases Arising from Securities-related False Statements), 6 *Faxue* (*Legal Science*) (2003) at 102. Both authors are from No. 1 Intermediate People's Court of Shanghai.

[171] Ibid.

producing evidence and reduce their burden of proof, so it was good for the protection of investors.[172]

Like the prerequisite rule, the joint action prescribed in the 2003 Rules of the SPC is another restrictive aspect of the procedure. Joint action (*gongtong susong*) is a form of action prescribed in the 1991 Civil Procedure Law.[173] It refers to an action where one party or both parties consist of two or more than two persons, their object of action is the same or of the same category, and the people's court considers that, with the consent of the parties, the action can be tried combined.[174] In a joint action, particularly those with a large number of parties on either side, one or more than one representative is elected to manage the case on behalf of other parties.[175] For this reason it is also known as a representative action (*daibiaoren susong*).

In accordance with the 2003 Rules of the SPC, where there are both individual actions and joint actions initiated by different plaintiffs suing the same defendants and on the same false statement alleged, the court may notify the plaintiff who initiated the individual action to join the joint action.[176] Similarly, where there is more than one joint action concerning the same defendants and with respect to the same false statement, the court may consolidate them into one joint action.[177] The number of

---

[172]   Ibid.
[173]   Arts 53, 54, 55, 1991 Civil Procedure Law.
[174]   Art. 53, the 1991 Civil Procedure Law.
[175]   Art. 54 of the 1991 Civil Procedure Law provides that if the number of parties on either side of the litigation is large, such parties may choose representatives to carry out the litigation. Art. 55 of the 1991 Civil Procedure Law provides that if many parties have similar claims but the actual number of parties is not known at the time the case is filed, the court may issue a notice detailing the case and the claims and notifying all persons whose rights are similarly affected to register with the court within a specified period. The parties who have registered may select representatives, failing which the people's court may decide representatives in consultation with the registered parties. Art. 55 also provides that the court's ruling or judgment is binding on all those who have registered with the court, and is applicable to those who have not registered with the court but who have brought lawsuits within the prescribed limitation period. Both Arts 54 and 55 provide that the acts of the representatives are binding on the parties whom they represent. However, if the representatives change or abandon claims, accept the claims of the opposing party, or settle the case, they must seek the consent of the parties whom they represent. According to Arts. 59 and 62 of the Supreme People's Court Opinions on Several Issues Relating to Application of the Civil Procedure Law of the PRC, 'large' parties are generally meant to be more than ten parties, and two to five representatives may be elected and they may entrust one or two persons as their legal representatives.
[176]   Art. 13, the 2003 Rules of the SPC.
[177]   Ibid.

plaintiffs in a joint action is to be determined before the hearing, and where the plaintiff is large in number, two to five representatives may be elected as litigation representatives who, on the strength of a special power of attorney granted to them by other plaintiffs, represent the plaintiffs to participate in the court hearing, to change or cancel claims made by the plaintiffs, and to settle or reach a mediation agreement with the defendants.[178] Each of the litigation representatives may entrust one or two legal representatives for the action.[179] Where the case involves a large number of plaintiffs, the court may give a total amount of compensation in the judgment itself, with an appendix attached to the judgment that lists the names of every plaintiff and the compensation awarded to each of them.[180] After the 2003 Rules of the SPC became effective on 1 February 2003, the first joint action case was accepted in February 2003 by the Intermediate People's Court of Ha'erbin City.[181] This was followed by more joint action cases coming into the people's court.[182]

It was advocated by Chinese scholars both inside and outside China that US style class actions were efficient and suitable for this type of

---

[178]   Arts 14 and 15, the 2003 Rules of the SPC.

[179]   Art. 14, the 2003 Rules of the SPC.

[180]   Art. 16, the 2003 Rules of the SPC.

[181]   On 9 February 2003, the Intermediate People's Court of Haerbin City formally accepted a case represented by Guohao Law Firm's Shanghai office involving an initial group of 107 plaintiffs and another 300 or more plaintiffs to be added to the case later in the middle of February. In March 2002, Guohao Law Firm's Shanghai and Beijing offices were entrusted respectively by 5 representatives on behalf of 679 investors to sue Daqing Lianyi, a listed company, for the losses caused by the false statement it made. But the case was not accepted by the court until after the Rules of the SPC became effective. For a news report, see M.A. Shiling, 'Gongtong Susong Diyi An Jian, Daqing Lianyi An Suopei Yu Qianwan' (The First Joint Action Case Was Filed, Daqing Lian Case Compensation Over Ten Million yuan) (February 11, 2003) (zhongguo fayuan wang) (on file with author).

[182]   The Dongfang Dianzi case was filed in the Intermediate People's Court of Qingdao city in July 2003, which involved an initial group of 141 shareholder plaintiffs with more to join; after 4 individual cases suing Guangxia (Yinchuan) Industrial Limited Company were accepted by the Intermediate People's Court of Yinchuan city on 31 July 2003, the lawyers representing the case were preparing more documents involving about 1,000 plaintiffs. See news reports concerning these two cases: *Jinan Gumin Zhuanggao Dongfang Dianzi, Suopei Jin E Da 300 Yu Wanyuan* (*Jinan Shareholders Sue Dongfang Dianzi, Claiming Figure Reaches Over 3 Million Yuan*), 10 July 2003; *Yinchuanshi Zhongyuan Zhengshi Shouli Yinguangxia Minshi Qinquan Peichang An* (*Yichuan City Intermediate People's Court Formally Accepted Yinuangxia Civil Tort Compensation Case*), 1 August 2002. Both news reports (zhongguo fayuan wang) are on file with author.

litigation and that the Supreme People's Court should adopt a form of class action for such litigation, subject to further amendments to the 1991 Civil Procedure Law.[183] Others, particularly judges from the people's courts, argued that the conditions were not ripe for such a move. They argued, among other points, that since China then had no organization similar to intermediaries in the United States who register hundreds and thousands of investors and calculate their losses, it was unrealistic to rely upon only the people's courts to make announcements, register plaintiffs and undertake the work in relation to the application of judgments; it was therefore necessary to make a distinction between a joint action with fixed plaintiffs and a joint action with a large number of indefinite plaintiffs, which is in line with the current conditions of the people's court.[184]

In December 2005, the Supreme People's Court issued a circular, instructing local people's courts concerning the changes made to the handling of cases of joint action.[185] Starting from January 2006, joint actions involving numerous parties either on one side or on both sides are to be dealt with by basic level people's courts; if the court that accepts such a joint action thinks that the case is not suitable for a joint action, the court may try the case individually; if a case of joint action is of major significance within the jurisdiction of a provincial high people's court, the case will be dealt with by an intermediate people's court; if, owing to special circumstances, a joint action case must be tried by a high people's court as the first instance court, the matter will be submitted to the Supreme People's Court for approval before the court accepts the case.[186]

The purpose of this change, as stated in the Circular, is to make it convenient for the parties to litigate as well as for the people's courts to

---

[183] See W Hutchens, 'Private Securities Litigation in China: Material Disclosure about China's Legal System?', 24 *University of Pennsylvania Journal of International Economic Law*, 599 (2003) at 643 and accompanying nn 173 and 174. S.V. Lawrence, 'Shareholder Lawsuits: Ally of the People', above n. 159 at 27. B. Tu, 'Zhengquan Xujia Chenshu Minshi Peichang Zheren Jizhi Lun' (On the Mechanism for Civil Compensation Liabilities for Securities-related False Statements), *Faxue* (*Legal Science*) No.6 (2005) at 97.

[184] See X. Xi and W. Jia, 'Guanyu Shenli Zhengquan Shichang Yin Xujia Chenshu Yinfa de Minshi Peichang Anjian de Ruogan Guiding de Lijie yu Shiyong' (Understanding and Application of 'Several Provisions of the Supreme People's Court on Hearing Civil Compensation Cases Arising from False Statements on the Securities Market'), *Renmin Sifa* (*People's Judiciary*) (2003) at 11.

[185] The Circular of the Supreme People's Court on the Issue of Acceptance of Joint Action Cases by the People's Court (*Zuigao Renmin Fayuan Guanyu Renmin Fayuan Shouli Gongtong Susong Anjian Wenti de Tongzhi*), issued by the Supreme People's Court on 30 December 2005 and effective as of 1 January 2006.

[186] Ibid.

mediate the cases locally, to increase efficiency of dealing with such type of cases as well as save court resources, and to strengthen the supervision and guidance by the Supreme People's Court on the adjudication work of the people's courts of lower levels.[187] These changes would be helpful to securities litigation in that investor plaintiffs in a joint action case may find it convenient and time saving to bring their case to a local basic level people's court in terms of availability of the court. But, overall, the changes have not brought about structural changes to the current system of joint action as prescribed in the 1991 Civil Procedure Law. The 2007 amendments to the 1991 Civil Procedure Law made no changes to the provisions concerning joint action in the 1991 Civil Procedure Law.[188]

On the whole, the 2003 Rules of the SPC established a procedural framework and made it possible for the first time for investors to claim their losses suffered as a consequence of false statements made on China's securities market. However, this procedural framework failed to provide investors with an easy and effective access to the court and judicial remedies. The cautiously chosen form of joint action, the limited number of intermediate people's courts designated, the priority given to the courts located at the places of issuer or listed company defendants, the lack of provisions on the determination and calculation of losses suffered on the issuing market, and practical difficulties concerning the determination of false statement dates and other crucial dates[189] mean that investors and their acting lawyers could face difficulties in bringing their cases to the people's court in a timely and efficient manner and in obtaining compensation successfully.

THE RULE OF LAW V. ADMINISTRATIVE ACTIONS

In December 2001, China formally became a member of the World Trade Organization (WTO) after 15 years' preparation, starting in 1986.[190] During the same period of time, China stepped up its constitutional

---

[187] Ibid. The opening first paragraph of the Circular.

[188] The 2007 Civil Procedure Law has the same provisions as those in Arts 53, 54, 55 of the 1991 Civil Procedure Law, which set out procedural conditions for joint action.

[189] See S. Zhu, 'Civil Litigation Arising from False Statements on China's Securities Market', 31 *North Carolina Journal of International Law & Commerce and Regulation*, 377 (2006).

[190] On 10 November 2001, a signing ceremony on China's accession to the WTO was held at Doha, following which China formally became a member of the WTO on 11 December 2001.

reform. In 1988, the 1982 Constitution was amended for the first time, which amendment, among other changes, paved the way for the significant rise of the private sector in later years.[191] In 1993, 1999 and 2004, the 1982 Constitution was further amended three times respectively, coinciding with the stages of China's economic, social and legal reforms.[192] One of the important changes in the 1999 amendments was, for the first time, the inclusion in the 1982 Constitution of a rule of law provision that states: 'The People's Republic of China governs the country according to law and makes it a socialist country ruled by law.'[193] However, the building of a rule-of-law state in China is not an easy task to achieve and real challenges exist with respect to the implementation of the constitutional principle in substance.[194]

In 2001, China began to implement its WTO commitments, including its commitments in the banking, insurance and auto-finance sectors and the commitment to open up China's securities market to foreign investment.[195] It was anticipated that more and more foreign securities investments would come into China following China's opening up of its securities and financial market in the post-WTO era.[196] It is important that continuous legal and judicial reforms are carried out to improve the environment of the legal system in post-WTO China and to promote and to protect foreign investment in China's securities market. The challenges include, for example, how the principles of impartiality and independence are to be truly implemented by the people's courts in their handling of securities disputes.

The judicial reform that has been carried out forms part of China's

---

[191]   Art. 11 was amended to the effect that the state permits the private sector of the economy to exist and develop within the limits prescribed by law and recognizes that the private sector of the economy is a complement to the socialist public economy.

[192]   Important amendments have been adopted, concerning, among others, the rule-of-law state, public ownership and other forms of ownership, protection of private property, and protection of human rights, etc. In total, 31 amendments have been adopted since 1988.

[193]   This is a new paragraph which was added to Art. 5 of the Constitution by the 1999 amendment 13.

[194]   See generally R. Peerenboom, *China's Long March Toward Rule of Law* (Cambridge: Cambridge University Press, 2002) (discussing the rule of law in China).

[195]   See S. Zhu, 'Implementing China's WTO Commitments in Chinese Financial Services Law', 6 *The China Review*, 2, 3–33 (2006) at 14–21.

[196]   For example, the Qualified Foreign Institutional Investors (QFII) scheme which started in 2003 has now grown to 82 institutional investors in the scheme in 2009. Ibid., at 27–30.

legal transformation process in the past decades.[197] Despite the progress that China has made in its judicial reform, some foundational aspects of China's judiciary have caused concerns, one of which is the institution of the judicial committee.[198] In accordance with the 1983 People's Court Organization Law, judicial committees are established at all levels of the people's courts.[199] The judicial committees are presided over by the president of the courts at each level, and consist of senior judges who are nominated by the president of the courts and appointed by the Standing Committee of the National People's Congress or the standing committees of local people's congresses.[200] In accordance with the provisions of the 1983 People's Court Organization Law and the 1991 Civil Procedure Law, the role of the judicial committee is to summarize and refine adjudicating experiences of the people's court, to discuss major or difficult cases and other issues concerning adjudication work, and to deal with the cases submitted to the judicial committee when an effective judgment or ruling of the court is found to have been wrongly decided, either on the facts of the case or the application of law.[201]

Securities disputes, particularly in the areas of sales and purchases of government bonds, securities repurchase agreements, and futures contracts, may involve a large sum of money or difficult issues. The judicial committee of the court where a securities dispute involving a large sum of money or difficult issues is tried is often involved in discussing and deciding such cases. For example, in *China Life Insurance Company Chengdu Branch v Sichuan Hualong Investment Consultant Co. Ltd*, a major and complicated case involving the purchase of 40 million yuan government bonds in 1999 by the plaintiff, China Life Insurance Company Chengdu Branch, the judicial committee of the Sichuan High People's Court was involved in discussing and deciding the case in the first instance level of hearing of the case.[202] In *Henan Province International Investment Trust Company v Wuhan Jinda Industrial Company Limited by Shares*, a case

---

[197] The most recent judicial reform programmes were carried out under 'The People's Court Second Five-Year Reform Outlines (2004–2008)'.
[198] Judicial committee (*Shenpan Weiyuanhui*) of the People's Court is also translated as adjudication committee of the people's court.
[199] Art. 11 of the People's Court Organization Law of the PRC, promulgated in July 1979, as amended in September 1983, requires that a judicial committee is established at each level of the people's court.
[200] Ibid.
[201] Arts. 11 and 14 of the 1983 People's Court Organization Law; Art. 177 of the 1991 Civil Procedure Law.
[202] See S. Zhu, *Securities Dispute Resolution in China* (Aldershot, England; Burlington, VT, USA: Ashgate, 2007) at 83.

involving difficult issues connected to a borrowing of 10 million yuan government bonds, the judicial committee of the first instance court Hubei High People's Court was involved in discussing and deciding the case.[203]

On the one hand, the outcome of such cases may have benefited from the collective thoughts of senior judges of the judicial committee on difficult and uncertain issues, but on the other hand, the judicial committee system operates on the basis that the members of the judicial committee are only briefed on the cases and do not fully participate in a hearing. Criticisms and debates about the system of the judicial committee have also focused on the way in which the cases are selected, summarized and dealt with by the judicial committee and on the adverse consequential impact on the appeal system.[204]

In The People's Court Second Five-Year Reform Outlines (2004–2008),[205] a set of proposals were outlined by the Supreme People's Court for the reform of the judicial committee.[206] It remains to be seen how the system of the judicial committee, which is deeply rooted as a key institutional mechanism in the judicial system in China, is to be reformed, and how the problems associated with this system are to be eliminated. The result of any reform would have a direct impact on all areas of dispute resolution by the people's court, including securities dispute resolution. Overall, it is an important reform project as it affects the way in which the people's court operates and affects the process of China's judicial reform, which should be guided by the principle of impartiality and independence in post-WTO China.

The role of the people's court in the regulation of China's emerging securities market has increased in past decades, as evidenced by the peo-

---

[203]   Ibid. at 86.

[204]   Recent years saw an increase in debate and discussion on the judicial committee system. See, for example, H Chu and J. Chen, 'Study on Several Problems of the System of Judicial Committee – Also on the Reform and Improvement of the System of Judicial Committee' (Shenpan Weiyuanhui Zhidu Ruogan Wenti Yanjiu – Jian Lun Shenpan Weiyuanhui Zhidu de Gaige He Wanshan), Falǔ Shiyong (Application of Law), No. 10 (2005) at 54–55; S Gua, 'Exploration and Improvement on Working Mechanism of the Judicial Committee' (Shenpan Weiyuanhui Gongzuo Jizhi Tansuo Ji Wanshan) (2005) at 27–30, *Renmin Sifa (People's Judiciary)*, No. 10, 2004.

[205]   The People's Court Second Five-Year Reform Outlines (Renmin Fayuan Di'erge Wunian Gaige Gangyao), announced by the Supreme People's Court on 26 October 2005, which covers 8 areas of the work of the people's court and includes altogether 50 entries of issues, proposals and measures.

[206]   Ibid., entries 23 and 24, outlines five proposals, such as the proposal to change the meeting (*huiyi*) of the judicial committee into a hearing (*shenli*).

ple's court's engagement in the resolution of disputes arising from the commodity and financial futures market and securities-related false statements, discussed above. Under certain circumstances, the role of the court and the role of the administrative securities regulator are entwined and the role of the court tends to be undermined. The 1998 Securities Law gives the administrative regulator a strong overall power to regulate China's securities market, including a power to impose administrative penalties, which occupies a central place in the regulation of China's securities market.[207] This is still the position in the current 2005 Securities Law.[208] While it is necessary for China's emerging securities market to have a strong administrative regulator, it is also necessary in China's context to promote the role of the courts in dealing with civil securities disputes and not to replace the role of the courts with that of the administrative securities regulator.

The prerequisite rules discussed above replaced the role of the court with that of the administrative authorities. Investors cannot go to the people's courts to claim compensation for their losses resulting from false statements unless the alleged false statement has already been investigated and there is an administrative penalty decision made by the CSRC, the Ministry of Finance or other competent administrative authorities, or a criminal court judgment, against the wrongdoers for their false statements. This procedural arrangement may lead to a situation where an alleged false statement is not investigated or punished by the administrative regulator for political or other reasons, such as the protection of local companies, and those investors who suffered losses as a result of the false statement will not be able to get remedies through civil compensation litigation.[209] As argued by some authors, this rule encourages false statement makers to make use of social connections or bribery to influence the process of administrative investigation in order to escape civil litigation and civil compensation.[210] Others have argued that the adoption of this rule was to prevent angry shareholders from flooding the people's court and thus generating adverse social and political repercussions.[211]

---

[207]   See Chapter 10 of the 1998 Securities Law: Securities Regulatory Authority, and Chapter 11 of the 1998 Securities Law: Legal Liability.

[208]   See Chapter 10 of the 2005 Securities Law: Securities Regulatory Authority, and Chapter 11 of the 2005 Securities Law: Legal Liability. A quick indicator shows that the Chinese word 'securities regulatory authority' (*zhengquan jiandu guanli jigou*) appeared 114 times in the 1998 Securities Law and 137 times in the 2005 Securities Law.

[209]   See above n. 168.

[210]   See Yin above n. 168, at 110.

[211]   See Lawrence, above n. 159, at 27.

An administrative investigation process in China, such as the one in which an alleged securities-related false statement is investigated by an administrative authority and an administrative penalty decision is subsequently made, is not as transparent as court proceedings where cases are tried openly. It is therefore possible that an administrative investigation process may be influenced behind the scenes by personal connections, local protectionism or political forces, and even hijacked by wrongdoers or their related persons without being noticed by the public and by aggrieved investors so that the case may never come to the people's court and the investors who suffered losses may never get compensation. It was said, for example, that the timing of the investigation, and the inability of the CSRC to pursue five directors involved in the case of Hainan Minyuan Modern Agricultural Company, was suspect for political reasons, and personal connections were also thought to be at play.[212] The abuse of the administrative investigation process could be prevented if the civil court played an active and decisive role in deciding whether a given statement or an activity amounts to false statement and whether it is subject to civil compensation. But this could happen only if the prerequisite rule were lifted by an amendment of the 2003 Rules of the SPC.

Those who support the 2003 Rules of the SPC have argued that the decision to have a prerequisite rule was in line with the provisions of the 1998 Securities Law with regard to the power of the administrative regulator and the role of administrative penalties for the regulation of China's securities market.[213] They have argued that it is therefore appropriate to

---

[212] Two of the largest shareholders of Hainan Minyuan Modern Agricultural Company apparently had ties to China's senior leader at that time. Hainan Minyuan Modern Agricultural Company made its public offering on 30 April 1993. The company's 1995 yearly report indicated a profit of 0.001 yuan per share and a stock price around 3.65 yuan. In January 1997, the company announced a profit in 1996 of 0.867 yuan per share, an improvement of 1290.68 times over profits in 1995. Minyuan's price rose to 26.18 yuan. The company released a mysterious 'supplemental report' on 1 February 1997, which changed some of the company's financial indicators. Towards the end of February 1997, trading of the company's stock was suspended and, in March 1997, five directors who had approved the false reports resigned and disappeared. Responding to requests from investors, an investigation into Minyuan's financial reports was launched on 5 March 1997. After a year-long investigation, the CSRC found that the company had fraudulently inflated accounts by 1.2 million yuan from illegal real estate transactions in Beijing. Minyuan refused to help the CSRC find the five directors, and the CSRC later released a notice stating that it was searching for the five directors but that Minyuan was under 'no obligation' to help. See Daniel M. Anderson, 'Taking Stock in China: Company Disclosure and Information in China's Stock Markets', 88 *Geo L.J.*, 1934–1935 (2002).

[213] See L. Kong and J. Ye, 'Zhengquan Shichang Yin Xujia Chenshu Yinfa de Minshi Peichang Anjian de shouli Tiaojian' (Conditions for Acceptance of Civil

first rely upon the role of the administrative regulator and administrative penalties before making use of the judicial process and the exclusive role played by civil litigation in compensating victims.[214] While arguing for the prerequisite procedure, these authors have also acknowledged that in cases where an alleged false statement is not punished by the administrative regulator or a criminal court, for one reason or another, those investors who suffered losses as a result of the false statement will not be able to get remedies through civil compensation litigation, which is a defect of the prerequisite procedure.[215]

In other areas of the securities market, the line between the role of the administrative authorities and the role of the people's court is sometimes crossed over. In the securities repurchase market, for example, the administrative regulators, in implementing the 1996 Circular of the State Council,[216] compiled a list of securities repurchase participants who owed debts to each other in a national chain of debt clearance. Correspondingly, the Supreme People's Court issued three circulars, in 1998, 2000 and 2001 respectively, instructing local people's courts to stop accepting, hearing and enforcing the cases of securities repurchase disputes listed on the national chain of debt clearance, which lasted about 18 months between 1998 and 2000.[217] On the futures market, the Supreme People's Court

---

Compensation Cases Arising from False Statements on the Securities Market), 4 *Falü Shiyong* (*Application of Law*) (2003) at 21, 22. One of the authors is from the Supreme People's Court. H. Sheng and C. Zhu, 'Zhengquan Xujia Chenshu Minshi Peichang Yinguo Guanxi Lun' (On Causal Link of Civil Compensation Cases Arising from Securities-related False Statements), 6 *Faxue* (*Legal Science*) (2003) at 102. Both authors are from No. 1 Intermediate People's Court of Shanghai.

[214]   Ibid.

[215]   Ibid.

[216]   See Zhu, above n. 202, at 120–122. Circular of the State Council Approving and Circulating the PBOC's Request for Instruction on Further Improving the Work of Clearing off Securities Repurchase Debts (*Guowuyuan Pizhuan Zhongguo Renmin Yinhang Guanyu Jinyibu Zuohao Zhengquan Huigou Zhaiwu Qingchang Gongzuo Qingshi de Tongzhi*), issued on 25 June 1996.

[217]   See Zhu, above n. 202, at 105. The first circular: The Circular of the Supreme People's Court on Stopping Hearing and Enforcing Securities Repurchase Economic Dispute Cases That Have Been Compiled into National Debt Clearance Chain Among Securities Repurchase Participants (*Zuigao Renmin Fayuan Guayu Zhongzhi Shenli, Zhongzhi Zhixing Yi Bianru Quanguo Zhengquan Huigou Jigou Jian Zhaiwu Qingqian Liantiao de Zhengquan Huigou Jingji Jiufen Anjian de Tongzhi*), was issued by the Supreme People's Court on 18 December 1998. The second circular: The Circular of the Supreme People's Court on Resuming Accepting, Hearing and Enforcing Securities Repurchase Economic Dispute Cases That Have Been Compiled into National Debt Clearance Chain Among Securities

instructed local people's courts that some disputes might be resolved
first by the administrative authorities, but if such attempts still could not
resolve the disputes, they should then be resolved through litigation, and
the people's courts should accept such cases.[218]

On the one hand, the involvement of administrative authorities and
regulators, and action taken by them, may speed up the process of resolving the problem, as in the case of securities repurchase triangle debt cases,
and thus save the resources of the people's courts and reduce the adverse
impact of the disputes on the securities market and on the economy as a
whole. But on the other hand, as in the case of civil compensation litigation arising from a false statement on the securities market, if there is an
abuse of the administrative investigation process, investors who suffered
losses as a result of the false statement will not be able to get remedies
through civil compensation litigation. Moreover, changing government
policies, formulated on economic, financial, social or political grounds,
may prevail in the process of securities dispute resolution, through actions
taken by administrative authorities and regulators, at the cost of the legal
rights and interests prescribed by law and regulations that should be
upheld by the people's courts through a judicial process.

Certainty is one of the things that a securities market and investors
seek. China's securities market and securities investors are no exception.
Financial security (*jinrong anquan*) and social stability (*shehui wending*),
emphasized by the Chinese government and the people's court in the regulation of China's emerging securities market, can help to bring certainty
to the market, but an overly-weighted emphasis on the social and financial
stability can, on the other hand, bring uncertainty to the market and also
generate negative effects with respect to the building of the rule of law in
China. In the commodity and financial futures market discussed above,
the closure of the government bond futures market in May 1995 and the

---

Repurchase Participants (*Zuigao Renmin Fayuan Guayu Huifu Shouli, Shenli he
Zhixing Yijing Bianru Quanguo Zhengquan Huigou Jigou Jian Zhaiwu Qingqian
Liantiao de Zhengquan Huigou Jingji Jiufen Anjian de Tongzhi*), was issued by the
Supreme People's Court on 26 July 2000. The third circular: The Circular of the
Supreme People's Court on the Issue of Statute Limitation in Connection With
Remaining Credits and Debts after National Coordinated Clearance among
Securities Repurchase Participants (*Zuigao Renmin Fayuan Guanyu Dui Quanguo
Zhengquan Huigou Jigou Jian Jing Tongyi Qingqian Hou Shangyu de Zhaiquan
Zhaiwu Susong Shixiao Wenti de Tongzhi*), was issued by the Supreme People's
Court on 20 January 2001. The statute of limitation restarts from 26 July 2000, the
day on which the Supreme People's Court instructed the people's courts to resume
accepting, hearing and enforcing the disputes.

[218]   See Point Four of the 1995 SPC Futures Judicial Guidelines.

crackdown campaign embarked upon by the government from 1993 to 1999 to stop chaotic situations and a blind development of the futures market show that the priority of the government was to maintain social stability, public confidence and the stability of the financial market.

Following the same approach, the default of repayments to bondholders by many enterprise bond issuers in the early 1990s was treated as a potential threat to social stability and a series of measures was taken by the government at both national and local levels to tackle the problem.[219] Similarly, the debt problem in the securities repurchase market was treated by the government as an urgent matter, as it was becoming a threat to social stability as well as to financial stability and to the implementation of government economic policy, which led the people's court to stop accepting, hearing and enforcing the cases of securities repurchase disputes listed on the national chain of debt clearance. In line with government policy, the people's court takes the protection of social stability as a priority in the resolution of securities disputes.[220]

Early in 1995, the Supreme People's Court instructed local people's courts that, in the case of disputes in the commodity and financial futures market that had a wider social coverage, or were related to social stability in other ways, the people's courts needed to listen to the opinion of futures regulators, and, where necessary, seek instructions from the courts of higher level, in order that such cases could be dealt with timely, properly and fairly.[221] In the same document, the Supreme People's Court instructed local people's courts to adhere to the principle of respecting

---

[219]   See Zhu, above n. 202, at 94–5. Notice of the State Council General Office for Circulating the Opinion of the People's Bank of China and the State Planning Commission on Dealing With the Problem of Default of Repayment Due of Enterprise Bonds (*Guowuyuan Bangongting Zhuanfa Zhongguo Renmin Yinhang, Guojia Jiwei Guanyu Qiye Zhaiquan Daoqi Buneng Duifu Wenti Chuli Yijian de Tongzhi*), issued on 22 September 1994. E.g., Point 6 of the Notice asked local governments to report to the State Planning Commission and the PBOC by the end of October 1994 on the measures taken to deal with the problem arising from possible default of repayments due in 1994 in their regions and related problems that may cause social unrest.

[220]   Li Guoguang, deputy president of the Supreme People's Court, speaking at a meeting on the trial of civil compensation cases arising from false statements on the securities market on 12–14 September 2002, emphasized that protecting social stability is the first and most important task of the people's court. For the news report, see W Yang and J Pan, 'Li Guoguang: Zhua Shenpan Bao Wending Shi Fayuan Shouyao Renwu' (Li Guoguan: To Work on Adjudication and to Protect Social Stability is the First and Important Task of the People's Court) (15 September 2002) (zhongguo fayuan wang) (on file with author).

[221]   Point Four of the 1995 SPC Futures Judicial Guidelines.

lawful agreements made between the parties; thus, as long as an agreement reached between the parties were not in violation of the provisions of law and administrative regulations and the practice of futures trading, the agreement should be treated as the basis for resolving the disputes between the parties.[222]

This cautious attitude towards the issues of social and financial stability, and an emphasis at the same time on the protection of lawful rights and interests of market participants and on the principle of respecting lawful contracts of the parties, continues to be found in the judicial guidelines of the Supreme People's Court. In 2004, for example, the Supreme People's Court issued procedures for the freezing and transferring of settlement funds related to securities trading, an important procedure that touches upon the interests of every shareholder and investor.[223] The aim of the procedures, as it was stated by the Supreme People's Court, is to ensure financial security and social stability, to protect lawful rights and interests of the parties, and to ensure lawful enforcement by the people's court.

Examining the way in which the people's court associates the resolution of securities disputes with the issue of financial security and social stability, it is obvious that the people's court assumes a dual role of maintaining financial and social stability on the one hand, while protecting lawful rights and the interests of market participants, and upholding the principle of freedom of contract and respect for lawful agreements of the parties, on the other hand. The process of resolution of securities disputes by the people's court during the government's clearing-up campaigns in the securities market became predominantly a process in which the people's court was implementing the government's clearing-up policy.[224] The Supreme People's Court had to strike a balance between the court, the government, social stability and the protection of state-owned listed companies on the one hand, and the need to protect and compensate investors who suffered losses as a result of securities frauds on China's securities market on the other.[225]

---

[222] Ibid.

[223] See above n. 33.

[224] For example, the people's courts stopped accepting, hearing and enforcing the cases of securities repurchase disputes listed on the national chain of debt clearance, which lasted about 18 months between 1998 and 2000. See above n. 217 and accompanying text.

[225] At a meeting on the trial of civil compensation cases arising from false statements on the securities market held on 12–14 September 2002 in Lanzhou city, Gansu province, Li Guoguang, deputy president of the Supreme People's Court, emphasized that the protection of social stability is the first and most important task of the people's court.

The development of China's emerging securities market is closely associated with China's overall social and economic policies. In November 2002, the 16th National Congress of the Communist Party of China set out a strategic goal of developing China into a 'well-off society' (*xiaokang shehui*).[226] In October 2003, the Third Plenary Session of the 16th Central Committee of the Communist Party of China outlined major tasks to further improve China's market economy to build a well-off society, seeking to further China's policy goals.[227] Subsequently, China's capital market was scrutinized by the central government under the policy decisions made by the 16th National Congress of the Communist Party of China and its Third Plenary Session, leading to the State Council's issuance of Several Opinions on Promoting the Reform, Opening-up and Steady Development of China's Capital Market in 2004 (the 'Nine-point Opinion').[228] The Nine-point Opinion represented the central government's assessment and comprehensive policy for the future of China's capital market. In 1992, the State Council had made a similar policy statement on China's capital market,[229] which focused more on the efficient regulation of China's emerging securities market; in contrast, the Nine-point Opinion focused on the opening-up and steady development of China's capital market.[230]

Over the next two years following the issuance of the Nine-point

---

[226] The 16th National Congress of the Communist Party of China was held on 8–14 November 2002, in which the then president Jiang Zemin made a speech entitled 'Build a Well-off Society in an All-Round Way and Create a New Situation in Building Socialism with Chinese Characteristics'. In his speech, President Jiang set out the goals for achieving a well-off society, one of which was China's GDP would be quadrupled by 2020 from the level in 2000.

[227] The Third Plenary Session of the 16th Central Committee of the Communist Party of China took place on 11–14 October 2003, in which the Decision on the Improvement of the Socialist Market Economic System was adopted. The Decision outlined tasks to further improve China's market economy to build a well-off society, covering a wide range of areas of the economic system, including, among others, state-owned enterprise reform (Section 3, points 7, 8 and 9), and financial system reform (Section 7, points 20–24).

[228] Several Opinions of the State Council on Promoting the Reform, Opening-up and Steady Development of China's Capital Market (*Guowuyuan Guanyu Tuijin Ziben Shichang Gaige Kaifang he Wending Fazhan de Ruogan Yijian*), announced on 31 January 2004.

[229] The Circular of the State Council on Further Strengthening Macro-administration of Securities Market (*Guowuyuan Guanyu Jinyibu Jiaqiang Zhengquan Shichang Hongguan Guanli de Tongzhi*), issued on 17 December 1992.

[230] See Point Four, in which it states that 'Steadily develop futures market . . . develop derivative products related with shares and bonds . . .' Several Opinions of the State Council on Promoting the Reform, Opening-up and Steady Development

Opinion, a re-establishment of the financial futures market in China took place. This shows that the development of China's securities and futures markets is guided by China's overall social and economic policies. Trading of government bond futures and financial bond futures, which was closed in the 1990s, resumed on 15 June 2005, via an inter-bank bond market, and a group of regulations and trading rules was promulgated by the People's Bank of China.[231] The establishment of the China Financial Futures Exchange in 2006 was a long-awaited and welcome move. It was accompanied by a new set of trading rules covering, among other things, financial futures trading,[232] financial futures settlement,[233] and risk control management by financial futures exchanges.[234] Unlike the uncontrolled growth in the early 1990s, the re-establishment of the financial futures market and the proposed introduction of financial futures products after 2004 formed part of the continuing and sustainable development of China's securities market. The specific regulations and rules promulgated to facilitate and regulate the re-establishment of the financial futures market were an extension of the securities and futures regulatory framework established by the 1998 Securities Law and the 2005 Securities Law and related regulations and judicial rules.

CONCLUSION

China's securities market is a new and transitional market, and has emerged during China's transformation from a previous socialist and planned economy to a market economy. In contrast to the tentative and ad hoc regulations and regulatory measures of the early 1990s, China has

---

of China's Capital Market (*Guowuyuan Guanyu Tuijin Ziben Shichang Gaige Kaifang he Wending Fazhan de Ruogan Yijian*), announced on 31 January 2004.

[231]   See primarily the Provisions on the Administration of Bond Futures Trading on National Inter-bank Bond Market (*Quanguo Yinhang Jian Zhaiquan Shichang Zhaiquan Yuanqi Jiaoyi Guanli Guiding*), issued by the People's Bank of China on 11 May 2005 and effective as of 15 June 2005.

[232]   Trading Rules of the China Financial Futures Exchange (*Zhongguo Jinrong Qihuo Jiaoyisuo Jiaoyi Guize*), effective as of 27 June 2007; Detailed Trading Rules of the China Financial Futures Exchange (*Zhongguo Jinrong Qihuo Jiaoyisuo Jiaoyi Xize*), effective as of 27 June 2007.

[233]   Detailed Settlement Rules of the China Financial Futures Exchange (*Zhongguo Jinrong Qihuo Jiaoyisuo Jiesuan Xize*), effective as of 27 June 2007.

[234]   Administrative Measures of the China Financial Futures Exchange on Risk Control (*Zhongguo Jinrong Qihuo Jiaoyisuo Fengxian Kongzhi Guanli Banfa*), effective as of 27 June 2007.

since gradually established a legal, regulatory and judicial framework for the regulation of the securities and futures market, which has promoted the healthy and sustainable growth of China's emerging securities market. Despite these developments and achievements, the securities law, regulations and judicial rules of China's emerging securities market are still at an early stage of development, compared with those of markets where the rule of law and governance are well established. Problems, such as those discussed in this chapter, give rise to concerns about the future development of the legal, regulatory and judicial framework of China's emerging securities market. The transformation of Shanghai into a prominent international financial centre calls for a well-established regulatory system and a respect for the rule of law and governance.

China's emerging securities market has developed and is regulated within the context of China's overall administrative, economic, legal, social and political systems. In particular, the development of the law, regulations and judicial rules governing China's emerging securities market cannot be separated from the development of China's legal system and judicial reform since 1978, in response to China's economic and legal transformation. The role of law, the role of courts, and the role of administrative authorities and their actions are entwined in the regulation of China's securities market. Constitutional developments in the past years have led to the inclusion of a rule-of-law provision in the 1982 Constitution. However, the building of a rule-of-law state in China is not an easy task to achieve and real challenges exist with respect to the implementation of the constitutional principle in substance. The story of China's emerging securities market tells that the establishment of a healthy and sustainable securities and futures market in China could not go far without a well-established regulatory system supported by a culture of rule of law and good governance.

The future development of China's securities markets depends upon, among other factors, continuing legal and judicial reforms in building the rule of law, good governance, and improvements to the operation of the legal system, such as improvements concerning the problematic gap between law on the books and the implementation and enforcement of law. The newly amended 2005 Securities Law and the 2005 Company Law have improved regulatory standards and corporate governance. When the Futures Trading Law is passed, China's securities and futures law will be a tripartite body of law, consisting of the Securities Law, the Securities Investment Fund Law and the Futures Trading Law, as well as related regulations and judicial rules. The regulatory experiences of China's commodity and financial futures market in the early 1990s demonstrated how crucial an appropriate and balanced legal, regulatory and judicial framework is to ensuring the healthy and sustainable development of a securities and futures market. The legal, regulatory and judicial developments in the regulation of China's securities and futures markets in post-WTO China suggest that China is moving a step closer to building a well-suited and well-balanced legal, regulatory and judicial framework for its securities and futures markets.

6. Of corporations and plumbers: Shareholder voting rights and securities clearing and settlement in Europe[1]

Agata Waclawik-Wejman[2]

INTRODUCTION

The framework for cross-border voting in Europe in the intermediated securities environment is currently being strengthened, reflecting its importance as a mechanism for promoting the integration of European capital markets. The fact that shareholdings in listed companies across Europe are evidenced as book entries on accounts maintained by intermediaries leads to the dependence of the core corporate relationship between the issuer and the shareholder on the soundness of the related cross-border securities clearing and settlement infrastructure – sometimes dubbed the plumbing of the capital markets. The barriers to cross-border exercise of shareholder rights in Europe show that it is not possible to create an effective corporate governance framework without a well-functioning capital markets infrastructure.

From the law reform perspective, the efficient and effective cross-border exercise of shareholder rights is not possible without a sound legal framework for cross-border intermediated securities holdings. Of particular importance are: (i) the identification of the shareholder to enable her to exercise her voting rights; (ii) communication between the issuer and

---

[1] This chapter was submitted to the Hart workshop in 2009 and updates an earlier paper based on the presentation given at the Seminar on Shareholder Rights on 19 May 2008 at the Stockholm Center for Commercial Law, Stockholm University, entitled 'Shareholder Rights in the Intermediated Holding Structures' (Stockholm, 2009).

[2] INPRIS Institute, Warsaw and Polish-German Banking Law Center, Jagiellonian University, Cracow. Member of the Legal Certainty Group of the European Commission, an expert group on the law of securities clearing and settlement.

shareholders before, during and after the general meeting; and (iii) third parties' actions on behalf of the investor.

The reforms at EU level in this sphere have proceeded in a fragmented way, which might increase the risk of an incomplete framework developing. While the EU Shareholder Rights Directive[3] (discussed below) introduces measures aimed at improving issuer–shareholder communication and otherwise strengthening foreign shareholders' voting rights, the core problems with cross-border voting are of a more technical nature and are related to the functioning of the securities clearing and settlement infrastructure.

The aim of this chapter is to provide an overview of the most important initiatives undertaken to remove legal barriers to the exercise of voting rights in Europe and to provide a basis for further deliberation on what has been achieved and what is still needed to create an efficient framework for the cross-border exercise of voting rights in Europe. The framework for the exercise of shareholder rights in Europe will need to be a joint product of a number of European and international initiatives, both in company law (best exemplified by the Shareholder Rights Directive) and in securities law (best exemplified by the EU's Legal Certainty Project as well as a range of other initiatives).

The facilitation of the cross-border exercise of shareholder voting rights is currently of particular importance for Europe.[4] In continental Europe in particular, where share ownership has traditionally been concentrated, in recent years levels of dispersed ownership have increased. At the same time, however, holdings by foreign shareholders and institutional shareholders in European corporations are increasing. In seven EU Member States (Finland, Belgium, Ireland, Slovakia, the Netherlands, Greece and Hungary),[5] domestic holdings constitute less than 50 per cent of total holdings in listed companies and there is a tendency towards an increase in international shareholdings.[6] In Poland, foreign investors hold 46 per cent (mostly institutional) of the Warsaw Stock Exchange capitalization,

---

[3] Directive 2007/37/EC OJ (2007) L184/17.

[4] For a political economy analysis of cross-border shareholder voting, see M C Schouten, *The Political Economy of Cross-Border Voting in Europe* (2009), available at: http://ssrn.com/abstract=1430507; for policy and corporate governance analysis related to UK law, see J Payne, 'Intermediated Securities and the Right to Vote in the UK', in L Gullifer and J Payne (eds), *Intermediated Securities: Legal Problems and Practical Solutions* (Oxford: Hart Publishing, 2010).

[5] Federation of European Securities Exchanges, *Share Ownership Structure In Europe, FESE Report* (2007) at 13.

[6] Schouten, above n. 4, at 13. It should be noted, however, that the trend towards the internationalization of shareholdings has slowed down or in some cases reversed as a result of the financial crisis.

while domestic institutional investors hold 39 per cent and owner-ship concentration is dropping in public companies.[7] But significantly fewer foreign shareholders vote their shares than domestic shareholders.[8] Reforms designed to strengthen shareholder voting rights are designed to solve the two consequential major barriers to voting: (i) the passivity of shareholders, particularly institutional shareholders; and (ii) barriers to the exercise of voting rights, in particular on a cross-border basis.

This chapter focuses on legal solutions related to the removal of barriers to the exercise of shareholder voting rights in the cross-border environment. Apart from voting rights, shareholders have, of course, a number of other corporate rights, such as the right to a dividend, subscription rights and rights to other distributions, information rights, etc. Securities other than shares also, of course, grant the security holders other specific rights – bondholders typically have the right to receive interest, as well as restricted voting rights, usually in the event of an issuer's insolvency. The particular problems related to barriers to cross-border voting are, however, analo-gous to the problems related to processing of other corporate actions, and so are the proposed solutions. At the same time, participation in general meetings and the exercise of voting rights are considered the most complex of all corporate actions. Therefore, their management in the intermediated securities context may require more steps and actions than is the case, for example, with dividend distributions or the exercise of subscription rights. The particular reform context which intermediated securities generate may also provide an opportunity to improve the framework for the exer-cise of voting rights generally.

Participation in the general meeting and voting are not mandatory for shareholders. For various reasons, these rights are not always exercised by shareholders – in contrast, for example, to dividend distribution rights. As a result, any formal impediments to the exercise of those non-mandatory rights are likely to bring the level of the exercise of those rights even lower. Therefore, the removal of those barriers is a necessary – although not a sole[9] – condition to overcome shareholder passivity in Europe.

---

[7] Warsaw Stock Exchange statistics, 1st quarter of 2008 (on file with author).

[8] European Commission, Annex to the Proposal for a Directive of the European Parliament and of the Council on the exercise of voting rights by shareholders of companies having their registered office in a Member State and whose shares are admitted to trading on a regulated market and amending Directive 2004/109/EC, Impact Assessment, COM (2005) 685 (Brussels: European Commission, 2005), at 9.

[9] The measures needed to decrease shareholder passivity go beyond merely granting the ability to exercise corporate rights. Careful analysis is required of

This chapter accordingly analyses the troublesome overlapping area between company law and securities law in the context of the legal nature of securities. The legal challenges are presented, as well as the opportunities related to shareholder voting in the intermediated securities environment. The chapter also outlines the current European and international legislative initiatives in the areas of company law and securities law that affect the way cross-border shareholder voting rights are exercised.

THE EXERCISE OF SHAREHOLDER RIGHTS AND BOOK-ENTRY SECURITIES: OVERLAPS BETWEEN COMPANY AND SECURITIES LAW

Company Law and Securities Law Cross-overs

Company law provides a framework for the corporate organization. Company law and the company statutes regulate the legal position of the shareholder as well as the requirements that have to be met in order for a shareholder to exercise her rights. With respect to the exercise of shareholder voting rights, company law generally regards voting rights as central shareholder rights and identifies those corporate decisions for which shareholder voice is required. It also tackles to a certain degree the voting process, at each of its stages: the collection of information necessary to make a decision, the decision itself, and its execution (the arrangements for the actual process of voting).[10]

The exercise of corporate rights is an area that links company law to the general law of securities and marks the overlap between company law and securities law. With respect to the exercise of voting rights, the cross-over between securities law and company law is particularly clear in the following processes:

1. The identification/evidencing of the person entitled to exercise corporate rights, as well as the discharge by the company of the company's

---

shareholder incentives to become engaged and of the regulation thereof. See e.g. A Wacławik-Wejman, *Mehr Macht für Aktionäre: Stärkung des Aktionärsstimmrechts in Europa*, in E Lemanska, T Bachner and R Cierpial (eds), *Aktuelle Entwicklungen im polnischen, deutschen und österreichischen Privatrecht. Vereinheitlichung oder Auseinanderentwicklung?* (Vienna: Nomos Verlag, 2010).

[10] D.A. Zetzsche, 'Shareholder Passivity, Cross-Border Voting and the Shareholder Rights Directive', 8 *Journal of Corporate Law Studies*, 23 (2008).

duty towards shareholders (for example, to register the shareholder's vote); and

2. Communication with the shareholder – where the company needs to address its shareholders rather than the general public,[11] for example with respect to voting, elective corporate actions, shareholder proposals or distributions to shareholders.

Securities in the Company Law Environment: Evidencing the Title of Shareholding vis-à-vis the Issue

A share can be understood as a bundle of corporate rights. But it also represents an agreement between the issuing company and the shareholder to use a certain form of evidence concerning the holder's status as shareholder.[12] The focus of this chapter is on the latter agreement and how it is constructed in the case of intermediated securities. How the shareholder evidences and exercises rights depends on the type and form of the evidencing instrument and it will differ for certificated and uncertificated securities. In modern securities markets, shares are not held in paper form. This affects how shareholder rights are exercised. These issues are central concerns of securities law.[13]

Securities law typically lays down a general framework for agreements that evidence legal entitlement through transferable documents – in effect,

---

[11] E.g., many corporate announcements do not require notification of company shareholders as such, but rather they are published and made accessible to the general public, including the shareholders. The traditional means of addressing the public through publication in official gazettes or daily newspapers is being substituted by the publication of information on the corporate website. See Art. 5 of the Shareholder Rights Directive.

[12] Cf. J.N. Druey in: T. Guhl, *Das Schweizerische Obligationenrecht* (Zürich: Schulthess Verlag, 2000), 84; F. Zoll, *Klauzule dokumentowe. Prawo dokumentów dłużnych ze szczególnym uwzględnieniem papierów wartościowych* (Warsaw: C.H. Beck, 2001); and A Wacławik, *Prawo krótkoterminowych papierów dłużnych* (Krakow: Zakamycze, 2002).

[13] Securities law here is understood as referring to the private law of negotiable instruments evidencing legal entitlement – securities and other negotiable instruments (e.g., German *Wertpapiere, Effekten*; French *valeurs mobilieres, titres, effets de commerce*, US *investment securities*, as governed by Art. 8 of the Uniform Commercial Code, Polish *papiery wartosciowe*). It stands in contrast to public-law-driven securities regulation, the focus of which is the efficiency of capital markets and investor protection through regulatory measures. Notably, the continental legal tradition does not clearly distinguish between negotiable instruments and investment securities – they all belong to the broader category of instruments.

the security. In case of company shares, the basic conditions for the exercise of shareholder rights are as follows:

1.   Those who hold company shares at a certain point in time, as determined by law/the company, are authorized to exercise shareholder rights, provided they meet any other requirements set forth in company law; and
2.   The company must be provided with evidence as to the identity of the shareholder.

If the securities are in the form of a paper document, the share certificate provides evidence of the shareholding. Thus, the share certificate has a double role: for the shareholder, it is the evidence of the holding, and for the company it is a means of identifying the shareholder. On one hand, the shareholder receives an assurance that the company will perform the obligations it owes to the proper holder of the evidence. On the other hand, the company has the assurance that if it performs its obligations owed to a formally entitled person, it will be released of its obligations vis-à-vis the shareholder.

As the capital markets have moved to a paperless world, the key evidentiary functions of paper have been taken over by another form of evidence. Currently, in order to hold and smoothly transfer shares of listed companies, the investor opens a securities account with an intermediary. All listed companies in Europe are required to introduce issues of securities into a securities settlement system in which the securities entitlements have the form of electronic book entries on securities accounts.[14] Typically, the account to which the whole issue is registered is kept by a top level intermediary, for example a central securities depository (CSD), and the individual shareholder account is kept by a lower level intermediary, who holds a corresponding amount of securities on account with the CSD. Between the account in which the whole issue of securities is registered and the individual investor account there may be additional accounts maintained by other intermediaries. Longer chains of intermediaries come into play

---

[14]   There are significant differences between the underlying legal concepts governing book entry systems: in some countries book entry systems are linked to dematerialized securities (e.g., France, Poland); in other countries, global share certificates are deposited with an intermediary and immobilized before the securities entitlements can be recorded in the system of electronic securities accounts (e.g., Germany). There are also differences between the rights considered to be registered on the securities account: are the securities themselves registered (e.g., Germany, Poland) or are entitlements registered (e.g., securities interests in the United Kingdom or securities entitlements in the United States)?

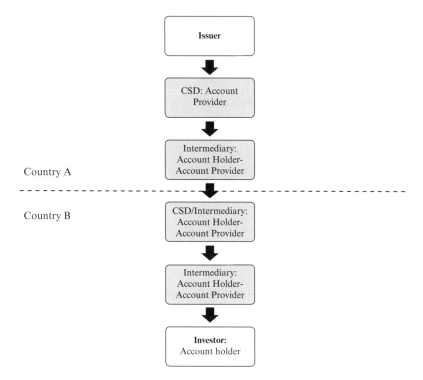

Figure 6.1   *Cross-border book-entry securities holdings – a simplified scheme*

when shareholders have their securities account in a country different to the country of the settlement system into which the securities of the issuer are entered (typically the country of the trading venue[15]). (See figure 6.1).

Book-Entry Securities – The Modified Relationship between the Company and Investor

In an intermediated securities environment, the book-entry system takes on the evidence function of certificated securities. The investor enters into a legal agreement with an intermediary account provider to keep

---

[15]   It can, however, also be the country of the issuer. In some Member States, there is still a requirement that the domestic issuer should register its issue with the local CSD, regardless of whether its securities will be traded at the local stock exchange.

accounts of the investor's securities holdings. Any acts related to those securities accordingly require the account provider's assistance: including the acquisition or disposal or holdings, the establishment of a secured interest in favour of a third party, and the exercise of any corporate rights by the investor. In all these cases, the investor alone cannot act as a legitimate shareholder vis-à-vis third parties or the issuer/company without the assistance of the account provider. This assistance may take the form of facilitating the evidencing of the investor vis-à-vis the issuer/company or other persons. It sometimes also takes the form of performing certain actions on behalf of the investor directly vis-à-vis the issuer/company or other parties – or, if the chain of intermediaries is longer, vis-à-vis the upper-tier intermediary who then performs these actions vis-à-vis their addressees.

Attempts have been made to apply the classical private law of negotiable instruments to book-entry securities. However, the law of certificated instruments does not capture the complexity of book-entry instruments. Indeed, by comparison with certificated securities there is far more complexity in the legal nature of intermediated securities. In the case of book-entry securities, the classic company/issuer–shareholder/investor relationship is substituted by a set of legal relationships and by a range of rights and obligations related to the administration of an evidentiary system by the account provider.

The Legal Problems of Intermediated Cross-border Securities Holdings

Because of the separation of the investor/shareholder from the issuer/company and the intermediation of their relationship, technological as well as legal uncertainties arise in relation to the exercise of voting rights and with respect to the information and corporate actions to which the shareholder is entitled. The longer the chain of account providers, the longer the processing of the voting right and thus the greater the risk and time pressure on the investor. The relationship between issuers and account providers must be identified, as must the relationships between account providers and shareholders/account holders. As a result, capital markets and securities law, rather than company law, is the body of law that deals with the legal intricacies of the intermediated securities holding systems.

The legal regime governing capital markets infrastructure in the EU is deeply fragmented, with significant differences between the Member States' legal frameworks for securities holding through account providers. The fragmentation of the legal chain of securities holdings can be property-law-driven or driven by regulation. Property-law-driven fragmentation is a product of differences among national property laws and the resulting differences among legal holding patterns. For example, some continental legal systems may not recognize the nominee–beneficial owner distinction applied in the intermediated securities holding system, which is typical for property law in common law countries. The regulatory fragmentation arises as not all EU Member States recognize multiple tiers or foreign holding patterns and foreign chains of intermediaries. In the case of such non-recognition, the nominee would be recognized as the actual shareholder in such continental systems, leaving the beneficial owner out of the legal picture. As a result, the actual foreign shareholder is cut from the holding chain in the country of the issuer, while certain regulations addressed to the shareholders are applied to the foreign intermediary who is the last link in the domestic intermediary chain.

Longer chains of intermediaries, combined with the fragmentation of the capital markets infrastructure in Europe, lead to legal uncertainty with respect to cross-border securities in a number of respects. First, communication between the issuer and the shareholder may be delayed or distorted by the long chain of intermediaries, which is governed by different national regulations and across which different standards of service may apply. Second, problems may arise with the core evidencing function as cross-country differences may arise between domestically-applied rules of identification. Some countries also may not recognize that foreign intermediaries are merely intermediaries (and not shareholders) and that the actual shareholder is a person at the very bottom of the holding chain, which may be located outside of the domestic chain of intermediaries.

Many legal systems attempt to create a legal framework for intermediated securities by means of a direct analogy to the concept of direct holding of certificated securities, and thus assume the investor has property rights over the securities (the form of those property rights varies; they can, for example, be defined as co-ownership rights over the pool of securities held by the account provider of the investor at the upper-tier account). In those systems, the shareholder is considered to be the legal securities owner and thus has the right to enforce his/her rights against the company. In other systems, the account provider is the legal owner of the securities and the shareholder is the beneficial owner. In these systems, the investor cannot act directly vis-à-vis the issuer and the terms and conditions governing the exercise of the rights from securities apply to the account provider, albeit subject to instructions from the shareholder-beneficial owner.

There are a number of impediments to the proper identification of the shareholder in a cross-border chain of intermediaries. In a number of countries, foreign nominee holdings or omnibus accounts are not permitted or recognized by the domestic system. As a result, the account holder recognized as the last link in the chain of intermediaries by a particular Member State is recognized as the shareholder for company law purposes. In some cases, a certificate confirming a shareholding issued by a foreign account provider will not be recognized as evidence of the shareholding in another country; thus only shareholders who are clients of a domestic intermediary can be recognized as shareholders for voting purposes. Further, in a number of countries there is uncertainty or a lack of legal rules with respect to vote splitting, in case of the exercise of voting rights by an account provider and where different votes are represented by securities of the same class registered with the omnibus account of the account provider. Impediments with respect to voting through proxies also arise across Europe.

There are also significant differences in national legal provisions with respect to the processing of corporate actions. The discrepancies between Member States' laws relate, for example, to the determination of the date relevant for identification of the person entitled to a security[16] for the purposes of the exercise of particular rights vested in the security, for example, for the exercise of voting rights or receipt of dividends. Some national systems do not recognize the concept of the record date (the date that sets a point in time at which the entitlement to vote is determined). In such cases, share blocking is required. Where share blocking applies, shares are deposited or blocked in the securities account, which effectively results in the inability of the shareholder to transfer blocked shares until the date of the general meeting. Where the concept of the record date is applied, national laws vary in their determination of the record date, providing, variously, that the date is the trade date, the intended settlement date or the actual settlement date.

The duties of account providers to facilitate the exercise of shareholder rights by their clients are not made clear in some national legal systems. Regardless of whether an investor in securities held through account providers is granted the right to act directly vis-à-vis the issuer under the particular national system, the exercise of rights by the shareholder always requires certain action by, or on the part of, the account provider. However, because of the nature of the holding of securities through an account provider (including the fact that the shareholder typically has no legal relationship with the upper-tier account provider), the shareholder is dependent on action by the account provider in order to enforce his/

---

[16]   This date is not the date of the security transfer; it is determined by the issuer for a particular class of securities.

her rights, either through providing certification vis-à-vis the issuer that the shareholder actually is the owner of securities, or through contractual means that authorize the account provider to act vis-à-vis the issuer on behalf of the shareholder.

To sum up, the exercise of shareholder rights is dependent on the efficient legal functioning of the securities clearing and settlement infrastructure. Any improvement envisaged by laws strengthening the exercise of shareholder rights generally could therefore be trumped where the relevant securities are held through long cross-border chains of intermediaries and where a fragmented legal framework governs securities clearing and settlement infrastructures.

The Classical Issuer–Shareholder Relationship and The Opportunities Presented by Book-Entry Systems

Book-entry systems for evidencing securities holdings contribute, however, to the technical facilitation and streamlining of the processes related to mass turnover in securities in the modern capital markets. Book-entry systems can channel certain communications between the issuer and the investor. This new communication channel presents certain opportunities for the simplification of the process, particularly by comparison with the traditional process that applies to the exercise of rights vested in certificated securities. This potential for simplification is particularly relevant in case of cross-border securities holdings. In the cross-border context, the application of the same rules to the voting process as in the case of certificated securities could therefore lead to unnecessary or excessive burdens on the investor or the issuing company.

For example, in many Member States there is a requirement to announce a general meeting in an official gazette of the country of the issuer[17] – although most shareholders, in particular foreign shareholders, do not have access to the official gazette. It is much more efficient to rely on electronic means of communication between the company and the shareholders, or to rely on the fact that the systems of securities accounts make it at least functionally possible to identify the shareholder at the end of the chain of intermediaries and so to rely on intermediated communication between the company and all its shareholders. It should therefore be the case that notifications reach the interested persons, including foreign shareholders, by the use of the Internet rather than printed

---

[17]   WSE Statistics, above n. 7, at 12 and 65–7.

announcements in local gazettes, or reach the actual shareholders through the chain of intermediaries.

Another example relates to the requirement that the shareholder personally present the proof of holding of shares to the company[18] and then physically attend the general meeting to vote.[19] In the intermediated securities environment, the process of proving to the issuer that one is the shareholder requires cooperation between the account provider and the shareholder. The shareholder requires assistance from his/her account provider in order to be able to prove to the issuer that s/he is entitled to participate in the general meeting and the law should determine the duties of the account provider in this context. On the other hand, electronic means of communication provide for a framework that allows the shareholder to participate in the general meeting – and vote – at a distance.[20]

Further, modern securities markets infrastructure, and in particular intermediated securities holding chains, create the possibility of streamlined communication where the intermediary connects with the issuer on behalf of the shareholder – through its existing connection to the chain of intermediaries and, ultimately, through the connection of the top-tier intermediary in the chain to the issuer. This chain of communication can be used both for passing the proof of entitlement to the issuer and for the voting process.

It is also worth noting another important assumption of classical company law that could be challenged in the intermediated securities environment. The intermediary chain creates the opportunity to track the shareholders of the company at a given moment. While traditionally the issuer would have to wait for the shareholders to identify themselves to the company by registering their shares with the company, book-entry securities make it possible to identify the shareholders at any time. An important policy issue arises, therefore, as to whether European issuers should be granted the right to use this opportunity. This issue may be gaining in importance owing to the policy of facilitating cross-border shareholdings through complex securities holding chains. The issue has not, however, been resolved so far in the current EU policy debate.

---

[18] See e.g. Poland, above n. 7, at 79.

[19] See the comparative data on electronic voting and voting per mail, above n 7, at 91–5.

[20] The above two issues are to a certain degree addressed by the Shareholder Rights Directive (Art. 5, Arts 7–9), which will be discussed below.

REMOVING OBSTACLES TO THE CROSS-BORDER EXERCISE OF SHAREHOLDER RIGHTS: EU AND INTERNATIONAL LEGISLATIVE INITIATIVES

EU Company Law

Despite recent developments, the current initiatives to strengthen shareholder voting rights in Europe are, to a large extent, still based on the 2003 Action Plan on Modernising Company Law and Enhancing Corporate Governance in the European Union[21] (the Action Plan), which adopted the recommendations of the Winter Report on the Modernisation of the European Company Law.[22] The Action Plan was presented to the Council and the European Parliament in 2003. As stated in the Action Plan, the European Commission aims to establish a real shareholder democracy in the EU over the medium to long term.[23] A major step towards this goal is the strengthening of shareholder rights to information and to participation in general meetings, in particular to vote.

The EU Shareholder Rights Directive

The main legal instrument addressing the issue of shareholder voting in Europe is the Shareholder Rights Directive (SRD).[24] The Shareholder Rights Directive, adopted in 2007, is a response to the growing importance of cross-border shareholdings and to related concerns about the low level of general meeting participation and exercise of voting rights, particularly by shareholders holding their shares on a cross-border basis. It aims to remove the existing barriers to voting and focuses on shareholders' access to information and the legal issues governing the process of voting. Currently, barriers result in significantly fewer foreign shareholders voting their shares than domestic shareholders.[25] The Directive was to be implemented by 3 August 2009.

The Directive applies to certain shareholder rights attaching to voting

---

[21] European Commission, *Communication from the Commission to the Council and the European Parliament – Modernising Company Law and Enhancing Corporate Governance in the European Union – A Plan to Move Forward* COM(2003)284 (Brussels: European Commission, 2003).

[22] *Report of the High Level Group of Company Law Experts on a Modern Regulatory Framework for Company Law in Europe* (2004).

[23] Commission, above n. 21, at 14.

[24] Above n. 3.

[25] WSE statistics, above n. 7, at 9.

shares in relation to the general meeting (GM) of companies with a registered office in an EU Member State and whose shares are admitted to
trading on a regulated market in a Member State.[26] The SRD covers
certain aspects of information collection (GM-related information) and
of execution.[27] It introduces rights and duties that aim to enhance shareholder control over the GM agenda (Article 6), improve the communication between the company and its shareholders (Article 9), minimize
barriers to the identification of shareholders' entitlement to vote and
remove restrictions on disposing of the security before the general meeting
(Article 7). The Directive acknowledges the use of means of distance
communication for the purpose of participation and voting at the GM
(Articles 8 and 12). It also aims to remove certain barriers to voting by
proxy (Articles 10–11) and by nominee shareholders (Article 13).

The SRD lays down the legal framework for the exercise of shareholder
rights in the cross-border context. The Directive explicitly confirms a
fundamental company law principle, the principle of equal treatment of
shareholders, in order to stress the need to remove any discrimination
between domestic and foreign shareholders within the EU.[28] A number of
the Directive's stipulations are relevant from the perspective of book-entry
systems. In particular, the SRD Regulatory Impact Assessment noted
that the key problem in cross-border voting related to the complexity of
the process. With respect to shareholder identification for the purpose of
voting at the GM, the Directive introduces the record date regime, pursuant to which the persons who hold shares of the issuer on a certain date
determined by the issuer are entitled to vote at the GM. This regime is
designed to replace any regimes based on share blocking.[29] The introduction of the record date regime has certain important consequences when
applied to book-entry securities. The Directive does not determine what
it means to 'hold shares' on a specified date, as a prerequisite for identification as shareholder. The determination as to 'holding shares' will rely
on national securities law and on the particular system of book entries
on securities accounts. Corporate governance issues, beyond the scope
of this chapter, also arise where shares are sold after the record date and
economic interests and voting power are split.[30]

The Directive also mandates removal of any excessive requirements con-

---

[26]   Art. 1 para 1, SRD.
[27]   Arts 5 and 14.
[28]   Art. 4.
[29]   Art. 7, paras 1–3.
[30]   H Hu and B Black, 'Empty Voting and Hidden (Morphable) Ownership:
Taxonomy, Implications, and Reforms', 31 *The Business Lawyer*, 3 (2006) at 1011.

cerning proof of qualification as shareholder[31] and requires the company laws of the Member States to accept persons acting as shareholders vis-à-vis the company who do not have an economic interest in the shares, but are nominees exercising the rights of the underlying shareholders. The Directive further recognizes the possibility of split voting. The Directive does not, however, explicitly require the mandatory recognition of nominees in those legal systems that currently do not recognize nominees – this is one of the most significant securities law issues related to the issue of recognition of cross-border multi-tiered intermediary chains.[32]

EU Securities Clearing and Settlement Law

The EU has for some time identified the fragmentation of the securities clearing and settlement infrastructure as a key barrier to capital markets integration in the EU. In 2001 and 2003, two key reports were written by a group of experts, led by Alberto Giovannini, which identified three types of barriers to cross-border clearing and settlement in Europe that required an EU solution: technological, legal and tax barriers.[33]

Overall, although EU action is becoming more intrusive, particularly in the wake of the crisis, the EU regards EU regulatory action as generally subsidiary, and gives priority to the securities clearing and settlement infrastructure integration processes initiated by the capital markets infrastructure industry itself. Private sector operating standards and best practices (including the 2006 Code of Conduct on Clearing and Settlement, which has been signed by the vast majority of European stock exchanges, CSDs and CCPs, and which is monitored by the Commission through the Code Monitoring Group) are regarded as the preferred primary solution. The industry work on harmonization is ongoing.[34] However, in areas such as the law and taxation, it is clear that there is a need for regulatory action. For this chapter's purposes, the legal barriers and the work of the Legal Certainty Group are the most relevant.

The ongoing EU initiatives in the sphere of securities clearing and settlement must also be viewed in the context of the parallel preparatory works on an international law of intermediated securities: the UNIDROIT draft

---

[31] Art. 7, para 4.

[32] See discussion below.

[33] Following the Giovannini reports, three expert groups were formed at the EU Commission level to provide detailed advice on the solutions needed in the three areas mentioned: CESAME, the Legal Certainty Group and FISCO.

[34] See e.g. the reports of the Monitoring Group at http://ec.europa.eu/internal_market/financial-markets/clearing/mog_en.htm.

Convention on substantive law applicable to intermediated securities; and the Hague Convention on the conflict of laws aspects of intermediated securities. If ratified, these conventions could form part of the EU legal framework. Therefore, they will be briefly presented to complete this outline of historical developments and of the future EU legislative framework.

International Legislative Initiatives

The UNIDROIT Convention

The UNIDROIT Convention on Substantive Rules for Intermediated Securities[35] is a proposed instrument of international law. After its adoption, it will become binding not only on European Union Members States, but also on other countries. While the scope of application of the draft Convention exceeds the scope of the EU legislative instruments, a number of issues have been left to contracting State law, which makes the UNIDROIT Convention a much more general legal document than the European legislative initiatives.

The Convention regulates the legal aspects of corporate action processing in Articles 8, 9, 10, 29 and 30. Pursuant to those provisions, an account holder has the right to enjoy shareholder rights, provided that the account holder is not an account provider at the same time. Article 9(1)(a) stipulates that a credit to a securities account confers on the account holder, for its own account, the right to receive and exercise rights attached to securities, including, inter alia, voting rights. Importantly, the Convention does not attempt to determine who is entitled to exercise rights vested in securities vis-à-vis the issuer. In fact, relations between the securities holder and the issuer have been left in their entirety outside the scope of the Convention.[36] Whether the investor can exercise rights against the intermediary or the issuer depends on the terms of the securities and the applicable non-Convention rules, or both.[37]

The Convention also mandates the removal of barriers to cross-border intermediated holdings of listed securities through the recognition of multi-tiered holding systems, including nominee and omnibus systems and partial or split exercise of corporate rights. In particular, Article 29(1) prescribes that contracting States must permit the holding through account

---

[35]　The Convention was adopted in October 2009 and is awaiting the required ratifications:　see　further　http://www.unidroit.org/english/implement/i-2009-intermediatedsecurities.pdf.

[36]　Art. 8.

[37]　Art. 9(2)(B).

providers of securities admitted to trading on an exchange or regulated market. With respect to nominee and omnibus holdings, Article 29(2) requires contracting States to recognize the holding of such securities by an account provider acting in its own name but on behalf of its clients and to permit such an account provider to exercise split voting or split the exercise of other corporate actions. Finally, Article 30 ensures that any set-off rights against the insolvent issuer not be precluded because the securities are held through account providers.

The Convention also provides a general description of the account provider's duties. Pursuant to Article 10(1), an account provider has the duty of the intermediary to enable the account holders to receive and exercise their rights. This obligation does not require the account provider to take actions that are not within its power or to establish new securities accounts with another account provider (Art. 10(2)).

Convention on the Law Applicable to Certain Rights in Respect of Securities held with on Intermediary

The Convention of 5 July 2006 on the Law Applicable to Certain Rights in Respect of Securities held with an Intermediary (the Hague Convention) also addresses cross-border intermediated securities holding. The Hague Convention addresses conflict of laws issues in international book-entry securities holdings. It deals with the law applicable to clearance, settlement and secured credit transactions that cross national borders. The Hague Convention has not been ratified by the European Union.[38]

The Legal Certainty Group's Advice

The Legal Certainty Group (LCG) deals with legal issues related to intermediated securities holding structures. Its mandate covers barriers to cross-border securities holdings, and covers all types of intermediated securities holdings and all corporate actions (Giovannini Barriers 13, 3 and 9).[39] The SRD, by contrast, applies only to shares of companies admitted to trading on a regulated market.[40] Three key areas have been subject to LCG deliberations:

---

[38]   It has, however, been ratified by the United States and Switzerland.

[39]   Two other key aspects of legal certainty related to cross-border securities holdings are: the issue of settlement finality and legal recognition of netting (Giovannini Barrier 14) and conflicts of laws issues (Barrier 15). These barriers have been addressed by other legal instruments (including the EU Collateral Directive and the Convention an the Law Applicable to Certain Rights in Respect of Securities held with on Intermediary) and are not within the scope of LCG works.

[40]   Art. 3, para 1.2, SRD.

1.   the absence of an EU-wide framework for the treatment of interests in securities held with an intermediary (Barrier 13);
2.   the differences in national legal provisions affecting corporate action processing (Barrier 3); and
3.   the restrictions relating to the issuer's ability to choose the location of its securities (Barrier 9).

The LCG was formed in 2004 and in 2006 delivered its First Advice to the EU Commission,[41] in which it recommended that a common EU-wide legal framework was needed for the treatment of interests in securities held with an intermediary as well as for the removal of existing restrictions to the issuer's ability to choose the location of its securities. In the area of legal obstacles to corporate actions, the LCG advised that the Commission wait until the finalization of related measures, including the Shareholder Rights Directive, and then assess which gaps required filling by the LCG. The Second Advice[42] of the Legal Certainty Group in 2008 builds upon the framework provided by the First Advice and reflects the UNIDROIT Convention on Substantive Rules Regarding Intermediated Securities. The 2008 recommendations of the LCG are divided into three groups, each corresponding to one of the Giovannini barriers addressed. In what follows, the recommendations relevant for the exercise of shareholder rights will be described.

First of all, the LCG Advice does not intervene in the terms of securities, for example, the rights and obligations of issuers. It focuses on the legal aspects of holding, transferring and exercising rights vested in securities held through intermediaries. The Group noted the need to remove the legal barriers to harmonization arising from differences in the legal frameworks of the Member States and the legal fragmentation of the securities holdings infrastructure. These barriers are particularly visible in the case of cross-border corporate actions processing and can lead to foreign shareholders being discriminated against relative to domestic investors.[43] Therefore the

---

[41]   Available at: http://ec.europa.eu/internal_market/financial-markets/docs/certainty/advice_final_en.pdf.

[42]   Available at: http://ec.europa.eu/internal_market/financial-markets/docs/certainty/2ndadvice_final_en.pdf.

[43]   The principle of equal treatment as foreseen in the Shareholder Rights Directive can be a guiding principle in the removal of barriers to cross-border clearing and settlement of securities. Non-discrimination means making the effective exercise of shareholder rights available to all shareholders, and the removal of the barriers to the enjoyment of rights and any discriminatory differentiation in the time frame of the exercise of shareholder rights.

LCG Advice recommends that Member States should recognize holding patterns of other jurisdictions (Recommendation 13). The desired result is to make cross-border chains of intermediaries 'visible' to the Member States' legal systems, including multiple tiers of intermediaries, and omnibus and nominee account structures.[44] This approach allows for proper enforcement of account holders' rights vis-à-vis the account providers. It also does not require any significant modification of domestic regimes governing holding patterns, which are deeply enrooted in the local property law system.

The legal relationship between the account holder and the account provider is the key relationship in the book-entry securities context (Recommendation 2). As noted above, account providers are entities who keep securities accounts for their clients – the account holders.[45] Account providing tends to be a regulated activity throughout Europe. It is performed by banks, investment firms, CSDs, international central securities depositories (ICSDs) and similar entities. The future EU legal regime, currently under development, will have to take a position on whether account providing can generally be performed by any entity or whether it is a regulated activity. The account holder can be a natural or legal person on whose behalf the securities are held by the account provider. Account holders can sometimes be, at the same time, account providers to their clients. The LCG has taken a functional approach in its Advice; it does not matter who the account provider is (CSD, custodian bank or another entity), as long as it performs the functions related to maintaining securities accounts.

As discussed above, investors require the assistance of these intermediaries in order to exercise the rights, and enjoy the benefits, vested in their securities. The LCG's recommendations related to the exercise of shareholder rights (Giovannini Barrier 3) accordingly focus on the role and duties of account providers in corporate actions processing. The LCG analysed the different types of assistance that could be provided by an account provider. In order of the relative intensity of the level of assistance, they are:

- assistance in the evidencing and identification of the investor vis-à-vis the issuer, for example, through providing the investor with a certificate that the investor can show to the issuer in order to be entered on a list of shareholders for a particular corporate event;

---

[44] Dermot Turing, Omnibus Accounts (2005), http://ec.europa.eu/internal_market/financial-markets/docs/certainty/background/31_8_5_turing_en.pdf.

[45] In the LCG's opinion, the Scandinavian-type account operators who effectively administer securities accounts, while technically the accounts are maintained by a CSD, should be subject to the same framework of duties as account providers. Ibid. at 33.

- operating a communication channel between the investor and the issuer and passing information between the issuer and the investor up and down the chain of account providers – the scope of the communication service may vary depending upon the agreement between the account provider and account holder; and
- the actual exercise of an investor's rights on behalf of the investor, including collecting and distributing any company distributions received, and exercising shareholder rights vis-à-vis the company, including voting rights. This highest degree of assistance is most relevant for custodian activity in those legal systems that attribute the legal ownership of securities to the intermediary, rather than to the investor.

The LCG accordingly recommends a minimum framework for account provider duties vis-à-vis account holders, in order to enable the enjoyment of account holder rights related to the security held (Recommendation 3). The Advice explicitly states the duty of account providers to facilitate the exercise of holders' rights vis-à-vis the issuer. Moreover, in certain cases the LCG recommends that the account provider act on behalf of the holder. These cases include the distribution of dividends and interests, the exercise of subscription or exchange rights, the acceptance of takeover bids, mergers and other purchase offers and conversions (Recommendation 14).

Where the account provider exercises the holder's rights vis-à-vis the issuer, the account provider should always act upon and in accordance with the account holder's instructions (Recommendation 10). The provider should not be permitted to act without instructions and, unless otherwise agreed, he cannot rely on instructions originating from a person other than the entitled shareholder. LCG Recommendation 15 also provides for the freedom of the issuer to enter its securities into a clearing and settlement system of its choice within any Member State.

The Future EU Legislation Harmonizing Securities Law

Following the Second Advice of the Legal Certainty Group, the ECOFIN Council, in its conclusions of 2 December 2008, urgently requested an outline of legislative measures for a harmonized legal framework for intermediated securities. In June 2009, the EU Commission launched a public consultation to consider possible legislative instruments to harmonize securities law in the European Union;[46] a second consultation followed

---

[46] European Commission, *Legislation on Legal Certainty of Securities Holding and Disposition* G2/PP D (2009) (Brussels: European Commission,

in November 2010.[47] While the outcome remains uncertain, any possible legislative instrument should address four issues:

1. the legal framework for the holding and disposition of securities held in securities accounts, covering substantive law as well as conflict of laws;
2. the legal framework governing the exercise of holder's rights flowing from securities through a chain of intermediaries, in particular in cross-border situations;
3. the establishment of free, EU-wide choice for issuers with respect to where the initial entry of their securities in the relevant holding structure is made, in particular with respect to CSDs; and
4. an appropriate supervisory regime governing the activities of safekeeping and administration of securities.

THE EUROPEAN MARKET STANDARDS FOR GENERAL MEETINGS – AN ALTERNATIVE TO LEGISLATION?

In December 2008, the Joint Working Group on General Meetings (JWGGM), comprising representatives of issuers, CSDs, intermediaries and stock exchanges,[48] published its proposal for European Market Standards for General Meetings (the Standards).[49] The Standards have been prepared in coordination with CESAME and as a measure complementary, and to some extent possibly alternative, to any new European legislative measure governing market participants' duties related to the exercise of shareholder voting rights in intermediated structures.

It is common to distinguish between three phases in relation to general

---

2009). Responses to the consultation are available at: http://ec.europa.eu/internal_market/consultations/2009/securities_law_en.htm.

[47] A second consultation was launched in November 2010: available at http://ec.europa.eu/internal_market/consultations/docs/2010/securities/consultation_paper_en.pdf.

[48] The following industry organizations were represented in the JWGGM: European Issuers (previously EALIC), ECSDA – the European Central Securities Depositories Association), EBF – the European Banking Federation, ESBG – the European Savings Bank Group, EACB – the European Association of Cooperative Banks and ESSF, previously ESF – the European Securities Services Forum and FESE – the Federation of European Securities Exchanges.

[49] Available at: http://www.europeanissuers.eu/_lib/newsflash/CAJWG%20 Standards%20Version%20for%20endorsement%208May09.doc.pdf.

meetings: the pre-meeting phase, the meeting, and post-meeting. The SRD reflects these distinctions, with Articles 5–7 referring to the pre-meeting phase, Articles 8–13 to the meeting itself, and Article 14 to the post-meeting phase. The JWGGM came to the conclusion that the most acute barriers to free exercise of voting rights are present in the pre-meeting phase and for this reason the Standards refer only to the processing of actions that need to take place before the GM. There are three main areas that the Standards deal with: (i) the meeting notice, (ii) the record date and related entitlements, and (iii) the notice of attendance at the GM.

The Standards provide for communication between the issuer and the end investor via the chain of intermediaries. The issuer should pass the notice of the GM with specified content (Standard 1.11) to the CSD, which then passes it through the chain of intermediaries to the end shareholder (Standards 1.1–1.3, 1.5–1.6 and 1.7–1.9). The issuer should decide whether it wants to receive notification of GM attendance (Standard 3) from the shareholder also through the chain of intermediaries, or whether it should be contacted directly by the shareholder (Standard 1.11). The issuer can also decide whether it wants to be informed about the shareholder entitlement and provided with the shareholder's proof of entitlement by the intermediary (Standard 1.11).

An important duty of the intermediary is the determination of persons entitled to vote on the statutory record date. The Standards set out requirements governing the determination of voting entitlements (Standard 2). The Standards propose the use of a 'uniform proof of entitlement throughout Europe'. Under Standard 2.9, the proof of entitlement should be the only valid proof of the entitlement to vote required by the issuer for participating and voting at the GM, irrespective of the means of participation chosen by the shareholder. The details of the uniform proof of entitlement are to be agreed during the implementation of the Standards.[50]

A question arises whether the Standards can be effectively implemented by means of endorsement by all the market participants involved, or whether a legislative instrument will be needed to codify certain aspects of the Standards. It seems that the Standards can do a good job in determining the degree to which the intermediary chain should be used for issuer–shareholder communication as an agreed level of service. On the other hand, uniformity with regard to the pan-EU acceptance of proof of entitlement issued by the shareholder's intermediary cannot be ensured with certainty without a legislative instrument mandating such acceptance. Another problematic issue concerns the ability of the issuer to

---

[50]   The Standards, introductory note to Standard 2.9.

request information on the entitlement and the proof of entitlement of the persons entitled to vote on the record date. There is at present no uniform EU policy on issuer access to shareholder information. Unless access to this information is granted, with shareholder permission, the existing restrictions on personal data processing may be a regulatory barrier to the passing of this information to the issuer. Therefore, there may be a need for a uniform legislative instrument to ensure that issuers and upper-tier intermediaries can obtain this information from the shareholder's intermediaries.

CONCLUSION

This chapter has provided an overview of how intermediated securities are held, the legal difficulties that arise, and the EU measures in train to remove the existing legal and regulatory barriers to the exercise of shareholder rights in cross-border intermediated securities holding structures. The following remarks can be offered by way of conclusion. First, in the context of the legal framework for exercising shareholder rights, there is an important link between company law and the law of intermediated securities. Second, the effective and efficient cross-border exercise of shareholder rights is not possible without a sound legal framework for cross-border intermediated securities holdings. Third, a modern framework for the exercise of shareholder rights should be a joint product of a number of legislative initiatives.

EU policy aims to facilitate the exercise of shareholder rights and to provide for closer coordination between company law and securities law matters. The Shareholder Rights Directive aims to modernize those requirements and to remove the related obstacles to cross-border voting. However, in order to achieve this goal, it is not sufficient to stipulate the specific duties and rights of the issuer and the shareholders. As the relationship between the shareholder and the issuer is intermediated, and the holding systems and the intermediaries are governed by fragmented Member States legal systems, the harmonization of voting rights requires the harmonization of the laws related to book-entry securities, and that similar standards apply to intermediaries with respect to assisting shareholders in the exercise of their rights. The LCG's recommendations and the Commission's current efforts to develop a Securities Law could fill the gaps in the existing EU law by providing a legal framework governing the basic contents of the legal rights of the shareholder and the duties of the intermediary.

PART III

Consumer and depositor protection

7. The crash that launched a thousand fixes: Regulation of consumer credit after the lending revolution and the credit crunch

Iain Ramsay and Toni Williams[1]

INTRODUCTION

The consumer lending 'revolution'[2] – with its promise of the democratisation of credit – was followed by the credit crunch. The credit crunch has stimulated both immediate regulatory initiatives and more fundamental reflection on consumer credit regulation.[3] As the Turner Review in the UK

---

[1] An earlier draft of this chapter was presented at the University of Tokyo, 9 March 2009. We thank those who made comments, in particular Professor Hi-san Hirose.

[2] See Federal Deposit Insurance Corporation, *Evaluating the Consumer Lending Revolution* (2003), available at http://www.fdic.gov/bank/analytical/fyi/2003/091703fyi.html and R. Brown and S. Burhouse, 'Implications of the Supply-Side Revolution in Consumer Lending', 24 *St. Louis University Public Law Review*, 363 (2005). This revolution included: financial liberalisation, deregulation of interest rates, securitisation, the application of sophisticated computer technology to develop predictive credit scores and risk-based pricing, and the increasing spread of all-purpose credit cards.

[3] In the UK these include: 'A New Approach to Consumer Credit' in *A Better Deal for Consumers: Delivering Real Help Now and Change for the Future,* Cm 7669 (London: TSO, 2009); 'Supporting and Protecting Consumers' in HM Treasury , *Reforming Financial Markets,* Cm 7667 (London: TSO, 2009); HM Treasury, *A New Approach to Financial Regulation: Judgment, Focus and Stability,* Cm 7874 (London: TSO, 2010), ch 4; Financial Services Authority, *Consultation Paper 10/16, Mortgage Market Review: Responsible Lending* (London: FSA, 2010); and HM Treasury/Department of Business Innovation and Skills, *Call for Evidence in Support of the Consumer Credit and Personal Insolvency Review* (2010), available at http://www.bis.gov.uk/assets/biscore/consumer-issues/docs/m/10-1185-managing-borrowing-call-for-evidence.pdf.

In the US, see US Department of Treasury, *A New Foundation: Rebuilding Financial Regulation and Supervision* (Washington DC: Department of Treasury,

notes, conventional regulatory assumptions – that reputable firms do not place risky products on the market, that innovation is stifled by regulation and that regulators are not as well placed as the market to judge the value of products – have been challenged by the financial crisis.[4]

This chapter explores an influential neo-liberal[5] approach to the fundamental problems of consumer credit regulation – availability and safety – that is promoted by the World Bank. We discuss the difficulties of achieving effective regulation that is fair and distributionally progressive within the framework of the World Bank's approach. We then turn to the role of public regulation of consumer credit markets. Neo-liberalism is often associated with a minimal role for the state, but even within neo-liberalism public regulation of consumer credit markets is necessary to achieve public confidence and fairness in credit markets.[6] Public regulation may take a variety of forms. In response to the financial crisis the US government has established a Consumer Financial Protection Bureau, with powers to regulate consumers credit so that 'all consumers have

---

2009), Department of Treasury, *Financial Regulatory Reform: A New Foundation* (Washington DC: Department of Treasury, 2009) at 55–70 and Title X of the Dodd-Frank Wall Street Reform and Consumer Protection Act (the Consumer Financial Protection Act of 2010). The Consumer Financial Protection Act 2010 establishes the Consumer Financial Protection Bureau (§1011). Although the safety of credit products is not listed among the Bureau's objectives (§1021), its powers to regulate the marketing and provision of consumer financial services would allow the Bureau to regulate safety related characteristics of financial product sales. See also the Credit Card Act 2009.

Gowan suggests the possibility of returning to a public utility model of financial services. See P. Gowan, 'Crisis in the Heartland: Consequences of the New Wall Street System', 55 *New Left Review*, 5 (2009). See also R. Wade, 'Financial Regime Change?', 54 *New Left Review*, 5 (2008). Bar-Gill and Warren earlier argued for a Consumer Credit Safety Commission that would screen credit products for safety. See O. Bar-Gill and E. Warren, 'Making Credit Safer', 157 *University of Pennsylvania Law Review*, 1 (2008). See also R. Shiller, *The Sub-Prime Solution* (Princeton: Princeton University Press, 2008) and M. Barr, S. Mullainathan and E. Shafir, *Behaviourally Informed Financial Services Regulation* (New America Foundation, 2008).

⁴ A. Turner, *The Turner Review: A Regulatory Response to the Global Banking Crisis* (London: FSA, 2009).

⁵ See generally D. Harvey, *A Brief History of Neoliberalism* (Oxford: Oxford University Press, 2005). See also S. Mudge, 'What is neo-liberalism?', 6 *Socio-Economic Review*, 703 (2008).

⁶ 'All commercial entities that . . . lend funds to consumers should be licensed and supervised by the appropriate prudential and market conduct regulator.' See World Bank, *Good Practices for Consumer Protection and Financial Literacy in Europe and Central Asia: A Diagnostic Tool* (Washington DC: World Bank, 2008), at 7.

access to markets for consumer financial products and services and that markets for consumer financial products and services are fair, transparent, and competitive'.[7] A variation on this model has existed in the UK since the Financial Services Authority (FSA) began to regulate secured credit (October 2004) and consumer insurance (January 2005) and we examine the role of the FSA in regulating sub-prime lending and payment protection insurance through its 'Treating Customers Fairly' initiative. This regulatory initiative provides important data for future regulation by the proposal Financial Conduct Authority.[8]

NEO-LIBERAL APPROACHES TO REGULATION

Neo-liberal regulation promotes access to consumer credit and the creation of confidence in an expanding and competitive consumer credit market.[9] Consumer choice and the promotion of individual management and responsibility for one's finances are assumptions guiding regulation. Regulation within neo-liberalism assumes that consumer credit is beneficial by permitting income smoothing over an individual's life cycle, for example permitting younger consumers to accumulate assets during periods of low income and addressing temporary income deficits.[10] Facilitating access to consumer credit is promoted as contributing, albeit indirectly, to alleviating poverty in developing countries.[11] The promotion of fairness in credit contracts is not, in itself, incompatible with neo-liberalism since a fair market promotes confidence and expansion of the market. This was the underpinning for the overall structure of the UK Consumer Credit Act 1974, which included a mandatory licensing scheme for all credit providers.

---

[7]   Consumer Financial Protection Act 2010, §1021.

[8]   HM Treasury, *A New Approach*, above n 3, ch 4; *Financial Conduct Authority: Approach to Regulation*, June 2011, http://www.fsa.gov.uk/pubs/events/fca-approach.pdf

[9]   See, e.g., Report of the Committee (The Crowther Committee), *Consumer Credit*, Cm 4596. The starting point for the report was that the 'state should interfere as little as possible with the consumer's freedom to use his knowledge of the consumer credit market to the best of his ability and according to his judgment of what constitutes his best interests': para. 3.9.1.

[10]   See World Bank, *Finance for All: Policies and Pitfalls in Extending Access* (Washington DC: World Bank, 2008), ch 3. See also D Karlan and J Zinman, 'Expanding Credit Access: Using Randomized Supply Decisions to Estimate the Impacts', 23(1) *Review of Financial Studies*, 433 (2006).

[11]   See Karlan and Zinman, above n. 10.

The central institutions and policies advocated for consumer credit markets within neo-liberalism are: (1) credit bureaux and positive credit reporting, (2) truth in lending and product disclosures, (3) financial literacy, and (4) financial ombudsmen.[12] Securitisation was also promoted as a measure to increase liquidity particularly in developing countries[13] but the institutional structure of securitisation created dangers for consumers and contributed to the instability of financial markets. Its future within consumer lending remains uncertain. The four institutions outlined above respond to information asymmetries facing both suppliers and borrowers and are intended to make consumer markets resemble more closely the conditions of the perfectly competitive market of neo-classical economics. Ombudsmen address individual enforcement costs. According to the World Bank these institutions will create the optimal 'rules of engagement' for creditors and debtors.[14]

This model assumes that it is possible to reduce the imbalance between consumers and credit providers by recreating the conditions of a neo-classical market – addressing informational market failures and redress costs. The premises of UK consumer policy (and the World Bank) are that the discipline of 'empowered' consumers will drive a virtuous circle of increased competition, innovation and productivity. While there is a role within these policies for greater protection of vulnerable consumers, this is an exception to the norm of empowerment.

---

[12]   See World Bank, *Consumer Protection and Financial Literacy: Good Practices for Consumer Protection and Financial Literacy in Europe and Central Asia – Consultative Draft* (Washington DC: World Bank, 2008); S Rutledge, *Policy Research Working Paper 5326, Consumer Protection and Financial Literacy; Lessons from Nine Country Studies* (Washington DC: World Bank, Europe and Central Asia Region, Finance and Private Sector Department, 2010). The World Bank studies drew on sources such as EU Directives, the reports of EU financial regulatory and supervisory bodies, the US Federal Trade Commission and Securities and Exchange Commission, OECD Guidelines for Protecting Consumers and the 1999 United Nations Guidelines on Consumer Protection.
[13]   See IMF, 'Household Credit Growth in Emerging Market Countries', in *Global Financial Stability Report: Market Developments and Issues* (Washington DC: IMF, 2006), ch. 2.
[14]   'Consumer protection ensures that consumers have access to information that will allow them to make informed decisions – and access to recourse mechanisms that allow them to resolve disputes when transactions go awry. Financial literacy gives consumers the skills to understand and evaluate the information that is provided. Together consumer protection and financial literacy set clear rules of engagement for dealings between financial firms and their retail customers – and help narrow the knowledge gap between consumers and their financial institutions.' World Bank, above n. 12, at iii.

Neo-liberalism is often associated with individualised enforcement through private rights. However, the need to maintain consumer confidence and the legitimacy of the credit system in the face of market failures and scandals often results in pressure for regulation and what Harvey describes as the paradox of 'intense state intervention' primarily through experts 'in a world where the state is supposed not to be interventionist'.[15] The introduction of financial ombudsmen (discussed below) provides a response to high enforcement costs and in the UK there is *ex ante* control of suppliers' access to the market.[16]

A neo-liberal model must also deal with the inevitable problem of consumer default in a society committed to high levels of credit. The system for regulating default is an integral aspect of a credit system and may affect levels of credit granting, although the actual effects are often difficult to measure and may depend on other aspects of the credit system such as the availability of high quality information to a creditor at the time of credit granting. In the business context the World Bank, influenced by the law and finance literature, underlines the importance of clear and easily enforced creditor rights in encouraging general credit availability.[17] Until recently, the Bank was silent, however, on the treatment of consumer over-indebtedness. In the consumer context, the potential costs of over-indebtedness for a debtor and third parties may not be accurately priced in the original transaction.[18] Moreover, if creditors are repeat players and are able to develop systematic advantages in using the courts as part of a collection routine there is a danger that rapid enforcement that does not scrutinise closely the validity of the underlying debt will result in overlending and the sanctioning of sharp practice.[19]

The relative roles of public and private actors in over-indebtedness

---

[15] D. Harvey, *A Brief History of Neo-Liberalism* (Oxford: Oxford University Press, 2005).

[16] Ibid. at 163.

[17] See World Bank, *Doing Business* (Washington DC: World Bank, 2004); and for an application to a developing country, A Kumar, *Access to Financial Services in Brazil* (Washington DC: World Bank, 2005).

[18] The UK Department of Business Innovation and Skills (DBIS) paper, *A Better Deal for Consumers: Economic Narrative* (London: 2009), which accompanied the White Paper on Consumer Reform, cites studies that indicate 'costs associated with debt problems to be in excess of £1000 per debt problem' (at 36), that 'the incidence of mental illness is associated with increased number of debts' (at 52) and that 'stress related to job problems caused 8.7 million lost working days in 2004 resulting in a cost to employers of £497 million' (at 52).

[19] See discussion in T.G. Ison, *Credit Marketing and Consumer Protection* (London: Croom Helm, 1979).

regulation are an issue for neo-liberalism. The state is involved through the court and enforcement system but neo-liberalism might encourage the use of privately negotiated settlements and assume a modest state 'intervention'. Consumer bankruptcy can function as both a consumer remedy and a crude brake on the perimeters of credit. The US debtor-oriented regime of open access to consumer bankruptcy, which existed before the adoption of the 2005 Bankruptcy Abuse Prevention and Consumer Protection Act,[20] promised an early re-entry to the credit society for a debtor and spread the costs of debt default among private creditors, creating incentives for them to monitor consumer behaviour. It co-existed with the most liberal credit regime in the world. There has also been the growth of a large over-indebtedness industry in the US and the UK over the past two decades, specialising in debt repayment programmes, consolidation loans, the purchase of delinquent consumer debts,[21] and debt counselling. While this growth fits with neo-liberal ideas of privatisation, regulation of this industry is necessary to protect against aggressive and misleading enforcement practices and ensure protection of individuals from professional malpractice.[22]

The detailed ground rules of consumer credit contract law have an impact on an individual's bargaining power[23] and create a model of how each party should treat the other throughout the transaction. The World Bank's 2008 discussion of the ground rules of consumer credit contracts recognises the necessity of controls on default interest rates as part of an effective consumer protection framework. However, it cautions that 'excessive regulation can stifle innovation'.[24] This underlying concern about restricting competition and innovation is also a theme in recent UK reform documents. The Labour government's economic narrative stated

---

[20]   2005 Public Law 109-8, 119 Stat. 23.

[21]   E.g., the Credit Services Association in the UK, which is the national association for debt recovery agencies, indicated in its submission to the Consumer Law Review (2009) that in excess of £15 billion is referred annually to members. In addition, it reports debt purchases of £6 billion. CSA, *Consumer Law Review: Response from the Credit Services Association* July 2008, in BIS, *Responses to the Consumer Law Review C-L* (London: BIS, 2009) at 1169–77.

[22]   See e.g. the interventions of the Office of Fair Trading in relation to the practices of providers of Individual Voluntary Arrangements and Debt Management Companies. The OFT's most recent report describes an industry where 'poor practices appear to be widespread'. See Office of Fair Trading, *Debt Management Guidance: Compliance Review,* OFT 1274 (London: OFT, 2010).

[23]   See discussion in I Ramsay, 'Consumer Credit Law, Distributive Justice and the Welfare State', *Oxford Journal of Legal Studies*, 177 (1995).

[24]   See World Bank, above n. 10, at ch 3.

that 'the future success of the UK financial services industry is therefore dependent on regulation not curtailing competition while ensuring the appropriate protection is in place for consumers'.[25] The current Treasury approach continues to emphasise issues of innovation and competitiveness in its mandate.

Neo-liberalism is sceptical of using market rules to redistribute the costs of market transactions, or protect consumers from the market, for example, through interest rate ceilings.[26] Any redistribution should be made by the state through the tax and transfer system. In the US the new Consumer Financial Protection Bureau does not have the power to impose interest ceilings. The UK Labour government set its face against any reintroduction of ceilings as part of reforms.[27] However, the new government in the coalition agreement promises to give regulators the power to determine and ban high rates on credit and store cards so that the issue of rate ceilings is once again in play. International agencies view interest ceilings as limiting the supply of microfinance[28] with effective competition, disclosure and financial literacy perceived to be the solutions to high interest rates.

Neo-liberalism does not mean, therefore, the absence of regulation. Nor is it limited to an 'informational' approach to consumer protection. This ideal type of neo-liberalism is often associated with contemporary Anglo-Saxon (common law) jurisdictions such as the UK, the US, Australia and Canada. French civil law jurisdictions, it is argued, are more likely to protect an individual from the market. However, the elasticity of the market failure concept and the need to respond to scandals and outrages (for example, concerns about 'loan sharks') and maintain the legitimacy of the financial system may result in a significant regulatory response.[29] In

---

[25] *Economic Narrative*, above n. 18, at 2–3.

[26] World Bank, above n. 10, at 160 and 179.

[27] See *A Better Deal*, above n. 3, at 37 (providing a 'Fact Box' outlining the detrimental effects of interest rate ceilings on consumer access to credit).

[28] See B. Helms and R. Xavier, *CGAP Occasional Paper No 9, Washington DC Consultative Group to Assist the Poor, Interest Rate Ceilings and Microfinance: The Story so Far* (September 2004).

[29] For example, in the UK in the early 2000s, the media highlighted the case of a couple whose mortgage loan had ballooned from £5000 to £348 000 because of compound interest on arrears. Questions were asked in Parliament and politicians promised to 'do something' about 'loan sharks'. See *London North Securities Ltd. v. Meadows* [2005] EWCA Civ 956 and the parliamentary response to the county court judgment, Hansard HC 15 Nov 2004 (Mr Sutcliffe): 'We have been paying close attention to this case and I have written to John Vickers, Chair of the Office of Fair Trading, alerting him to the complaints made to me about this lender by

societies of high inequality, such as the UK and the US, where low income consumers pay much higher credit costs than middle-class consumers, thereby undermining the impact of state transfers, the legitimacy of the credit system is always in question.

LIMITATIONS OF THE NEO-LIBERAL APPROACH TO CONSUMER CREDIT REGULATION

Competition for Innovation or Exploitation of Behavioural Biases?

A neo-liberal model assumes that more competition is a good thing for consumer markets and this is certainly the approach adopted in UK reform documents. Competition in credit markets can foster innovation and increased access. However, innovation in credit products and aggressive competition in the credit market pose challenges for regulators. Given the long-term nature of many credit relationships and the often short-term behavioural biases of consumers, competition may lead consumers to focus on short-term costs and contingencies rather than on long-term or lower probability events such as default costs. The case of credit cards is a well-known example where firms may exploit consumers' behavioural biases – individuals underestimate their future borrowing on cards – and competition focuses on short-term benefits such as the absence of annual fees. High prices are, however, charged on longer-term contingencies such as borrowing costs and default charges.[30] Bar-Gill has drawn attention to the potentially regressive and socially harmful aspects of this form of pricing. This general structure of pricing seems to exist in both prime and sub-prime consumer credit markets and was a subject of much criticism in

---

a number of Hon. Members. In order to ensure that in the future consumers are not faced with this situation we will be introducing the Consumer Credit Bill, once Parliamentary time permits.'

[30]   See e.g. O. Bar-Gill, 'Seduction by Plastic', 98 *Northwestern University Law Review*, 80 (2004). See also L. Ausubel, 'The Failure of Competition in the Credit Card Market', 81 *American Economic Review*, 50 (1991). For a study on the effect of psychological factors in credit marketing see M. Bertrand, D. Karlan, S. Mullainathan, E. Shafir and J. Zinman, *What's Psychology Worth? A Field Experiment in the Consumer Credit Market* (2005), available via http://ssrn.com/abstract=770389, concluding that 'even in a market setting with large stakes and experienced customers, subtle psychological features that normatively ought to have no impact appear to be extremely powerful drivers of behaviour'. See also R. Harris and E. Albin, 'Bankruptcy Policy in Light of the Manipulation in Credit Advertising', *Theoretical Inquiries in Law*, 431 (2006).

the early 2000s.[31] The Competition Commission concluded that high cost payment protection insurance might be compensating for low margins on credit prices. Competition drives innovation but the question is whether financial innovations result in 'a large range of subtly different products rather than . . . increasing market focus on the types of products which consumers might reasonably be expected to want'.[32]

Barr, Mullainathan and Shafir describe the quandary of 'high road' firms – those that view themselves as good corporate citizens – which may not wish to adopt pricing practices that exploit consumers' biases. However, they do so because they fear being at a competitive disadvantage in a market where it is difficult to correct consumers' short-term preferences and convince them that an alternative product, for example a credit card with an annual fee and a lower interest rate, might be more suitable.[33] And even if this bias is addressed through some form of 'debiasing intervention', other forms of marketing will sprout such as the use of high default fees. Regulators are continually chasing the latest 'innovation'.

The behavioural literature challenges the view that consumer choices always reflect consumer preferences. Preferences may be inconsistent over time. A common argument against regulation of sub-prime lending practices, such as payday loans, is that it interferes with individual choice. But if choices do not always accurately reflect preferences – or there is a clear possibility that a consumer may display inconsistent preferences – then the argument against regulation becomes weaker and any a priori presumptions against regulation based on abstract concepts such as markets versus regulation are undermined. A close scrutiny of the potential harmful effects of biases in particular credit markets, particularly the higher costs of credit mistakes for lower income consumers, may justify regulation.

Behavioural economics has stimulated several distinct policy responses from better disclosures to greater product regulation. There is the search for 'debiasing interventions' through more imaginative disclosures as well as the exploitation of behavioural findings to design more effective

---

[31] See e.g. O. Bar-Gill, *New York University Law and Economics Working Paper, The Law, Economics and Psychology of Sub-Prime Mortgage Contracts* (2008). On payment protection insurance, see the *Final Report* (2009) and associated documents published by the UK Competition Commission's *Market Inquiry into Payment Protection Insurance*, available at http://www.competition-commission.org.uk/inquiries/ref2007/ppi/. The pricing of overdrafts in the UK may also reflect these biases. See Office of Fair Trading, *Personal Current Accounts in the UK, An OFT Market Study* (London: OFT, 2008).

[32] HM Treasury, *Reforming Financial Markets,* above n. 3, at 154.

[33] See Barr et al., above n 3.

'choice architectures'[34] for consumers. Barr et al. propose a 'behaviourally informed financial regulation'.[35] This might include vanilla mortgages
with a consumer opt-out only after heightened disclosure, or the use of
'traffic light' disclosure for risks in financial products similar to those used
in food labelling.[36] Although disclosure remains a central aspect of regulation, there is much scepticism about the effectiveness of existing regulation
and uncertainty as to what might work, particularly where consumers'
decision-making problems are cognitive rather than informational.[37] The
application of social science methods to understanding and measuring
policy alternatives does not necessarily promise clear solutions.

The above approaches retain consumer choice and autonomy, compatible with a form of libertarian paternalism.[38] Product regulation through
standardisation of subsidiary terms in credit contracts is a further option
where there is unlikely to be substantial competition between providers
and/or where individuals are unlikely to be able to assess the risks of the
term in advance.[39] Standardisation already exists in some financial con-

---

[34] See R. Thaler and C. Sunstein, *Nudge: Improving Decisions about Health,
Wealth, and Happiness* (New Haven: Yale University Press, 2008) for a discussion
of choice architectures.

[35] Above n 3.

[36] Caisse d'Epargne use these indicators in France and the Netherlands
has a similar scheme. See Consumers International, *Consumers International
Position on the Financial Crisis*, available at http://www.consumersinternational.
org/media/164238/consumersinternationalandgfc-1-210509.pdf, 9. The US Dodd-
Frank Act creates a category of 'qualified mortgages' (§ 1412). If the mortgage
meets the required criteria there is a rebuttable presumption that the consumer can
pay back the loan.

[37] See e.g. National Consumer Council, *Warning: Too Much Information Can
Harm* (2007); S. Block-Lieb, R. Wiener, J.A. Cantone and M. Holtje, 'Disclosure as
an Imperfect Means for Addressing Over-Indebtedness: An Empirical Assessment
of Comparative Approaches', in J. Niemi-Kiesilainen, I. Ramsay and E. Whitford,
Consumer Credit: Debt and Bankruptcy: Comparative and International Perspectives
(Oxford: Hart, 2009); and I Ramsay, 'From Truth in Lending to Responsible
Lending', in G. Howells, A. Janssen and R. Schulze, *Information Rights and
Obligations* (Aldershot: Ashgate, 2005) at 48–57. In relation to disclosure in US
sub-prime markets see L Willis, 'Decisionmaking and the Limits of Disclosure:
The Problem of Predatory Lending: Price', *University of Maryland Law Review*,
707 (2006). Similarly, D. De Meza, B. Irlenbusch and D. Reyniers, *FSA Consumer
Research 69, Financial Capability: A Behavioural Economics Perspective* (London:
FSA, 2008). Research does suggest that consumers do use the APR to compare
credit choices. See Bar-Gill, above n. 31, at 57.

[38] C. Sunstein and R. Thaler, 'Libertarian Paternalism is not an Oxymoron',
70 *University of Chicago Law Review*, 1159 (2003).

[39] See e.g. in relation to credit cards R. Mann, *Charging Ahead: The Growth
and Regulation of Payment Card Markets* (2007) at 143. An example of the latter

tracts such as insurance where there is strong competition and substantial switching. The OFT has standardised default charges in credit cards.[40]

Increased Supply Side Information for Profit Maximisation or Risk Reduction and Responsible Lending?

In a famous paper, Stiglitz and Weiss[41] highlighted the credit rationing effects of information asymmetry in credit markets. A major antidote to the suppliers' informational problem in consumer credit markets has been the development of credit scoring and credit bureaux. Sophisticated computer technology has substantially reduced creditors' costs of storing and using credit information on an individual's creditworthiness. Standardised 'credit-scoring' systems for assessing creditworthiness have been developed by many major creditors. These techniques have facilitated the management of large numbers of small credit accounts – such as credit cards. Credit scoring has also facilitated 'risk based pricing' in the credit card market where credit card companies differentiate more finely between customers in relation to the level of interest payable on outstanding balances and use behavioural scorecards to determine whether to change interest rates on existing accounts.

The development of credit bureaux and credit scoring is a central plank in the World Bank's vision of the development of credit markets[42] and the UK policy-making has viewed better data sharing as an important aspect of the control of over-indebtedness.[43] The Competition Commission concluded that better credit bureaux information on low income repayment patterns for

---

is changing the interest rate on a card retroactively, e.g., by applying it to existing balances. See the recent US Credit Card Act 2009.

[40] Effectively reducing credit card penalty fees from £25 to £12. See OFT, *Calculating Fair Default Charges in Credit Card Contracts*, OFT 842 (London: OFT, 2006). The Financial Times reported on 24 August 2006 that all 36 main credit card issuers had reduced their penalty fees to £12 in response to the OFT paper and the OFT threat to take further action against the previous level of default fees. The work of the OFT under the Unfair Terms in Consumer Contracts Regulations has also resulted in greater standardisation of subsidiary terms.

[41] J. Stiglitz and A. Weiss, 'Credit Rationing in Markets with Imperfect Information', *American Economic Review,* 393 (1981).

[42] See e.g. World Bank, above n. 10, and World Bank, *Doing Business Project*, above n 17. M Miller, *Credit Reporting Systems in the International Economy* (Cambridge MA: MIT, 2003). For a discussion of credit information systems in Europe see F Ferreti, *The Law and Consumer Credit Information in the European Community* (London: Routledge, 2008).

[43] See DBERR, *Removing Barriers to the Sharing of Non-Consensual Credit Data*, 08/591 (London: DBERR, 2008).

home credit would facilitate individuals' access to lower cost credit.[44] Article 8 of the EU Consumer Credit Directive indicates that credit databases should be consulted 'when appropriate' by prospective lenders and the EU is investigating the possibility of harmonising databases throughout Europe,[45] an important step toward the integration of European credit markets.

The perceived economic benefits of credit bureaux and credit scoring are well known:[46] better assessment of risks and reduction of bad debts, more accurate pricing of credit, facilitating new entry by reducing the competitive advantages of incumbent bank and increased penetration among higher risk groups. There is an international distinction between positive and negative credit reporting, the former providing a relatively full picture of an individual's payment history, the latter being limited to negative events such as bankruptcies, court judgments and defaults in payment. International financial interests and institutions have favoured positive credit reporting as a method of facilitating credit in developing countries and the entry of foreign financial institutions that can upset the informational advantages of local banks.[47] Countries with negative credit reporting (for example, France and Australia) have lower levels of consumer credit outstanding than the UK and the US. Negative credit reporting may, however, be expected to produce greater incentives to repay because in a positive system a borrower knows that one default may be discounted by a lender with a full picture of the financial position of the borrower.[48]

---

[44] See Competition Commission, *Home Credit Inquiry* (available at http://www.competition-commission.org.uk/inquiries/current/homecredit/).

[45] But the Report of the Expert Group on Credit Histories (2009) (available at http://ec.europa.eu/internal_market/consultations/docs/2009/credit_histories/egch_report_en.pdf) indicates a number of barriers to such integration. Under the Consumer Credit (EU Directive) Regulations 2010, adding section 55B to the Consumer Credit Act 1974, a lender will have to make an assessment of creditworthiness before granting or increasing credit. This may, where necessary, include information obtained from a credit reference agency.

[46] See ibid. Expert Group on Credit Histories.

[47] See e.g. PERC Center for Competitive Credit, *Economic Fairness Through Smarter Lending: Some Factors to Consider on the Eve of Brazilian Credit Reporting Reform* (2007), available at http://perc.net/files/downloads/WEB_Brazil_White_Paper_full_study.pdf. A review of the current regime of negative credit reporting in Australia concluded that the benefits of moving to a positive credit reporting system had not been sufficiently substantiated to outweigh the potential costs in terms of privacy and other costs. See *Report of the Consumer Credit Review* (2006), available at http://www.consumer.vic.gov.au/CA256902000FE154/Lookup/CAV_Credit_Review_Documents/$file/credit_review_complete.pdf, at 280.

[48] A. Padilla and M. Pagano, 'Sharing Default Information as a Borrower Discipline Device', 44 *European Economic Review*, 1951 (2000).

Credit information is not used only to minimise risk but also to maximise profits.[49] Information may be used by credit card companies to segment markets, develop 'behavioural scorecards' and target consumers who are likely to generate high profits through late payments and borrowing on a card. Less profitable consumers may be terminated. Thus, the Egg credit card company terminated contracts with those customers who did not use the card frequently and regularly paid off their balances. Ronald Mann argues that, through increased segmentation of the credit card market, companies target some consumers with high fees while attempting to profit from higher income consumers through affinity cards with relatively high annual fees, whose benefits consumers often mistakenly assume outweigh their costs.[50] During the 1990s it was argued that credit scoring was used in the UK to exclude individuals from mainstream markets and facilitated the development of sub-prime lending.[51] Most recently, credit card companies use risk-based pricing to change the interest rate (sometimes by as much as 10 per cent) for existing holders of cards.[52]

Extensive information sharing may facilitate a deeper consumer credit market but not necessarily result in lower levels of indebtedness or even default. One study claims that 'countries with positive registries such as the UK, the US and Sweden . . . have high levels of indebtedness'.[53] These comments suggest some ambiguity about the overall effects of more creditor information: greater competition that could create incentives to 'oversell', more access to credit but not necessarily a reduction in the level of default.

---

[49] See e.g. L. Thomas, *Consumer Credit Models; Pricing Profits and Portfolios* (Oxford: Oxford University Press, 2009). The description of this text indicates that 'models allow one to make decisions that maximise the profitability of the borrower to the lender'.

[50] See Mann, above n. 39, at 137–8.

[51] See D. Burton, D. Knights, A. Leyshon, C. Alferoff and P. Signoretta, 'Making a Market: The UK Retail Financial Services Industry and the Rise of the Complex Sub-Prime Credit Market', 8 *Competition and Change*, 3, (2004) at 12–13: 'complex sub-prime providers actually use much more sophisticated credit rating technologies through differential pricing according to the risk profile. This ensures that they make a profit regardless of the level of risk'.

[52] The Government and the credit card industry have now signed a voluntary agreement with the credit card companies that includes the right of a consumer not to receive a credit limit increase. See statement by UK Department of Business Innovation and Skills (on file with authors).

[53] European Credit Research Institute, *Briefing on consumer credit, indebtedness and overindebtedness,* prepared for the European Parliament Hearing on the Consumer Credit Directive 29 April 2003, available at http://www.europarl. europa.eu/hearings/20030429/juri/ecri_en.pdf, 5.

Credit scoring also facilitates forms of lending where lending is centralised, staff costs are reduced through the absence of face-to-face contact through branches, and credit processing is computerised. This may reduce the possibility of determining whether credit is suitable or appropriate to the needs of a particular individual rather than the profit maximisation of the lender. There is therefore a tension between this form of credit granting and the development of an individualised responsible lending standard.[54]

There is remarkably little 'hard' regulation of several aspects of credit bureaux and credit scoring practices in the UK,[55] notwithstanding their central role in segmenting, including and excluding individuals from the credit market.

Upskilling Consumers through Financial Literacy?

During the past ten years governments, regulators and international institutions have joined with financial firms to promote financial literacy as a core element of consumer financial services market regulation. This development illuminates how neo-liberal policy-making organises consumer protection policy around individualisation, responsibilisation and market expansion.

In 2003, the OECD launched an international 'Financial Education Project', sponsored by Prudential plc's corporate responsibility programme. This project is based on a belief that 'financially illiterate' consumers cannot cope with the proliferation of consumer financial products that has resulted from neo-liberalism's expansion of financial markets, and on concerns about the long-term implications for public policy of consumers making unwise financial choices. Identifying financial education as an important aspect of the solution to the problem of consumers spending too much and saving too little, the OECD project encourages countries to develop effective regulatory policies to enhance financial literacy within their populations. The OECD project's early policy documents, published before the recent crisis erupted, make bold claims to the effect that financially literate consumers will improve economic growth, help to reduce poverty and potentially moderate the volatility of financial markets in emerging economies.[56] These publications characterise financial illiteracy

---

[54] See Consumer Credit Directive, Art. 5.
[55] Referred to primarily in the Consumer Credit Act 1974 and the 1998 Data Protection Act.
[56] OECD, *Improving Financial Literacy: Analysis of Issues and Policy* (Washington DC: OECD, 2005), 35. See also OECD, 'OECD's Financial Education

as an urgent and pervasive problem for financial markets, and represent literate financial consumers as 'regulatory subjects' whose decisions will increase price competition among suppliers and stimulate innovation and may ultimately reduce the need for regulatory action in consumer financial markets.[57] The OECD has continued to promote the improvement of consumer financial literacy as an important policy initiative after the crash, and other international organisations and development institutions – including the World Bank and the UK's Department for International Development – have become advocates of financial literacy programmes.[58]

Since 2003, several countries have launched high profile national programmes to promote financial literacy (sometimes termed financial capability). Some early initiatives include: Australia's Consumer and Financial Literacy Task Force (2004), which led to the establishment of the Financial Literacy Foundation in 2005; L'institut pour l'Education Financière du Public (IEFP), created in France in 2006; the New Zealand Retirement Commission's 'Sorted' programme; the US Federal Government's Financial Literacy and Education Commission;[59]

Project', 87 *Financial Market Trends*, 223 (2004); OECD, *Recommendation on Principles and Good Practices for Financial Education and Awareness* (Washington DC: OECD, 2005).

[57] OECD, *Improving Financial Literacy*, above n 56, at 35. For extensive discussion of the financial consumer as regulatory subject, see T Williams, 'Empowerment of Whom and for What? Financial Literacy Education and the New Regulation of Consumer Financial Services', 29(2) *Law & Policy*, 226 (2007).

[58] OECD publications since 2007 include: OECD, *Improving Financial Education and Awareness on Insurance and Private Pensions* (Washington DC: OECD, 2008); OECD, *Recommendation on Good Practices for Enhanced Risk Awareness and Education on Insurance Issues* (Washington DC: OECD, 2008); OECD, *Recommendation on Good Practices for Financial Education Relating to Private Pensions* (Washington DC: OECD, 2008); and OECD, *Financial Literacy and Consumer Protection: Overlooked Aspects of the Crisis – OECD Recommendation on Good Practices on Financial Education and Awareness Relating to Credit* (Washington DC: OECD, 2009). See also the OECD's International Gateway for Financial Education, 'a global clearinghouse on financial education', available at http://www.financial-education.org/pages/0,29 87,en_39665975_39666038_1_1_1_1,00.html. For recent publications by other international organisations, see S L Rutledge, *World Bank Policy Research Working Paper, Consumer Protection and Financial Literacy: Lessons From Nine Country Studies* (Washington DC: The World Bank, 2010) and a report jointly published by the World Bank, the UK's Department for International Development, the OECD and CGAP, *The Case for Financial Literacy in Developing Countries: Promoting Access to Finance by Empowering Consumers* (Washington DC, 2009).

[59] This agency was established to 'coordinate the financial education efforts throughout the federal government, support the promotion of financial literacy by

and the UK's National Financial Capability strategy. The UK's multi-
agency programme of consumer literacy enhancement, originally led by
the FSA and now the responsibility of the Consumer Financial Education
Body, has been heavily backed by HM Treasury since 2003.[60] Although
the particular mandates and specific goals of these initiatives vary, it is
common for their work to be characterised as 'empowering consumers'
at a minimum through the provision of information, the development
of financial skills and the activation of a consumers' sense of financial
responsibility. These policy initiatives link the enhancement of consumers' financial capabilities to their responsibilisation, through the idea that
financial literacy improves the capacity of consumers to protect themselves against risks of 'mis-buying' and mis-selling of financial products.
A second important linkage is the idea that financial literacy generates
demand for financial products as consumers become more active and
more self-reliant – that is, more self-regulating – about how they manage
income smoothing and their future economic security. As consumers
become more capable and therefore responsible they in turn are supposed
to reduce the need for regulatory intervention.

Financial literacy enhancement has begun to resemble an international
crusade and it is difficult to find balanced discussion of its role in financial
services regulation. The idea of 'responsibilising' consumers by upgrad-
ing their financial capabilities fits neatly into strategies of governance in
neo-liberalism where suitably upgraded consumers in the credit market
will become part of the supposed virtuous circle of driving competition,
innovation and productivity in financial services. Consumers will also,

---

the private sector while also encouraging the synchronization of efforts between the
public and private sectors': The Financial Literacy and Education Improvement
Act (Title V of the Fair and Accurate Credit Transactions (FACT) Act of 2003).
National financial education initiatives in the US are now under the auspices of
the Consumer Financial Protection Bureau, Consumer Financial Protection Act
2010 (§1013(d)). There is a vast array of state, private and NGO financial literacy
initiatives in the US, most are very recent; e.g. a 2006 report found that only
about one in four US financial literacy programmes started before the late 1990s:
Financial Literacy and Education Commission, *Taking Ownership of the Future:
The National Strategy for Financial Literacy* (Washington: Financial Literacy and
Education Commission, 2006), at 97.

[60]   Basic Skills Agency (BSA) and Financial Services Authority (FSA), 'Adult
Financial Capability Framework' (London: BSA and FSA, 2003); FSA; 'Towards
a National Strategy for Financial Capability' (London: FSA, 2003); and HM
Treasury, 'Financial Capability: The Government's long-term approach' (London:
TSO, 2007). See also HM Treasury and FSA, 'Helping You Make the Most of
Your Money: A Joint Action Plan for Financial Capability', available at http://
www.cfebuk.org/uk/pdfs/mostofyourmoney.pdf

it is argued, be able to avoid the problems of over-indebtedness through better financial management. Financial literacy has become part of the professional discourse of policymakers and the helping professions. There remains, however, much that is untested in the financial literacy literature. The World Bank comments that 'improving financial literacy is a long term process for which little is clearly understood as to what works (and what does not) in improving financial behaviour'.[61] A review of behavioural finance suggests that it is not absence of information but behavioural biases that cause consumers to make repeated mistakes in credit markets.[62]

Reducing Enforcement Costs: Financial Ombudsmen

A financial ombudsman disposes of disputes between consumers, small businesses and financial institutions. The financial ombudsman has become an international institution, since its emergence in the UK in the early 1980s.[63] Its characteristics are its ability to determine issues on broad fairness grounds, specialist knowledge, the absence of costs to consumers, the requirement for firms to develop internal complaint systems, and the possibility of identifying patterns of misconduct that can be addressed by regulators. An ombudsman can be therefore part of a meta-regulatory strategy to ensure the responsiveness of large organisations.

Experience in the UK indicates that the FOS has provided a useful service to primarily middle- and upper-middle-class consumers.[64] The FOS now has a large caseload with 163012 new cases in 2010. An ombudsman may, however, be limited in addressing issues where large numbers of consumers might have rights to compensation.

Ombudsmen in developed countries may often be perceived as consumer-oriented institutions providing greater access to justice than through the courts. However, the international embrace of ombudsmen for developing credit markets may also be driven by concerns that courts

---

[61] See World Bank, above n. 10, at 5.

[62] In a study conducted for the FSA, De Meza et al., above n. 37, conclude that: 'The best empirical work finds that financial education is not likely to have major lasting effects on knowledge and especially on behaviour' and that 'There is a lack of direct evidence that the National Strategy for Financial Capability will substantially improve long-term financial decision making.'

[63] See the discussion in I. Ramsay, *Consumer Law and Policy*, 2nd edn (Oxford: Hart, 2007), at 239–54.

[64] The 2008 Annual Review indicates increasing numbers of consumers using the service in the C1 and C2 categories, reflecting the growth of its consumer credit jurisdiction and the decline in mortgage endowment cases: Financial Ombudsman Service, *Annual Report* (2008).

are too debtor oriented, too willing to do equity on behalf of debtors when lenders attempt to enforce contracts. A World Bank study of access to credit in Brazil critiques Brazilian judicial decisions as 'perceived to be pro-debtor, reflecting judicial social activism' rather than a rigorous interpretation of the law.[65] The study also claims that there is substantial uncertainty because 'jurisprudence and patterns of judicial behaviour play a role as or more important than the law itself in regulating disputes' and that 'especially for small loans, judicial processes are avoided as far as possible due to the uncertainty, expense and time-consuming nature of the judicial processes'.[66]

Ensuring that the Poor Do Not Pay More?

It is a commonplace that lower income consumers generally pay more, often much more, for secured and unsecured credit. This seems unfair and regressive, contributing further to the large inequalities that currently exist in countries such as the UK and the US. Achieving competitive and fair markets, where there is an absence of deception, will not prevent the poor paying more or being excluded by the market. This is a continuing challenge for neo-liberalism, committed to a modest welfare state and flexible labour markets that may increase insecurity among low income consumers. This challenge has resulted in several policies: (1) facilitating the development of non-profit lenders; (2) establishing public institutions dedicated to providing funds for the poor; and (3) creating obligations on the mainstream financial sector to serve lower income consumers. The UK government proposes to expand choices through a revitalisation of the mutual and credit union sector, and a possible 'Big Society' bank, harnessing funds from dormant bank accounts for social investment. In the US the Community Reinvestment Act, enacted in response to the practice of 'redlining', requires banks to have regard to the credit needs of low and moderate income neighbourhoods 'consistent with the sound and safe operation' of a bank. It is the best-known method of attempting to expand access, and is certainly compatible with the conception of expanding the reach of the market.[67]

---

[65] See A. Kumar, *Access to Financial Services in Brazil* (Washington: World Bank, 2005) at 346.

[66] Ibid. at 349.

[67] See generally M. Barr, 'Credit where it Counts: The Community Reinvestment Act and its Critics', 80 *New York University Law Review*, 513 (2005).

A CONSUMER CREDIT SAFETY COMMISSION? THE UK REGULATORY TRIANGLE

Public regulation is an accepted part of credit regulation within neo-liberalism but its contours differ between countries. In the US the Obama administration's 'new deal' Consumer Financial Protection Bureau is endowed with supervision rule-making and enforcement powers including *ex ante* credit product regulation.[68] The Consumer Financial Protection Act reflects ideas elaborated by Elizabeth Warren that the 'agency would be charged with responsibility to establish guidelines for consumer disclosure, collect and report data about the uses of different financial products, review new financial products for safety, and require modification of dangerous products before they can be marketed to the public'.[69]

The new Financial Conduct Authority in the UK will continue many of the powers of the FSA in its conduct of business regulation so that a variation of the US model already existed in the UK (see comparison in Table 7.1) where the Office of Fair Trading (OFT) licensed unsecured credit providers and the Financial Services Authority (FSA) licensed secured credit providers. Both the OFT and the FSA had the power to monitor and regulate the business model of credit providers and the addition of irresponsible lending to the criteria for licence revocation provides the OFT with a significant lever for regulating lending practices throughout the course of a transaction.[70]

---

[68]   Above n. 3.

[69]   Warren above n. 3, at 17; Consumer Financial Protection Act 2010.

[70]   The 2006 amendments to the 1974 Act now permit the OFT to take into account the business model of a firm in assessing its fitness to hold a licence and 'irresponsible lending' is included as a criterion in deciding whether to grant or revoke a credit licence. See Consumer Credit Act s25 (2), (2A(e) and (2B). The OFT is under an obligation to provide guidance on the fitness test (s25A). Under s26 it may make conduct of business regulations. The OFT has intermediate powers to impose requirements on a licensee where it is dissatisfied with the manner in which it is carrying on its business (s33A). The Office is to prepare guidance on how it proposes to exercise these powers (33E). The Office also has information-gathering powers (36C) and power to require access to observe the carrying on of business and to inspect documents (36C). The Office proposes a risk assessment approach to credit licensing so that it can focus on higher risk areas such as debt collection, debt management and sub-prime lending. Sub-prime and home lenders will be required to provide a credit risk profile to ensure that they are not lending irresponsibly. See *Consumer Credit Licensing*, OFT 969 (London: OFT, January 2008). See also *Irresponsible Lending-OFT Guidance for Lenders*, OFT 1107 (London: OFT, 2010). The FSA's rule-making powers are found in Part X of the Financial Services and Markets Act 2000.

Table 7.1   Comparison of powers

	CFPB	OFT	FSA	Proposed FCA
Rule-making	✓	✓ (guidance)	✓	✓
Monitoring/supervision	✓	✓	✓	✓
Ex ante licensing for safety, fairness	?	✓	✓	✓
Enforcement	✓	✓	✓	✓
'Outcomes based approach'	✓	?	✓	Likely
Measures to ensure responsiveness to consumer interests	✓	✓	✓	✓
Funding by industry	Partly	Licensing activity funded	✓	✓
Separate from prudential regulator?	✓	✓	✕	✓
Promoting credit access to underserved groups	✓	✕	?	?

Credit licensing by the OFT in the UK had both efficiency and distributional objectives. From an efficiency perspective licensing compensated for general information and enforcement costs facing consumers. The distributional goal was the protection of lower income and vulnerable consumers who would have difficulties in seeking individual remedies against unfair credit practices. The licensing provisions under the 1974 Act did confer broad powers on the OFT to police 'unfair practices' irrespective of whether they were proscribed by law. The Annual Reports of the OFT during the 1980s and 1990s indicate that they used the licensing process as a method of identifying unfair practices, for example developing guidelines on unfair practices in the sub-prime (non-status) lending market. These practices included irresponsible lending, the use of dual interest rates, and negative option selling of credit insurance. The licensing process did function therefore as a nascent form of industry rule-making of credit products. The perception was, however, that the OFT's information-gathering and enforcement powers and practices were not effective and that the agency was under-resourced. Although self-regulation also developed during this period, its coverage was least effective in higher risk lending. There was also little political support for the OFT during the 1990s while the Conservative government was in power. Indeed reform during this period focused primarily on deregulation and whether the costs of licensing (over-inclusive and costly to administer) outweighed its benefits.[71] In contrast the regulatory impact analysis for the 2006 amendments to the Consumer Credit Act concluded that the costs to consumers and reputable businesses from deregulation would far outweigh the costs saved through deregulation.[72]

The 2006 changes resulted effectively in two-tier licensing by the OFT. Businesses classified as high risk because of potential consumer detriment, such as lenders offering consolidation loans or debt management companies, are subject to heightened scrutiny of their business model by the Office and subject to detailed rule-making.

The OFT has also engaged in credit industry rule-making through its general power to prohibit unfair contract terms under the UTCC regulations implementing the related EU Directive. Thus it has effectively set the terms for default rates on credit cards.[73]

The new OFT licensing model is based on the licensing powers of the Financial Services Authority whose jurisdiction includes first charge mortgages (since October 2004) and credit insurance (since January 2005). Retail financial services are regulated through conduct of business rules but in recent years the FSA adopted what regulatory scholars describe as a meta-regulatory approach, requiring financial firms to embed general principles such as 'treating customers fairly' within their business model and organisational culture. The FSA more recently has emphasised the 'outcome' orientation of this form of regulation and has formulated the Treating Customers Fairly (TCF) requirements in terms of firms achieving a number of 'consumer outcomes'.[74] These include: 'consumers can be confident that they are dealing with firms where the fair treatment of customers is central to corporate culture and is automatically taken into account in all relevant business decisions'; 'products and services marketed and sold in the retail market are designed to meet the needs of identified consumer groups and are targeted accordingly': and 'consumers are provided with products that perform as firms have led them to expect

---

[71] See discussion in Ramsay, above n. 63, 499 et seq.

[72] See *Consumer Credit Bill, Full Regulatory Impact Assessment* (2004) available at: http://webarchive.nationalarchives.gov.uk/+/http://www.berr.gov.uk/files/file24434.pdf, at 48–9.

[73] See discussion in Ramsay, above n. 63, 476–85.

[74] See FSA, *Treating Customers Fairly: Measuring Outcomes* (London: FSA, 2007), which lists the six consumer outcomes: 'We are moving towards a greater reliance on principles and outcome-focused rules rather than detailed rules prescribing how outcomes must be achieved' (at 4).

and the associated service is both of an acceptable standard and as they have been led to expect'. The FSA expects fair treatment to be 'established throughout the firm not just in systems and controls but in business culture including strategy, training, remuneration, and staff behaviours'. Senior management must have adequate information to monitor TCF. Firms must not rely solely on consumer satisfaction studies to determine whether there is fair treatment of consumers, since consumers may be satisfied with an unsuitable product and dissatisfied with a fair product. The FSA's approach does not depend on prescriptive rules and action against deviant firms but is intended to embed attentiveness to consumer welfare throughout the product life cycle, that is, financial product design, development and marketing and financial contract formation, performance, complaint handling and redress. While this approach ultimately harnesses self-regulation, the FSA has required financial firms to identify progress in implementing TCF, monitored firms for TCF compliance during routine supervision and taken enforcement action, including the levying of substantial fines, where it identifies significant violations of the principles.[75] In the wake of the crash, the FSA has developed an Intensive Supervision model, which emphasises 'outcomes testing' to a much greater extent than before and which may include greater product regulation.[76]

The FSA has been active in its regulation of the sub-prime credit industry since taking over this jurisdiction in 2004. In 2005 the FSA highlighted to firms the importance of making a suitability assessment and treating consumers fairly when selling payment protection insurance. The 2005 review concluded that many firms visited had inadequate documentation to demonstrate suitability when advising on mortgage products. The Authority responded through individual feedback, a 'Dear CEO letter' – alerting senior management to the problems with sales of PPI – and enforcement actions. In 2007 it conducted a further review of substantial numbers of lenders and intermediaries in the sub-prime lending market. The review revealed that in the case of intermediaries one third of files showed an inadequate assessment of consumers' ability to afford the mortgage and in almost half the files there was an inadequate assessment of customers' suitability for the mortgage.

---

[75] In November 2008, the FSA announced that the TCF initiative was to become 'embedded' into its 'core supervisory work'. FSA, *FSA update on the Treating Customers Fairly Initiative and the December Deadline* (London: FSA, 2008), at 1.

[76] Several FSA speeches and other communications since March 2009 have explained its Intensive Supervision model, which aims to achieve 'credible deterrence'. See, e.g., FSA, *Business Plan 2009/10* (London: FSA, 2009).

It concluded that 'significant numbers of consumers were advised to re-mortgage, thereby incurring early repayment charges, without the adviser being able to demonstrate that this was beneficial to the customer. None of the lenders adequately covered all relevant responsible lending considerations in their policies' and 'there were also failings by lenders to monitor the application of their policies, which resulted in the approval of potentially unaffordable mortgages.' Five firms were referred for enforcement action.

Payment protection insurance, which is often sold with sub-prime loans[77] and is part of the business model of selling sub-prime credit,[78] has been a target of FSA regulation. Problems with mis-selling were identified in the 2005 visits to firms in the sub-prime market and from 2006 the FSA took high profile action against large institutions such as HFC, GE Capital and Citigroup (Egg Credit Card) concerning the mis-selling of credit insurance.[79] HFC (Household Finance), a subsidiary of HSBC, was fined over £1 million for its mis-selling practices. It sold single premium insurance with 75 per cent of its consumer loans, which are primarily made to working-class and lower-middle income consumers. The investigation by the FSA of its internal practices revealed that its procedures for training and monitoring staff were inadequate and that these resulted in an 'unacceptable risk of unsuitable sales'. The need to monitor staff was heightened by the existence of a bonus structure for meeting sales targets of PPI. In addition to a substantial fine, HFC undertook an independent audit of its compliance and contacted consumers who may have been mis-sold insurance to identify possible compensation.[80] The report of the FSA

---

[77]   See Competition Commission, above n. 31, at para 11: 'PPI consumers are more likely to earn less than the national average income or come from socio-economic groups C and D.'

[78]   The practice of finance companies selling insurance with credit is known in the US as 'insurance packing', 'shoving as much insurance onto the customer as possible without the customer's knowledge or without the customer's understanding': Statement of Jim Dough to Hearings Before the Special Committee on Aging, US Senate (105th Congress) (2d Session) (March 16, 1998).

[79]   From 2005 to 2010, the FSA took action against 24 firms for failings in their PPI sales practices and imposed fines totalling close to £13 million. See FSA, *FSA/PN/132/2010, Press Release* (London: FSA, 2010).

[80]   The decision indicates: 'As a result of the review HFC is in the process of making a significant number of changes to its sales processes. It has also agreed to strengthen its compliance monitoring and oversight arrangements. HFC has also committed to a robust remedial action plan, overseen by third party accountants, involving a programme of customer contact and, if appropriate, steps to ensure that its customers are not disadvantaged': *Final Notice: HFC Bank Ltd.* (16 January 2008), at para. 6.10.

action also revealed the business model of HFC, which involved much refinancing of loans that provided opportunities for selling larger loans, more insurance and settlement fees. The FSA has now required all firms not to sell single premium PPI.[81] A consequence of these and other investigations (by the Competition Commission) is that payment protection insurance may no longer be a major supra-normal profit centre for financial institutions.[82] The demise of single premium PPI might be analogised to recall of a potentially dangerous product.

There are several points of interest in the FSA's approach to regulation. First, treating customers fairly is a form of *ex ante* regulation in the sense that firms must not market dangerous products or have marketing structures that create an unreasonable risk of mis-selling. Second, the regulator opens up the black box of corporate decision-making, requiring firms to develop a business model that does not create this unacceptable risk.[83] Third, the FSA has significant informational and monitoring powers. Firms must make monthly reports and are subject to audit visits, particularly if they are operating in a potentially higher risk sector. Fourth, the agency has the power to award redress and in a number of cases required companies to write to existing customers with policies outlining the possibility of redress.[84] Fifth, the FSA has gradations of penalties ranging from informal feedback and 'Dear CEO letters' through to financial penalties and the possibility of licence revocation.

The FSA approach attempts to change organisational culture. There are difficulties in achieving this objective. First, Baldwin has pointed to the difficulties of regulators attempting to harness internal organisational structures where there may be confusion and conflict over roles and a

---

[81]   FSA, *FSA/PN/031/2019, Press Release* (London: FSA, 2010).

[82]   The Competition Commission calculated a return on equity of 490 per cent for PPI. See Competition Commission, *Final Report: Payment Protection Insurance* (2009), available at http://www.competition-commission.org.uk/inquiries/ref2010/ppi_remittal/final_report.htm.

[83]   This point is developed in T. Williams, 'Open the Box: an exploration of the Financial Services Authority's model of fairness in consumer financial transactions', in M. Kenny, J. Devenney and L. Fox O'Mahony (eds), *Unconscionability in European Private Financial Transactions: Protecting the Vulnerable* (Cambridge: CUP, 2010). For an insightful empirical study of financial firms' responses to the FSA's initiative, see S Gilad, *CARR Discussion Paper No. 64, Enlisting Commitment to Internal Compliance via Reframing and Delegation* (2010), available at http://www2.lse.ac.uk/researchAndExpertise/units/CARR/publications/discussionPapers.aspx.

[84]   See e.g. FSA, *Final Notice, Egg Credit Card*, 9 December 2008 (FSA: London, 2008).

tension between shareholder return and regulatory risk.[85] The continued mis-selling of payment protection insurance by large 'reputable' organisations after being warned of the dangers by the regulator – and in some cases the receipt of a 'Dear CEO letter' – might support Baldwin's argument or simply suggest that these firms were amoral calculators and unlikely to change their culture. Second, there is the perennial problem of 'capture' of agencies by particular interests. Since the onset of the financial crisis a number of commentators have argued that the FSA was 'captured' by the financial services industry. Willem Buiter argued to the Treasury Select Committee that there had been 'universal capture of the regulators and the political process by the financial sector'.[86] The UK consumer group Which? claims that the FSA has been captured by the financial services industry. This judgement may be justified in relation to its prudential regulation although a better interpretation might be that any agency would find it difficult to regulate in the teeth of influential opinion against regulation. However, the capture theory does not seem justified in relation to its jurisdiction over consumer credit where it has been relatively active since assuming the jurisdiction in 2004/05. The capture theory does not in any event adequately describe the complex interdependence between powerful actors in particular regulatory spaces where 'no single actor can hope to dominate the regulatory process'.[87]

An assessment of 'capture' and other regulatory theories about the FSA must also account for the role of the Financial Ombudsman Service (FOS) and the OFT within the regulatory structure. The FOS, given statutory authority by the Financial Services and Markets Act 2000, decides disputes that remain unsettled after having been considered by the mandatory complaints handling institutions of the relevant financial institution. It has a large caseload, with 127 000 new cases in 2008/09 and 8764 cases resolved.[88] The FOS plays an informational role in identifying potentially unfair credit practices in its dispute settlement work and acting as a catalyst for regulatory action. High levels of complaints signal problems in existing regulation. The existence of the OFT with some overlapping jurisdiction provides the possibility of regulatory competition and

---

[85]   R. Baldwin, 'The New Punitive Regulation', 67 *Modern Law Review*, 351 (2004).

[86]   See HC Treasury Committee, *Banking Crisis: Regulation and Supervision,* 14th Report HC 767 (2009), at para. 18.

[87]   J. Black, 'Decentring Regulation: Understanding the Role of Regulation and Self-Regulation in a Post-Regulatory World', 54 *Current Legal Problems*, 103 (2001), at 109.

[88]   Financial Ombudsman Service, *Annual Review 2008–09.*

the existence of regulatory redundancy.[89] This UK regulatory triangle is complemented by the existence of the 'super-complaints' process, which permits consumer groups to place issues (such as PPI) on the regulatory agenda.[90]

A key question raised by the contemporary financial crisis is the regulation of 'new' products, balancing protection against the value of fostering innovation. The 1980s and 1990s witnessed much financial innovation in credit card and other markets. How should an agency react to novel products, such as payday loans or equity release mortgages aimed at older consumers, where there may be uncertainty as to who will benefit or the risks associated with a product? The analogy to product safety suggests the possibility of applying a precautionary principle to a new product with an initial burden on credit providers to indicate the benefits of the product.[91] The benefits of swift innovation in credit markets are, as others have suggested, unlikely to be the same as those in the case of pharmaceutical products.[92] History suggests that there are often substantial costs for some consumers as new markets develop. The application of a precautionary principle to credit products might possibly have protected consumers against some of the initial problems with equity release products. In the early stage of development some inappropriate products were marketed that resulted in some consumers losing their homes.

The effectiveness of credit safety licensing depends on high quality information to identify potentially unsafe credit products and the ability to devise a regulation that can achieve an optimal level of safety without unnecessarily decreasing the availability of credit or innovation. Experience of consumer safety regulation indicates that private groups inevitably play an important role in information gathering and standard setting in regulation. There is a danger that existing firms may oppose new entrants that pose a competitive threat. Establishing product safety standards is a complex blend of technical expertise and responsiveness to politi-

---

[89]   See C. Scott, 'Analysing Regulatory Space: Fragmented Resources and Institutional Design', *Public Law*, 329 (2001).

[90]   See section 11 Enterprise Act 2002. Super-complaints have been made in relation to PPI, home credit and credit card practices.

[91]   See the proposal in the US whereby firms will have a burden to update their disclosures where they introduce a new product that is not covered by existing rules. If they introduce a new product then they could get a 'no action' letter from the regulator This addresses the problem of slow reaction by agency and the regulatory ratchet.

[92]   See A. Turner, *Prospect Magazine* (August 2009).

cal pressures. The FSA is in a continuing dialogue with its stakeholders so that there is the potential to blend both technical expertise and political responsiveness.[93]

The increasing use of broad standards such as responsible lending[94] also argues in favour of the FSA outcomes-based approach. A standard such as responsible lending is subject to the critique that it may increase costs (for example, legal advice) and uncertainty for lenders, which may in turn result in hesitation to lend to more marginal credit risks. Reliance on private litigation to develop the concept of responsible lending suffers from several drawbacks: the difficulties of courts establishing useful standards to be applied within bureaucratic organisations; the reactivity and lack of expertise of courts, and lack of knowledge about how to change organisational behaviour; and the likelihood of being subject to the biases of the litigation strategies of repeat players. The experience of the long period of strategic litigation by the banks in relation to standard setting to protect bank loan guarantors illustrates these limitations.[95] A public regulator will be in a better position to develop guidance, encourage the development of best practices within an industry and monitor the potentially changing nature of the concept of responsible lending. The history of credit regulation indicates that detailed rules result in a cat-and-mouse game between the legislator and the regulated with increased regulatory complexity.

The current government will separate prudential regulation from conduct of business regulation, establishing a Financial Conduct Authority as part of their reform of the architecture of financial regulation in the UK. The Authority will become the primary regulator of conduct of business in retail financial markets and may include the current responsibilities of the OFT concerning unsecured credit. The government promises that it will be 'a strong consumer champion in pursuit of a single objective' and 'build on the progress recently made by the FSA towards a more interventionist and pre-emptive approach to retail conduct regulation . . . which will necessarily be backed by a strong approach to enforcement to ensure credible deterrence'.[96] It is likely to have similar powers to the FSA. Class actions

---

[93] The US proposals include the possibility of developing 'plain vanilla' mortgages to be offered alongside other products.

[94] A form of responsible lending is implicit in Art. 5.6 of the 2008 EU Consumer Credit Directive currently being implemented in the UK.

[95] See the discussion of this in H. Collins, 'Regulating Contract Law', in C. Parker, C. Scott, N. Lacey and J. Braithwaite (eds), 'Regulating Law' (Oxford: OUP, 2004).

[96] See HM Treasury, *A New Approach*, above n. 3, para 4.24.

may also be a significant part of the regulatory landscape. These were not ultimately adopted in the UK Financial Services Act 2010, although the FSA was given power to require firms to develop redress schemes where there are widespread contraventions of regulations and consumers have suffered loss.[97] The development of new consumer credit regulatory agencies in both the US and the UK invites comparative analysis of the effectiveness of different styles of regulation although there are substantial difficulties in carrying out such research.[98]

CONCLUSION

Examination of the neo-liberal model suggests that there are limits on consumers as 'a market discipline' in credit markets and that financial literacy remains a relatively untested method of upskilling consumers.[99] Regulation of the supply side is therefore crucial for achieving fairness as to the appropriateness of products and the manner of product marketing. We have suggested that the outcomes-based approach of a suitably resourced FCA or OFT has the potential to meet this need. There are, however, limits to this regulation. Regulation promises greater safety, perhaps slightly lower prices and greater choice for lower income consumers. This approach does not, however, prevent the poor from paying more than middle income consumers for credit. It may be desirable therefore to include financial inclusion as an objective of any future consumer credit agency.

Affordable access to credit for low income consumers, particularly for short-term loans, remains a problem. A recent history of working-class credit concludes that 'cheap credit remains elusive for the depressingly large number of families who still have to manage on limited budgets . . . unfortunately the liberalization of credit that accompanied the great leap into the consumer society has not produced a simple solution for the

---

[97]   See Financial Services Act 2010 s 14 amending s 404 Financial Services and Markets Act 2000.

[98]   See H.E. Jackson, 'Variation in the Intensity of Financial Regulation: Preliminary Evidence and Potential Implications', 24 *Yale Journal of Regulation*, 253 (2007). One of the authors has drawn attention to the difficulties of comparing consumer bankruptcy across jurisdictions: I. Ramsay, 'Comparative Consumer Bankruptcy', *Illinois Law Review*, 241 (2007).

[99]   'Questions still remain as to how far consumers can actively drive fair and efficient competitive outcomes and whether some consumers will ever be able to make effective decisions in a market which is inherently complex': Office of Fair Trading, *Financial Services Plan, OFT 1106* (London: OFT, 2009), 17.

economic problems of the poorest groups. For them easy terms remain elusive.'[100] One question is whether credit regulation can achieve the goal of cheap credit for lower income consumers. If this does not seem possible then policy should focus more on ensuring adequate income support, better safety nets and methods to address income shocks among lower income consumers. Conceptualisation of financial services as a public utility or 'a service of general interest' might provide a framework for exploring these issues further.

---

[100] S. O'Connel, *Credit and Community: Work Class Debt in the UK since 1880* (Oxford: OUP, 2009) at 291.

APPENDIX

Table A7.1   Significant fines imposed on firms selling PPI for TCF failures, 2006–2008

Year–Month	Firm	Amount	Summary
2006–09	Regency Mortgage	£56 000	Failures in mortgage related PPI sales in the sub-prime market
2006–10	Loans.co.uk Limited (LCUK)	£455 000	PPI selling failures
2006–11	Capital Mortgage Connections Ltd (CMC)	£17 500	Breaches including cold calling potential customers and PPI failings
2006–12	Redcats (Brands) Ltd	£270 000	Failing to treat customers fairly when selling PPI in connection with home shopping products
2006–12	Home and County Mortgages Limited (HCML)	£52 500	Management failures and a lack of skill, care and diligence
2007–01	GE Capital Bank	£610 000	Systems and controls failings in selling insurance including PPI, and failing to treat its customers fairly
2007–02	Capital One Bank (Europe) plc	£175 000	Not having adequate systems and controls in place to sell PPI and for failing to treat its customers fairly
2007–09	Hadenglen Home Finance	£133 000	For inadequate systems and controls when recommending re-mortgages and PPI to customers
2007–09	Richard Hayes, Chief Director of Hadenglen	£49 000	For inadequate systems and controls when recommending re-mortgages and PPI to customers
2008–01	HFC Bank Ltd	£1 085 000	For failing to take reasonable care to ensure that the advice it gave customers to buy PPI was suitable, and for failing to have adequate systems and controls for the sale of PPI

Year–Month	Firm	Amount	Summary
2008–05	Land of Leather	£210 000	For allowing its sales force to sell PPI on loans without effective monitoring or training in place to ensure that the insurance was being sold fairly
2008–05	Mr Briant in relation to Land of Leather	£14 000	For failing to properly oversee the sale of PPI by Land of Leather Limited
2008–07	Liverpool Victoria Banking Services	£840 000	For serious failings in the sale of single premium PPI
2008–08	GK Group Limited	£51 100	For serious breaches relating to the sale of PPI
2008–08	George White Motors Ltd	£28 000	For serious breaches relating to the sale of PPI
2008–08	Park's of Hamilton Holdings Ltd	£61 600	For serious breaches relating to the sale of PPI
2008–08	Ringways Garages (Leeds) Limited & Ringways Garages (Doncaster) Limited	£35 000	For serious breaches relating to the sale of PPI
2008–09	Alliance and Leicester	£7 000 000	For serious failings in its telephone sales of payment protection insurance
2008–12	Egg Banking plc	£721 000	For serious failings in its sales of credit card PPI

8. Deposit protection schemes in British offshore finance centres

Philip Morris*

INTRODUCTION

The British Isles offshore jurisdictions of Jersey, Guernsey and the Isle of Man enjoy a 'unique' constitutional status.[1] Neither part of the United Kingdom nor colonies they are British Crown dependencies with near complete domestic self-government. This is cemented by an historic constitutional convention that prevents the United Kingdom Parliament from legislating on their internal affairs without first engaging in consultation with and obtaining the prior consent of the insular authorities. Recent political concordats[2] struck between the insular authorities and the United Kingdom government further develop this position by granting all three jurisdictions autonomy to create a separate international identity; this is expressed in concrete terms by the United Kingdom entering into formal agreements with supranational institutions and sovereign states. These arrangements are, however, subject to the undisputed sovereign right, in technical constitutional law terms, of the United Kingdom Parliament to legislate for the Crown dependencies, if need be in defiance of their wishes, and an overarching, ill-defined power of unilateral intervention on grounds of good government. The insular perspective construes the latter narrowly as requiring a serious breakdown of civil order, but its precise content has never been defined and it is arguably capable

---

* Independent Researcher.

[1] See generally Report of the Royal Commission on the Constitution 1969–73, Vol I, Cmnd 5460, paras 1347–1348, 1361–1363, 1469 and 1473 (the Kilbrandon Report)..

[2] Department for Constitutional Affairs/States of Guernsey, *Framework for Developing the International Identity of Guernsey* (1 May 2007); Department for Constitutional Affairs/States of Jersey, *Framework for Developing the International Identity of Jersey* (1 May 2007); and Department for Constitutional Affairs/Isle of Man Government, *Framework for Developing the International Identity of the Isle of Man* (1 May 2007).

of extending to a systemic failure of financial regulation resulting in structural economic dislocation.

These sweeping powers of self-government have permitted, since the late 1960s, all three jurisdictions to construct finance-magnet fiscal structures and a portfolio of niche, international business-friendly special purpose vehicles, which have fuelled their rapid development as leading international offshore finance centres (OFCs). The insular economies are now heavily dependent on the OFCs, which account for around 20 per cent of employment and 50 per cent of national income.[3] Such high levels of dependence and the absence of credible alternative economic strategies mean there is no turning back; policies have been compelled to focus on diversification within the OFCs and the evolution of financial regulation regimes that conform to the highest international standards. Stringent financial regulation is conceptualised as a critical factor in attracting good quality business that in turn sharpens the OFCs' competitive edge.[4] In summary, the long-term regulatory process in these jurisdictions, in terms of official policies at least, is arguably a 'race to the top' in sharp contrast to the corrosive and on occasion degradatory 'race to the bottom' encountered in some aspects of OFC activities in Caribbean and Pacific Basin small island jurisdictions. In global terms, therefore, the Channel Islands and Manx OFCs can be characterised as professionally regulated and geared toward the conduct of reputable international business.[5]

This chapter is a critical analysis of bank deposit protection schemes in these jurisdictions. The Isle of Man has operated a scheme since 1991 that has been triggered on two occasions. Guernsey has recently enacted a scheme with distinctive features and Jersey committed to a new structure that became operational in 2009. There are interesting points of comparison among all three schemes, and the Foot Review of financial regulation in the Crown Dependencies and Overseas Territories, commissioned by the United Kingdom Treasury, has focused on deposit protection arrangements as a key theme.

Before embarking on this overview, it is worthwhile briefly commenting on the status of deposit protection in international financial regulation and the enduring economic critique of it. Notwithstanding its rapid proliferation, deposit protection is still not a required or recommended

---

[3] Home Office, *Review of Financial Regulation in the Crown Dependencies*, Cmnd 4109-1 (1998) (Edwards Report), paras 2.9.1 and 2.12.2.

[4] Ibid., para. 17.2.4.

[5] Ibid., para. 3.1.1.

international regulatory standard; it simply exists de facto in most developed jurisdictions as an acknowledged investor protection mechanism.[6] The Foot Review may, in the context of British Isles OFCs, advance its status by recommending its introduction as an exemplar of good regulatory practice. Neo-classical economic critique posits deposit protection as fuelling moral hazard by removing the incentive for depositors to perform checks on the financial soundness of banks since they will in any event receive compensation following a bank collapse.[7] There is a distinct air of unreality about this given that most depositors are in no position to perform such checks and, even if they could access relevant information, they lack the interpretive financial and business acumen to properly evaluate it. Nonetheless, such thinking continues to exert influence amongst policymakers, regulators and legislators in the design and implementation of deposit protection schemes. Failure to incorporate such concerns is regarded as a serious design flaw and this is likely to continue even if deposit protection crystallises into a required or recommended international regulatory standard; recent EU reforms, for example, have focussed on deposit protection post-crisis.

Despite this hostility grounded in classical economic orthodoxy, deposit protection is increasingly recognised as both a valuable depositor protection technique and a vehicle for reducing systemic risk in removing the incentive for depositors to trigger bank runs by withdrawing funds once news breaks that a bank is in financial difficulty. The British Isles offshore dimension adds third and fourth distinctive rationales for deposit protection schemes: furnishing their vitally important offshore banking sectors with a buffer against capital flight should a bank fail and preservation of their competitive edge with each other and other OFCs in the continuous (and highly competitive) project to attract liquid funds. These policy factors rooted in economic self-interest have tended to be paramount in the decisions of all three jurisdictions to launch deposit protection schemes. Depositor protection often seems, as the policy formation and implementation process unfolds, simply an inevitable by-product of secondary importance to the interests of their OFCs.

---

[6]   See the detailed global survey in: D.S. Hoelscher, M. Taylor and U.H. Klueh, *The Design and Implementation of Deposit Insurance Systems, IMF Occasional Paper 251* (Washington DC. IMF, 2006).

[7]   For fuller discussion see: A.C. Page and R.B. Ferguson, *Investor Protection* (London: Weidenfeld & Nicolson, 1992), at 39–40, 72.

THE ISLE OF MAN

Located in the middle of the Irish Sea equidistant from the coasts of North-West England, South-West Scotland, Northern Ireland and the Republic of Ireland, the Isle of Man has a population of approximately 80 000 and traditionally lags behind its Channel Islands rivals in OFC development. Its offshore banking sector has, however, rapidly expanded in terms of its deposit base and now holds £65.59 billion in liquid funds.[8]

The island's development as an OFC was seriously impeded for over a decade by the notorious Savings and Investment Bank collapse in 1982, which left over 4000 aggrieved depositors bereft of access to compensation. This scandal led to the creation of a Manx deposit protection structure in 1991 whose avowed purpose has been that of shoring up confidence in the offshore banking sector. First recourse to it took place in the 1990s in the aftermath of the collapse of BCCI: all investors in the island subsidiary received compensation although this took several years; and the banks recouped in full levies imposed in the form of payments from the multi-jurisdictional liquidation.

During the autumn of 2008, international bank instability spilled over into the island resulting in the collapse of Kaupthing, Singer and Friedlander Isle of Man (KSF IoM), a local subsidiary of a major Icelandic banking group, resulting in depositors' losses and fears of contagion. Despite strong government support for a customised Manx High Court supervised scheme of arrangement, as an alternative to invocation of the deposit protection scheme, larger depositors overrode this solution in favour of the greater rapidity and certainty provided by placing the bank into formal liquidation and activation of the deposit protection scheme.[9] This has now been completed and the net effect is an Isle of Man government £193 million funding package[10] providing 100 per cent return of deposits (within the scheme's £50 000 ceiling) for 75 per cent of depositors during a six-week time frame. Government funding takes the form of £73 million in direct support and a £120 million interest free loan. The support is recoverable via levies from banks and dividends payable by the liquidator.

The KSF IoM affair highlights a couple of points that are not

---

[8] Isle of Man Financial Supervision Commission, *Annual Report 2007–2008*, at 16.

[9] Depositors' compensation claims are being handled by international accountancy firm KPMG LLC as the designated scheme agent for these purposes.

[10] For full details, see Isle of Man Government, *Government Funding will speed up compensation for KSF IoM depositors*, Press Release (17 July 2009).

necessarily unique to the Isle of Man. First, active government intervention in the form of early repayment schemes (in this instance of £1000 and £10000[11]) can go a long way towards quickly alleviating small-scale investor distress caused by bank failure. Moreover, it created valuable time for the provisional liquidator to pursue corporate resale, restructuring and scheme of arrangement alternatives to formal activation of the deposit protection scheme. Secondly, in the offshore context reputational interests can serve as a disincentive to activation of a deposit protection scheme inasmuch as publicity generated by this may simply exacerbate external depositor concerns regarding bank soundness in the jurisdiction.

Recourse to a deposit protection scheme is therefore arguably a double-edged sword: although providing depositor redress and cutting down the risk of bank runs, it may paradoxically, in an intangible psychological sense, inflict damage on the perceived safeness of the offshore banking sector. Government and regulator preferences for alternative corporate rescue, restructuring and scheme of arrangement options witnessed in the KSF IoM affair may well be replicated in Jersey and Guernsey in the future. Placing a deposit protection scheme on the statute book does not of itself guarantee it will be triggered; private alternative options are likely to prove more attractive where the asset base of the failed bank permits this. Key substantive features of the Isle of Man deposit protection scheme[12] are as follows:

(i) It is triggered only when a participant is in default, which means when it cannot satisfy claims against it in connection with its deposit-taking activities *and* it is being wound up, a creditors' meeting has been summoned or a receiver appointed or there has been a voluntary arrangement with its creditors or an event equivalent to these has occurred outside the jurisdiction.

(ii) The scheme manager entrusted with administration of it is the Isle of Man Financial Supervision Commission, which is the lead bank regulator

---

[11] See Kaupthing, Singer and Friedlander (Isle of Man) Limited Early Payment Scheme (Isle of Man Government Circular 1/09); Kaupthing, Singer and Friedlander (Isle of Man) Limited Early Payment (No.2) Scheme (Isle of Man Government Circular 4/09); and Compensation of Depositors (Amendment) Regulations 2009 (Tynwald, Isle of Man).

[12] Detailed rules in the text can be located in: Compensation of Depositors Regulations 2008 (Tynwald, Isle of Man, 9 October 2008), issued pursuant to section 25 of the Financial Services Act 2008 (Tynwald, Isle of Man). See also, 'Isle of Man Government, Depositors Compensation Scheme' (not dated). The scheme does not extend to building societies registered under insular (or equivalent United Kingdom) legislation.

charged with ensuring compliance with the burgeoning raft of international regulatory standards.

(iii) Funds are paid out of an ad hoc compensation fund created once the bank has been declared in default. Payments are in respect of eligible deposits up to a maximum of £50 000. Separate deposits held with a single participant are aggregated and treated as single deposits for this purpose. Where full immediate payment would not be prudent, part payment may be made. If a balance remains in the fund after meeting claims the residue is distributed to depositors pro rata.

(iv) Ad hoc levies imposed once a bank has been declared in default can range from a minimum of £35 000 per participant per year to a corresponding maximum of £350 000 or 0.125 per cent of the bank's entire deposit base, whichever is the lower.

(v) Regarding defaults, between 23 October 2008 and 23 October 2009, the liability cap of banks collectively was set at £200 million. The cap was prompted by fears of contagion unleashed by the Icelandic banking crisis and wider international banking instability, which in turn could result in catastrophic compensation liability threatening the viability of the off-shore banking sector. This so-called 'sunset clause' will survive beyond its termination date on an interim basis until a full-scale consultation on and review of the entire deposit protection scheme has been completed.

(vi) The Manx Treasury is empowered to provide funding support of compensation sums per depositor in excess of £20 000 subject to an overall cap of £150 million. This is contained in a 'sunset clause' which automatically expired on 23 October 2009 and was designed to bolster the credibility of the scheme during the period of international banking instability in 2008–2009. Sums paid out are recoverable via bank levies and dividends from the liquidator. As with and on the same basis as the banks' collective cap this 'sunset clause' is set to be extended as a temporary measure.

(vii) Depositors applying for compensation are required to subrogate their existing rights against the bank to the Isle of Man FSC. Compensation within the £50 000 ceiling may be reduced in respect of any liability that existed at the time of default or payments made under any early repayments scheme or any dividend or distribution relating to that deposit.

(viii) There are no explicit time limits for payment of compensation although the implicit expectation appears to be that payments ought to be made as rapidly as possible. In practice payments can range from a few weeks in Manx Treasury-administered early repayment schemes to several years in complex, multi-jurisdictional bank insolvencies, as the aftermath of the BCCI collapse on the island demonstrated during the 1990s.

The Isle of Man scheme is thus entirely ad hoc post-funded apart from Manx government financial support, which was and probably still is a rapid temporary response to international bank instability in 2008 and the threat this posed to the insular economy. Assessment of its effectiveness is difficult since it has been invoked only on two occasions. Alternative corporate rescue and restructuring responses to bank failure exist in separate legislative regimes. Although there is no legislatively defined hierarchy of preferences, insular policy where the asset position of the failed bank permits is clearly to utilise these rather than deposit protection, which in general terms is regarded as a last resort option. The longer-term future of the Manx structure is very uncertain. In the short term it will continue in its current form with continued Manx Treasury funding capacity, pending results of the consultation exercise that will doubtless draw on the Foot Review and features of the Jersey and Guernsey schemes. Whether the final outcome will be a fine-tuning or a radically different structure remains to be seen.

GUERNSEY

The Bailiwick of Guernsey is located off the north-west coast of France in the English Channel with a population of around 62 000. It comprises the Island of Guernsey itself as the principal geographical unit and the neighbouring Islands of Herm, Alderney and Sark. The latter two islands are separate jurisdictions with their own legislatures (although bank regulation is in practice the responsibility of the Bailiwick's States of Deliberation (legislature)) and in which branch and office banking activity takes place.

Guernsey is now an established international OFC enjoying a strong reputation in the specialist areas of captive insurance, international banking, investment funds and offshore trusts. In captive insurance, it is generally regarded as a world-leading centre. Rapid OFC development has resulted in overall bank deposits of £119 billion,[13] the bulk of which are held in international private and corporate banks servicing the needs of inter-bank depositors, multinational corporations and high net worth individuals. The banking sector provides 3000 well paid, skilled jobs and contributes £40 million tax revenues annually to the insular economy.[14]

[13] Guernsey Financial Services Commission, *Annual Report and Financial Statements 2007*, at 17, 31 and 37.
[14] States of Guernsey Commerce and Employment Department, Deposit Protection Scheme, *Billet d' Etat* XIX (Wednesday 26 November 2008), at paras 5.1–5.14.

Offshore banking is now clearly a vital feature of the OFC; and it is on the future security of the OFC that employment levels and public revenues depend.

The historic position of the insular authorities in Guernsey has been that deposit protection is unnecessary since a rigorously selective licensing policy in conjunction with a more demanding stance towards capital adequacy ratios than under Basel II rules is sufficient to protect the interests of depositors. This policy was dealt a crippling blow in autumn 2008 when international banking instability spilled over into the island, resulting in the collapse of, and depositors' losses in, Landsbanki Guernsey (LG),[15] the wholly-owned subsidiary of a major Icelandic banking group that was effectively nationalised by the Icelandic government amidst an unfolding national economic crisis triggered and fuelled by banking sector meltdown.[16]

Around 2000 depositors were left without access to guaranteed restitution other than the minimum guarantee of 30 pence in the pound arising out of its liquidation. The States of Guernsey (insular government) adopted an unflinching position to the effect that its role was the restricted one of placing political pressure on the parent group to honour comfort letter commitments and, more recently, pressing the Icelandic government, regulator and administrator of LG's parent, Landsbanki Islands hf, to ensure equitable treatment of LG depositors in the protracted liquidation currently taking place.[17] It has unreservedly rejected any suggestion of *ex gratia* payments or retrospective extension of its recently enacted deposit compensation scheme.

Reacting with remarkable speed the insular authorities designed and implemented, virtually from scratch, within the space of a couple of months a comprehensive deposit protection scheme. The driving force behind this is not principally to provide depositors with redress; rather, it is to shore up external investor confidence in the offshore banking sector and provide a hedge against contagion.

Fundamental features of the scheme[18] can be summarised as follows:

---

[15] For a full account of its collapse and the insular political and legislative responses, see P.E. Morris, 'Bank Failure and Deposit Protection in Offshore Britain: The Case of Guernsey', 17 *Journal of Financial Regulation and Compliance* (2009).

[16] Details of which are fully documented in: House of Commons Treasury Committee (2009), *Banking Crisis: The Impact of the Failure of the Icelandic Banks*, HC 402, Fifth Report of Session 2008–2009 (4 April 2009), ch. 2.

[17] States of Guernsey, 'Chief Minister Urges Fair Treatment For Landsbanki Guernsey Depositors', *Press Release* (10 August 2009).

[18] The detailed rules in the text can be found in: The Banking Deposit Compensation Scheme (Bailiwick of Guernsey) Ordinance 2008 (*Billet d'Etat*

(i) It covers the entire Bailiwick and is administered by an institutionally separate Guernsey Banking Deposit Protection Board, which is operationally independent of the States of Guernsey and the Bailiwick's bank regulator, the Guernsey Financial Services Commission.

(ii) The scheme does not become operative until the Guernsey FSC has made a formal declaration of default, which it is required to do when a bank has been wound up, placed into administration, entered into an arrangement and/or compromise with its creditors, or its affairs have been declared *en desastre*.

(iii) Alternative corporate restructuring and resale options are built into the scheme as valid alternatives to the scheme, particularly where this is less costly than invoking the scheme. These powers also exist independently pre-declaration of default.

(iv) The funding model used is an innovative, mixed pre- and post-funding based on administration and insurance levies used respectively to meet the costs of administering the scheme and gradually build up £100 million in a captive insurance special purpose vehicle. Banks' collective liability is capped at £100 million over a five-year period.

(v) Some £70 million of this accumulated fund will take the form of risk-based premiums calculated according to the risk-assessed profiles of covered deposit institutions. This will result in some banks obtaining discounts of up to 30 per cent with others paying up to double their initial contribution.[19]

(vi) Compensation levies are imposed once a bank has been formally declared in default; these are intended as a 'top-up' in the sense that, in calculating them, monies paid out of the captive insurance vehicle have to be taken into account. Banks' individual compensation levies are capped at £1 million per annum or 50 per cent of their average profits over the previous three years, whichever is the lower.

(vii) The total amount of compensation payable is the aggregate amount of qualifying deposits or £50000, whichever is the lower. Compensation payments cannot be made in respect of more than one account with a single participant in default.

The Guernsey scheme is embodied, unlike its Manx counterpart, in a comprehensive code that provides a flexible range of solutions to bank col-

---

XLVIII of 2008, States of Guernsey), enacted pursuant to section 46 of the Banking Supervision (Bailiwick of Guernsey) Law of 1994 (*Billet d'Etat* XIII of 1994, States of Guernsey).

[19]   States of Guernsey Commerce and Employment Department, Deposit Protection Scheme, *Billet d' Etat* XIX 2008 (Wednesday 26 November 2008) at paras 10.1–10.10.

lapses. The potentially serious flaw is its reliance on risk-related premiums as the main source of funding. These are technically very difficult to quantify with confidence and possess an in-built tendency to become excessively expensive. Although they provide a private insurance solution that is prima facie more attractive than government financial support (which the Isle of Man is persisting with as an interim measure, and the projected use of which is causing real concern regarding public finances risk exposure in Jersey) there remains a danger of unwelcome business costs imposed on certain types of banks with higher risk profiles at a time when international banks are taking strategic decisions regarding business distribution offshore. In the longer term, it may be that prudently measured government financial backing is a risk worth taking in terms of banking business retention rates in the Bailiwick.

This point carries particular weight given the 'level playing field' created by the fact that all three jurisdictions will operate deposit protection schemes as part of their regulatory architecture. With the removal of competitive disadvantage, in terms of investor perceptions of the OFC being professionally regulated, a new form of impediment may emerge: a scheme seen as having excessive business costs and bereft of government financial backing. Guernsey appears to be in a vulnerable position on this and may in the longer term regret its rushed legislative reaction to the LG debacle.

JERSEY

Located around 20 miles south-east of Guernsey and 14 miles off the coast of Normandy, Jersey is both the most populous of the Crown dependencies (91 000) and furthest advanced in its offshore development. The total value of bank deposits at the end of 2008 was £206 billion – a more than doubling in size over a decade.[20] Like Guernsey, Jersey has historically placed great faith in a 'club of quality' admission policy that restricts award of banking licences to those banks in the global top 500. This stance was rapidly re-evaluated following the very real risk of contagion generated in small offshore finance centres by Icelandic bank collapses in the Isle of Man and Guernsey. The immediate response to this has been an implicit deposit scheme in the form of a States of Jersey (insular government) political guarantee[21] that Island residents' deposits are protected,

---

[20] Jersey Financial Services Commission, *Annual Report 2008* (2008) at 8 and 48.
[21] For full details see: States of Jersey Hansard, *Official Report*, 2 December 2008, paras 4.2, 4.2.1 and 6.1.10 (Chief Minister Walker); and States of Jersey Hansard, *Official Report*, 3 October 2008, para. 11.1.4 (Chief Minister Walker).

without a financial ceiling, should a bank collapse. A response along these lines was never going to be a permanent solution given the open-ended commitment of taxpayers' money involved and risks of competitive disadvantage flowing from operation of the deposit protection principle in its rival jurisdictions of Guernsey and the Isle of Man.

Not surprisingly therefore the government of Jersey, acting on the advice of external consultants who provided a cost–benefit analysis and comparative legal perspectives,[22] secured the approval in principle of the States Assembly (the insular legislature) for introduction of a deposit protection structure that was operationalised in 2009. This was subject to pre-legislative scrutiny by Jersey politicians independent of the insular government that endorsed the main thrust of the scheme subject only to debate regarding the level and nature of government financial support.

Justifications for the scheme are frankly admitted[23] as maintenance of the Jersey banking sector's competitive edge given anecdotal evidence of lost deposits to OFC rivals caused by perceived deficient depositor protection and the overriding political imperative of responding to the Foot Review agenda, which is depicted as virtually mandating deposit protection as good regulatory practice. Failure to unequivocally make this commitment is regarded as detrimental to Jersey's international regulatory reputation. Concern for consumer protection in banking and the hardship caused to economically vulnerable savers by bank default scarcely figures in these political and regulatory debates.

Key substantive features of the Jersey structure[24] are as follows:

(i) The scheme is administered by the Jersey Bank Depositors Protection Board, which is required to be independent of the Minister and insular government. It is under a duty to declare a bank in default once it is bankrupt, establish administrative arrangements for the payment of compensation and operate a compensation fund post-default.

---

[22]   Oxera, *Deposit Guarantee Arrangements for the States of Jersey: A Review and Evaluation of Options* (May 2009).

[23]   See the statements to this effect by senior members of the Jersey government at: States of Jersey Hansard, *Official Report*, 14 July 2009, para. 8.1 (A J H Maclean, Minister for Economic Development); and States of Jersey Hansard, *Official Report*, 14 July 2009, para. 8.9 (Chief Minister le Sueur).

[24]   Detailed rules discussed in the text are located in: States of Jersey, Draft Banking Business (Depositers Compensation) (Jersey) Regulations 200- (Lodged au Greffe on 2 June 2009 by the Minister for Economic Development). These were approved largely in 2009. See also: States of Jersey, Draft Public Finances (Depositers Compensation) (Jersey) Regulations 200- (Lodged au Greffe on 2 June 2009 by the Minister for Treasury and Resources).

(ii) Within the overall ceiling of £50 000 the Board is required to pay the first £5000 within seven days of an application being submitted and the remainder within three months. The quantum of compensation may be reduced by the Board to reflect payments made by schemes outside Jersey (or the claim may be dealt with entirely by the foreign scheme administrator with the agreement of the Board) or to take account of payments made to the depositor during administration. Generally, compensation is required to be paid by the Board within six months of it declaring a covered bank or financial institution bankrupt.

(iii) Funding of the scheme is by means of levies imposed after a bank defaults; there is no pre-funding whatsoever. Prima facie compensation liability is the total amount of eligible deposits held by the bank in default divided by the total amount of eligible deposits held by all the banks liable to pay a levy. The liability of a bank is capped at 0.3 per cent of its deposit base per annum and a five-year periodic cap of £10 million if this amount were to exceed £10 million (in any other case £5 million). When the £10 million cap comes into play a maximum annual cap of £2 million per bank operates (in any other case £1 million); and the collective cap on banks' liability under the scheme as a whole is £100 million over a five-year period.

(iv) Where there is a shortfall between the Board's compensation obligations and the collective £100 million cap the Board is entitled to make use of a loan facility provided by the States of Jersey Strategic Fund for a further £100 million. Interest is chargeable and the loan is repayable within a maximum five-year period. Support is envisaged as including short-term borrowing.

These arrangements bear a resemblance to those in the Isle of Man during 2008–2009 in the sense that they share the fundamental features of *ex post* funding and potentially large-scale government support. A clear point of divergence is the tight and non-negotiable time limits for payment of compensation under the Jersey scheme. These will considerably mitigate depositor distress in the immediate aftermath of a bank collapse. The scale of the LG (£82 million) and KSF IoM (£191 million) liabilities suggests this opening up of government reserves for possible use in large-scale deposit compensation exercises is potentially irresponsible in the context of an offshore jurisdiction facing a challenging economic climate for the foreseeable future. The States Strategic Fund is 'only to be used in exceptional circumstances to insulate the Island's economy from severe structural decline such as the collapse of a major Island industry or from major natural disaster'.[25] Failure of an individual bank does not, despite

---

[25] States of Jersey Strategic Reserve Fund, Use for Bank Depositors' Compensation Scheme (Lodged au Greffe on 2 June 2009 by the Minister for

inherent risks of contagion, pose this type of risk. The insular authorities, however, regard the £100 million exposure as theoretical: in practice recoveries from liquidation in large-scale bank failures would have de facto caps on exposure of £35 million, and a political directive is expected to limit the scheme's use to one of the top six Jersey licensed banks.[26] This could well prove over-sanguine in the event of multiple bank failure triggering catastrophic compensation liabilities resulting in loans that the Board may struggle to repay.

In terms of reputational interests and preservation of the banking sector's competitive edge, Jersey has had little option but to rapidly react to bank default and to the legislative responses of its OFC competitor jurisdictions Guernsey and the Isle of Man. Despite use of external expert advice and detailed pre-legislative scrutiny, the scheme was still being fast-tracked on to the statute book ahead of the Foot Review in a blatantly obvious attempt to 'look good'. A higher quality scheme may have been attained by a more reflective response that absorbed anticipated guidance in the Foot Review and comparative experiences of deposit protection schemes in small offshore jurisdictions.

CONCLUSIONS

Deposit protection reform was undertaken in the offshore jurisdictions of the UK Crown dependencies post-crisis. The motive for this is not enhanced depositor protection; rather, it is to bolster the external perceptions of these jurisdictions as financial centres that are attractive OFCs where foreign banks, investment firms and the professionals who advise them can do business. This reform is also designed to gain political credit by providing a proactive response to the external reviews conducted on behalf of the United Kingdom Treasury and International Monetary Fund. The latter feeds through into the former, creating, it is thought, a virtuous circle that clearly demarcates them from rival OFCs subscribing to less stringent regulatory standards. In narrower domestic terms, the Channel Islands OFCs have closed a depositor protection deficit between

---

Treasury and Resources) 2. Hence, the need for amending regulations to confer legality on its projected extended use as a support mechanism for the deposit protection scheme.

[26] See the statements to this effect in: *States of Jersey Hansard* (2009), Official Report (14 July 2009) at para. 8.1 (A J H Maclean, Minister for Economic Development); and *States of Jersey Hansard* (2009), Official Report, 15 July, at para. 1.11.3 (PFC Ozouf, Minister for Treasury and Resources).

themselves and the Isle of Man at a time of international banking instability that created a significant risk of lost business.

Despite common problems in regulating the offshore banking sector, in particular intractable barriers to exerting influence on group management and securing observance of comfort letter commitments, the schemes adopted exhibit fundamental differences. The Isle of Man scheme relies on ad hoc levies and does not incorporate into its code alternative or concurrent corporate rescue responses. It has been strengthened by government financial backing; but the continuation of this is uncertain. In dealing with the BCCI and KSF IoM collapses it has proved robust and efficient. The Jersey structure replicates funding aspects of the Manx model but there remain potential risks to public finances in the event of large-scale or multiple bank failures, which, in a protracted economic cycle subjecting these to considerable strain, places a question mark over its long-term credibility. Guernsey's scheme relies primarily on risk-related premiums and development of what is effectively a private insurance fund. This private sector solution eschews any government funding and the LG collapse suggests that the continuing political position of the government of Guernsey will reflect its legislative scheme. The longer-term effect may, however, be that Guernsey becomes a more expensive place in which to do business for certain types of banks with higher risk profiles, possibly triggering relocations and consequential employment and tax losses in a small island economy heavily dependent on its OFC. There are fine judgments in the small offshore jurisdiction context between beneficial reduction of systemic risk on the one hand and erosion of competitiveness vis-à-vis rival jurisdictions on the other.

Finally, it is important to place deposit protection in its proper perspective. It is a valuable means of alleviating depositor distress caused by bank failure but no substitute for prudential regulation as a technique deployed in reducing systemic risk. In jurisdictions seeking to regulate subsidiaries of major international banking conglomerates and lacking full constitutional sovereignty, there is a need, as the Foot Review recognises, to broaden the range of policy instruments necessary to deal with economic volatility, including additional powers of intervention, improved resolution procedures and capacity to provide emergency funding following bank failure.[27] All three structures provide for this in varying ways, but as an adjunct or alternative to deposit protection. The British Isles OFCs remain handicapped by structural problems of limited influence on group

---

[27] M. Foot, 'Progress report of the independent review of British Offshore Finance Centres' (April 2009) at paras 1.7 and 2.20.

management, absence of lender of last resort facilities, and the lack of regulatory benefits generated by a central bank able to exert its political and commercial muscle in sponsoring corporate rescue operations that preserve banks as business operations. Offshore dependencies' deposit protection schemes operating in this straightjacket are inevitably a limited banking regulation mechanism.

PART IV

The role of the lender of last resort and EU
sovereign debt restructuring

9. Exigent and unusual circumstances:* The Federal Reserve and the US financial crisis

Christian A. Johnson**

INTRODUCTION

In response to the greatest economic upheaval experienced by the US economy since the Great Depression, the Board of Governors of the Federal Reserve System (the Federal Reserve), through the Federal Reserve Bank of New York and other Federal Reserve Banks, embarked upon a series of unparalleled and unprecedented actions, repeatedly injecting hundreds of billions of liquidity into the US credit markets. Some of the most innovative approaches occurred during the extraordinarily volatile months of September and October of 2008. Measured in the tens and hundreds of billions of dollars, all of the actions were bold and innovative, providing fodder for decades of academic debate and discussion.

This chapter focuses initially on the economic carnage facing the Federal Reserve as it contemplated how to deal with the crisis. It will then address the different tools employed by the Federal Reserve to contain the different crises and financial fires, especially those experienced during the months of September and October of 2008, and will quantify how much liquidity was injected under each of the different programs and facilities employed by the Federal Reserve.[1] Finally, the chapter will discuss the actions of the US Congress in the aftermath of the crisis with respect to the

* Section 13(3) of the Federal Reserve Act.
** Professor, University of Utah College of Law. The initial research for this chapter was developed for and presented at the W.G. Hart Workshop on Law Reform and Financial Markets, Institute of Advanced Legal Studies, University of London, 24 June 2009. The author gratefully acknowledges the thorough research assistance provided by D. Gardiner and S. Anderson.
[1] The lending and purchase amounts were taken from the Federal historical releases entitled 'Federal Reserve Statistical Releases H.4.1' (Factors Affecting Reserve Balances).

statutory powers of the Federal Reserve and the extent to which they were exercised and the reforms that have been adopted in the Dodd-Frank Act.

THE US FINANCIAL CRISIS

That the United States has passed through its worst financial crisis since the Great Depression is both beyond debate and well chronicled.[2] There is an enormous amount of both technical and popular literature describing the crisis and actions to combat the financial collapse.[3] Ben Bernanke summarized the state of the US economy near the apex of the crisis in the Stamp Lecture given at the London School of Economics on 13 January, 2009:

> The abrupt end of the credit boom has had widespread financial and economic ramifications. Financial institutions have seen their capital depleted by losses and writedowns and their balance sheets clogged by complex credit products and other illiquid assets of uncertain value. Rising credit risks and intense risk aversion have pushed credit spreads to unprecedented levels, and markets for securitized assets, except for mortgage securities with government guarantees, have shut down. Heightened systemic risks, falling asset values, and tightening credit have in turn taken a heavy toll on business and consumer confidence and precipitated a sharp slowing in global economic activity. The damage, in terms of lost output, lost jobs, and lost wealth, is already substantial.[4]

The various stock market indices may be one of the most accurate barometers of the crisis. The US DOW Industrial Average peaked on 9 October 2007 at 14 164, a historic high for the DOW. By the time of the Lehman insolvency, it was at 11 422. By 9 March 2009, it had reached its low point of the crisis at 6440, representing a 55 per cent decline from its peak. It has

---

[2]   The Federal Reserve Bank of Saint Louis and the Federal Reserve Bank of New York have each prepared a financial crisis timeline that helped chronicle the crisis. See also D Wessel, *In Fed We Trust: Ben Bernanke's War on the Great Panic* (New York: Crown Business, 2009).

[3]   J.B. Foster and F. Magdoff, *The Great Financial Crisis: Causes and Consequences* (New York: Monthly Review Press, 2009); A.R. Sorkin, *Too Big to Fail: The Inside Story of How Wall Street and Washington Fought to Save the Financial System and Themselves* (London: Allen Lane, 2009); R.J. Shiller, *The Subprime Solution: How Today's Global Financial Crisis Happened, and What to Do about It* (Princeton: Princeton University Press, 2008); L. McDonald, *A Colossal Failure of Common Sense: The Inside Story of the Collapse of Lehman Brothers* (London: Ebury Press, 2009); D. Wessel, *In Fed We Trust: Ben Bernanke's War on the Great Panic* (New York: Crown Business, 2009).

[4]   B. Bernanke, 'The Crisis and the Policy Response', *Stamp Lecture, London School of Economics*, London (13 January 2009).

experienced a significant recovery in 2010, closing on 2 April 2010 at 10 927, although it is still nowhere near the high from more than two years ago.

The most volatile month of the crisis was arguably September of 2008. During that particular period, Fannie Mae and Freddie Mac failed, Bank of America purchased Merrill Lynch, Lehman Brothers filed for bankruptcy, AIG was effectively nationalized. In addition, the Reserve Primary Money Fund 'broke' the buck, Goldman Sachs and Morgan Stanley became bank holding companies, Washington Mutual Bank became insolvent, and Citigroup and Wells Fargo entered into a bidding war to purchase Wachovia Bank.[5]

Although there were some indications that the financial crisis began as early as February of 2007,[6] the Business Cycle Dating Committee of the National Bureau of Economic Research reported that the US economy's economic activity peaked in December of 2007,[7] ending an economic expansion of 73 months and signifying the beginning of the recession for the United States.[8] This recession is considered to be the longest and the deepest since the Great Depression. The recession continued from December of 2007 through the middle of 2009, with the third and fourth quarter eventually showing return to growth in the GDP.[9]

The Federal Reserve Response

The US government's response to the financial crisis was led principally by the Federal Reserve and the US Treasury, although the Federal Deposit Insurance Corporation (FDIC) and the Securities and Exchange

---

[5]   For a complete breakdown of September 2008, see St Louis Fed Financial Crisis Timeline, above n. 2.

[6]   The financial crisis timeline of the Federal Reserve Bank of St Louis shows the first cracks beginning as early as 27 February 2007 when Freddie Mac announced that 'it will no longer buy the most risky subprime mortgages and mortgage-related securities'. See St Louis Fed Financial Crisis Timeline, above n. 2. For an example of the valuation issues with mortgage-backed securities, see R. Lowenstein, 'Triple-A Failure', *The New York Times* (27 April 2008); A. Sloan and D. Burke, 'Once Upon a Time in Mortgage Land', *Fortune* (21 December 2009) at 106.

[7]   National Bureau of Economic Research, *Determination of the December 2007 Peak in Economic Activity* (11 December 2008).

[8]   For a discussion of the determination as to when a recession begins and ends, see R. Hall, M. Feldstein, J. Frankel, R. Gordon, C. Romer, D. Romer and V. Zarnowitz, 'Business Cycle Dating Committee', *National Bureau of Economic Research* (21 October 2009).

[9]   C. Isidore, *Best Economic Growth in Six Years* (29 January 2010), available at http://money.cnn.com.

Commission (SEC) also made their own contributions. Both the Federal Reserve's and the US Treasury's responses were extraordinary by any standard. The Federal Reserve, in particular, developed unique solutions to unique problems, often under intense time pressures as different segments of the US financial markets imploded owing primarily to a lack of liquidity.

Overview of the US Governmental Actions

It is important to distinguish between the Federal Reserve's activities and those conducted by Congress, the US Treasury, the FDIC and the SEC during the financial crisis. By statute, the Federal Reserve is effectively limited to secured lending activities and purchasing securities. This is done through creating reserves by crediting US dollars to a borrower's account at a Federal Reserve Bank, a process that at times is pejoratively referred to as 'printing money'. The Federal Reserve activities are directed by the Board of Governors of the Federal Reserve System (a US Federal government agency) and are coordinated and funded through the Federal Reserve Bank of New York and the 11 other Federal Reserve Banks.[10]

Congress responded initially by passing the Economic Stimulus Act of 2008, signed into Law by President Bush on 13 February 2008, estimated to cost approximately US$152 billion, and focused on tax rebates and incentives.[11] On 30 July 2008, President Bush signed into law the Housing and Economic Recovery Act of 2008,[12] which principally reformed the regulation of government-sponsored enterprises such as Fannie Mae and Freddie Mac. On 3 October 2008, Congress passed the Emergency Economic Stabilization Act of 2008, which established the Troubled Asset Relief Program ('TARP'), a US$700 billion fund established to fight the financial crisis.[13] Finally, on 17 February 2009, Congress passed the US$787 billion economic stimulus package, formally referred to as the American Recovery and Reinvestment Act of 2009.[14]

The US Treasury was able to intervene in other ways beyond the lending powers provided to the Federal Reserve. The most important activities of the US Treasury were the equity investments and lending activities

---

[10]   For an overview of the Federal Reserve System, see A.H. Meltzer, *A History of the Federal Reserve*, 2 vols (Chicago: University of Chicago Press, 2002 and 2010).

[11]   Public Law 110–185.

[12]   Public Law 110–289. See P Muolo, *US$700 Billion Bailout*, p. 178 (London: John Wiley & Sons, 2008).

[13]   Public Law 110–343, ibid., n.12.

[14]   Public Law 111–5.

through its use of the US$700 billion TARP fund in numerous depository institutions, and institutions such as AIG, Fannie Mae and Freddie Mac, as well as making loans and equity investments in the auto industry.[15] As of January of 2010, the US Treasury had expended approximatelyUS$470 billion on equity investments and lending and had been 'repaid' approximately US$125 billion.[16] Other significant activities include its general involvement in government-sponsored enterprises,[17] the nationalization of Fannie Mae and Freddie Mac,[18] the creation of the Fund Stabilization Program to help money market funds,[19] the creation of various programs such as the Financial Stability Plan,[20] the Federal Homeowners Stability Plan,[21] the Auto Supplier Support Program,[22] and the Public-Private Investment Program for Legacy Assets,[23] and the development of regulatory reforms.[24]

Although working more in the shadows, the FDIC also extended its resources.[25] To provide greater assurances to depositors as banks continued to slide into crisis, the FDIC raised the deposit insurance limit from

---

[15] For a discussion of the TARP program, see Thomson Hine, Summary of the Troubled Assets Relief Program (8 October 2008).

[16] For a summary of expenditures under the TARP to date, see US Treasury Department, *Office of Financial Stability, Troubled Asset Relief Program, Transactions Report for Period Ending* (15 January 2010).

[17] US Treasury Press Release, *Paulson Announces GSE Initiatives* (13 July 2008) at HP-1079.

[18] US Treasury Press Release, *Statement by Secretary Henry M. Paulson, Jr. on Treasury and Federal Housing Finance Agency Action to Protect Financial Markets and Taxpayers* (7 September 2008) at HP-1129.

[19] US Treasury Press Release, *Treasury Announces Guaranty Program for Money Market Fund* (19 September 2008) at HP-1147.

[20] US Treasury Press Release, *Secretary Geithner Introduces Financial Stability Plan* (10 February 2009) at TG-18.

[21] US Treasury Press Release, *Homeowner Affordability and Stability Plan* (18 February 2009) at TG-33.

[22] US Treasury Press Release, *Treasury Announces Auto Supplier Support Program* (19 March 2009) at TG-64.

[23] US Treasury Press Release, *Treasury Department Releases Details on Public Private Partnership Investment Program* (23 March 2009) at TG-65.

[24] *Ibid.*, n 23.

[25] The FDIC actions can be easily traced through a review of their press releases during the financial crisis (available at fdic.gov). For example, see FDIC Press release, 'Agencies encourage participation in Treasury's Capital Purchase Program', FDIC's Temporary Liquidity Guarantee Program (10/20/2008), available at http://www.fdic.gov/news/press/2008/pro08103.html. See also C. Johnson, *Doing Whatever it Takes: The FDIC and the U.S. Financial Crisis* (to be published in 2012).

US$100000 to US$250000 on 7 October 2008.[26] Only a week later, the FDIC created the Temporary Liquidity Guarantee Program to guarantee the senior debt of depository institutions and their holding companies.[27]

The SEC was much less active than its sister agencies and departments. On 15 July 2008, the SEC issued a temporary order prohibiting the '"naked" short selling in the securities of Fannie Mae, Freddie Mac, and primary dealers at commercial and investment banks.'[28] This was followed up by a ban on short selling of 'the securities of all public companies, including all companies in the financial sector'.[29] In addition, the SEC has also focused on regulation of credit rating agencies[30] and proposed amendments to strengthen financial regulation.[31]

The Federal Reserve's response to the financial crisis can be divided and summarized into six different categories:

- lowering the Federal Funds interest rate essentially to zero per cent;
- lending through the Discount Window and the Term Auction Facility;
- swapping US dollars for foreign currencies with other central banks;
- direct lending to non-depository institutions pursuant to Section 13(3) of the Federal Reserve Act;
- creating new lending programs to non-depository institutions pursuant to Section 13(3); and
- purchasing mortgage-backed securities through the large-scale asset purchase programs developed by the Federal Reserve.

The sections below describe in detail the actions taken by the Federal Reserve with respect to each of these categories.[32]

---

[26] FDIC Press Release, *Emergency Economic Stabilization Act of 2008 Temporarily Increases Basic FDIC Insurance Coverage from US$100,000 to US$250,000 per Depositor* (7 October 2008).

[27] FDIC Press Release, *FDIC Announces Plan to Free Up Bank Liquidity: Creates New Program to Guarantee Bank Debt and Fully Insure Non-Interest Bearing Deposit Transaction Accounts* (14 October 2008).

[28] SEC Press Release, *SEC Enhances Investor Protections Against Naked Short Selling*, 2008-143 (15 July 2008).

[29] SEC Press Release, *SEC Issues New Rules to Protect Against Naked Short Selling Abuses*, 2008-204 (17 September 2008).

[30] SEC Press Release, *SEC Approves Measures to Strengthen Oversight of Credit Rating Agencies*, 2008-28 (3 December 2008).

[31] SEC Press Release, *SEC Proposes Rule Amendments to Strengthen Regulatory Framework for Money Market Funds*, 2009-142 (24 June 2009).

[32] For a statistical analysis of these various actions, see SIFMA Research and Statistics.

Lowering Interest Rates

Beginning in the fall of 2007, the Federal Reserve began to lower interest rates in hopes of loosening the credit markets. Using its monetary authority to lower interest rates,[33] the Federal Reserve began to target lowering the Federal Funds rate.[34] As the smaller interest rate cuts failed to have the desired effect, the Federal Reserve became more aggressive in targeting the Federal Funds rate until it eventually neared zero by January of 2009. Unfortunately, these aggressive actions appear not to have had the impact on credit markets hoped for by the Federal Reserve.[35]

Table 9.1 below summarizes the Federal Reserve's actions to lower the Federal Funds interest rate from a high of 4.25 per cent in September of 2007 to essentially zero per cent by the end of 2008.

Lending Directly to Depository Institutions

Some trace the beginning of the 'credit crunch', often defined as 'a severe shortage of money or credit', to the problems experienced by BNP Paribas in August of 2007.[36] During this time period, it became difficult for banks to borrow in the interbank lending markets such as the LIBOR and Federal Funds markets.[37] Without access to these interbank lending markets, banks were unable to make new loans and found it increasingly difficult to meet their current lending commitments.[38]

---

[33]   For a discussion of the Federal Reserve's ability to influence interest rates, see T. Cook and T. Hahn, 'The Effect of Changes in the Federal Funds Rate Target on Market Interest Rates in the 1970s', *Working Paper 88-4*, Federal Reserve Bank of Richmond (July 1988).

[34]   12 USC §355; for a discussion of open market operations, see C Edwards, *Open Market Operations in the 1990s*, Federal Reserve Bulletin (November 1997) at 859. See also A.M. Meulendyke, *U.S. Monetary Policy and Financial Markets* (New York: Federal Reserve Bank of New York, 1999) at 18–47 (for a general discussion of monetary policy).

[35]   D.L. Kohn, Vice Chairman of the Federal Reserve, *Monetary Policy in the Financial Crisis* (speech) (2009).

[36]   O. Armantier, S. Krieger and J. McAndrews, 'The Federal Reserve's Term Auction Facility', 14 *Current Issues in Economics and Finance*, 5 (July 2008) 2.

[37]   BBC News, 'Timeline: Credit Crunch to Downturn' (7 August 2009), stating '[t]he moves are the latest in a series of steps orchestrated by the Fed to relieve a credit crunch triggered earlier this year by problems in the subprime mortgage business'.

[38]   Armantier, Krieger and McAndrews, above n. 36, at 3 ('depository institutions also faced large expected future demands for funds as they anticipated further calls on their promises to provide credit').

Table 9.1   Federal Reserve's actions to lower the Federal Funds interest rate

Announcement date of intended Fed Funds rates	Intended Fed Funds rates
16 December 2009	0%–0.25%
11–12 August 2009	0%–0.25%
24 June 2009	0%–0.25%
16 January 2009	0%–0.25%
16 December 2008	0%–0.25%
29 October 2008	1%
8 October 2008	1.5%
30 April 2008	2.0%
18 March 2008	2.25%
30 January 2008	3.0%
22 January 2008	3.5%
11 December 2007	4.25%
31 October 2007	4.5%
18 September 2007	4.75%

As credit became tighter, the Federal Reserve began to encourage depository institutions that were members of the Federal Reserve to borrow from the Discount Window (described further below).[39] The Federal Reserve through the different Federal Reserve Banks is authorized to lend to member institutions pursuant to section 10B of the Federal Reserve Act.[40] Banks have generally resisted borrowing from the Discount Window because the Federal Reserve is often viewed as a lender of last resort, suggesting that a bank is unable to fund itself through normal market channels. In September of 2007, under pressure from the

---

[39]   Reuters, *Top International Banks Tap Fed Discount Window* (22 August 2007).

[40]   Section 10B(a) of the Federal Reserve Act states:

'Any Federal Reserve Bank, under rules and regulations prescribed by the Board of Governors of the Federal Reserve System, may make advances to any member bank on its time or demand notes having maturities of not more than four months and which are secured to the satisfaction of such Federal Reserve Bank. Notwithstanding the foregoing, any Federal Reserve Bank, under rules and regulations prescribed by the Board of Governors of the Federal Reserve System, may make advances to any member bank on its time notes having such maturities as the Board may prescribe and which are secured by mortgage loans covering a one-to-four family residence. Such advances shall bear interest at a rate equal to the lowest discount rate in effect at such Federal Reserve Bank on the date of such note.' Codified at 12 USC §347b(a).

Federal Reserve, Citibank, JP Morgan Chase, Wachovia and Bank of America all borrowed amounts through the Discount Window from the Federal Reserve in order to reverse the stigma often associated with such borrowing.[41]

Borrowing from the Federal Reserve is typically done through what is historically referred to as the 'Discount Window' and is always done on a secured basis with an overnight maturity. The categories of Discount Window borrowings are primary credit, secondary credit, and seasonal credit. As it became clear that the Discount Window was inadequate to meet the liquidity demands being placed on the market, the Federal Reserve announced, on 12 December 2007, the creation of the Term Auction Facility.

The Term Auction Facility permits banks to borrow funds over a 28 or 84 day time period as opposed to the overnight maturity for the Discount Window.[42] The Term Auction Facility proved to be an extraordinarily important source of liquidity for the interbank market with an outstanding high balance of over US$490 billion in March of 2009. Currently the amount outstanding to the different Federal Reserve Banks under the Discount Window and Term Auction Facility is approximately US$55 billion.

The current outstanding and high balance amounts in these four categories are set out in Table 9.2 below.

Central Bank Liquidity Swaps

In addition to the credit crisis occurring in the United States, a severe liquidity crisis emerged worldwide with respect to US dollars in the fall of 2007. Not only was credit difficult to obtain in the United States, but there was also a shortage of US dollars that could be lent outside the United States. Central banks as well as other credit worthy financial institutions found it extremely difficult to borrow in dollars. To meet that demand, the Federal Reserve created the Central Bank Liquidity Swap Facility on 12 December 2007 under Section 14 of the Federal Reserve Act.

The Federal Reserve provides a detailed description of the mechanics of these dollar liquidity swap lines:

---

[41]   A. Barr and R. Nutting, *Market Watch – U.S. Banking Giants Borrow US$2 Billion from Fed* (22 August 2007).

[42]   For a discussion of the terms and conditions of the Term Auction Facility, see Term Auction Facility, Armantier, Krieger and James, above n. 36, at Box 2 (Operation of TAF Auctions).

Table 9.2   Current outstanding and high balance amounts

Program	Current balances (31 Mar 10) US$	Highest balance (and date) US$
Primary Credit	7.6 billion	112 billion (29 Oct 08)
Secondary Credit	600 million	973 million (20 Jan 10)
Seasonal Credit	0	361 million (30 Aug 2006)[43]
Term Auction Facility	3.4 billion	493 billion (11 Mar 09)

These swaps involve two transactions. When a foreign central bank draws on its swap line with the Federal Reserve, the foreign central bank sells a specified amount of its currency to the Federal Reserve in exchange for dollars at the prevailing market exchange rate. The Federal Reserve holds the foreign currency in an account at the foreign central bank. The dollars that the Federal Reserve provides are deposited in an account that the foreign central bank maintains at the Federal Reserve Bank of New York. At the same time, the Federal Reserve and the foreign central bank enter into a binding agreement for a second transaction that obligates the foreign central bank to buy back its currency on a specified future date at the same exchange rate. The second transaction unwinds the first. At the conclusion of the second transaction, the foreign central bank pays interest, at a market-based rate, to the Federal Reserve.[44]

The facilities appear to have been highly effective in meeting the global dollar liquidity crisis.[45]

These dollar liquidity swap lines were entered into with the Reserve Bank of Australia, the Banco Central do Brasil, the Bank of Canada, Danmarks Nationalbank, the Bank of England, the European Central Bank, the Bank of Japan, the Bank of Korea, the Banco de Mexico, the

---

[43]   US$361 million is the highest balance in seasonal credit since 2003.

[44]   For a discussion of the swap lines with the Brazilian Central Bank, see World Bank, *Currency Swaps: Fed to Brazilian Central Bank to Real Sector, Crisis Talk: Emerging Markets and the Financial Crisis* (27 July 2009).

[45]   J.H.E. Christensen, J.A. Lopez and G.D. Rudenbusch, *Do Central Bank Liquidity Facilities Affect Interbank Lending Rates*, Federal Reserve Bank of San Francisco Working Paper Series (June 2009), Working Paper 2009-13; M. Obstfeld, J.C. Shambaugh and A.M. Taylor, *Financial Instability, Reserves and Central Bank Swap Lines in the Panic of 2008*, Working Paper 14826; R. Auer and S. Kraenzlin, *Money Market Tensions and International Liquidity Provision during the Crisis*, NBER Working Paper Series (14 October 2009).

Reserve Bank of New Zealand, Norges Bank, the Monetary Authority of Singapore, Sveriges Riksbank, and the Swiss National Bank. The Central Bank Liquidity Swap Facility was initially very active, with an outstanding balance of US$582 billion on 12 December 2008. The balance is now down to zero as these arrangements were officially ended on 1 February 2010.[46]

Lending under Section 13(3) of the Federal Reserve Act

The Federal Reserve actions that generated the most controversy involved the unprecedented lending to non-depository institutions pursuant to the Federal Reserve's lending powers under Section 13(3) of the Federal Reserve Act. The action was unprecedented for three reasons. First, the Federal Reserve had not exercised this lending power since the Great Depression, and even then it had done so in a relatively limited fashion. Second, the dollar amount of the intervention was measured in the hundreds of billions of dollars. Third, the Federal Reserve has no supervisory responsibility or examination authority over the borrowers receiving help.

Section 13(3) permits the Federal Reserve to lend to non-depository institutions provided that the borrower and the situation meet specific requirements. Section 13(3), codified in Section 343 of Title 12 of the US Code, states:

> In unusual and exigent circumstances, the Board of Governors of the Federal Reserve System, by the affirmative vote of not less than five members, may authorize any Federal reserve bank, during such periods as the said board may determine, at rates established in accordance with the provisions of section 14, subdivision (d), of this Act, to discount for any individual, partnership, or corporation, notes, drafts, and bills of exchange when such notes, drafts, and bills of exchange are indorsed or otherwise secured to the satisfaction of the Federal Reserve bank: *Provided*, That before discounting any such note, draft, or bill of exchange for an individual, partnership, or corporation the Federal reserve bank shall obtain evidence that such individual, partnership, or corporation is unable to secure adequate credit accommodations from other banking institutions. All such discounts for individuals, partnerships, or corporations shall be subject to such limitations, restrictions, and regulations as the Board of Governors of the Federal Reserve System may prescribe.[47]

---

[46] J. Wardell, *Central Banks End US Dollar Emergency Swap Lines* (27 January 2010).

[47] As added by act of 21 July 1932 (47 Stat. 715); and amended by acts of 13 August 1935 (49 Stat. 714) and 19 December 1991 (105 Stat. 2386).

The language is anachronistic at best, employing terms and processes that were best understood in the early 1900s, but these still represent the power to lend to an 'individual, partnership or corporation' that is not a member bank of the Federal Reserve System.

In approving the emergency loan to The Bear Stearns Companies Inc. under Section 13(3) in March of 2008, the Federal Reserve summarized the key Section 13(3) requirements in its approval of the transaction:

> As required by the Federal Reserve Act when fewer than five Board members were available to approve an extension of credit to any individual, partnership, or corporation under section 13(3) of the Federal Reserve Act, all available Board members then in office unanimously determined, in connection with the authorization of the extension of credit, that (1) unusual and exigent circumstances existed; (2) Bear Stearns, and possibly other primary securities dealers, were unable to secure adequate credit accommodations elsewhere; (3) this action was necessary to prevent, correct, or mitigate serious harm to the economy or financial stability . . .[48]

The Board of Governors exercised its authority under Section 13(3) not only for systemically important institutions such as Bear Stearns, AIG, Citigroup and Bank of America Corporation but also to create a host of Section 13(3) lending facilities.

To appreciate why the Federal Reserve's actions were so controversial, it is important to understand the historical context in which Section 13(3) was passed and later amended.[49] The original Federal Reserve Act did not authorize the Federal Reserve to lend to a non-depository institution.[50] Section 13(3) was added later during the Great Depression to provide an additional source of liquidity.[51] Although helpful, the statute required that the same quality of collateral be used that was eligible for borrowings from the Discount Window.[52] Because this type of collateral was normally not

---

[48] Minutes of the Board of Governors of the Federal Reserve System (14 March 2008).

[49] See D. Fettig, 'The History of a Powerful Paragraph: Section 13(3) Enacted Fed Business Loans 76 Years Ago' (The Federal Reserve Bank of Minneapolis, June 2008) at 33.

[50] Federal Reserve Act of 1913, 38 Stat. 362.

[51] Emergency Relief and Construction Act (1932), ch. 520, 47 Stat. 709, enacted 21 July 1932.

[52] This would have included certain US Treasury obligations and 'notes, drafts, and bills of exchange issued or drawn for agricultural, industrial, or commercial purposes' with a maturity of not more than 90 days. Section 13(2), 12 U.S.C. 343; W. Todd, 'FDICIA's Emergency Liquidity Provisions', *Federal Reserve Bank of Cleveland, Economic Review*, Third Quarter (1993) at 18 n. 10.

held by non-depository institutions, especially those in a liquidity crisis, Section 13(3)'s help was probably illusory at best.

In spite of the collateral restrictions, the Federal Reserve did some lending to non-depository institutions under Section 13(3) during the Great Depression. The volume of lending, however, was very small.[53] Only 123 loans were made under Section 13(3), in a total amount of only US$1.5 million from 1932 through 1936.[54]

Although Section 13(3) remained a tool for the Federal Reserve, the Federal Reserve had not invoked its authority until it intervened in the Bear Stearns crisis.[55] It has been suggested by commentators anecdotally that the Federal Reserve had considered lending under Section 13(3) several times during past market stress. The most prominent examples include the Penn Central crisis,[56] the potential bankruptcy of New York City in 1975,[57] the Crash of 1987,[58] and the financial difficulties experienced by the airline industry after 9/11.[59] One article suggested that the Federal Reserve's Section 13(3) lending powers could potentially have been helpful with respect to liquidity pressures faced with respect to Y2K.[60] In surveying some of these examples in 1991, Anna Schwartz, a senior research fellow at the National Bureau of Economic Research, questioned 'whether [the Federal Reserve] will be firm in the future in resisting pressures to fund insolvent firms that are politically well-connected'.[61]

In assessing the markets' reaction to the 1987 financial crisis, Congress

---

[53] Fettig, above n 49, at 18.

[54] Todd, above n 52, at 18; Fettig, above n 49; H.H. Hackley, *Lending Functions of the Federal Reserve Bank* (Washington: Federal Reserve System, 1961) at 130.

[55] For a review of the Bear Stearns failure, see K. Kelly, *Streetfighters: The Last 72 Hours of Bear Stearns, the Toughest Firm on Wall Street* (Portfolio Hardcover, 2009).

[56] See Fettig, above n. 49, at 46; A.J. Schwartz, 'The Misuse of the Fed's Discount Window', 74(5) *Federal Reserve Bank of St. Louis, Review* (5 September/ October 1992) at 62.

[57] See Fettig, above n. 49, at 46; Schwartz, above n. 56, at 62.

[58] Fettig, above n. 49, at 46. For a discussion of the 1987 crisis, see D. Wessel, 'Fed Opposed Any Rise in Interest Rates Following the Oct. 19 Market Collapse', *Wall Street Journal* (21 December 1987); T.E. Ricks and M. Langley, 'Congress Puts On Fast Track Regulations for Wall Street', *Wall Street Journal* (21 October 1987); K.H. Bacon, 'A Repeat of '29? Depression in '87 Is Not Expected', *Wall Street Journal* (20 October 1987) at 1.

[59] Fettig, above n. 49, at 47.

[60] T. Baxter and J. Sommer, 'Liquidity Crisis', 34 *International Lawyer*, 87 (Spring 2000).

[61] Schwartz, above n. 56, at 63.

was concerned that the collateral limitations imposed by Section 13 were too restrictive for the section to be useful during a future crisis.[62] Section 13(3) at that time required non-depository institutions to pledge the same 'near substitute for cash' quality of collateral eligible for the Discount Window. In response, Congress amended Section 13(3) in Section 473 of the Federal Deposit Insurance Corporation Act of 1991:

> Sec. 473. Emergency Liquidity.
> Section 13 of the Federal Reserve Act (12 U.S.C. 343) is amended in the third paragraph by striking 'of the kinds and maturities made eligible for discount for member banks under other provisions of this Act'.[63]

By deleting this collateral requirement, it permitted the Federal Reserve to accept less liquid collateral for loans made under Section 13(3) than it was permitted to accept for loans made through the Discount Window. One commentator prophetically noted that the loosening of this requirement 'effectively expanded the safety net',[64] making possible the Federal Reserve's lending efforts under Section 13(3) during the recent financial crisis.

Section 13(3) lending to systemically important non-depositor institutions

The section 13(3) lending that has drawn the most attention to the Federal Reserve is the credit extended directly to what are often euphemistically referred to as systemically important non-depository institutions.[65] The Federal Reserve stepped in aggressively in lending directly to Bear Stearns and AIG as these companies' financial difficulties threatened entire financial markets. Additional help in the form of guarantees was provided under Section 13(3) to both Citigroup and Bank of America Corporation.

The Federal Reserve first exercised its Section 13(3) power in March of 2008 when it lent US$12.9 billion to The Bear Stearns Companies Inc. After this amount was repaid, the Federal Reserve lent US$29 billion to a special purpose investment vehicle named 'Maiden Lane'. Money was

---

[62]   Todd, above n. 52.

[63]   FDIC Improvement Act of 1991, Pub. Law No. 102-242, 105 Stat. 2236 (1991). (S. 473) Subtitle J (Sense of the Congress Regarding the Credit Crisis).

[64]   Todd, above n. 52.

[65]   As the dust began to settle in January of 2010, US Treasury Secretary Geithner, as well as other Federal Reserve and US Treasury officials, testified before Congress with respect to the Federal Reserve's actions with AIG. See Bloomberg (2010), *Geithner Recounts AIG Rescue in Testimony to U.S. House (Text)*.

lent to Maiden Lane on a non-recourse basis. These funds were then used to acquire certain illiquid assets of Bear Stearns in order to facilitate the acquisition of Bear Stearns by JP Morgan Chase. The Maiden Lane facility currently has an outstanding balance of US$26.2 billion.[66]

The Federal Reserve also stepped into a liquidity void after Lehman Brothers failed in September of 2008. As the financial crisis continued to grow, the Federal Reserve believed that it needed to help contain the AIG meltdown.[67] The Federal Reserve in September of 2008 entered into a US$85 billion credit facility with AIG, of which US$82 billion was drawn down. AIG has reduced the amount outstanding under the credit facility first by applying the US$40 billion of the TARP money received from the US Treasury to purchase AIG preferred stock. The amount outstanding was further reduced by US$25 Billion in exchange for an interest in two life insurance subsidiaries of AIG.

The Federal Reserve also made two additional loans to AIG (similar to the Bear Stearns Maiden Lane facility) through two special purpose vehicles referred to as Maiden II and Maiden III. The Federal Reserve lent funds on a non-recourse basis to Maiden Lane II in order to 'purchase residential mortgage-backed securities from the U.S. securities lending portfolio of AIG subsidiaries'.[68] The Federal Reserve lent funds on a non-recourse basis to Maiden Lane III in order to purchase 'multi-sector collateralized debt obligations on which AIG Financial Products had written on credit default swaps'.[69] As the economy stabilized, the Federal Reserve came under scrutiny from Congress regarding its actions to rescue AIG.[70]

---

[66] ('Maiden Lane LLC (ML LLC), was formed to facilitate the merger of the Bear Stearns Companies, Inc. and JP Morgan Chase & Co. The New York Fed extended credit to ML LLC to acquire certain assets of Bear Stearns.') See also Federal Reserve Press Release, Statement on Financing Arrangement of JP Morgan Chase's Acquisition of Bear Stearns ('This action is being taken by the Federal Reserve, with the support of the Treasury Department, to bolster market liquidity and promote orderly market functioning').

[67] For a discussion of the AIG's actions, see Report Pursuant to Section 129 of the Emergency Economic Stabilization Act of 2008: Restructuring of the Government's Financial Support to the American International Group, Inc. on 10 November 2008; GAO, Federal Financial Assistance: Preliminary Observations on Assistance Provided to AIG (18 March 2009) GAO-09-490T.

[68] GAO, Federal Financial Assistance, Preliminary Observations on Assistance Provided to AIG (18 March 2009) GAO-09-490T, at 3.

[69] Ibid.

[70] See, e.g., Press Release from the House Committee on Oversight and Government Reform, 'Chairman Towns Announces Hearing to Examine AIG's Federal Financial Assistance' (22 January 2010).

Recently, the Federal Reserve has agreed to turn over all of its records regarding AIG to the US Comptroller General.[71]

Because of concerns about the effects that the collapse of Citigroup and Bank of America Corporation could have on the financial recovery, the Federal Reserve also provided financial assistance to Citigroup[72] and Bank of America Corporation[73] under its Section 13(3) authority in the form of loss sharing guarantees in conjunction with the Treasury and the FDIC. It was estimated that the Federal Reserve was potentially liable for up to US$280 billion for Citigroup alone in the event that the protection was required.[74] As the companies have stabilized, both Citigroup[75] and Bank of America Corporation[76] have paid exit fees and terminated the loss sharing guarantees.

Table 9.3 below summarizes the lending made by the Federal Reserve to systemically important non-depository institutions under Section 13(3).

Section 13(3) lending facilities
In addition to the individual assistance required by certain large systemically important non-depository institutions as discussed above, the Federal Reserve found itself having to react on an ad hoc basis as different financial sectors of the economy collapsed. In response, the Federal Reserve developed a series of lending facilities to assist non-depository institutions under its Section 13(3) lending authority.[77] Each of these facilities provided liquidity in the hundreds of billions of dollars to non-depository institutions unable to obtain necessary credit otherwise. Although the balances in these facilities were measured in the hundreds of

[71] See Letter from Ben Bernanke dated 19 January 2010 to Mr Gene L. Dodaro.
[72] See Joint Statement by Treasury, Federal Reserve, and the FDIC on Citigroup (23 November 2008); term sheet. For a description of the loss sharing program, see Summary of Terms of USG/Citigroup Loss Sharing Program.
[73] Press Release, Treasury, Federal Reserve, and the FDIC Provide Assistance to Bank of America; term sheet. For a discussion of the Bank of America Corporation guarantee, see Report Pursuant to Section 129 of the Emergency Economic Stabilization Act of 2008, Authorization to Provide Residual Financing to Bank of America Corporation Relating to a Designated Asset Pool.
[74] B. Keoun and M. Pittman, *Citigroup's Asset Guarantees to Be Audited by TARP* (Washington DC, 2010).
[75] The termination agreement for Citigroup.
[76] See Bank of America Corporation Press Release, dated 21 September 2009, Bank of America Terminates Asset Guarantee Term Sheet.
[77] For a general discussion of these programs, see Davis Polk Wardwell, *Financial Crisis Manual*, 20–40 (2009).

Table 9.3   Federal Reserve lending under Section 13(3)

Program name	Description	Current balance 31 Mar 10 US$	High balance US$
Bear Stearns Loan (14 Mar 08)	Emergency Discount Window loan to Bear Stearns secured by US$13.8 billion of Bear Stearns assets (repaid 17 Mar 08).	0	12.9 billion (17 Mar 08)
Maiden Lane (SPV) (Mar 08)	Facilitated the acquisition of Bear Stearns by JPMorgan Chase by non-recourse loan to SPV (Bear Stearns) (collateral value US$26 billion 12 Aug 09).	27.3 billion	30 billion (02 July 08)
AIG Revolving Credit Facility (16 Sept 08)	Revolving loan for general corporate purposes to AIG. (Commitment has been reduced to US$60 billion.)	26.2 billion	89.5 billion (29 Oct 08)
AIG Secured Borrowing Facility (08 Oct 08)	Secured loan for general corporate purposes. Repaid and terminated (originally authorized to US$37.8 billion).	0	20 billion (08 Oct 08)
Maiden Lane II (SPV) (12 Dec 08)	Formed to purchase residential mortgage security assets from AIG.	15.4 billion	20 billion (07 Jan 09)
Maiden Lane III (SPV) (25 Nov 08)	Formed to purchase multi-sector CDOs on which the Financial Products group of AIG had written credit default swap and similar contracts.	22.1 billion	28 billion (24 Dec 08)
AIA Aurora LLC and ALICO Holdings LLC (2 March 09)	Part of the restructuring of aid extended to AIG. The revolving credit outstanding and revolving credit available to AIG was reduced in exchange for preferred interests in two special purpose vehicles that will hold all of the common stock of two AIG life insurance subsidiaries.	25 billion	25 billion
Citigroup Loss Sharing Facility (25 Nov 08)	Obligated to fund non-recourse loan of approximately US$250 billion after US$300 billion asset pool has suffered approximately US$50 billion in losses.	0	0
Bank of America Corp Loss Sharing Facility (15 Jan 09)	Obligated to fund non-recourse loan of US$97 billion after pool of Merrill Lynch assets incurs US$18 billion of mark-to-market losses.	0	0

billions of dollars, the majority of these programs have wound down to a significant extent.

These Section 13(3) lending facilities consisted of the following:

- Primary Dealer Credit Facility
- Term Securities Lending Facility (not technically a 13(3) program)
- Asset-Backed Commercial Paper Money Market Mutual Fund Liquidity Facility
- Commercial Paper Funding Facility
- Money Market Investor Funding Facility
- Term Asset-Backed Securities Loan Facility.

The *Primary Dealer Credit Facility*[78] was created in response to the liquidity crisis facing primary dealers in the spring of 2008.[79] In contrast to other lending programs, this is an overnight fully collateralized loan facility for primary dealers that deal and trade with the Federal Reserve Bank of New York in US Treasury securities.[80] The facility had an outstanding US$147 billion on 1 October 2008, although it currently has a zero balance. Initially, the facility was intended to provide liquidity for only six months. After almost two years, the program officially expired on 1 February 2010.

The *Term Securities Lending Facility*[81] was announced (in conjunction with similar programs announced by other central banks) during the same time as the Primary Dealer Credit Facility.[82] Although the program was

---

[78]   For a complete discussion of the Primary Dealer Credit Facility, see T. Adrian, C.R. Burke and J.J. McAndrews, 'The Federal Reserve's Primary Dealer Credit Facility', *Current Issues in Economics and Finance*, 15 (Federal Reserve Bank of New York, 4 August 2009).

[79]   The facility was created too late for Bear Stearns to benefit.

[80]   Primary dealers are the financial institutions that trade and deal in the US Treasury securities market and include institutions such as BNP Paribas Securities Corp., Banc of America Securities LLC, Barclays Capital Inc., Cantor Fitzgerald & Co., Citigroup Global Markets Inc., Credit Suisse Securities (USA) LLC, Daiwa Securities America Inc., Deutsche Bank Securities Inc., Goldman Sachs & Co., HSBC Securities (USA) Inc., Jefferies & Company, Inc., J.P. Morgan Securities Inc., Mizuho Securities USA Inc., Morgan Stanley & Co. Incorporated, Nomura Securities International, Inc., RBC Capital Markets Corporation, RBS Securities Inc., UBS Securities LLC.

[81]   Federal Reserve Press Release, *Summary of Terms and Conditions and FAQs* (11 March 2008).

[82]   For a study of the effectiveness of the facility, see M.J. Fleming, W.B. Hrung and F.M. Keane, 'Repo Market Effects of the Term Securities Lending Facility', *Staff Report No. 426* (January 2010); M.J. Fleming, W.B. Hrung and F.M. Keane,

intended for primary dealers (non-depository institutions), authority for the program was not based on Section 13(3). Instead it was viewed as an expansion of the Federal Reserve's existing securities lending programs. As opposed to a 'lending' facility, this facility permitted primary dealers to swap less liquid securities for US Treasury securities for 28 days. The facility had an outstanding balance of US$234 billion on 1 October 2008. The auctions under the facility were suspended on 1 July 2009. The program was terminated on 1 February 2010.

The *Asset-Backed Commercial Paper Money Market Mutual Fund Liquidity Facility* was created in September of 2008 to provide liquidity to money market mutual funds in order to meet redemption requests.[83] The facility provided 'funding to U.S. depository institutions and bank holding companies to finance their purchases of high-quality asset-backed commercial paper (ABCP) from money market mutual funds under certain conditions'. The facility had a high balance on 8 October 2008 of US$145 billion, although it now has a zero balance and expired on 1 February 2010.

The *Commercial Paper Funding Facility*[84] was announced in October of 2008 in response to the market for commercial paper drying up.[85] Companies that relied on commercial paper for financing their businesses found it extremely difficult to raise the debt financing that they needed. Although the maturity for commercial paper can be up to 270 days, the average maturity for the majority of the paper issued during 2008 was less than a week.[86]

The Federal Reserve provided a description of the mechanics of the facility:

> The CPFF will provide a liquidity backstop to U.S. issuers of commercial paper through a special purpose vehicle (SPV) that will purchase three-month

---

'The Term Securities Lending Facility: Original, Design and Effects', *Current Issues in Economics and Finance* (February 2009).

[83]   D.M. Covitz, N. Liang and G.A. Suarez, 'The Evolution of a Financial Crisis: Panic in the Asset-Backed Commercial Paper Market, Finance and Economics Discussion Series', *Divisions of Research & Statistics and Monetary Affairs, Federal Reserve Board* (Washington DC: August 2009) at 18.

[84]   See also T. Adrian, K.J. Kimbrough and D. Marchioni, *The Commercial Paper Funding Facility* (January 2010).

[85]   For a discussion of the commercial paper market during the financial crisis, see G.R. Anderson and C.S. Gascon, *The Commercial Paper Market, the Fed, and the 2007-2009 Financial Crisis* (Federal Reserve Bank of St. Louis Review, November/December 2009) at 589.

[86]   D. M. Covitz, N. Liang and G. A. Suarez, see above, n.83.

unsecured and asset-backed commercial paper directly from eligible issuers. The Federal Reserve will provide financing to the SPV under the CPFF and will be secured by all of the assets of the SPV and, in the case of commercial paper that is not asset-backed commercial paper, by the retention of up-front fees paid by the issuers or by other forms of security acceptable to the Federal Reserve in consultation with market participants.

The facility had a high balance of US$349 billion on 21 January 2009 and had a balance of $7.8 billion as of 31 March 2010. The program expired on 1 February 2010 and no new lending has been done under the program since that date.

The impetus for the creation of the *Money Market Investor Funding Facility* was in response to a run on money market mutual funds after the Lehman failure. The crisis began when the shares issued by the Reserve Primary Fund broke the 'buck' owing to the Lehman failure, meaning that shares in this money market fund traded below one US dollar per share.[87] Money market funds were under pressure not only from potential losses on commercial paper and other assets that they were holding, but also owing to redemption requests from investors.

Under the facility, 'the Federal Reserve Bank of New York provided senior secured funding to a series of special purpose vehicles to facilitate an industry-supported private-sector initiative to finance the purchase of eligible assets from eligible investors'.[88] For a variety of reasons, there

---

[87]   S. Anand and D. Gullapalli, 'Fear that Had Gripped US$3.4 trillion Market Abates, Ending the Reluctance of Funds to Buy Vital Commercial Paper', *Wall Street Journal* (20 September 2008); D. Gullapalli, S. Anand and D. Maxey, 'Big Money-market Fund "Breaks the Buck"', *Wall Street Journal* (18 September 2008) at 20.

[88]   The actual mechanics are more complex than many of the other facilities and may explain why it proved to be unpopular: the Federal Reserve Bank of New York will provide senior secured funding to a series of special purpose vehicles (SPVs) established by the private sector to finance the purchase of certain money market instruments from eligible investors. Eligible assets will include US dollar-denominated certificates of deposit, bank notes and commercial paper issued by highly rated financial institutions. Assets must be DTC cleared and have remaining maturities of at least 7 days and no more than 90 days. Eligible investors will include US 2a-7 money market mutual funds and certain other money market investors. Each SPV will finance its purchases of eligible assets by selling asset-backed commercial paper (ABCP) and by borrowing under the MMIFF. The SPV will issue to the seller of the eligible asset subordinated ABCP equal to 10 per cent of the asset's purchase price. The ABCP will be rated at least A-1/P-1/F1 by two or more major nationally recognized statistical rating organizations (NRSROs), S&P, Moody's and Fitch, respectively. The New York Fed will lend to each SPV, on a senior secured basis, 90 per cent of the purchase price of each eligible asset.

were never any borrowings under this facility and the authorization for this program expired in October of 2009.

The *Term Asset-Backed Securities Loan Facility*[89] was initially considered one of the most important initiatives and potentially one of the largest of the various Section 13(3) lending facilities. Although the facility was announced in November of 2008, it did not begin operations until March of 2009. The facility was intended to support the market for asset-backed securities that securitized 'floorplan loans, insurance premium finance loans, loans guaranteed by the Small Business Administration, residential mortgage servicing advances or commercial mortgage loans'.

In response to the further deterioration of the financial markets, the Federal Reserve and the Treasury jointly announced in February of 2009 the expansion of the facility up to US$1 trillion. Such large-scale expansion, however, either proved not to be needed or too difficult to achieve.[90] The program had a balance of US$47 billion as of 27 January 2010 and an expiration date for new credit of 30 June 2010 for loans collateralized by newly issued CMBS and 31 March 2010 for loans collateralized by all other eligible securities.[91]

Table 9.4 below is a summary of the liquidity programs created by the Federal Reserve, listing their current and high balances.

Large-Scale Asset Purchase Programs

As part of its efforts to control monetary policy, the Federal Reserve has always been a large buyer and seller of US Treasury securities and also a securities lender. However, in an effort to stabilize the residential housing market, the Federal Reserve has become an extremely active purchaser of mortgage-backed securities and Federal agency debt securities, providing enormous liquidity for the home mortgage residential lending industry. These purchases are part of a strategy that the Federal Reserve euphemistically refers to as its 'large-scale asset purchase programs', of which the

---

The SPVs will hold the eligible assets until they mature, and proceeds from the assets will be used to repay the Federal Reserve loan and the ABCP.

[89]   A.B. Ashcraft, A. Malz and J. V. Rosenberg, *The Term Asset-Backed Securities Lending Facility* (17 March 2009) available at SSRN: http://ssrn.com/abstract=1361712.

[90]   See N. Irwin, 'Federal Program to Boost Private Lending Struggles to Get Money to Consumers', *Washington Post* 23 April 2009.

[91]   See Circular 12130 (2009), 15 August.

Table 9.4   Liquidity programs created by the Federal Reserve

Program name	Current balance 31 Mar 10 US$	High balance US$ (date)
Term Securities Lending Facility (11 Mar 08)	0	234 billion (01 Oct 08)
Primary Dealer Credit (16 Mar 08)	0	147 billion (01 Oct 08)
Asset-Backed Commercial Paper Money Market Mutual Fund Liquidity Facility (19 sep 2008)	0	145 billion (08 Oct 08)
Commercial Paper Funding Facility (07 Oct 08)	7.78 billion	349 billion (21 Jan 09)
Money Market Investor Funding Facility (21 Oct 08)	0	0
Term Asset-Backed Securities Loan Facility (TALF) (25 Nov 08)	47.3 billion	48 billion (20 Jan 10)

Mortgage-Backed Securities Purchase Program (MBS Purchase Program) is the largest component.[92]

Throughout the crisis, the Federal Reserve has targeted interest rates through the buying and selling of US Treasury securities. As of 3 February 2010, the Federal Reserve owned US$776 billion of Treasury securities as part of these actions. That amount has fluctuated, however, from the Federal Reserve holding US$780 billion in August of 2007 to holding only US$476 billion in October of 2008. (Although not a large-scale asset purchase program, the Federal Reserve's historical securities lending program[93] has also not varied much. Currently it has only US$4 billion outstanding under the facility with a high balance of US$25 billion in October of 2008.)

Apart from the traditional Federal Reserve activities of buying and selling US Treasury securities, the Federal Reserve has become an active purchaser of fixed-rate mortgage-backed securities guaranteed by Fannie Mae, Freddie Mac and Ginnie Mae through the MBS Purchase Program.[94] The expressly stated purpose of the program is 'to support the mortgage and housing markets and foster improved conditions in financial markets

---

[92]   Federal Reserve Press Release (Federal Reserve Announces the Creation of the Mortgage-Backed Securities Purchase Program), December 30, 2008.
[93]   The historical securities lending program should be distinguished from the Term Securities Lending Facility discussed above, which was much more active.
[94]   Federal Reserve Bank of New York, Frequently Asked Questions: Mortgage-Backed Securities Purchase Program.

Table 9.5   Current balances of Federal Reserve large-scale purchases

Program or asset class	Description	Current holdings 31Mar10 US$
Treasury Securities Held Outright	Treasury securities held outright	776 billion
Securities Lending Facility	Overnight securities lending to primary dealers of Treasury securities for agency debt securities and agency MBS	7.1 billion
Mortgage-Backed Securities Purchase Program (25Nov08)	Purchased of fixed-rate mortgage-backed securities guaranteed by Fannie Mae, Freddie Mac and Ginnie Mae	1.06 trillion
Federal Agency Debt Securities (25Nov08)	Includes purchases of direct obligations of housing-related GSEs	169 billion

more generally'. Since 31 March 2010, the Federal Reserve has purchased over US$1.06 trillion in mortgage-backed securities, an amount that is then recycled back into the housing lending market, permitting banks to make additional residential real estate loans. The Federal Reserve intends to continue buying mortgage-backed securities through the spring of 2010, with total purchases to equal approximately US$1.25 trillion.

In addition to the MBS Purchase Program, the Federal Reserve also has a less formal program to purchase direct obligations of housing-related government-sponsored enterprises such as Fannie Mae, Freddie Mac and the Federal Home Loan Banks. The Federal Reserve intended to purchase up to US$200 billion of non-callable senior benchmark debt securities through the end of 2009.[95] As of the end of March 2010, the Federal Reserve holds approximately US$169 billion of these obligations.

Table 9.5 above summarizes the current balances of these large-scale purchases and also that of its historical securities lending program (as distinguished from the Term Securities Lending Facility).

---

[95] Federal Reserve Bank of New York, Frequently Asked Questions: Purchasing Direct Obligations of Housing-Related GSEs.

ASSESSING THE FEDERAL RESERVE'S ACTIONS

There is an enormous amount of assessment and analysis that needs to be done with respect to both the actions of the Federal Reserve during the financial crisis and the apparent expansion of its mission.[96] First, there are questions about the effectiveness of the Federal Reserve's actions in combating the financial crisis. In other words, would we be in the same position had the Federal Reserve not intervened so aggressively? Second, there are concerns about the effect of the Federal Reserve's actions on the US economy and on the Federal Reserve's balance sheet. Friends and critics alike have questioned whether the Federal Reserve's actions of injecting hundreds of billions of liquidity into the US financial markets will inevitably lead to an inflationary spiral and whether the Federal Reserve will be able to exit from its role as the key supplier of liquidity. Finally, there are questions about whether changes should be made to the Federal Reserve's leadership and lending authority, especially with respect to its lending authority to non-depository institutions under section 13(3) of the Federal Reserve Act.

Combating the Financial Crisis

While there is still debate about whether the financial crisis has ended, the fears of a repetition of the Great Depression and the continued free fall of US financial markets appear to have been arrested.[97] In particular, economists and others focus on the surge in the US gross domestic product at the end of 2009.[98] In addition, inflation has remained almost flat.[99] A variety of studies suggest that the different Federal Reserve programs had a positive effect on the financial crisis.[100]

---

[96] D. Malpass, 'Fed Should Go Back to Basics', *Forbes*, 8 (15 February 2010).
[97] D. Wessel, 'Government's Trial and Error Helped Stem Financial Panic', *Wall Street Journal* (14 September 2009).
[98] C. Isidore, 'Best Economic Growth in Six Years', *The Wall Street Journal* (29 January 2010).
[99] L. Di Leo and J. Burns, *Inflation Remains Subdued* (15 January 2010).
[100] J.H.E. Christensen, J.A. Lopez and G.D. Rudenbusch, 'Do Central Bank Liquidity Facilities Affect Interbank Lending Rates', *Federal Reserve Bank of San Francisco Working Paper Series No. 13* (June 2009); M. Obstfeld, J.C. Shambaugh and A.M. Taylor, 'Financial Instability, Reserves, and Central Bank Swap Lines in the Panic of 2008', *Working Paper 14826* (2009); M.J. Fleming, W.B. Hrung and F.M. Keane, 'Repo Market Effects of the Term Securities Lending Facility', *Staff Report No. 426* (January 2010); M.J. Fleming W.B. Hrung and F.M. Keane, 'The Term Securities Lending Facility: Origin, Design and Effects', *Current Issues in Economics and Finance* (February 2009).

The health of the US economy, however, continues to falter in spite of all of the programs and actions taken. Unemployment is still hovering at 10 per cent in the United States and shows no signs of abating in the near future.[101] Although residential real estate appears to be recovering somewhat, there are serious concerns about commercial real estate and the availability of financing.[102] Although the economy does appear to be recovering, there are several areas of the economy that continue to suffer. Currently, the DOW Industrial stock index is trading above 10 000, which is much better than its bottom of 6440 in the spring of 2009. There appears, however, little hope of it returning to its high of 14 000 that it reached in October of 2007 anytime in the near future. The bond market has begun to return to normal, but banking lending still remains weak.[103]

The Federal Reserve itself recently provided its own assessment of the state of the financial crisis:

> Information received since the Federal Open Market Committee met in December suggests that economic activity has continued to strengthen and that the deterioration in the labor market is abating. Household spending is expanding at a moderate rate but remains constrained by a weak labor market, modest income growth, lower housing wealth, and tight credit. Business spending on equipment and software appears to be picking up, but investment in structures is still contracting and employers remain reluctant to add to payrolls. Firms have brought inventory stocks into better alignment with sales. While bank lending continues to contract, financial market conditions remain supportive of economic growth. Although the pace of economic recovery is likely to be moderate for a time, the Committee anticipates a gradual return to higher levels of resource utilization in a context of price stability.[104]

A reasonable assumption that could be gathered from this assessment is that things might have been much worse had the Federal Reserve not intervened so aggressively in the US financial markets. It may take scholars decades, however, to fully quantify the effectiveness of the Federal Reserve's actions.

---

[101] See also J. Idaszak, *The Kiplinger Letter*, 'Double-Digit Unemployment Through 2010' (2009).

[102] R. Parkus and J. An, 'The Future Refinancing Crisis in Commercial Real Estate', *CMBS Research (Deutsch Bank)* (23 April 2009); C. Mollenkamp and L. Wei, *Unfinished Projects Weigh on Banks* (20 January 2010); L. Wei and M. Spector, *Tishman Venture Gives Up Stuyvesant Project* (25 January 2010).

[103] P. Lattman and M. Spector (2010), *Yield Junkies Return to Bond Market*, 19 January.

[104] Federal Reserve, *Press Release* (27 January 2010) (on file with author).

Consequences of the Federal Reserve's Actions

As the Federal Reserve escalated its battle with the financial crisis, critics raised numerous questions about future consequences. In particular, questions were raised about whether the Federal Reserve would be able to exit from its role as the principal liquidity provider in the US economy; whether such actions were inflationary; and whether in the Federal Reserve's efforts to maintain stability of the financial system and to contain systemic risk, it may have lost its ability to conduct monetary policy. Finally, there is great concern that by injecting historically unparalleled amounts of liquidity into the financial system, the Federal Reserve may have set a precedent with respect to its willingness to intervene in future crises.

Exit strategy

Since the beginning of the Federal Reserve's intervention, there has been a concern that the Federal Reserve would be unable to exit from its expanded role as primary liquidity provider that it assumed during the financial crisis. As discussed above, the Federal Reserve literally transformed both its mission and its lending activities as it dealt with the various crises. Many are concerned that the Federal Reserve will be unable to return to the role that it held prior to the crisis.

With respect to its Discount Window activities, the Federal Reserve is almost back to its pre-crisis levels. Currently the Federal Reserve has approximately US$11.6 billion outstanding through the Discount Window and the Term Auction Facility, compared with almost US$500 billion outstanding under the Term Auction Facility at its high point. The Federal Reserve's current exposure is roughly only 4 per cent of what it was back in March of 2009.

The Central Bank Liquidity Swap Facility and the Section 13(3) Lending Facilities, with the exception of a US$47 billion balance in the Term Asset-Backed Securities Loan Facility and the $7.6 billion balance in the Commercial Paper Funding Facility, have also been reduced to almost zero from aggregate high balances of US$930 billion. Vice President Brian P. Sack of the Federal Reserve Bank of New York noted that 'creating these liquidity facilities and implementing them was a lot harder than exiting from them'.[105] He further noted that by design, these

---

[105] 'The Fed's Expanded Balance Sheet (2009), Targeted News Service, December' (text of speech given by Executive Vice President Brian P. Sack).

facilities became an 'unattractive source of funding once markets returned toward more normal functioning'.[106]

In addition to the lending programs unwinding on their own, the Federal Reserve announced at the end of January 2010 that it is officially discontinuing the majority of its liquidity programs,[107] a tremendous validation for the Federal Reserve's strategy of providing liquidity and reserves when needed, and then withdrawing them from the US financial markets as conditions return to normal. The Federal Reserve announced that it was closing, as of 1 February 2010, the Asset-Backed Commercial Paper Money Market Mutual Fund Liquidity Facility, the Commercial Paper Funding Facility, the Primary Dealer Credit Facility, and the Term Securities Lending Facility. The Central Bank Liquidity Swap Facility was also allowed to expire on 1 February 2010. A definitive end to these programs was important given the Federal Reserve's history over the past two years of extending the different facility expiration dates.[108]

The Federal Reserve also announced that the Term Auction Facility, which did not have an official expiration date, would have a final auction on 8 March 2010. Finally, the Federal Reserve announced that the 'anticipated expiration dates for the Term Asset-Backed Securities Loan Facility remain set at 30 June, 2010 for loans backed by new-issue commercial mortgage-backed securities and 31 March, 2010 for loans backed by all other types of collateral'.

A key caveat to the announcement, however, was that the 'Federal Reserve is prepared to modify these plans if necessary to support financial stability and economic growth'.[109] Such an announcement was probably given to provide comfort to the market that the Federal Reserve would intervene again if it proved that it exited too early from the various facilities.

The problem children for the Federal Reserve, however, will continue to be the Section 13(3) lending made to systemically important institutions. The good news is that both Citigroup and Bank of America Corporation terminated the guarantee provided by the Federal Reserve. The balances, however, in the Maiden Lane, Maiden Lane II and Maiden Lane III facilities have been only nominally lowered, and it is unclear whether that is from the collateral self-liquidating or from the Federal Reserve writing off

---

[106]   Ibid.
[107]   Federal Reserve, *Press Release* (27 January 2010).
[108]   For example, on 25 June 2009 the Federal Reserve extended its liquidity programmes through 1 February 2010. See Federal Reserve, *Press Release* (25 June 2009).
[109]   Federal Reserve, *Press Release* (27 January 2010).

the worthless pieces. Because the collateral taken for those loans was problematic assets and the loans were made on a non-recourse basis, demand for repayment cannot be made and these loans may be impossible to sell without incurring large losses. It may be years before the amounts owing to the Federal Reserve under the Maiden Lane facilities are paid down in any meaningful way.

The Federal Reserve has made some progress in reducing the revolving loan facility to AIG. When the US Treasury invested in the preferred stock of AIG, US$40 billion of that amount was used to pay down the Federal Reserve loan. Another US$25 billion was paid down by converting debt into preferred interests in AIA Aurora LLC and ALICO Holdings LLC, special purpose vehicles holding stock in AIG subsidiaries. It is unclear, however, how soon the remaining US$20 billion loan will be repaid or when the Federal Reserve will be able to liquidate its interests in the two special purpose vehicles.

The most important question with respect to the Federal Reserve's lending and purchasing activities is whether it will be able to exit the MBS Purchase Program and sell the US$1.5 trillion in mortgage-backed securities and government-sponsored enterprise debt securities that it will be holding by the spring of 2010. Many believe that the principal reason behind the recovery of the residential lending market has been the Federal Reserve's purchases of approximately 70 per cent of the mortgages (in the form of mortgage-backed securities) that Fannie Mae and Freddie Mac are purchasing from mortgage lenders. It could be argued that the Federal Reserve is still providing most of the liquidity in the residential housing market.

The Federal Reserve is developing an exit strategy for liquidating its portfolio of mortgage-backed securities.[110] Some commentators, and even members of the Federal Reserve's Federal Open Market Committee, have argued, however, that the residential market will have a difficult time dealing with the Federal Reserve stopping its purchases of mortgage-backed securities, much less liquidating its portfolio.[111] Joseph Stiglitz, former chairman of the Council of Economic Advisors, noted that 'the Fed is basically underwriting all of the mortgages . . . to keep up the mort-

---

[110]   E. Andrews, 'Fed Begins Testing a Strategy to Exit a Securities Program', *New York Times* (Economy Section) (30 November 2009).

[111]   'The Fed will Still Intervene in MBS Markets If Needed', *National Mortgage News* (11 January 2010); L. Rappaport and J. Hilsenrath, 'U.S. News: Fed Plan to Stop Buying Mortgages Feeds Recovery Worries', *The Wall Street Journal* (8 January 2010) at A3; 'U.S. News: Mortgage Program Splits Fed Officials', *The Wall Street Journal* (7 January 2010) at A3.

gage market'.[112] In contrast, some commentators and scholars see little effect of the Federal Reserve curtailing its activities.[113]

The possibility that the Federal Reserve could incur losses as it exits its various activities is also a possibility. Any losses incurred by the Federal Reserve impact the US Treasury directly since the Federal Reserve returns its profits to the US Treasury.[114] Chairman Bernanke has stated that '[t]he Federal Reserve has never suffered any losses in the course of its normal lending to banks and, now, to primary dealers'.[115] This comment on past history, however, does not take into account the changes in the Federal Reserve's activities during the crisis and the expansion of its balance sheet. However, the nature of the Federal Reserve's activities and balance sheet has changed dramatically over the past two years. In particular, there is certainly a possibility that the Federal Reserve may never collect what is owed under the three Maiden Lane facilities, given that the loans are non-recourse and are secured by illiquid collateral. The value of the assets in the large-scale asset purchase programs could also swing widely as interest rates move, perhaps generating losses as it liquidates its portfolio.[116]

Inflation and monetary policy

Critics of the Federal Reserve's efforts to inject liquidity into the US monetary system have argued that the US is risking a period of high

---

[112]   S.L. Beckner, 'Fed Could Do More MBS Buys if Needed After March', *The Main Wire* (4 January 2010), 7:09 PM GMT; 'The Fed's Expanded Balance Sheet', *Targeted News Service* (2 December 2009) (text of speech given by Executive Vice President Brian P. Sack) (discussing exit strategy).

[113]   'Fed to Wind Down Purchases', *National Mortgage News* (28 December 2009). Some scholars have questioned whether the Federal Reserve's purchases have had any effect on residential mortgage interest rates. See J. Stroebel and J.B. Taylor, 'Estimated Impact of the Fed's Mortgage-Backed Securities Purchase Program' (December 2009) *NBER Working Paper No. w15626* (only finding evidence of statistically insignificant or small effects of the MBS purchase program). But see 'The Fed's Expanded Balance Sheet', *Targeted News Service* (2 December 2009) (text of speech given by Executive Vice President B.P. Sack, arguing that the Federal Reserve's purchases have had an effect on interest rates).

[114]   For a discussion of the effect of losses suffered by Discount Window borrowing, see Schwartz, above n. 56, at 65.

[115]   Stamp Lecture, above n. 4.

[116]   Heard on the Street/Financial Analysis and Commentary, 'Dream Mortgage Bailout Has a Darker Side', *The Wall Street Journal* (3 April 2009) at C14.

inflation.[117] Charles Plosser, President of the Federal Reserve Bank of Philadelphia, noted that '[w]hile the lending programs are designed to improve the flow of credit, they are currently injecting enormous amounts of liquidity into the system. I believe that we need to monitor that liquidity and its composition closely so that we are able to withdraw it when the time comes or else we risk fueling inflation in the future.'[118]

Although many of the lending facilities developed by the Federal Reserve have a low or even a zero balance, a significant portion still remains unpaid. In particular, the Federal Reserve is currently holding almost US$1 trillion in mortgage-backed securities as described above. Because employment in particular has not yet bounced back, however, the anticipated inflationary impact has not occurred. The twin results of high unemployment and lower consumer spending appear to have neutralized the inflationary impact in the short run. In fact, the consumer price index over the past 12 months has not only not been inflationary, but has actually been approximately zero.[119] Some commentators fear, however, that inflation will reignite if the Federal Reserve is unable to exit from its strategies.[120]

The Federal Reserve's efforts to inject liquidity into the economy, particularly with respect to the MBS Purchase Program, could hinder the Federal Reserve's general ability to influence monetary policy. Brian Sack, Executive Vice President of the Federal Reserve Bank of New York, noted that the large holdings of mortgage-backed securities, if 'left on their own, would keep reserve balances high, potentially complicating the Fed's efforts to tighten monetary policy when appropriate.'[121] Similar concerns were echoed by Charles Plosser, President of the Federal Reserve Bank of Philadelphia:

> [e]ventually economic conditions will improve, demand for excess reserves will fall, and in order to maintain price stability, the Fed will have to begin

---

[117]   See A.H. Meltzer, *The Fed's Anti-Inflation Exit Strategy Will Fail* (27 January 2010); D. Thorton, 'The Case for 'Inflation First', *Monetary Policy, Economic Synopses*, No. 4 (2009).

[118]   C.L. Plosser, 'The Economic Outlook and Some Challenges Facing the Federal Reserve', *Economic Panel Outlook* (University of Delaware, 14 January 2009).

[119]   Bureau of Labor Statistics; see also L. Di Leo and J. Burns, *Inflation Remains Subdued* (15 January 2010).

[120]   Meltzer, above n. 117, at 134.

[121]   'The Fed's Expanded Balance Sheet', *Targeted News Service* (December 2009) (text of speech given by Executive Vice President Brian P. Sack) (on file with author).

withdrawing the extraordinarily large supply of liquidity with which it has flooded the market. Under normal operating procedures, this isn't a problem, as the Fed holdings are mainly short-term Treasuries, which can be liquidated to reduce reserves and increase interest rates. However, under current circumstances, the Fed has substituted less liquid assets for Treasuries.[122]

In contrast to the holding and use of US Treasury securities in the past to influence monetary policy, these mortgage-backed securities are less liquid and may be more difficult to liquidate if needed to reduce reserves in the US economy.

Moral hazard and too big to fail
As legislators, regulators and academics sort out the Federal Reserve's actions, there is enormous concern that 'moral hazard' has been reintroduced into the financial system and that the Federal Reserve is now in the business of saving those institutions 'too big to fail'.[123] Although the Federal Reserve and the US Treasury allowed Lehman Brothers to fail, the Federal Reserve provided key liquidity with respect to the 'bail-outs' of Bear Stearns, AIG, Citigroup and Bank of America Corporation. As described above, it also provided hundreds of billions of dollars of key liquidity to depository institutions and non-depository institutions such as primary dealers, money market mutual funds and issuers of commercial paper.

Going forward, bankers may become less risk averse, believing that the Federal Reserve will step in once again if the economy experiences a liquidity crisis and/or credit crunch in its credit sector. Lenders may also believe that the Federal Reserve will bail them out if a systemically important institution teeters on the brink of insolvency, similar to what was done for the creditors of AIG.

Reforming the Federal Reserve

As the economy slowly returns to normal, the inevitable assessment of the Federal Reserve and its actions by the US Congress has already begun. Although the Federal Reserve appears to have emerged from the financial

---

[122] C. Plosser, 'Ensuring Sound Monetary Policy in the Aftermath of Crisis', *U.S. Monetary Policy Forum, The Initiative on Global Markets* (University of Chicago Booth School of Business, New York, 27 February 2009).
[123] K.S. Okamoto, 'Essay After the Bailout: Regulating Systemic Moral Hazard', 57 *UCLA Law Review*, 183 (2009); S. Labaton (25 October 2009), 'Trying to Rein in "too Big to Fail" Institutions'; 'How Big is Too Big to Fail?', *Conversation with George Shultz* (15 December 2009).

crisis, there is a tiny minority in Congress who will never be happy until the Federal Reserve is abolished.[124] Hearings on the Federal Reserve's performance and actions have also begun.[125]

The first question raised, which has already been answered, is the future of Ben Bernanke, the chairman of the Board of Governors of the Federal Reserve System. Second, the current legislative proposals before Congress with the Federal Reserve should be assessed and the potential consequences of such reforms should be weighed. Finally, beyond what Congress is already planning, it must be decided whether the Federal Reserve's lending authority, especially under Section 13(3), should be reassessed and perhaps limited.

The fate of Ben Bernanke

The most pressing decision to be made as the crisis began to abate was the coincidental timing of the reappointment and reconfirmation by the US Senate of Ben Bernanke as chairman of the Federal Reserve. As the scope of the Federal Reserve's actions during the crisis became clear, the press put Bernanke himself under a microscope.[126] In a show of his support and confidence, President Obama reappointed Benjamin Bernanke for a second term as chairman of the Federal Reserve System in October of 2009. Although there was some initial concern about opposition to his reappointment, he was confirmed by the Senate in January of 2010.[127]

Current Congressional legislative agenda

Congress has moved to limit the Federal Reserve's lending authority and powers, although much of its Section 13(3) lending powers remain substantively intact. Congress initially required the Federal Reserve to report

---

[124]   Ron Paul, a Texas Congressman, has been particularly outspoken, publishing his book *End the Fed* in an attempt to publicize his criticism of the Federal Reserve.

[125]   D. Reilly, 'Secret Banking Cabal Emerges from AIG Shadows' (29 January 2009).

[126]   The most notable example of press coverage was *Time Magazine*'s selection of Bernanke as Person of the Year. See 'Person of the Year: Ben Bernanke', *Time Magazine* (28 December 2009) at 44. A Google search of the term 'Bernanke' shows 9 960 000 results. Books with his name in the title include D. Wessel, *In Fed we Trust: Ben Bernanke's War on the Great Panic* (2009); see also S.H. Axelrod, *Inside the Fed: Monetary Policy and Its Management, Martin through Greenspan to Bernanke* (2009).

[127]   S. Reddy, *Senate Votes to Confirm Bernanke* (28 January 2010).

its Section 13(3) lending activities on a confidential basis to Congress.[128] Given the expansive power that Section 13(3) provides, such reporting is necessary and is useful for Congress as it assesses the Federal Reserve's powers and actions.[129]

There initially appeared to be little incentive to amend Section 13(3) in the immediate aftermath of the financial crisis. Such reform, however, took root as the US House and Senate began to consider statutory reforms to the US financial system. Congress, in fact, enacted numerous amendments to Section 13(3) when it passed the Dodd-Frank Wall Street Reform and Consumer Protection Act (Dodd-Frank Act).[130] Although these reforms provide some important limitations and checks and balances with respect to the Federal Reserve's authority, the Federal Reserve still retains substantial power and discretion with respect to its Section 13(3) lending powers, principally through what is described above as the Section 13(3) Lending Facilities.

The Dodd-Frank Act amendments first limit the Federal Reserve's Section 13(3) lending authority to lending done through a *program* or *facility* 'with broad-based eligibility', as opposed to lending targeted to a specific party or company needing assistance. The term 'broad-based eligibility' under Section 13(3) excludes any program or facility 'that is structured to remove assets from the balance sheet of a single and specific company, or that is established for the purpose of assisting a single and specific company avoid' insolvency. Under the Dodd-Frank Act amendments, it would appear that the Federal Reserve would have been unable to lend directly to Bear Stearns or AIG unless Bear Stearns or AIG would

---

[128]   Emergency Economic Stabilization Act of 2008, Section 129. For an example of the reporting on the Commercial Paper Funding Facility, see Report Pursuant to Section 129 of the Emergency Economic Stabilization Act of 2008: Commercial Paper Funding Facility.

[129]   Section 129 reads as follows: 'Not later than 7 days after the date on which the Board [of Governors of the Federal Reserve System] exercises its authority under the third paragraph of section 13 of the Federal Reserve Act (12 U.S.C. 343; relating to discounts for individuals, partnerships, and corporations) the Board shall provide to the Committee on Banking, Housing, and Urban Affairs of the Senate and the Committee on Financial Services of the House of Representatives a report which includes (1) the justification for exercising the authority; and (2) the specific terms of the actions of the Board, including the size and duration of the lending, available information concerning the value of any collateral held with respect to such a loan, the recipient of warrants or any other potential equity in exchange for the loan, and any expected cost to the taxpayers for such exercise'. Codified at 12 USC §5235.

[130]   Dodd-Frank Wall Street Reform and Consumer Protection Act (2010), *Public Law 111-203*, 111th Cong., 2d sess, 21 July.

have otherwise qualified for the terms of a facility or program in place 'with broad-based eligibility'.

It is unclear what would have been the consequences had the Federal Reserve not been able to lend to Bear Stearns and AIG. Clearly the Federal Reserve believed that the consequences would have been systemically disastrous had it not intervened. In a noticeable exercise of restraint, the Federal Reserve refused to lend to Lehman Brothers under Section 13(3) as it had done for Bear Stearns. In spite of such restraint, however, the Federal Reserve actually suffered severe criticism for its unwillingness to lend to Lehman:

> Now, the consequences of [allowing Lehman to fail] look more dire than almost anyone imagined. Lehman's **bankruptcy** filing . . . sparked a chain reaction that sent credit markets into disarray. It accelerated the downward spiral of [AIG] and precipitated losses for everyone . . . Within days, the chaos enveloped even Wall Street pillars Goldman Sachs Group Inc. and Morgan Stanley.[131]

Such actions today, however, would appear not be to be possible regardless of the consequences of the failure of a systemically important institution such as AIG.

In addition to this limitation, the Dodd-Frank Act amendments impose the requirement in Section 13(3) that 'the Board may not establish any program or facility under this paragraph without the prior approval of the Secretary of the Treasury'. The notion appears to be that such approval would introduce more accountability into the process and would provide oversight of the Federal Reserve's actions by the US Treasury. However, because the US Treasury serves at the direction of the US President, the secretary of the Treasury would be less insulated from outside political pressure than the Federal Reserve, creating a risk of politicizing the approval process. An important advantage of the Federal Reserve as it carries out its mandates is that it has historically been independent from day-to-day political pressures and control.

The Dodd-Frank Act amendments to Section 13(3) also require the Federal Reserve to promulgate regulations to

> ensure that any emergency lending program or facility is for the purpose of providing liquidity to the financial system, and not to aid a failing financial

---

131   C. Mollenkamp, M. Whitehouse, J. Hilsenrath and I.J. Dugan, 'Lehman's Demise Triggered Cash Crunch Around Globe', *Wall Street Journal*, 29 September 2008, at A1.

company, and that the security for emergency loans is sufficient to protect taxpayers from losses and that any such program is terminated in a timely and orderly fashion.

Such a requirement is probably timely given the lack of guidance on exercising its Section 13(3) powers and the ad hoc actions that it took with respect to those powers during the financial crisis.

The Dodd-Frank Act amendments to Section 13(3) have also expanded the amount of disclosure required under Section 13(3) to the US Senate Committee on Banking, Housing and Urban Affairs and the US House of Representatives Financial Services Committee. These disclosures include identifying the recipients, material terms, etc. of any assistance under Section 13(3). Such disclosure requirements probably reflect Congress's concerns that the Federal Reserve is able to lend extraordinary sums to virtually any institution, whether subject to regulation by the Federal Reserve or not, without Congress's knowledge. The chairman of the Federal Reserve, however, can also request that such disclosures be kept confidential.

Such disclosures are probably healthy although they can risk politicizing the process. It is clear, however, that Congress probably never contemplated how the Federal Reserve would push its authority to lend and purchase assets. If the high balances in the Term Auction Facility, the Central Bank Liquidity Swap Facility, and the Section 13(3) lending activities are added together, the Federal Reserve extended liquidity of more than US$2.223 trillion into the US economy.

Other possibilities

Although Congress enacted a series of reforms, it does not appear to have considered simply repealing Section 13(3). Such an option would have been a simplistic and easy solution for those unhappy with the Federal Reserve's role in the Bear Stearns and AIG 'bail-outs' in particular. H.L. Menken is attributed with the adage that for every problem, there is a solution that is simple, elegant and wrong. Repealing Section 13(3) would close the door on any hope of generating the same level of emergency liquidity for the US economy in the future that was required by the current crisis. Unlike the depository institutions that were members of the Federal Reserve, non-depository institutions have no similar institution to look to for help in the event that liquidity vanishes. Preserving such access to the Federal Reserve ensures that there is an institution with sufficient wherewithal to meet similar demands in a future crisis.

Congress also wisely never placed dollar limitations on the total amount of liquidity that can be provided under different Section 13(3) programs or facilities or to individual participants in these programs. Currently, the Federal Reserve still essentially has a blank check under Section 13(3) to combat any unforeseen future events involving non-depository institutions. While it is tempting to impose a dollar limitation on that power, it is unclear what those amounts should be. As shown above, certain sectors of the US financial markets found themselves requiring hundreds of billions of dollars of liquidity on literally no notice. It is unclear if the Federal Reserve was able to develop any kind of accurate estimate as to what the eventual demands on those facilities were going to be prior to extending credit. With statutory caps placed on the amount of lending permitted under Section 13(3), the Federal Reserve may find itself only able to provide half the liquidity (and thus only half the solution) necessary with no other partner available to make up the difference.

Limitations on the Federal Reserve's large-scale asset purchase program might also be considered when one considers the extraordinary commitment made by the Federal Reserve to purchase US$1.25 trillion of mortgage-backed securities. Currently, the Federal Reserve's ability to purchase mortgage-backed securities appears to be limited only by its ability to create reserves to purchase them. While the amount is disquieting, it is still unclear whether even US$1.25 trillion will be enough to ensure the continued recovery of the US housing market. Similar to the argument immediately above, restricting the total amount of securities that could be purchased risks limiting the Federal Reserve to providing only half the solution. It is unclear whether it would be prudent to limit the Federal Reserve's purchase powers that may be required in a future liquidity crisis.

CONCLUSION

It may be too early to claim total victory for the Federal Reserve (along with the US Congress and other US agencies) over the recent financial crisis. Unemployment and bank failures unfortunately continue and the memories of the extraordinary events of September and October of 2008 have been seared into participants' memories. The Federal Reserve, however, has begun a cautious exit from its strategy of injecting unprecedented amounts of liquidity into the US financial system. Congress and commentators have already begun the process of analysing the Federal Reserve's actions in an effort to determine if laws and regulations should be changed or if the Federal Reserve should have responded differently. Until the US economy returns again to full prosperity, it will be difficult to determine whether the hundreds of billions of dollars of liquidity provided by the Federal Reserve were instrumental in averting an even deeper crisis. The long-term consequences of the Federal Reserve's actions are also not yet fully understood. Congress should be wary of dramatically changing the Federal Reserve's powers beyond what it did through the Dodd-Frank Act amendments until it fully appreciates the consequences of doing so.

10. Sovereign debt restructuring in the EU: Lessons from the recent crisis

Kern Alexander*

INTRODUCTION

The global financial crisis has led to a severe recession in Europe culminating in sovereign debt problems for many eurozone governments. Greece was particularly hard hit because of fiscal mismanagement and unsustainably high levels of public debt, resulting in an extraordinary and unprecedented bailout by eurozone governments and the International Monetary Fund (IMF), with the creation of the European Financial Stabilization Mechanism[1] and the European Financial Stability Facility (EFSF).[2] The

---

* I would like to thank Karin Lorez for her research assistance. In a previous commissioned report, entitled 'Market Impact of an Orderly Sovereign Debt Restructuring' (September 2010), the author proposed the mandatory use of collective action clauses (CACs) for EU sovereign bond contracts and a permanent sovereign liquidity mechanism. The CAC proposal was later adopted by the European Council in December 2010 in a Regulation that would require all EU states to use CACs in their sovereign bond contracts from 2013 onwards.

[1] The EU created the EFSM in 2008 to lend up to 60 billion euros to EU Member States who were experiencing difficulties in financing international trade resulting from the global credit crunch and the collapse of Lehman Brothers in 2008. Council Regulation (EU) No. 407/2010 of 11 May 2010 establishing a European Financial Stability Mechanism, *OJ L 118/1* (12/05/2010). The EU used the fund along with additional IMF financial support to help pay the EUR 110 billion bailout for Greece that was approved on May 2010. The EFSM is not the focus of this chapter.

[2] See Council Regulation (EU) No 407/2010 of 11 May 2010 establishing a European Financial Stability Mechanism, *OJ L 118/1* (12/05/2010). The Regulation also authorised the creation of the EFSF to provide financial support to euro–area member states in difficulties caused by exceptional circumstances beyond such euro–area member states' control with the aim of safeguarding the financial stability of the euro area as a whole and of its member states. As discussed below, the EFSF provides financial support in conjunction with the IMF: the terms of these support loans are comparable to the terms of the loans advanced by euro–area member states and the IMF Greece on 8 May 2010.

Greek crisis demonstrates the inadequate macroeconomic crisis management framework in the EU and the need to establish a more orderly sovereign debt restructuring process.

Europe has not had a legal or formal institutional framework to resolve a sovereign debt default or restructuring. Indeed, the Greek crisis and the growing sovereign debt problems of other EU states raise important questions about whether EU policymakers should establish a formalized institutional process across the EU to promote more orderly sovereign debt restructurings. This chapter analyses a number of corollary questions about how such a process could work without undermining market discipline, and what powers, if any, should be allocated to EU institutions to oversee sovereign debt restructurings and whether these comply with the EU treaties. It further examines what set of principles should guide policymakers in devising such an institutional framework and whether this could help indebted countries avoid a damaging loss of investor confidence and destabilizing market volatility.

The chapter examines what type of orderly sovereign debt restructuring arrangements should be established in the EU and how it can address the type of liquidity and solvency problems that Member States have been experiencing in the recent sovereign debt and financial crisis. In evaluating the first question, the chapter reviews the proposal for a European Monetary Fund (EMF) and the operational structure of the EFSF. These approaches intend to remove the risk of disorderly default, which is the main risk that countries in a fiscal crisis pose to financial stability in the euro-area. The establishment of the EFSF brought some stability to European financial markets when it was established in July 2010, which resulted in lower spreads on the sovereign debt of Greece, Ireland and other vulnerable euro-area states, but spreads in late 2010 for Greece and other countries, such as Italy and Spain, sharply increased in 2011 reflecting a loss of market confidence in their fiscal positions and a concern that the EFSF is only a short-term measure designed to restore investor confidence in eurozone sovereign debt.

A major focus of the chapter examines the weaknesses of the existing institutional framework for sovereign debt restructuring and sets forth some principles and guidelines for reform of the sovereign debt restructuring process. The chapter argues that the EU should adopt a decentralized sovereign debt default and restructuring process that emphasizes the use of collective action clauses (CACs) to facilitate negotiations and restructuring creditor claims when a sovereign is experiencing financial difficulties. EU legislation should harmonize the principles and guidelines that govern the operation of CACs, but parties should be permitted some freedom to decide certain CAC repayment terms and some of the parameters of the restructuring process. The chapter also suggests that the EU should create an EU sovereign debt agency that would oversee the application of EU principles and guidelines for Member State sovereign debt negotiations and contract formation and would provide market data on sovereign debt markets to market participants and sovereigns. The EU sovereign debt agency could also administer a European Financial Stability Fund that would be created to provide liquidity to states experiencing financial distress if the state in question fulfils the requisite conditions for obtaining support. The Fund would be financed by a small transaction tax on all sovereign bond trading and derivative instruments.

THE GREEK CRISIS AND THE SOVEREIGN DEBT PROBLEM

The Greek Crisis

The problems arising from the Greek sovereign debt crisis raise important issues regarding how the EU and the eurozone institutions should assist Member States that are experiencing liquidity and/or solvency problems.[3] The EU Stability and Growth Pact (SGP) presently requires Member States not to run annual budget deficits in excess of 3 per cent of gross domestic product (GDP) and not to have national debt in excess of 60 per cent of GDP. The Pact's effectiveness has been undermined because of the failure of the EU Council to enforce its rules consistently across states and the inflexible application of its deficit and debt rules regardless of a state's position in the economic cycle. Indeed, the Pact's inflexible rules can be characterized as having resulted in neither growth nor stability.

The SGP has failed, in part, because the EU lacks a fiscal policy dimension to assist states experiencing financial difficulties in crisis situations. Article 125 of the Treaty on the Functioning of the European Union (TFEU) prohibits EU institutions from bailing out EU states experiencing fiscal problems.[4] Article 122 TFEU, however, provides the legal basis for EU institutional and Member State support, as it calls for political and financial solidarity with Member States that are in severe difficulties. Paragraph 2 of Article 122 authorizes the Council to grant financial assist-

---

[3]   L.C. Buchheit, C. Lee and G. Mitu Gulti, 'How to Restructure Greek Debt', 7 May 2010 (unpublished paper on file with author).
[4]   Article 125 (1) TFEU excludes the allocation of liability to the Union and the Member States for the commitments of another Member State.

ance from the Union to a Member State if the state in question is in, or seriously threatened with, severe difficulties caused by natural disasters or 'exceptional occurrences beyond its control'. Although a state facing serious budgetary constraints and financing problems would certainly not qualify for the natural disaster exception, it might qualify under the language of 'exceptional occurrences beyond its control' on the grounds that a self-inflicted budgetary limitation in combination with a global financial crisis that caused a substantial reduction in the country's GDP is an exceptional occurrence beyond its control.

Based on the TFEU provisions, the EU could adopt institutional reforms that provide state guarantees to Member States experiencing serious financial difficulties the causes of which are partly beyond their control. The mismanagement of the Greek economy, exacerbated by the collapse of world trade and hence the collapse of shipping revenues, led to cumulative severe pressures on the bond sales necessary to fund the Greek government deficit. Since Greek government bonds are denominated in euros, investors faced no currency risk. However, they did face increasing fears of default. The reaction in European capitals was to initiate a protracted, indecisive debate on raising the funds for a Greek 'bailout'. As vague pronouncements were piled on indecision, the fear of default increased, so that when the EUR 120 billion bailout was at last agreed, it proved inadequate as a defence against the rising tide of default pessimism. The Greek crisis, along with the recent sovereign debt difficulties of a number of EU states, has defined the shape of the necessary institutional and market reforms to be considered in this chapter.

The Mexican 'Tesobono' Crisis

The confused handling of the Greek crisis stands in stark contrast to the rapid and effective measures taken by the United States Government in the Mexican debt crisis of December 1994, which was very similar in important respects to the Greek crisis. The Mexican government had borrowed billions of dollars of short-term US dollar denominated debt when the economy was growing. When Mexico fell into a severe recession in 1994, it was forced to devalue the peso. This drove up the value of its sovereign bonds or 'tesobonos', as they were known. Investors in Mexican government tesobonos faced a complex mixture of currency risk and default risk.

By late 1994, Mexican government finances were collapsing with USD 25 billion coming due in a few months while central bank reserves had fallen to less than USD 6 billion. In devising a rescue plan, US policymakers and the IMF had not forgotten the Latin American debt crisis of 1982 in which the Mexican government had defaulted on USD 80 billion in loans from large – mainly US – banks, creating a contagion that spread rapidly across Latin American countries, causing them to seek emergency refinancing of their US dollar denominated loans from foreign banks. The US government intervened with guarantees for the loans only after defaults led to the near failure of several large US banks: the US's slow response in providing emergency liquidity support in the form of loan guarantees worsened the crisis and plunged Latin America into a severe recession that stunted its economic development for nearly a decade.

In contrast, during the 1994 Mexican crisis, the Clinton administration, acting with support from the IMF, assembled a USD 50 billion emergency package in a few days, predominantly in the form of guarantees, which stemmed the investor run and rapidly restored confidence.[5] Although the 1994 crisis was smaller than the Latin American crisis of the early 1980s, it could have threatened financial stability throughout Latin America and in other developing countries.[6] Moreover, the growing integration of international trade and financial markets suggests that the negative externalities of financial risk-taking can spread more quickly across borders and threaten global financial stability.

If a credible eurozone or EU institution had guaranteed Greek bonds at the outset and had imposed adequate fiscal adjustments and facilitated restructuring of bondholder claims, the immediate crisis would probably have been over sooner, at much lower costs. Instead, the eurozone's leading states – Germany and France – dithered and allowed the Greek crisis to worsen considerably. It was not until the emergency meeting of EU finance ministers held on 9 May 2010 that they agreed to adopt an extraordinary rescue package that provided a EUR 110 billion bailout for Greece that would be financed from the EFSM and the IMF and would be distributed in three EUR 37 billion tranches. The EU finance ministers also agreed to guarantee all of Greece's sovereign bonds and the bonds of other eurozone members by establishing an off-balance sheet entity that would issue bonds worth up to EUR 660 billion (including an IMF USD 250 billion facility) to banks and other investors that would be fully guaranteed by eurozone states. The emergency rescue package essentially

---

[5]   As Alan Greenspan recounts in his autobiography: 'Mexico ended up using only a fraction of the credit. The minute confidence was restored, it paid the money back – the United States actually profited USD 500 million on the deal.' A Greenspan, *The Age of Turbulence* (New York: Penguin, 2007).

[6]   The North American Free Trade Agreement had liberalized much of cross-border finance and trade between Mexico and the US with the result that the two economies were increasingly integrated and exposed to the economic and social problems that both experienced.

bailed out the banks and other creditors who had purchased Greek sovereign debt and it imposed the burden of adjustment almost entirely on the taxpayers of Greece and indirectly on the taxpayers of all eurozone states. The Greek rescue package will have the effect of increasing moral hazard for the creditors of EU sovereign states by incentivizing them to make more and riskier loans to eurozone states with the cost of any adjustment borne by the debtor state and indirectly by European taxpayers.

The confusion and delay in putting together the guarantee fed the flames of volatility and it is now not clear that even this sum will be enough. A more damaging sequence of events would be difficult to imagine, but worse may come. Having at last chosen to follow a sensible guarantee strategy as discussed below, the eurozone governments continue to be gripped by deficit hysteria, with all governments being forced to commit to massive cuts in public expenditure. It appears that the path to recovery may be paved with higher unemployment and bankruptcy.[7]

European Monetary Fund

The absence of an EU sovereign debt restructuring framework and sovereign default mechanism has led to a proposal for an EMF that could provide financial support to EU states that have already adopted the euro. The proponents of the EMF, such as Daniel Gros and Thomas Mayer, argue that a sovereign default mechanism is necessary for the following reason:

> The strongest negotiating asset of a debtor is always that default cannot be contemplated because it would bring down the entire financial system. This is why it is crucial to create mechanisms to minimise the unavoidable disruption resulting from a default. Market discipline can only be established if default is possible because its costs can be contained.[8]

The idea of the EMF is premised on the notion that sovereign defaults are good economic policy if a state has assumed unsustainable debt and that an orderly default can be permitted because its costs can be contained. This is an important assumption that drives the EMF proposal. The

---

[7]   As the *Financial Times* leader argued on 25 May 2010: 'growth is a precondition for stability, not something to be traded off against it. Putting countries on the rack of debt deflation will not stabilise their economies, only destabilise their politics.'

[8]   D. Gros and T. Mayer, 'How to Deal with the Threat of Sovereign Default in the EU: Towards a Euro(pean) Monetary Fund', *Intereconomics*, 2 (2010), Forum, at 64–8.

proposed EMF has been supported by the German Finance Minister and the IMF Managing Director.[9]

The mechanics of the EMF would work as follows. The EMF will be financed by euro-area states paying a 1 per cent levy on the value of their annual deficit exceeding 3 per cent of GDP and on the value of their national debt exceeding 60 per cent of GDP. The levy creates additional incentives for states to comply with the SGP's national debt limits by allowing the EMF to guarantee a Member State's debt up to a value of 60 per cent of GDP. It would have responsibility for organizing an orderly sovereign default as a matter of last resort.[10]

The EMF will be allowed to borrow money on the capital markets. A Member State encountering financial difficulties would be allowed to submit a request for support but must submit a fiscal adjustment plan. If approved, the Member State can receive up to the amount of its contribution paid so far into the Fund. Proponents of the EMF assert that it can be implemented within the framework of enhanced cooperation, recognized by Article 20 of the Treaty on European Union (TEU) and by Articles 236ff. of the TFEU. The enhanced cooperation framework requires that once Council affirms that the measure in question has a valid Treaty objective, it must decide whether the Union acting as a whole can achieve the objective within a reasonable amount of time. If it cannot, Council can authorize enhanced cooperation in this area by a group of at least nine Member States, thus enabling those states to move ahead with the legislation in question and to adopt it for themselves. However, other states must be allowed to participate in the enhanced cooperation process if they comply with all the conditions laid down by the Council in its authorizing decision.

The EMF proposal is an important development in the debate over whether to establish a centralized sovereign default support mechanism in the EU. Under the proposal, it would be operated by the eurozone states but would be open to participation by all EU states if they satisfy the requisite conditions. Serious legal concerns have been raised about whether the EMF can be established through the enhanced cooperation framework and whether it violates the no-bailout prohibition of Article 125 TFEU and whether it qualifies for the exceptions in Article 122 TFEU.[11] It is submitted that in addition to the legal concerns, the adoption of the proposed

---

[9] Dominique Strauss-Kahn, IMF Managing Director, Lecture at King's College, Cambridge, Institute for the Teaching of Economics Conference (10 April 2010).

[10] Gros and Mayer, *supra* n. 8.

[11] U. Häde, 'Legal Evaluation of a European Monetary Fund', *Intereconomics*, 2 (2010), Forum, 69–72.

EMF would represent a substantial centralization of EU institutional authority to provide guarantees to ailing EU sovereign debtors without an adequate framework to encourage or facilitate negotiations between creditors and sovereigns over the restructuring of sovereign debt. Nevertheless, the EMF proposal is under serious consideration by EU policymakers and will continue to play an important role in the debate over a reformed sovereign default mechanism in the EU.

EUROPEAN FINANCIAL STABILITY FACILITY (EFSF)

The EFSF was approved by Council on 10 May 2010 to provide funding support to eurozone states that are in financial difficulties.[12] Eurozone states (excluding Greece) pledged EUR 440 billion in 2010 to the fund, which will be guaranteed by these 15 states according to their respective contributions to the capital of the European Central Bank.[13] To enhance its creditworthiness, the fund has a cash reserve of 20 per cent in addition to the amount pledged by each member. It was designed to be a short-term financing arrangement that would be available to eurozone states experiencing financial difficulties for only three years, after which the fund would be dissolved if no member had drawn on it.[14] However, the EFSF issued bonds to pay for loan facility agreements to the Irish government of EUR 67.5 billion bailout; these bonds are scheduled to be paid off over a 10- to 20-year period. This required that the EFSF would need to be established on a more permanent basis beyond 2013. To ensure this, the Council of Ministers met in January 2011 and agreed that the EU Treaty (TFEU) would need to be amended to provide a permanent EU bailout fund and that the EFSF should be transformed into a permanent European Stability Mechanism (ESM). The details of the ESM will be agreed in 2011 followed by the necessary proposed amendments to the TFEU to be submitted for ratification in late 2011 and 2012. In a statement dated 21 July 2011 the Heads of State

---

[12] Council Regulation No. 9606/2010. See also Decision of the 16 euro-area Member States (7 June 2010) (Luxembourg). The EFSF has a basic securitization structure but with no tranches. Unlike other securitizations, there is no actual exchange of collateral.

[13] For example, Germany's pro rata share of the fund is EUR 122.85 billion, while France's share is EUR 92.3 billion and Italy has a EUR 81 billion share.

[14] The EFSF will close down on 30 June 2013, unless there is a financial operation in which a eurozone state draws on the fund, in which case the EFSF's existence would be prolonged until the last obligation was fully repaid.

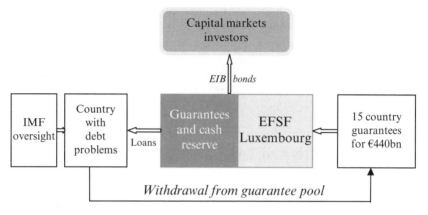

Source: The German Debt Office.

Figure 10.1   The European Financial Stability Facility

of the euro-area and EU institutions stated their intention to improve the effectiveness of the EFSF and address contagion by agreeing to increase the flexibility of the EFSF and to link its financial support to appropriate conditionality. As a consequence, whilst originally financial assistance was provided solely by way of loan facility agreements, financial assistance may now be granted in the form of financial assistance facility agreements. These financial facility agreements will provide financial assistance by way of loan disbursements, precautionary facilities, facilities to finance the recaptalisation of financial institutions in a euro-area member state experiencing difficulties, and facilities for the purchase of bonds in the secondary markets on the basis of an ECB analysis recognizing the existence of exceptional financial market circumstances and risks to financial stability.[15]

The EFSF relies for the most part on operational support from the German Debt Office and the European Investment Bank. It is an off-balance sheet special purpose vehicle that can issue bonds to the market and transfer the proceeds of the bond issuance to the eurozone states who have been approved for financial assistance.[16] Before a euro-area member

---

[15]   See Amendment to the EFSF Framework Agreement, Execution Version (21 July 2011).

[16]   The EFSF received a triple A rating in September 2010. The EFSF argues that the Triple-A rating is justified based on its 20 per cent reserve fund it will have in addition to the amounts contributed by each eurozone state.

receives assistance, the Eurogroup must ask the IMF, the European Commission and the ECB to analyse the request and visit the country seeking assistance. Based on the Greek and Irish experiences, this may take about two weeks. The IMF and the EU institutions can then deliberate for another week or two before making the final decision to authorize the euro-area finance ministers to authorize the EFSF to raise money. At that point, the German Debt Office will work closely with the European Investment Bank (EIB) to issue the bonds as agent for the EFSF. Initially the EFSF could guarantee bonds up to EUR 440 billion but it was actually much less at an amount of about EUR 250 billion.[17] Under the 2011 agreement, the EFSF will be able to provide financial facility support of up to EUR 2 trillion (including guarantees).

Much uncertainty surrounds the fund: little is known about whether investors will continue buying the bonds it issues if the fiscal positions of more eurozone states (who are guarantors) continue to deteriorate and they too apply for support from the fund, which is a strong possibility now for Portugal, Spain, Italy and Belgium.[18] The fund has attracted criticism as 'an attempt to resolve the crisis with imaginary money rather than providing real money and having to find it somewhere'.[19] Moreover, if several countries seek assistance at once, there is a risk that the fund could be exhausted, but fund proponents argue that this is unlikely because foreign investors are returning to the sovereign debt markets and China has even promised to buy the bonds of several ailing eurozone sovereigns.[20] Euro-area states can also use the fund to bail out their banks. The recent sovereign debt problems of Ireland arising from it assuming substantial liabilities from its largest banking and financial institutions resulted in the EFSF's first bailout. The Irish experience suggests that other eurozone states with unsustainable fiscal positions will probably have to tap the EFSF as well.

The creation of the EFSF initially brought some stability to European financial markets and restored some investor confidence in Greek sovereign debt and in the debt of other vulnerable eurozone sovereign debtors.

---

[17] See, EFSF Framework Agreement, Execution version (7 June 2010) (on file with author).

[18] The EFSF is incorporated and domiciled under Luxembourg law and Klaus Regling was appointed as chief executive on 1 July 2010.

[19] Liz Chong, 'Klaus Regling Explains the EU's Stability Fund', *The Financial News*, 8 (July 2010), quoting David Watts.

[20] See comments of EFSF CEO Klaus Regling proponents citing the Chinese foreign exchange department's announcement in July 2010 that it would buy more Spanish government bonds. 'Special Purpose Vehicle Set on Rescue Mission', *The Financial News*, 9 (July 2010).

Nevertheless, EU financial markets remain fragile in 2011: Ireland was forced to seek a bailout because of the huge pre-tax losses of its largest banks, which increased the costs of the country's credit default swaps (CDSs) by 40 per cent since 1 August 2010. Ireland's fiscal position remains unsustainable and the probability is high that restructuring Irish bondholder claims will be necessary with significant 'haircuts'.[21] The persistent troubles with Ireland's state-owned banks suggest that the newly created EFSF has not sufficiently eased investor concerns about EU financial institutions and by extension has rekindled fears about the solvency of some deeply indebted EU sovereigns, such as Greece, Belgium, Spain, Portugal and Italy. These concerns have led financial institutions in these countries to increase significantly their borrowing from the ECB in 2010 and early 2011. Moreover, as part of its emergency programme begun in May at the height of the Greek crisis to purchase eurozone sovereign bonds, the ECB continued to purchase substantial amounts of short-dated Irish bank bonds in an effort to reduce growing volatility in the Irish bond market based on investor concerns that the government will have to continue massive public support for Ireland's weakened banking sector. These developments suggest that volatility is returning to EU sovereign debt markets and that investor concerns have not been allayed by the much-heralded bank stress tests and the creation of the EFSF.

REFORMING SOVEREIGN DEBT RESTRUCTURING IN THE EU

This chapter argues that a reformed institutional structure at the EU level to oversee sovereign debt restructurings and, in exceptional circumstances, sovereign defaults should be established based on a coherent set of principles that are linked to a new decentralized EU institutional structure with clear lines of responsibility and decision-making to facilitate negotiations between creditors and sovereigns during periods of financial distress. The desirability of a level playing field in the EU internal market suggests that

---

[21]   Indeed, there is agreement among most economists, including IMF economists, that Greece will have to restructure most of its existing debt, which is forecast to exceed 150 per cent of GDP in late 2011. It should be noted that in the case of Ireland the EU Council and the IMF agreed in July 2011 to reduce the interest rate on its loan from the EFSF to 3.5% and to seek a restructuring of the payment terms to bondholders of Irish banks in order to impose a limited 'haircut' on their claims. See C. Forrelle, 'A Comprehensive Guide to Ending Europe's Crisis', *Wall Street Journal (Europe)* (25 January 2011), 4.

such an approach can be based on a harmonized set of principles and guidelines across EU states that governs the application and operation of this sovereign debt restructuring process.

A Decentralized EU Institutional Approach

The recent sovereign debt crisis and ongoing financial turbulence in global and European financial markets demonstrate the need for a more coherent and rational sovereign debt default and restructuring process. Such a process could reduce the uncertainty and thus the moral hazard for states to reach unsustainable debt levels by creating a more predictable sovereign debt restructuring process. A clearer procedural framework and set of principles applicable throughout Europe would lead to improved and more timely sovereign debt management decisions, thus reducing the likelihood of crises occurring and mitigating the associated costs. The aim for creating a more orderly sovereign debt restructuring process in Europe would be to increase the incentives that sovereigns have to pay their debts in full and on time. This will allow sovereigns to have continued access to capital at reasonable interest rates. To achieve this, a clearer EU legal and institutional framework should be established to reduce the uncertainty that now surrounds sovereign defaults and restructurings.

Recent proposals as discussed above for an EMF or the creation of a new EU agency with powers to arbitrate and resolve sovereign debt disputes would probably require amending the EU Treaty, which may not be a feasible political proposition at present.[22] Instead, this section suggests that EU policymakers should consider the following principles and rules to provide more certainty to sovereign debt risk management for both sovereigns and investors. These would not necessitate Treaty changes, but would be feasible within the existing legislative instruments.

Collective action clauses (CACs)
CACs – also known as majority action clauses – allow a super-majority of, for example, bondholders holding a particular class of bond contracts to vote to restructure the financial or repayment terms of the bond.[23] The

---

[22] See discussion in Häde, *supra* n. 11.
[23] The financial terms of the contract would generally include the rate of interest (the coupon rate), the amount of the principal, and related financing terms, while the repayment terms would include the date of periodic payments and the means and place of payment, the loan's maturity date, and in some cases what amount of interest and principal would be included in each payment.

bond contract could require, for instance, that 75 per cent of creditors –
rather than 100 per cent – of a certain creditor class vote to restructure the
financial and repayment terms (i.e., lower the interest rate or extend the
maturity of the debt, respectively). The super-majority's decision would
bind the minority bondholders of the same class, thus preventing a small
minority from delaying or otherwise disrupting a restructuring agreement,
thereby making the restructuring process more predictable.[24]

First, sovereign debtors and investors should agree henceforth to incorporate CACs into sovereign bond contracts or sovereign loan contracts
(i.e., bank loans) governed under the law of an EU state. Although investors and sovereigns are increasingly using CACs in their sovereign bond
contracts following the Argentine default, significant differences in the
structure of these contracts still exist, thus increasing uncertainty regarding the renegotiation of repayment terms and how the overall restructuring process would operate. Sovereign bond contracts issued by EU states
should have harmonized legal templates governing their overall structure
but would allow the parties to agree on some of the specific repayment
terms.

Although a growing number of EU sovereign bond contracts contain
CACs, the majority do not, which means that for most EU sovereign bond
contracts the consent of 100 per cent of the bondholders of a particular
class of bonds is necessary to change the repayment terms of the bond.[25]
As a result, a small minority of bondholders can prevent a restructuring
that the majority believe to be in their best interests. Rather, EU directives and regulations should require that all sovereign bond and loan
contracts contain majority action clauses, but allowing the parties to
agree on certain repayment terms, such as specifying the percentage of
creditors holding a certain value of the debt (e.g., 85 per cent, 75 per cent
or 65 per cent) to approve a change in payment terms (e.g., lower interest
rate). EU law should also require that sovereign bond or loan contracts

---

[24]   CACs are in all sovereign bonds issued under English law and are increasingly being used under New York law sovereign bond contracts, which by tradition required unanimity or 100 per cent of creditors of the same class to vote to
restructure the financial or repayment terms of the bond contract.

[25]   See E.B. Koch, *Challenges at the Bank for International Settlements: An
Economist's (Re)view* (Basel: Bank for International Settlements, 2003) 56–60,
stating '[t]raditionally, CACs were included in sovereign bonds governed by
English, Japanese and Luxembourgian law. Sovereign bonds issued under US,
German, Italian and Swiss law did not include CACs', and thus required unani-
mous approval by bondholders of a particular class of bonds to change repayment
terms. Ibid. 60–65, providing data of the value of sovereign bond issuance with
CACs.

contain a clause describing the process through which sovereign debtors and creditors would negotiate if a restructuring event were to occur. This clause would specify how the creditors would be represented and by whom and on what date, or within what period of time, the debtor must provide financial and other information to the creditors' representative. The representative would be authorized to act on behalf of the creditors in the negotiations and have discretion to act based on the instructions of creditors with a specified percentage value of claims.[26]

Another important area concerns how the sovereign would initiate a restructuring. EU law could require that this be provided in a clause describing the permitted period of time – e.g., four weeks – for creditors to come together to obtain the relevant information regarding the sovereign's financial situation, choose a representative, and decide a timeline for the negotiation process. The notion of a 'cooling off' period or automatic stay on creditor action against non-sovereign corporate or individual debtors is already recognized in the insolvency laws of some countries, such as Chapter 11 of the US Bankruptcy Code.[27] The contract would be required to state when the 'cooling off' period would begin, e.g., the date when the sovereign notifies its creditors that it wants to restructure its payments and/or the date that the creditors appoint their representative. The duration of the cooling off period would be mandated by EU law at, say, 60 or 75 days. During this period, a temporary suspension or deferral of payments would be required and enforced by an EU court of law. EU law should mandate that the bond or loan contract should provide for the possibility of a suspension or deferral of payments and provide for damages or penalties for any creditor who violates the provision by seeking to enforce its claim without prior court approval.

---

[26] The specified percentage value of claims would be provided in the repayment terms of the contract. Moreover, the representative, and not individual creditors, would have the authority to initiate litigation for breach of the bond or loan covenants, but only with the approval of creditors with a specified value of claims.

[27] Although Ch. 11 of the US Bankruptcy Code does not apply to sovereign debt default or restructuring, Ch. 9 of the US Bankruptcy Code does provide insolvency proceedings and an automatic stay against creditor claims against a municipal or county government debtor while the sovereign debtor is formulating a repayment plan for judicial and creditor approval. While the automatic stay is in effect, secured creditors can petition the court for adequate protection of their collateral rights in eligible property owned or possessed by the debtor. In Chs 9 and 11, the automatic stay can remain in effect for up to a six-month period to allow the debtor an opportunity to negotiate with creditors and devise a comprehensive payment plan.

Implementation

The decentralized approach that relies on regulating EU sovereign bond and loan contracts so that they contain CACs is not the only option that has been proposed for reforming the sovereign debt restructuring process. Of course, the IMF staff had proposed an international sovereign debt restructuring mechanism (SDRM) in 2002 that attracted much attention but was not approved because of US opposition. The SDRM would have provided a more centralized approach that would have involved amending the IMF Articles of Agreement in order to create a legally binding arbitration process in which a designated IMF tribunal would have mediated and approved any disputes regarding the restructuring of sovereign debt.[28] The IMF's SDRM was criticized on the grounds that it was insufficiently market-oriented and required too much centralized authority at the international level by concentrating too much power in the IMF. These same criticisms are perhaps also applicable to recent proposals to create an EU Monetary Fund that would provide guarantees on sovereign debt and liquidity assistance for ailing EU sovereign debtors while negotiating creditor claims, or to the creation of the EFSF, which also provides liquidity support and issues guarantees for eurozone sovereigns having financial difficulties.

On the other hand, one can question the viability of the decentralized approach on the grounds that there are multiple legal systems of contract law in the EU and that this might be difficult to harmonize in order to facilitate sovereign debt negotiations and restructurings. Another question is what the scope of the debt subject to the CACs should be. In theory, there would be no reasonable justification on economic grounds to restrict the scope of such clauses to bond contracts. For instance, Taylor observes that '[i]t would be appropriate, for example, to include such clauses in bank debt along with bonded debt'.[29] It is observed that such clauses are already incorporated in many syndicated bank loans.[30] Another question is whether during a restructuring all the claims of different bond issues should be consolidated into a single class of creditors or, alternatively,

---

[28]   Anne Krueger, *A New Approach to Sovereign Debt Restructuring*, 16 April 2002, Washington DC, International Monetary Fund, www.imf.org/external/pubs/ft/exrp/sdrm/eng/sdrm.pdf ('SDRM – April version', 11–14).

[29]   J.B. Taylor, 'Sovereign Debt Workouts: Hopes and Hazards', conference address (Washington DC, Institute for International Economics) (on file with author).

[30]   See S.L. Schwarcz, 'Sovereign Debt Restructuring: A Bankruptcy Reorganization Approach', *Cornell Law Review* 85 (2000), 975, 982–4; and 'Facing the Debt Challenge of Countries that are Too Big to Fail', *Duke Law Working Paper* (2008), 1–7.

whether all the claims of bondholders should be consolidated with the claims of other creditors (i.e., bank loans). Market-based practitioners appear to prefer an approach that consolidates the CACs and other clauses into debt on an issue-by-issue or loan-by-loan basis. Any inconsistency in legal terms or requirements created by different types of issues or jurisdictions should be resolved by arbitration provided in the contracts or by an EU agency established (as discussed below) to apply the EU principles and guidelines governing sovereign debt restructuring.

Finally, the EU must have the institutional capacity to monitor the implementation of such debt contracts to ensure that vital data is communicated to creditors and debtors and that the parties negotiate terms and conditions with full access to relevant information. An EU sovereign debt agency could be created by Regulation to exercise such a function and would have authority to collect data and perform surveillance of sovereign debt markets and report market developments to the European Commission, Parliament and market participants. The responsibilities of an EU sovereign debt agency could include overseeing EU Member State sovereign debt practices and providing data to the market regarding the risks that certain bond and loan contracts pose and making recommendations to and, if necessary, 'naming and shaming' states that appear to be developing unsustainable debt positions.

The agency could also exchange information with the ECB, the European Supervisory Authorities and the European Systemic Risk Board regarding financial stability issues in the sovereign debt markets. Moreover, it would clarify the process by which market participants could enforce their rights and obligations under the debt contracts in a court of law of an EU state, especially to ensure that any restructuring process is occurring according to contractual requirements.

EU Financial Stability Fund

This chapter's proposed EU sovereign debt agency with responsibility for overseeing the implementation of the CAC approach to sovereign debt restructuring based on harmonized EU principles and guidelines could also administer the establishment of a EU 'stability' fund to which EU states experiencing short-term funding problems would have access for short-term funding during financial distress and crises until they regain access to capital markets. The EU 'financial stability' fund would be paid for by a small transaction tax on all sovereign bond sales.[31] The tax could be imposed at

---

[31] See K. Alexander, J. Eatwell, A. Persaud and R. Reoch, 'Crisis Management,

a very low level – ten basis points/0.10 per cent, or five basis points/0.05 per cent – so as not to distort significantly the sovereign bond market and it would be easily implemented by requiring the intermediary banks who execute the transactions to deduct the tax at the point of purchase and sale and pay on to national treasuries, who would then have an obligation to pay the sums into the fund. The tax could also apply to sovereign debt derivative instruments (i.e., sovereign credit default swaps (CDSs)) or other instruments that use sovereign debt as a referenced asset. The tax would apply uniformly to all EU sovereign bond issuance and could even be extended to include a tax on bank loans to EU governments. The tax could provide a sustainable source of finance to assist EU sovereigns experiencing sovereign liquidity problems and help assist the implementation of any restructuring plans. In return for accessing the fund, states would be required to implement appropriate fiscal adjustments in order to bring their sovereign debt to sustainable levels over the medium term.

If instead the country is not merely illiquid, but insolvent, more drastic measures should be taken and the EU stability fund would continue to be available, but would need to be supplemented by a mechanism for determining collective guarantees.[32] These should be offered on the basis of strict conditionality, in which the state in question may be required to undertake significant structural reforms to, for example, the fiscal system, the structure of macroeconomic management, or the labour market. Short-term austerity measures may be a necessary component of a rescue package. But their impact should always be assessed against the needs of medium-term recovery. This also means that the rules of the SGP that have so conspicuously failed should be reconsidered and possibly replaced.

The approach suggested above would involve a major rethink of the political economy of the EU in general and the eurozone in particular. It would require a significant change of direction in fiscal policy, including a harmonized EU framework consisting of principles and guidelines to govern the restructuring and default of a sovereign debtor. The absence of an EU regime governing the restructuring of sovereign debt resulted in an under-pricing of sovereign bonds and other sovereign debt-linked instruments, which created a moral hazard for investors to invest too much in sovereign debt because they perceived that euro-states would find a way to bail out their brethren to prevent a collapse of the eurozone.

Burden Sharing and Solidarity Mechanisms in the EU' (Brussels: European Parliament, 2010), 43.

[32] This means that EU authorities should adopt criteria for determining whether a state is either illiquid or insolvent; or, if it is illiquid, at what point it becomes insolvent.

This has led to an under-pricing of sovereign debt, which means that the full cost of sovereign debt has not been internalized by those who invested in it, thereby resulting in too much of it being issued. Moreover, investors would be able to price sovereign debt more efficiently if they had more certainty regarding the rules of debt renegotiation and their ability to coordinate their claims collectively with other creditors in a crisis and to obtain relevant information from sovereigns. Whether an EU agency could be established to assist creditors and sovereigns with these function is a policy matter and raises legal issues that go beyond the scope of this brief study.

EU Stability Mechanism

The above proposals for EU collective action clauses and an EU sovereign debt agency were made by the author in a report commissioned by the European Parliament in September 2010. Following this report in December 2010. The European Council, considering it necessary to establish a more permanent emergency financing mechanism for sovereign debtors, approved in March 2011 a Treaty amendment to Article 136 TFEU that would create a permanent. European Stability Mechanism[33] (ESM), based on the current EFSF, capable of providing financial assistance programmes for eurozone member states under strict conditionality.[34] Significantly, the ESM will enjoy preferred creditor status for its loans to sovereign debtors, which means that the claims of private sector creditors, such as bondholders, will be subordinated to ESM loans. ESM loans will be disbursed to a eurozone state only if it appears insolvent and has agreed to a debt sustainability plan with the Commission and the IMF that must involve both an economic and fiscal adjustment programme and a comprehensive restructuring of creditor claims.

Under the proposal, the restructuring of creditor claims must involve the use of standardized and identical collective action clauses (CACs) to facilitate the bailing in of the private creditors while maintaining market

---

[33]   European Council Decision of 25 March 2011 amending Article 136 of the Treaty on the Functioning of the European Union with regard to a stability mechanism for Member States whose currency is the euro. OJ L 91/1 (04/06/2011).

[34]   The European Central Bank has called the ESM *an ultima ratio safeguard* against imbalances in individual countries. It is expected that the new ESM will enter in to one on 1 July 2013, following an amendment to the Treaty (TFEU) and the signing of an ESM Treaty by the euro area countries. See ECB, 'European Stability Mechanism', *ECB Monthly Bulletin* (July 2011), pp. 71–84.

liquidity.[35] Eurozone governments will be required to issue CACs starting in June 2013 when the ESM begins its operations. The CACs would be similar to the CACs already in use under English and US law, which are modelled in part on a G10 Report in 2002 recommending the use of CACs with 'aggregation clauses' that allow all debt securities issued by a state to be considered and voted on together as part of restructuring negotiations with the sovereign. Crucially, bondholders would be allowed to pass by a qualified majority vote a legally binding change to the terms of payment, such as a payment standstill, maturity extension, interest rate cut or reduction in principal, if the sovereign is unable to pay. This sweeping reform of the legal framework of sovereign debt finance and restructuring is expected to take effect in June 2013 once eurozone member states have approved the amendment to the TFEU. The effectiveness of the ESM will be evaluated by the Commission and the ECB in 2016.

CONCLUSION

The EU sovereign debt crisis of 2010 involving Greece and a growing number of eurozone countries demonstrates how financial distress in one Member State can rapidly spread through contagion channels to threaten the macroeconomic and financial stability of both the eurozone and the European Union and also destabilize global financial markets. Although EU bank stress tests, reported in July 2010 and July 2011, calmed concerns about the health of EU banks by showing generally that EU banks were not inadequately capitalized or dangerously exposed to sovereign debt, EU financial markets remain fragile. Falling bank share prices, rising interbank loan rates and volatile credit defaut swap spreads suggest that the stress test results have not sufficiently eased investor concerns about EU financial institutions and by extension have rekindled fears about the solvency of some deeply indebted EU sovereigns, especially Greece, Ireland, Portugal, Italy and Spain.

These developments suggest that volatility is returning to EU sovereign debt markets and that EU policymakers should consider whether Europe needs a formal EU sovereign default process to incentivize states to manage their sovereign debt more effectively and to promote a more orderly resolution of creditors' claims. This chapter has examined a number of options, including the newly created EFSF, and suggests that

---

[35] See Kern Alexander, 'Market Impact of an Orderly Sovereign Debt Restructuring' (Sept. 2011), Brussels: European Parliament.

European policymakers should focus reform efforts on adopting a decentralized sovereign debt restructuring process that emphasizes the use of CACs to facilitate negotiations and information flow between creditors and sovereigns regarding sovereign debt risks. EU directives and regulations, not necessitating Treaty changes, should harmonize the principles and guidelines that govern the operation of CACs, but parties should be permitted some freedom to decide the parameters of CAC negotiations and some aspects of the restructuring process.

An EU sovereign debt agency should be created to facilitate such negotiations and to serve as an information warehouse for creditors and sovereigns to obtain data on market developments relevant to the pricing of sovereign debt risk. The EU sovereign debt agency could also administer a European Financial Stability Fund that would be created to provide liquidity to states experiencing financial distress and undergoing a restructuring if the state in question fulfils the requisite conditions for obtaining support. The EU Financial Stability Fund would be financed by a transaction tax on all EU sovereign bond issuance, CDSs and other derivative transactions that reference EU sovereign bonds. The tax would be at a very low rate so as not to unduly limit the market and to raise adequate revenue to assist states with temporary liquidity problems.

Index